DESSERTS

DESSERTS

365 Delicious Step-By-Step Recipes

Martha Day

HERMES
HOUSE

This edition is published by Hermes House, an imprint of Anness Publishing Ltd,
Hermes House, 88–89 Blackfriars Road, London SE1 8HA;
tel. 020 7401 2077; fax 020 7633 9499
www.hermeshouse.com; www.annesspublishing.com

If you like the images in this book and would like to investigate using them for publishing, promotions or advertising, please
visit our website www.practicalpictures.com for more information.

Publisher: Joanna Lorenz
Project Editor: Finny Fox Davies
Designer: Ian Sandom
Recipes: Catherine Atkinson, Alex Barker, Michelle Berriedale-Johnson, Angela Boggiano, Janet Brinkworth,
Carla Capalbo, Jacqueline Clark, Francis Cleary, Carol Clements, Roz Denny, Patrizia Diemling, Nicola Diggins,
Joanna Farrow, Christine France, Sarah Gates, Shirley Gill, Rosamund Grant, Carole Handslip, Deh-Ta Hsiung,
Shehzad Husain, Sheila Kimberley, Gilly Love, Norma MacMillan, Sue Maggs, Maggie Mayhew, Maggie Parnell,
Anne Sheasby, Liz Trigg, Laura Washburn, Stephen Wheeler, Kate Whiteman, Elizabeth Wolf-Cohen, Jeni Wright
Photographers: William Adams-Lingwood, Karl Adamson, Edward Allwright, David Armstrong, Steve Baxter,
James Duncan, Michelle Garrett, Amanda Heywood, David Jordan, Don Last, Patrick McLeavy,
Michael Michaels, Thomas Odulate

ETHICAL TRADING POLICY
Because of our ongoing ecological investment programme, you, as our customer, can have the pleasure and reassurance of
knowing that a tree is being cultivated on your behalf to naturally replace the materials used to make the book you are holding.
For further information about this scheme, go to www.annesspublishing.com/trees

Previously published as *Desserts All Around the Year*

NOTES
For all recipes, quantities are given in both metric and imperial measures and, where appropriate, measures are also given in
standard cups and spoons. Follow one set, but not a mixture, because they are not interchangeable.

Standard spoon and cup measures are level. 1 tsp = 5ml, 1 tbsp = 15ml, 1 cup = 250ml/8fl oz

Australian standard tablespoons are 20ml. Australian readers should use 3 tsp in place of 1 tbsp for measuring
small quantities of gelatine, cornflour, salt, etc.

American pints are 16fl oz/2 cups. American readers should use 20fl oz/2.5 cups in place of 1 pint when measuring liquids.

Electric oven temperatures in this book are for conventional ovens. When using a fan oven, the temperature will probably need to be
reduced by about 10–20°C/20–40°F. Since ovens vary, you should check with your manufacturer's instruction book for guidance.

Medium eggs are used unless otherwise stated.

Portion sizes: The recipes in this book are generally for four people. They can be halved or quartered, depending
on the number of servings required.

Contents

Introduction

DESSERT RECIPES CAN RANGE from the lightest sorbet to the most substantial steamed chocolate pudding, so there are several decisions to be made when planning a menu. Your choice of what to serve will be influenced by the season, the occasion and the dietary requirements of your guests. If you are serving a filling main course you will invariably choose a light or fruity dessert to follow it, or if you plan to make a rich, creamy dessert you will deliberately pick a light main course. To help you maintain a healthy balance this book includes a wide range of delicious low-fat desserts that can make the decision reassuringly easy.

Many of the desserts in this selection can be made a day or two in advance, others can be started early in the day and finished off just before you eat, while frozen desserts and ice creams can be made weeks in advance, ready to serve whenever you need them. If you are planning a festive meal or entertaining a large number of people make sure you leave plenty of time for preparation, choose one of the desserts that can be made in advance and do at least some of the work for the other courses earlier in the day. That way your guests *and you* can enjoy the meal.

Many of the recipes have clear instructions, so that even the potentially difficult desserts, such as soufflés and roulades, will be easy to make, and look and taste delicious. For certain results, read the recipe through before you start and follow the step-by-step instructions.

The book is divided into two sections. *Best-ever Desserts* contains all the old favourites, such as Sticky Toffee Pudding, Crème Caramel and Trifle, along with some more unusual recipes that are destined to become your new favourites. There are chapters on hot puddings and desserts, cold puddings and desserts, and many more, to make sure you serve a best-ever dessert for every occasion. *Low-fat Desserts* contains recipes that are just as delicious, but are carefully designed to fit into a healthy, lighter diet. Nearly all recipes have no more than 5g of fat per portion, and many have fewer than 200 calories.

Best-ever Desserts

Desserts are irresistible at any time of day: with morning coffee or afternoon tea, as the perfect end to a lazy lunch, as a special indulgence or treat, or as the grand finale to a romantic evening. This section of the book presents recipes for the most luxurious, sumptuous desserts imaginable, including classics such as Peach Melba and Black Forest Gâteau, as well as innovative ideas such as Chocolate and Cherry Polenta Cake and Kiwi Ricotta Cheese Tart. There are six easy-to-use chapters that cover every kind of dessert for all occasions — hot and cold puddings, cakes and gâteaux, pastries and pies, custards and soufflés, fruit salads, ices and sorbets.

❖ ◆ ❖

Making Shortcrust Pastry

A meltingly short, crumbly pastry sets off any filling to perfection, whether sweet or savoury. The fat content of the pastry dough can be made up of half butter or margarine and half white vegetable fat or with all one kind of fat.

INGREDIENTS

For a 23cm/9in pastry case

225g/8oz/2 cups plain flour

1.5ml/¼ tsp salt

115g/4oz/8 tbsp fat, chilled and diced

1 Sift the flour and salt into a bowl. Add the fat. Rub it into the flour with your fingertips until the mixture is crumb-like.

2 Sprinkle 45ml/3 tbsp of iced water over the mixture. With a fork, toss gently to mix and moisten it.

3 Press the dough into a ball. If it is too dry to hold together, gradually add another 15ml/1 tbsp of iced water.

4 Wrap the ball of dough with cling film or greaseproof paper and chill it for at least 30 minutes.

5 To make pastry in a food processor: combine the flour, salt and cubed fat in the work bowl. Process, turning the machine on and off, just until the mixture is crumbly. Add 45–60ml/3–4 tbsp iced water and process again briefly – just until the dough starts to pull away from the sides of the bowl. It should still look crumbly. Remove the dough from the processor and gather it into a ball. Wrap and chill.

SHORTCRUST PASTRY VARIATIONS

For Nut Shortcrust
Add 30g/1oz/¼ cup finely chopped walnuts or pecan nuts to the flour mixture.

For Rich Shortcrust
Use 225g/8oz/2 cups flour and 175g/6oz/¾ cup fat (preferably all butter), plus 15ml/1 tbsp caster sugar if making a sweet pie. Bind with 1 egg yolk and 30–45ml/ 2–3 tbsp water.

For a Two-crust Pie
Increase the proportions for these pastries by 50%, thus the amounts needed for basic shortcrust pastry are: 340g/12oz/3 cups flour, 2.5ml/½ tsp salt, 175g/6oz/¾ cup fat, 75–90ml/5–6 tbsp water.

Making French Flan Pastry

The pastry for tarts and flans is made with butter or margarine, giving a rich and crumbly result. The more fat used, the richer the pastry will be – almost like a biscuit dough – and the harder to roll out. If you have difficulty rolling it, you can press it into the tin instead, or roll it out between sheets of cling film. Flan pastry, like shortcrust, can be made by hand or in a food processor. Tips for making, handling and using shortcrust pastry apply equally to this type of pastry.

INGREDIENTS

For a 23cm/9in flan case

200g/7oz/1¾ cups plain flour

2.5ml/½ tsp salt

115g/4oz/½ cup butter or margarine, chilled

1 egg yolk

1.5ml/¼ tsp lemon juice

1 Sift the flour and salt into a bowl. Add the butter or margarine. Rub into the flour until the mixture resembles fine breadcrumbs.

2 In a small bowl, mix the egg yolk, lemon juice and 30ml/ 2 tbsp of iced water. Add to the flour mixture. With a fork, toss gently to mix and moisten.

3 Press the dough into a rough ball. If it is too dry to come together, add 15ml/1 tbsp more water. Turn on to the work surface or a pastry board.

4 With the heel of your hand, push small portions of dough away from you, smearing them on the surface.

5 Continue mixing the dough in this way until it feels pliable and can be peeled easily off the work surface or pastry board.

6 Press the dough into a smooth ball. Wrap in cling film and chill for at least 30 minutes.

FLAN PASTRY VARIATIONS

For Sweet Flan Pastry
Reduce the amount of salt to 1.5ml/¼ tsp, add 15ml/1 tbsp caster sugar with the flour.

For Rich Flan Pastry
Use 200g/7oz/1¾ cups flour, 2.5ml/½ tsp salt, 150g/5oz/10 tbsp butter, 2 egg yolks, and 15–30ml/ 1–2 tbsp water.

For Rich Sweet Flan Pastry
Make rich flan pastry, adding 45ml/3 tbsp caster sugar with the flour and, if liked, 2.5ml/½ tsp vanilla essence with the egg yolks.

Making Choux Pastry

Unlike other pastries, where the fat is rubbed into the flour, with choux pastry the butter is melted with water and then the flour is added, followed by eggs. The result is more of a paste than a pastry. It is easy to make, but care must be taken in measuring the ingredients.

INGREDIENTS

For 18 profiteroles or 12 eclairs

115g/4oz/½ cup butter, cut into small pieces
10ml/2 tsp caster sugar (optional)
1.5ml/¼ tsp salt
150g/5oz/1¼ cups plain flour
4 eggs, beaten to mix
1 egg, beaten with 5ml/1 tsp cold water, for glaze

1 Preheat the oven to 220°C/ 425°F/Gas 7. Combine the butter, sugar, if using, salt and 250ml/8fl oz/1 cup of water in a large heavy-based saucepan. Bring to the boil over moderately high heat, stirring occasionally.

2 As soon as the mixture is boiling, remove the pan from the heat. Add the flour all at once and beat vigorously with a wooden spoon to mix the flour smoothly into the liquid.

3 Return the pan to moderate heat and cook, stirring, until the mixture will form a ball, pulling away from the side of the pan. This will take about 1 minute. Remove from the heat again and allow to cool for 3–5 minutes.

4 Add a little of the beaten eggs and beat well to incorporate. Add a little more egg and beat in well. Continue beating in the eggs until the mixture becomes a smooth and shiny paste.

5 While still warm, shape choux puffs, éclairs, profiteroles or rings on a baking sheet lined with baking parchment.

6 Glaze with 1 egg beaten with 1 teaspoon of cold water. Put into the preheated oven, then reduce the heat to 200°C/400°F/ Gas 6. Bake until puffed and golden brown.

SHAPING CHOUX PASTRY

For Large Puffs
Use two large spoons dipped in water. Drop the paste in 5–6cm/ 2–2½in wide blobs on the paper-lined baking sheet, leaving 4cm/1½in between each. Neaten the blobs as much as possible. Alternatively, for well-shaped puffs, pipe the paste using a piping bag fitted with a 2cm/¾in plain nozzle.

For Profiteroles
Use two small spoons or a piping bag fitted with a 1cm/½in nozzle and shape 2.5cm/1in blobs.

For Eclairs
Use a piping bag fitted with a 2cm/¾in nozzle. Pipe strips 10–13cm/4–5in long.

For a Ring
Draw a 30cm/12in circle on the paper. Spoon the paste in large blobs on the circle to make a ring. Or pipe two rings around the circle and a third on top.

BAKING TIMES FOR CHOUX PASTRY	
Large puffs and éclairs	30–35 minutes
Profiteroles	20–25 minutes
Rings	40–45 minutes

Rolling Out and Lining a Tin

A neat pastry case that doesn't distort or shrink in baking is the desired result. The key to success is handling the dough gently. Use the method here to line a round pie or tart tin that is about 5cm/2in deep.

Remove the chilled dough from the fridge and allow it to soften slightly at room temperature. Unwrap and put it on a lightly floured surface. Flatten the dough into a neat, round disc. Lightly flour the rolling pin.

1 Using even pressure, start rolling out the dough, working from the centre to the edge each time and easing the pressure slightly as you reach the edge.

2 Lift up the dough and give it a quarter turn from time to time during the rolling. This will prevent the dough sticking to the surface, and will help keep the thickness even.

3 Continue rolling out until the dough circle is about 5cm/2in larger all round than the tin. It should be about 3mm/⅛in thick.

4 Set the rolling pin on the dough, near one side of the circle. Fold the outside edge of the dough over the pin, then roll the pin over the dough to wrap the dough round it. Do this gently and loosely.

5 Hold the pin over the tin and gently unroll the dough so it drapes into the tin, centring it as much as possible.

6 With your fingertips, lift and ease the dough into the tin, gently pressing it over the bottom and up the side. Turn excess dough over the rim and trim it with a knife or scissors, depending on how you want to finish the edge.

Finishing the Edge

1 *For a forked edge*
Using a knife, trim the dough even with the rim and press it flat. Firmly and evenly press the prongs of a fork all round the edge. If the fork sticks, dip it in flour every so often.

2 *For a crimped edge*
Using scissors, trim the dough to leave an overhang of about 1.5cm/½in all round. Fold the extra dough under. Put the knuckle or tip of the index finger of one of your hands inside the edge, pointing directly out. With the thumb and index finger of your other hand, pinch the dough edge around your index finger into a "V" shape. Continue all the way round the edge.

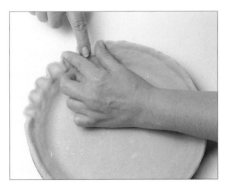

3 *For a ruffled edge*
Using scissors, trim the dough to leave an overhang of about 1.5cm/½in all round. Fold the extra dough under. With the thumb and index finger of one hand about 2.5cm/1in apart, gently pinch the dough around the index finger of your other hand. Continue this all the way round the edge.

4 *For a cutout edge*
Using a knife, trim the dough even with the rim and press it flat. With a small pastry cutter, cut out decorative shapes from the dough trimmings. Moisten the edge of the pastry case and press the cutouts in place, overlapping them slightly if you like.

5 *For a ribbon edge*
Using a knife, trim the dough even with the rim and press it flat. Cut long strips about 2cm/¾in wide from the dough trimmings. Moisten the edge and press one end of a strip on to it. Twist the strip gently and press it on to the edge again. Continue this all the way round the edge.

Preparing Fresh Fruit

Citrus fruit
To peel completely: cut a slice from the top and from the base. Set the fruit base down on a work surface. Using a small sharp knife, cut off the peel lengthways in thick strips. Take the coloured rind and all the white pith (which has a bitter taste). Cut, following the curve of the fruit.

To remove rind: use a vegetable peeler to save off the rind in wide strips, taking none of the white pith. Use these strips whole or cut them into fine shreds with a sharp knife, according to recipe directions. Or rub the fruit against the fine holes of a metal grater, turning the fruit so you take just the coloured rind and not the white pith. Or use a special tool, called a citrus zester, to take fine threads of rind. (Finely chop the threads as an alternative method to grating.)

Kiwi fruit
Follow the citrus fruit technique, taking off the peel in thin lengthways strips.

Apples, pears, quinces, mangoes, papayas
Use a small sharp knife or a vegetable peeler. Take off the peel in long strips, as thinly as possible.

Peaches, apricots
Cut a cross in the base. Immerse the fruit in boiling water. Leave for 10–30 seconds (according to ripeness), then drain and immerse in iced water. The skin should slip off easily.

Pineapple
Cut off the leafy crown. Cut a slice from the base and set the pineapple upright. With a sharp knife, cut off the peel lengthways, cutting thickly to remove the brown "eyes" with it.

Bananas, lychees, avocados
Make a small cut and remove the peel with your fingers.

Passion fruit, pomegranates
Cut in half, or cut a slice off the top. With a spoon, scoop the flesh and seeds into a bowl.

Star fruit (carambola)
Trim off the tough, darkened edges of the five segments.

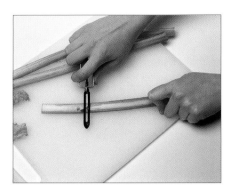

Rhubarb
Cut off the leaves and discard them (they are poisonous). Peel off any tough skin.

Fresh currants (red, black, white)
Pull each cluster through the prongs of a fork to remove the currants from the stalks.

Fresh dates
Squeeze gently at the stalk end to remove the rather tough skin.

CORING AND STONING OR SEEDING FRUIT

Apples, pears, quinces
For whole fruit: use an apple corer to stamp out the whole core from stalk end to base. Alternatively, working up from the base, use a melon baller to cut out the core. Leave the stalk end intact.

For halves: use a melon baller to scoop out the core. Cut out the stalk and base using a small sharp knife.
For quarters: cut out the stalk and core with a serrated knife.

Citrus fruit
With the tip of a pointed knife, nick out pips from slices or segments.

Cherries
Use a cherry stoner to achieve the neatest results.

Peaches, apricots, nectarines, plums
Cut the fruit in half, cutting round the indentation. Twist the halves apart. Lift out the stone, or lever it out with the tip of a sharp knife.

Fresh dates
Cut the fruit lengthways in half and lift out the stone. Or, if the fruit is to be used whole, cut in from the stalk end with a thin-bladed knife to loosen the stone, then remove it.

Mangoes

Cut lengthways on either side of the large flat stone in the centre. Curve the cut slightly to follow the shape of the stone. Cut the flesh from the two thin ends of the stone.

Papayas, melons

Cut the fruit in half. Scoop out the seeds from the central hollow, then scrape away any fibres.

Pineapple

For spears and wedges: cut out the core neatly with a sharp knife.
For rings: cut out the core with a small pastry cutter.

Gooseberries

Use scissors to trim off the stalk and flower ends.

Grapes

Cut the fruit lengthways in half. Use a small knife to nick out the pips. Alternatively, use the curved end of a sterilized hair grip.

Star fruit (carambola), watermelon

With the tip of a pointed knife, nick out pips from slices.

Strawberries

Use a special huller to remove the leafy green top and central core. Or cut these out with a small sharp knife.

Avocado

Cut the fruit in half lengthways. Stick the tip of a sharp knife into the stone and lever it out without damaging the surrounding flesh.

Apples, quinces

For rings: remove the core and seeds with an apple corer. Set the fruit on its side and cut across into thick or thin rings, as required.

For slices: cut the fruit in half and remove core and seeds with a melon baller. Set one half cut side down and cut it across into neat slices, thick or thin according to recipe directions. Or cut the fruit into quarters and remove core and seeds with a knife. Cut lengthways into neat slices.

Pears

For fans: cut the fruit in half and remove the core and seeds with a melon baller. Set the halves cut side down and cut lengthways into thin slices, not cutting all the way through at the stalk ends. Gently fan out the slices so they are overlapping each other evenly. Transfer the pear fans to the plate or pastry case using a palette knife.
For slices: follow apple technique.

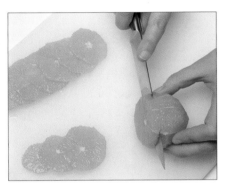

Citrus fruit
For slices: using a serrated knife, cut the fruit across into neat slices.

For segments: hold the peeled fruit in your cupped palm, over a bowl to catch the juice. Working from the side of the fruit to the centre, slide the knife down one side of a separating membrane to free the flesh from it. Then slide the knife down the other side of that segment to free it from the membrane there. Drop the segment into the bowl. Continue cutting out the segments, folding back the membrane like the pages of a book as you work. When all the segments have been cut out, squeeze all the juice from the membrane.

Peaches, nectarines, apricots, plums
For slices: follow apple technique.

Papayas, avocados
For slices: follow apple technique. Or cut the unpeeled fruit into wedges, removing the central seeds or stone. Set each wedge peel side down and slide the knife down the length to cut the flesh away from the peel.
For fans: follow pear technique.

Melon
For slices: follow papaya technique.
For balls: Use a melon baller.

Mangoes
Cut the peeled flesh into slices or cubes, according to recipe directions.

Pineapple
For spears: cut the peeled fruit lengthways in half and then into quarters. Cut each quarter into spears and cut out the core.
For chunks: cut the peeled fruit into spears. Remove the core. Cut across each spear into chunks.
For rings: cut the peeled fruit across into slices. Stamp out the central core from each slice using a pastry cutter.

Kiwi fruit, star fruit (carambola)
Cut the fruit across into neat slices; discard the ends.

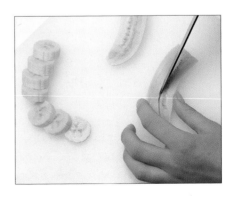

Banana
Cut the fruit across into neat slices. Or cut in half and then lengthways into quarters.

Gelatine

DISSOLVING GELATINE

It's important to dissolve gelatine correctly, or it can spoil the texture and set of your finished dessert.

1 Place 45ml/3 tbsp of very hot water per sachet of gelatine in a small bowl.

2 Sprinkle the gelatine over the liquid. Always add the gelatine to the liquid.

3 Stir briskly until the gelatine is completely dissolved. There should be no visible crystals and the liquid should be clear. If necessary, stand the container in a pan of hot water over a low heat until dissolved. Do not allow the gelatine to boil.

VEGETARIAN ALTERNATIVE

There is a vegetarian alternative to gelatine, which can be used in the appropriate recipes, if you wish. Follow the instructions on the packet, but in general you should sprinkle the alternative on to cold liquids and stir until completely dissolved. Next, heat the mixture to near boiling. (If setting proves difficult add more of the gelatine alternative to the mixture and reheat.) It is now ready to be used as specified in the recipe, but should be allowed to set for about 1 hour, or until firm and should always be allowed to cool.

Redcurrant and Raspberry Coulis

A dessert sauce for the height of summer to serve with light meringues and fruit sorbets. Make it particularly pretty with a decoration of fresh flowers and leaves.

INGREDIENTS

Serves 6

225g/8oz/2 cups redcurrants
450g/1lb/2⅔ cups raspberries
50g/2oz/½ cup icing sugar
15ml/1 tbsp cornflour
juice of 1 orange
30ml/2 tbsp double cream, to decorate

1 Strip the redcurrants from their stalks using a fork. Place in a food processor or blender with the raspberries and sugar, and purée until it it smooth.

2 Press the mixture through a fine sieve into a bowl and discard the seeds and pulp.

3 Blend the cornflour with the orange juice then stir into the fruit purée. Transfer to a saucepan and bring to the boil, stirring continuously, and cook for 1–2 minutes until smooth and thick. Leave until cold.

4 Spoon the sauce over each plate. Drip the cream from a teaspoon to make small dots evenly around the edge. Draw a cocktail stick through the dots to form heart shapes. Place the meringue or scoop sorbet into the middle and decorate with flowers.

Crème Anglaise

Here is the classic English custard, light, creamy and delicious – far superior to packet versions. Serve hot or cold.

INGREDIENTS

Serves 4

1 vanilla pod
450ml/¾ pint/1⅞ cups milk
40g/1½oz/3 tbsp caster sugar
4 egg yolks

1 Split the vanilla pod and place in a saucepan with the milk. Bring slowly to the boil. Remove from the heat, then cover and infuse for 10 minutes before removing the pod.

2 Beat together the sugar and egg yolks until thick, light and creamy.

3 Slowly pour the warm, infused milk on to the egg mixture, stirring constantly.

4 Transfer to the top of a double boiler or place the bowl over a saucepan of hot water. Stir constantly over a low heat for 10 minutes or until the mixture coats the back of the spoon. Remove from the heat immediately as curdling will occur if the custard is allowed to simmer.

5 Strain the custard into a jug if serving hot or, if serving cold, strain into a bowl and cover the surface with buttered paper or clear film.

VARIATION

Infuse a few strips of thinly pared lemon or orange rind with the milk, instead of the vanilla pod.

Sabayon

Serve this frothy sauce hot over steamed puddings or chill and serve just as it is with light dessert biscuits or whatever you prefer. Never let it stand for any length of time, as it will collapse.

INGREDIENTS

Serves 4-6

1 egg
2 egg yolks
75g/3oz/⅔ cup caster sugar
150ml/¼ pint/⅔ cups sweet white wine
finely grated rind and juice of 1 lemon

1 Whisk the egg, yolks and sugar until they are pale and thick.

2 Stand the bowl over a saucepan of hot – not boiling – water. Add the wine and lemon juice, a little at a time, whisking vigorously and constantly.

3 Continue whisking until the mixture is thick enough to leave a trail. Whisk in the lemon rind. If serving hot serve immediately over pudding or fruit salad.

4 To serve cold, place over a bowl of iced water and whisk until chilled. Pour into small glasses and serve at once.

Butterscotch Sauce

A deliciously sweet sauce which will be loved by adults and children alike! Serve with ice cream or with pancakes or waffles.

INGREDIENTS

Serves 4–6

75g/3oz/6 tbsp butter

175g/6oz/¾ cup soft dark brown sugar

175ml/6fl oz/¾ cup evaporated milk

50g/2oz/½ cup hazelnuts

1 Melt the butter and sugar in a heavy-based pan, bring to the boil and boil for 2 minutes. Cool for 5 minutes.

2 Heat the evaporated milk to just below boiling point, then gradually stir into the sugar mixture. Cook over a low heat for 2 minutes, stirring frequently.

3 Spread the hazelnuts on a baking sheet and toast under a hot grill.

4 Tip the nuts on to a clean dish towel and rub them briskly to remove the skins.

5 Chop the nuts roughly and stir into the sauce. Serve hot, poured over scoops of vanilla ice cream, or warm waffles or pancakes.

Brandy Butter

This is traditionally served with Christmas pudding and mince pies but a good spoonful on a hot baked apple is equally delicious.

INGREDIENTS

Serves 6

100g/4oz/½ cup butter

100g/4oz/½ cup icing, caster or soft light brown sugar

45ml/3 tbsp brandy

1 Cream the butter until very pale and soft, then beat in the sugar gradually until mixed.

2 Add the brandy, a few drops at a time, beating continuously. Add enough for a good flavour but take care it does not curdle.

3 Pile into a small serving dish and allow to harden. Alternatively, spread on to aluminimum foil and chill until firm. Cut into shapes with small fancy cutters.

VARIATION

Cumberland Rum Butter
Use soft light brown sugar and rum instead of brandy. Grate the rind of 1 orange and beat in with the sugar, adding a good pinch of mixed spice.

Chocolate Fudge Sauce

A real treat if you're not counting calories. Fabulous with scoops of vanilla ice cream.

INGREDIENTS

Serves 6
150ml/¼ pint/⅔ cup double cream
50g/2oz/4 tbsp butter
50g/2oz/¼ cup granulated sugar
175g/6oz plain chocolate
30ml/2 tbsp brandy

VARIATIONS

White Chocolate and Orange Sauce:
40g/1½oz/3 tbsp caster sugar, to replace
  granulated sugar
175g/6oz white chocolate, to replace plain
  chocolate
30ml/2 tbsp orange liqueur, to replace
  brandy
finely grated rind of 1 orange

Coffee Chocolate Fudge:
50g/2oz/¼ cup light brown sugar, to
  replace granulated sugar
30ml/2 tbsp coffee liqueur or dark rum, to
  replace brandy
15ml/1 tbsp coffee essence

1 Heat the cream with the butter and sugar in the top of a double boiler or in a heatproof bowl over a saucepan of hot water. Stir until smooth, then cool.

2 Break the chocolate into the cream. Stir until it is melted and thoroughly combined.

3 Stir in the brandy a little at a time, then cool to room temperature.

4 For the White Chocolate and Orange Sauce, heat the cream and butter with the sugar and orange rind in the top of a double boiler, until dissolved. Then, follow the recipe to the end, but using white chocolate and orange liqueur instead.

5 For the Coffee Chocolate Fudge, follow the recipe, using light brown sugar and coffee liqueur or rum. Stir in the coffee essence at the end.

6 Serve the sauce over cream-filled profiteroles, and serve any that is left over separately.

Glossy Chocolate Sauce

Delicious poured over ice cream or on hot or cold desserts, this sauce also freezes well. Pour into a freezer-proof container, seal, and keep for up to three months. Thaw at room temperature.

INGREDIENTS

Serves 6
115g/4oz/½ cup caster sugar
175g/6oz plain chocolate, broken into
  squares
30ml/2 tbsp unsalted butter
30ml/2 tbsp brandy or orange juice

1 Place the sugar and 60ml/ 4 tbsp of water in a saucepan and heat gently, stirring occasionally, until the sugar has dissolved.

2 Stir in the chocolate, a few squares at a time, until melted, then add the butter in the same way. Do not allow the sauce to boil. Stir in the brandy or orange juice and serve warm.

Hot Puddings & Desserts

✦ ✦ ✦

Warm Lemon and Syrup Cake

The combination of pears, sticky syrup and lemon makes this a real winner. Drizzle with single cream for extra luxury.

Serves 8

3 eggs

175g/6oz/¾ cup butter, softened

175g/6oz/¾ cup caster sugar

175g/6oz/1½ cups self-raising flour

50g/2oz/½ cup ground almonds

1.5ml/¼ tsp freshly grated nutmeg

50g/2oz/5 tbsp candied lemon peel, finely chopped

grated rind of 1 lemon

30ml/2 tbsp lemon juice

poached pears, to serve

For the syrup

175g/6oz/¾ cup caster sugar

juice of 3 lemons

1 Preheat the oven to 180°C/350°F/Gas 4. Grease and base-line a deep, round 20cm/8in cake tin.

2 Place all the cake ingredients in a large bowl and beat well for 2–3 minutes, until the mixture is light and fluffy.

3 Tip the mixture into the prepared tin, spread level and bake for 1 hour, or until golden and firm to the touch.

4 Meanwhile, make the syrup. Put the sugar, lemon juice and 75ml/5 tbsp water in a pan. Heat gently, stirring until the sugar has dissolved, then boil, without stirring, for 1–2 minutes.

5 Turn out the cake on to a plate with a rim. Prick the surface of the cake all over with a fork, then pour over the hot syrup. Leave to soak for about 30 minutes. Serve the cake warm with thin wedges of poached pears.

Chocolate and Orange Scotch Pancakes

Fabulous baby pancakes in a rich creamy orange liqueur sauce.

INGREDIENTS

Serves 4

115g/4oz/1 cup self-raising flour

30ml/2 tbsp cocoa powder

2 eggs

50g/2oz plain chocolate, broken into
    squares

200ml/7fl oz/⅞ cup milk

finely grated rind of 1 orange

30ml/2 tbsp orange juice

butter or oil for frying

60ml/4 tbsp chocolate curls, for sprinkling

For the sauce

2 large oranges

30ml/2 tbsp unsalted butter

45ml/3 tbsp light muscovado sugar

250ml/8fl oz/1 cup crème fraîche

30ml/2 tbsp Grand Marnier or Cointreau

chocolate curls, to decorate

1 Sift the flour and cocoa into a bowl and make a well in the centre. Add the eggs and beat well, gradually incorporating the surrounding dry ingredients to make a smooth batter.

2 Mix the chocolate and milk in a saucepan. Heat gently until the chocolate has melted, then beat into the batter until smooth and bubbly. Stir in the grated orange rind and juice.

3 Heat a large heavy-based frying pan or griddle. Grease with a little butter or oil. Drop large spoonfuls of batter on to the hot surface. Cook over a moderate heat. When the pancakes are lightly browned underneath and bubbly on top, flip them over to cook the other side. Slide on to a plate and keep hot, then make more in the same way.

4 Make the sauce. Grate the rind of 1 of the oranges into a bowl and set aside. Peel both oranges, taking care to remove all the pith, then slice the flesh fairly thinly.

5 Heat the butter and sugar in a wide, shallow pan over a low heat, stirring until the sugar dissolves. Stir in the crème fraîche and heat gently.

6 Add the pancakes and orange slices to the sauce, heat gently for 1–2 minutes, then spoon over the liqueur. Sprinkle with the reserved orange rind. Scatter over the chocolate curls and serve the pancakes at once.

Gingerbread Upside-down Pudding

A proper pudding goes down well on a cold winter's day. This one is quite quick and easy to make and looks very impressive.

Serves 4–6

sunflower oil, for brushing

15ml/1 tbsp soft brown sugar

4 medium peaches, halved and stoned, or canned peach halves

8 walnut halves

For the base

130g/4½ oz/generous 1 cup wholemeal flour

2.5ml/½ tsp bicarbonate of soda

7.5ml/1½ tsp ground ginger

5ml/1 tsp ground cinnamon

115g/4oz/½ cup molasses sugar

1 egg

120ml/4fl oz/½ cup skimmed milk

50ml/2fl oz/¼ cup sunflower oil

1 Preheat the oven to 180°C/ 350°F/Gas 4. For the topping, brush the base and sides of a 23cm/9in round springform cake tin with oil. Sprinkle the sugar over the base.

2 Arrange the peaches cut-side down in the tin with a walnut half in each.

3 Sift together the flour, bicarbonate of soda, ginger and cinnamon, then stir in the sugar. Beat together the egg, milk and oil, then mix into the dry ingredients.

4 Pour the mixture evenly over the peaches and bake for 35–40 minutes, until firm to the touch. Turn out and serve hot.

Rhubarb-Strawberry Crisp

Strawberries, cinnamon and ground almonds make this a luxurious and delicious version of rhubarb crumble.

INGREDIENTS

Serves 4

225g/8oz strawberries, hulled

450g/1lb rhubarb, diced

90g/3½oz/½ cup granulated sugar

15ml/1 tbsp cornflour

85ml/3fl oz/⅓ cup fresh orange juice

115g/4oz/1 cup plain flour

90g/3½oz/1 cup rolled oats

115g/4oz/½ cup light brown sugar,
   firmly packed

2.5ml/½ tsp ground cinnamon

50g/2oz/½ cup ground almonds

150g/5oz/generous ½ cup cold butter

1 egg, lightly beaten

1 If the strawberries are large, cut them in half. Combine the strawberries, rhubarb and granulated sugar in a 2.4 litre/ 4 pint/10 cup baking dish. Preheat the oven to 180°C/350°F/Gas 4.

2 In a small bowl, blend the cornflour with the orange juice. Pour this mixture over the fruit and stir gently to coat. Set the baking dish aside while making the crumble topping.

3 In a bowl, toss together the flour, oats, brown sugar, cinnamon and ground almonds. With a pastry blender or two knives, cut in the butter until the mixture resembles coarse bread-crumbs. Stir in the beaten egg.

4 Spoon the oat mixture evenly over the fruit and press down gently. Bake until browned, 50–60 minutes, then serve warm.

Baked Apples with Caramel Sauce

The creamy caramel sauce turns this simple country dessert into a more sophisticated delicacy.

INGREDIENTS

Serves 6

3 Granny Smith apples, cored but not peeled

3 Red Delicious apples, cored but not peeled

150g/5oz/¾ cup light brown sugar

2.5ml/½ tsp grated nutmeg

1.5ml/¼ tsp freshly ground black pepper

40g/1½ oz/¼ cup walnut pieces

40g/1½ oz/scant ¼ cup sultanas

50g/2oz/4 tbsp butter or margarine, diced

For the caramel sauce

15g/½oz/1 tbsp butter or margarine

120ml/4fl oz/½ cup whipping cream

1 Preheat the oven to 190°C/ 375°F/Gas 5. Grease a baking tin just large enough to hold the apples.

2 With a small knife, cut at an angle to enlarge the core opening at the stem-end of each apple to about 2.5cm/1in in diameter. (The opening should resemble a funnel in shape.)

3 Arrange the apples in the prepared tin, stem-end up.

4 In a small saucepan, combine 175ml/6fl oz/¾ cup of water with the brown sugar, nutmeg and pepper. Bring the mixture to the boil, stirring. Boil for 6 minutes.

5 Mix together the walnuts and sultanas. Spoon some of the walnut-sultana mixture into the opening in each apple.

6 Top each apple with some of the diced butter or margarine.

7 Spoon the brown sugar sauce over and around the apples. Bake, basting occasionally with the sauce, until the apples are just tender, 45–50 minutes. Transfer the apples to a serving dish, reserving the brown sugar sauce in the baking tin. Keep the apples warm.

8 For the caramel sauce, mix the butter or margarine, cream and reserved brown sugar sauce in a saucepan. Bring to the boil, stirring occasionally, and simmer until thickened, about 2 minutes. Leave the sauce to cool slightly before serving.

VARIATION

Use a mixture of firm red and gold pears instead of the apples, preparing them in the same way. Cook for 10 minutes longer.

Cabinet Pudding

A rich, baked custard, flavoured with glacé and dried fruit.

INGREDIENTS

Serves 4

25g/1oz/2½ tbsp raisins, chopped
30ml/2 tbsp brandy (optional)
25g/1oz/2½ tbsp glacé cherries, halved
25g/1oz/2½ tbsp angelica, chopped
2 trifle sponge cakes, diced
50g/2oz ratafias, crushed
2 eggs
2 egg yolks
30ml/2 tbsp sugar
450ml/¾ pint/1⅞ cups single cream or
    milk
few drops of vanilla essence

1 Soak the raisins in the brandy, if using, for several hours.

2 Butter a 750ml/1¼ pint/3 cup charlotte mould and arrange some of the cherries and angelica in the base.

3 Mix the remaining cherries and angelica with the sponge cakes, ratafias and raisins and brandy, if using, and spoon into the mould.

4 Lightly whisk together the eggs, egg yolks and sugar. Bring the cream or milk just to the boil, then stir into the egg mixture with the vanilla essence.

5 Strain the egg mixture into the mould, then leave for 15–30 minutes.

6 Preheat the oven to 160°C/ 325°F/Gas 3. Place the mould in a roasting tin, cover with baking paper and pour in boiling water to come halfway up the side of the mould. Bake for 1 hour, or until set. Leave for 2–3 minutes, then turn out on to a warm plate, to serve.

Eve's Pudding

The tempting apples beneath the sponge topping are the reason for the pudding's name.

INGREDIENTS

Serves 4–6

115g/4oz/½ cup butter
115g/4oz/generous ½ cup caster sugar
2 eggs, beaten
grated rind and juice of 1 lemon
90g/3½oz/scant 1 cup self-raising flour
40g/1½oz/⅓ cup ground almonds
115g/4oz/scant ½ cup soft brown sugar
675g/1½lb cooking apples, cored and
    thinly sliced
25g/1oz/¼ cup flaked almonds

1 Beat together the butter and caster sugar in a large mixing bowl until the mixture is very light and fluffy.

2 Gradually beat the eggs into the butter mixture, beating well after each addition, then fold in the lemon rind, flour and ground almonds.

3 Mix the brown sugar, apples and lemon juice, tip into the dish, add the sponge mixture, then the almonds. Bake for 40–45 minutes, until golden.

Chocolate Crêpes with Plums and Port

A good dinner party dessert, this dish can be made in advance and always looks impressive.

INGREDIENTS

Serves 6

50g/2oz plain chocolate, broken into
    squares
200ml/7fl oz/⅞ cup milk
120ml/4fl oz/½ cup single cream
30ml/2 tbsp cocoa powder
115g/4oz/1 cup plain flour
2 eggs

For the filling

500g/1¼lb red or golden plums
50g/2oz/¼ cup caster sugar
30ml/2 tbsp port
oil, for frying
175g/6oz/¾ cup crème fraîche

For the sauce

150g/5oz plain chocolate, broken into
    squares
175ml/6fl oz/¾ cup double cream
30ml/2 tbsp port

1 Place the chocolate in a saucepan with the milk. Heat gently until the chocolate has dissolved. Pour into a blender or food processor and add the cream, cocoa powder, flour and eggs. Process until smooth, then tip into a jug and chill for 30 minutes.

2 Meanwhile, make the filling. Halve and stone the plums. Place them in a saucepan and add the sugar and 30ml/2 tbsp of water. Bring to the boil, then lower the heat, cover, and simmer for about 10 minutes or until the plums are tender. Stir in the port and simmer for a further 30 seconds. Remove the pan from the heat and keep warm.

3 Have ready a sheet of non-stick baking paper. Heat a crêpe pan, grease it lightly with a little oil, then pour in just enough batter to cover the base of the pan, swirling to coat it evenly.

4 Cook until the crêpe has set, then flip it over to cook the other side. Slide the crêpe out on to the sheet of paper, then cook 9–11 more crêpes in the same way.

5 Make the sauce. Combine the chocolate and cream in a saucepan. Heat gently, stirring until smooth. Add the port and heat gently, stirring, for 1 minute.

6 Divide the plum filling between the crêpes, add a dollop of crème fraîche to each and roll them up carefully. Serve in shallow plates, with the chocolate sauce spooned over the top.

Pears in Chocolate Fudge Blankets

Warm poached pears coated in a rich chocolate fudge sauce – who could resist?

Serves 6

6 ripe eating pears

30ml/2 tbsp lemon juice

75g/3oz/scant ½ cup caster sugar

1 cinnamon stick

For the sauce

200ml/7fl oz/⅞ cup double cream

150g/5oz/scant 1 cup light muscovado
   sugar

25g/1oz/2 tbsp unsalted butter

60ml/4 tbsp golden syrup

120ml/4fl oz/½ cup milk

200g/7oz plain dark chocolate, broken
   into squares

1 Peel the pears thinly, leaving the stalks on. Scoop out the cores from the base. Brush the cut surfaces with lemon juice to prevent browning.

2 Place the sugar and 300ml/ ½ pint/1¼ cups of water in a large saucepan. Heat gently until the sugar dissolves. Add the pears and cinnamon stick with any remaining lemon juice, and, if necessary, a little more water, so that the pears are almost covered.

3 Bring to the boil, then lower the heat, cover the pan and simmer the pears gently for 15-20 minutes.

4 Meanwhile, make the sauce. Place the cream, sugar, butter, golden syrup and milk in a heavy-based saucepan. Heat gently until the sugar has dissolved and the butter and syrup have melted, then bring to the boil. Boil, stirring constantly, for about 5 minutes or until thick and smooth.

5 Remove the pan from the heat and stir in the chocolate until it has melted.

6 Using a slotted spoon, transfer the poached pears to a dish. Keep hot. Boil the syrup rapidly to reduce to about 45–60ml/3–4 tbsp. Remove the cinnamon stick and gently stir the syrup into the chocolate sauce.

7 Serve the pears in individual bowls or on dessert plates, with the hot chocolate fudge sauce spooned over.

Sticky Toffee Pudding

Filling, warming and packed with calories, but still everyone's favourite pudding.

INGREDIENTS

Serves 6

115g/4oz/1 cup toasted walnuts, chopped
175g/6oz/¾ cup butter
175g/6oz/scant 1 cup soft brown sugar
60ml/4 tbsp single cream
30ml/2 tbsp lemon juice
2 eggs, beaten
115g/4oz/1 cup self-raising flour

1 Grease a 900ml/1½ pint/ 3¾ cup pudding basin and add half the walnuts.

2 Heat 50g/2oz/4 tbsp of the butter with 50g/2oz/4 tbsp of the sugar, the cream and 15ml/ 1 tbsp lemon juice in a small pan, stirring until smooth. Pour half into the pudding basin, then swirl to coat it a little way up the sides.

3 Beat the remaining butter and sugar until light and fluffy, then gradually beat in the eggs. Fold in the flour and the remaining nuts and lemon juice and spoon into the bowl.

4 Cover the bowl with greaseproof paper with a pleat folded in the centre, then tie securely with string.

5 Steam the pudding for about 1¼ hours, until it is set in the centre.

6 Just before serving, gently warm the remaining sauce. Unmould the pudding on to a warm plate and pour over the warm sauce.

Chocolate and Orange Soufflé

The base in this soufflé is an easy-to-make semolina mixture, rather than the thick white sauce that most soufflés call for.

INGREDIENTS

Serves 4

600ml/1 pint/2½ cups milk
50g/2oz/generous ⅓ cup semolina
50g/2oz/scant ¼ cup brown sugar
grated rind of 1 orange
90ml/6 tbsp fresh orange juice
3 eggs, separated
65g/2½oz plain chocolate, grated
icing sugar, for sprinkling

1 Preheat the oven to 200°C/400°F/Gas 6. Butter a shallow 1.75 litre/3 pint/7½ cup ovenproof dish.

2 Pour the milk into a heavy-based saucepan and sprinkle over the semolina and brown sugar. Bring to the boil, stirring the mixture all the time, until thickened.

3 Remove the pan from the heat, beat in the orange rind and juice, egg yolks and all but 15ml/ 1 tbsp of the grated chocolate.

4 Whisk the egg whites until stiff, then lightly fold into the semolina mixture in three batches. Spoon into the buttered dish and bake for about 30 minutes, until just set in the centre. Sprinkle with the reserved chocolate and the icing sugar.

Queen of Puddings

This hot pudding was developed from a seventeenth-century recipe by Queen Victoria's chefs and named in her honour.

INGREDIENTS

Serves 4

75g/3oz/1½ cups fresh breadcrumbs

60ml/4 tbsp caster sugar, plus 5ml/1 tsp

grated rind of 1 lemon

600ml/1 pint/2½ cups milk

4 eggs

45ml/3 tbsp raspberry jam, warmed

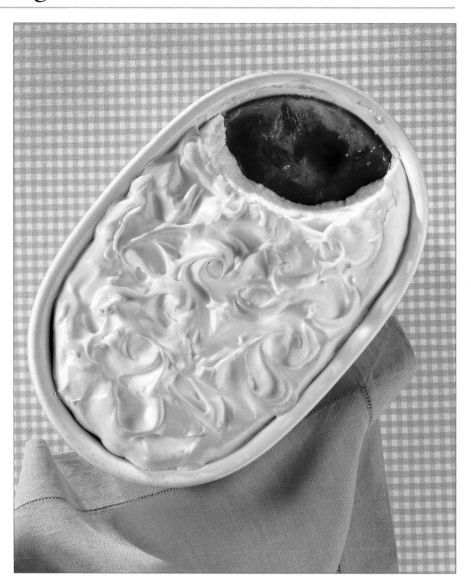

1 Preheat the oven to 160°C/ 325°F/Gas 3. Stir the breadcrumbs, 30ml/2 tbsp of the sugar and the lemon rind together in a bowl. Bring the milk to the boil in a saucepan, then stir into the breadcrumb mixture.

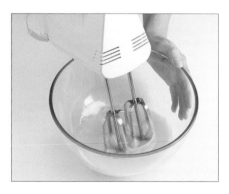

2 Separate three of the eggs and beat the yolks with the whole egg. Stir into the breadcrumb mixture, pour into a buttered baking dish and leave to stand for 30 minutes, then bake the pudding for 50–60 minutes, until set.

COOK'S TIP

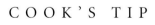

Ring the changes by using another flavoured jam, lemon curd, marmalade or fruit purée.

3 Whisk the three egg whites in a large, clean bowl until stiff but not dry, then gradually whisk in the remaining 30ml/2 tbsp caster sugar until the mixture is thick and glossy, taking care not to overwhip.

4 Spread the jam over the pudding, then spoon over the meringue to cover the top completely. Sprinkle the remaining sugar over the meringue, then bake for a further 15 minutes, until the meringue is beginning to turn a light golden colour.

Magic Chocolate Mud Pudding

A popular favourite, which magically separates into a light and luscious sponge and a velvety chocolate sauce.

INGREDIENTS

Serves 4

50g/2oz/4 tbsp butter

200g/7oz/generous 1 cup light muscovado sugar

475ml/16fl oz/2 cups milk

90g/3½oz/scant 1 cup self-raising flour

5ml/1 tsp ground cinnamon

75ml/5 tbsp cocoa powder

Greek-style yogurt or vanilla ice cream, to serve

1 Preheat the oven to 180°C/350°F/Gas 4. Lightly grease a 1.5 litre/2½ pint/6 cup ovenproof dish and place on a baking sheet.

2 Place the butter in a saucepan. Add 115g/4oz/¾ cup of the sugar and 150ml/¼ pint/⅔ cup of the milk. Heat gently, stirring from time to time, until the butter has melted and all the sugar has dissolved. Remove the pan from the heat.

COOK'S TIP

A soufflé dish will support the sponge as it rises above the sauce.

3 Sift the flour, cinnamon and 15ml/1 tbsp of the cocoa powder into the pan and stir into the mixture, mixing evenly. Pour the mixture into the prepared dish and level the surface.

4 Sift the remaining sugar and cocoa powder into a bowl, mix well, then sprinkle over the pudding mixture.

5 Pour the remaining milk over the pudding.

6 Bake for 45–50 minutes or until the sponge has risen to the top and is firm to the touch. Serve hot, with the yogurt or vanilla ice cream.

Christmas Pudding

This recipe makes enough to fill one 1.2 litre/2 pint/5 cup basin or two 600ml/1 pint/2½ cup basins. It can be made up to a month before Christmas and stored in a cool, dry place. Steam the pudding for 2 hours before serving. Serve with brandy or rum butter, whisky sauce, custard or whipped cream, topped with a decorative sprig of holly.

INGREDIENTS

Serves 8

115g/4oz/½ cup butter

225g/8oz/1 heaped cup soft dark brown sugar

50g/2oz/½ cup self-raising flour

5ml/1tsp ground mixed spice

1.5ml/¼ tsp grated nutmeg

2.5ml/½ tsp ground cinnamon

2 eggs

115g/4oz/2 cups fresh white breadcrumbs

175g/6oz/generous 1 cup sultanas

175g/6oz/generous 1 cup raisins

115g/4oz/½ cup currants

25g/1oz/3 tbsp mixed candied peel, chopped finely

25g/1oz/¼ cup chopped almonds

1 small cooking apple, peeled, cored and coarsely grated

finely grated rind or 1 orange or lemon

juice of 1 orange or lemon, made up to 150ml/¼ pint/⅔ cup with brandy, rum or sherry

1 Cut a disc of greaseproof paper to fit the base of the basin(s) and butter the disc and basin(s).

2 Whisk the butter and sugar together until soft. Beat in the flour, spices and eggs. Stir in the remaining ingredients thoroughly. The mixture should have a soft dropping consistency.

3 Turn the mixture into the greased basin(s) and level the top with a spoon.

4 Cover with another disc of buttered greaseproof paper.

5 Make a pleat across the centre of a large piece of greaseproof paper and cover the basin(s) with it, tying it in place with string under the rim. Cut off the excess paper. Pleat a piece of foil in the same way and cover the basin(s) with it, tucking it around the bowl neatly, under the greaseproof frill. Tie another piece of string around and across the top, as a handle.

6 Place the basin(s) in a steamer over a pan of simmering water and steam for 6 hours. Alternatively, put the basin(s) into a large pan and pour round enough boiling water to come halfway up the basin(s) and cover the pan with a tight-fitting lid. Check the water is simmering and top it up with boiling water as it evaporates. When the pudding(s) have cooked, leave to cool completely. Then remove the foil and greaseproof paper. Wipe the basin(s) clean and replace the greaseproof paper and foil with clean pieces, ready for reheating.

TO SERVE

Steam for 2 hours. Turn on to a plate and leave to stand for 5 minutes, before removing the pudding basin (the steam will rise to the top of the basin and help to loosen the pudding). Decorate with a sprig of holly.

Steamed Chocolate and Fruit Puddings

Some things always turn out well, including these wonderful little puddings. Dark, fluffy chocolate sponge with tangy cranberries and apple is served with a honeyed chocolate syrup.

INGREDIENTS

Serves 4

115g/4oz/⅔ cup dark muscovado sugar

1 eating apple

75g/3oz/¾ cup cranberries, thawed if frozen

115g/4oz/½ cup soft margarine

2 eggs

75g/3oz/⅔ cup plain flour

2.5ml/½ tsp baking powder

45ml/3 tbsp cocoa powder

For the chocolate syrup

115g/4oz plain chocolate, broken into squares

30ml/2 tbsp clear honey

15ml/1 tbsp unsalted butter

2.5ml/½ tsp vanilla essence

1 Prepare a steamer or half fill a saucepan with water and bring it to the boil. Grease four individual pudding basins and sprinkle each one with a little of the muscovado sugar to coat well all over.

2 Peel and core the apple. Dice it into a bowl, add the cranberries and mix well. Divide equally among the prepared pudding basins.

3 Place the remaining muscovado sugar in a mixing bowl. Add the margarine, eggs, flour, baking powder and cocoa; beat until combined and smooth.

4 Spoon the mixture into the basins and cover each with a double thickness of foil. Steam for about 45 minutes, topping up the boiling water as required, until the puddings are well risen and firm.

5 Make the syrup. Mix the chocolate, honey, butter and vanilla essence in a small saucepan. Heat gently, stirring, until melted and smooth.

6 Run a knife around the edge of each pudding to loosen it, then turn out on to individual plates. Serve immediately, with the chocolate syrup.

COOK'S TIP

The puddings can be cooked very quickly in the microwave. Use non-metallic basins and cover with greaseproof paper instead of foil. Cook on High (100% power) for 5–6 minutes, then stand for 2–3 minutes before turning out.

Hot Chocolate Cake

This is wonderfully wicked served as a pudding with a white chocolate sauce. The basic cake freezes well – thaw, then warm in the microwave before serving.

INGREDIENTS

Makes 10–12 slices

200g/7oz/1¾ cups self-raising wholemeal
  flour
25g/1oz/¼ cup cocoa powder
pinch of salt
175g/6oz/¾ cup soft margarine
175g/6oz/¾ cup soft light brown sugar
few drops vanilla essence
4 eggs
75g/3oz white chocolate, roughly chopped
chocolate leaves and curls, to decorate

For the white chocolate sauce
75g/3oz white chocolate
150ml/¼ pint/⅔ cup single cream
30–45ml/2–3 tbsp milk

1 Preheat the oven to 160°C/
  325°F/Gas 3. Sift the flour,
cocoa powder and salt into a bowl,
adding in the whole wheat flakes
from the sieve.

2 Cream the margarine, sugar
  and vanilla essence together
until light and fluffy, then gently
beat in one egg.

3 Gradually stir in the remaining
  eggs, one at a time, alternately
folding in some of the flour, until
the mixture is blended in.

4 Stir in the white chocolate and
  spoon into a 675–900g/
1½–2lb loaf tin or a 18cm/7in
greased cake tin. Bake for 30–40
minutes, or until just firm to the
touch and shrinking away from the
sides of the tin.

5 Meanwhile, prepare the sauce.
  Heat the white chocolate and
cream very gently in a pan until
the chocolate is melted. Add the
milk and stir until cool.

6 Serve the cake sliced, in a pool
  of sauce and decorated with
chocolate leaves and curls.

Bread Pudding with Pecan Nuts

A version of the British classic deliciously flavoured with pecan nuts and orange rind.

INGREDIENTS

Serves 6

400ml/14fl oz/1⅔ cups milk

400ml/14fl oz/1⅔ cups single or whipping
 cream

150g/5oz/¾ cup caster sugar

3 eggs, beaten to mix

10ml/2 tsp grated orange rind

5ml/1 tsp vanilla essence

24 slices of day-old French bread,
 1.5cm/½in thick

75g/3oz/½ cup toasted pecan nuts,
 chopped

icing sugar, for sprinkling

whipped cream or soured cream and
 maple syrup, to serve

1 Put 350ml/12fl oz/1½ cups each of the milk and cream in a saucepan. Add the sugar. Warm over low heat, stirring to dissolve the sugar. Remove from the heat and cool. Add the eggs, orange rind and vanilla and mix well.

2 Arrange half of the bread slices in a buttered 23–25cm/9–10in baking dish. Scatter two-thirds of the pecans over the bread. Arrange the remaining bread slices on top and scatter on the rest of the pecans.

3 Pour the egg mixture evenly over the bread slices. Soak for 30 minutes. Press the top layer of bread down into the liquid once or twice.

4 Preheat the oven to 180°C/350°F/Gas 4. If the top layer of bread slices looks dry and all the liquid has been absorbed, moisten with the remaining milk and cream.

5 Set the baking dish in a roasting tin. Add enough water to the tin to come halfway up the sides of the dish. Bring the water to the boil.

6 Transfer to the oven. Bake for 40 minutes or until the pudding is set and golden brown on top. Sprinkle the top of the pudding with sifted icing sugar and serve warm, with whipped cream or soured cream and maple syrup, if you like.

Chocolate Chip and Banana Pudding

*Hot and steamy, this superb light
pudding tastes extra special served
with chocolate sauce.*

INGREDIENTS

Serves 4

200g/7oz/1¾ cups self-raising flour

75g/3oz/6 tbsp unsalted butter or
    margarine

2 ripe bananas

75g/3oz/⅓ cup caster sugar

60ml/4 tbsp milk

1 egg, beaten

60ml/4 tbsp plain chocolate chips or
    chopped chocolate

Glossy Chocolate Sauce (see Basic
    Techniques) and whipped cream, to serve

1 Prepare a steamer or half fill a
saucepan with water and bring
it to the boil. Grease a 1 litre/
1¾ pint/4 cup pudding basin. Sift
the flour into a bowl and rub in
the butter or margarine until the
mixture resembles breadcrumbs.

2 Mash the bananas in a bowl.
Stir them into the creamed
mixture, with the caster sugar.

3 Whisk the milk with the egg in
a jug or bowl, then beat into
the pudding mixture. Stir in the
plain chocolate chips or chopped
chocolate.

4 Spoon the mixture into the
prepared basin, cover closely
with a double thickness of foil, and
steam for 2 hours, topping up the
water as required during cooking.

5 Run a knife around the top of
the pudding to loosen it, then
turn it out on to a warm serving
dish. Serve hot, with the
chocolate sauce and a spoonful of
whipped cream.

COOK'S TIP

If you have a food processor,
make a quick-mix version by
processing all the ingredients,
except the chocolate, until
smooth. Stir in the chocolate and
proceed as in the recipe.

Hot Plum Batter Pudding

Other fruits can be used in place of plums, depending on the season. Canned black cherries are a convenient substitute to keep in the storecupboard.

INGREDIENTS

Serves 4

450g/1lb ripe red plums, quartered and stoned
200ml/7fl oz/⅞ cup skimmed milk
60ml/4 tbsp skimmed milk powder
15ml/1 tbsp light muscovado sugar
5ml/1 tsp vanilla essence
75g/3oz/⅔ cup self-raising flour
2 egg whites
icing sugar, to sprinkle

1 Preheat the oven to 220°C/ 425°F/Gas 7. Lightly oil a wide, shallow ovenproof dish and add the plums.

2 Pour the milk, milk powder, sugar, vanilla, flour and egg whites into a blender or food processor. Process until smooth.

3 Pour the batter over the plums. Bake for 25–30 minutes, or until puffed and golden. Sprinkle with icing sugar and serve immediately.

> ### COOK'S TIP
> ∿
>
> If you don't have a food processor, then place the dry ingredients for the batter in a large bowl and gradually whisk in the milk and egg whites.

Glazed Apricot Sponge

Proper puddings can be very high in saturated fat, but this healthy version uses the minimum of oil and no eggs.

INGREDIENTS

Serves 4

10ml/2 tsp golden syrup
411g/14½oz can apricot halves in fruit juice
150g/5oz/1¼ cups self-raising flour
75g/3oz/1½ cups fresh breadcrumbs
90g/3½oz/½ cup light muscovado sugar
5ml/1 tsp ground cinnamon
30ml/2 tbsp sunflower oil
175ml/6fl oz/¾ cup skimmed milk

1 Preheat the oven to 180°C/ 350°F/Gas 4. Lightly oil a 900ml/1½ pint/3¾ cup pudding basin. Spoon in the syrup.

2 Drain the apricots and reserve the juice. Arrange about 8 halves in the basin. Purée the rest of the apricots with the juice and set aside.

3 Mix the flour, breadcrumbs, sugar and cinnamon then beat in the oil and milk. Spoon into the basin and bake for 50–55 minutes, or until firm and golden. Turn out and serve with the puréed fruit as an accompaniment.

Crunchy Gooseberry Crumble

Gooseberries are perfect for traditional family puddings like this one. When gooseberries are out of season, other fruits such as apples, plums or rhubarb could be used instead.

INGREDIENTS

Serves 4

500g/1¼lb/5 cups gooseberries
50g/2oz/4 tbsp caster sugar
75g/3oz/scant 1 cup rolled oats
75g/3oz/⅔ cup wholemeal flour
60ml/4 tbsp sunflower oil
50g/2oz/4 tbsp demerara sugar
30ml/2 tbsp chopped walnuts
natural yogurt or custard, to serve

1 Preheat the oven to 200°C/ 400°F/Gas 6. Place the gooseberries in a pan with the caster sugar. Cover the pan and cook over a very low heat for about 10 minutes, until the gooseberries are just tender. Tip the contents of the pan into an ovenproof dish.

2 To make the crumble, place the oats, flour and oil in a bowl and stir with a fork until evenly mixed.

3 Stir in the demerara sugar and walnuts, then spread evenly over the gooseberries. Bake for 25–30 minutes, or until golden and bubbling. Serve hot with yogurt, or custard made with skimmed milk.

COOK'S TIP

The best gooseberries to use for cooking are the early, small, firm green ones.

Chocolate Amaretti Peaches

Quick and easy to prepare, this delicious dessert can also be made with fresh nectarines or apricots.

INGREDIENTS

Serves 4

115g/4oz amaretti biscuits, crushed
50g/2oz plain chocolate, chopped
grated rind of ½ orange
15ml/1 tbsp clear honey
1.5ml/¼ tsp ground cinnamon
1 egg white, lightly beaten
4 firm ripe peaches
150ml/¼ pint/⅔ cup white wine
15ml/1 tbsp caster sugar
whipped cream, to serve

1 Preheat the oven to 190°C/375°F/Gas 5. Mix together the crushed amaretti biscuits, chocolate, orange rind, honey and cinnamon in a bowl. Add the beaten egg white and mix to bind the mixture together.

2 Halve and stone the peaches and fill the cavities with the chocolate mixture, mounding it up slightly.

3 Arrange the stuffed peaches in a lightly buttered, shallow ovenproof dish which will just hold the peaches comfortably. Pour the wine into a measuring cup and stir in the sugar.

4 Pour the wine mixture around the peaches. Bake for 30–40 minutes, until the peaches are tender. Serve at once with a little of the cooking juices spooned over and the whipped cream.

Apple Fritters

Make sure you buy plenty of apples for this recipe. They taste so good you'll probably have to cook an extra batch.

INGREDIENTS

Serves 4–6

130g/4½oz/1⅓ cups plain flour

10ml/2 tsp baking powder

1.5ml/¼ tsp salt

150ml/¼ pint/⅔ cup milk

1 egg, beaten

oil for deep-frying

150g/5oz/¾ cup granulated sugar

5ml/1 tsp ground cinnamon

2 large tart-sweet apples, peeled, cored, and cut in 5mm/¼ in slices

icing sugar, for dusting

1 Sift the flour, baking powder and salt into a bowl. Beat in the milk and egg with a wire whisk.

2 Heat at least 7.5cm/3in of oil in a heavy frying pan to 185°C/360°F or until a cube of bread browns in 1–2 minutes.

3 Mix the granulated sugar and cinnamon in a shallow bowl or plate. Toss the apple slices in the sugar mixture to coat all over.

4 Dip the apple slices in the batter, using a fork or slotted spoon. Drain off excess batter. Fry, in batches, in the hot oil until golden brown on both sides, about 4–5 minutes. Drain the fritters on kitchen paper.

5 Sprinkle with icing sugar, and serve hot.

Cherry Compote

Sweet cherries in syrup to serve with cream or ice cream.

INGREDIENTS

Serves 6

120ml/4fl oz/½ cup red wine

50g/2oz/¼ cup light brown sugar, firmly packed

50g/2oz/¼ cup granulated sugar

15ml/1 tbsp honey

2 2.5cm/1in strips of orange rind

1.5ml/¼ tsp almond extract

675g/1½lb sweet fresh cherries, pitted

ice cream or whipped cream, for serving

1 Combine all the ingredients except the cherries in a saucepan with 120ml/4fl oz/½ cup of water. Stir over medium heat until the sugar dissolves. Raise the heat and boil until the liquid reduces slightly.

2 Add the cherries. Bring back to the boil. Reduce the heat slightly and simmer for 8–10 minutes. If necessary, skim off any foam.

3 Let cool to lukewarm. Spoon warm over vanilla ice cream, or refrigerate and serve cold with whipped cream, if desired.

Ginger Baked Pears

This simple French dessert is the kind that would be served after Sunday lunch or a family supper. Try to find Comice or Anjou pears – this recipe is especially useful for slightly under-ripe fruit.

INGREDIENTS

Serves 4

4 large pears

300ml/½ pint/1¼ cups whipping cream

50g/2oz/¼ cup caster sugar

2.5ml/½ tsp vanilla essence

1.5ml/¼ tsp ground cinnamon

pinch of freshly grated nutmeg

5ml/1 tsp grated fresh root ginger

1 Preheat the oven to 190°C/375°F/Gas 5. Lightly butter a large shallow baking dish.

2 Peel the pears, cut in half lengthways and remove the cores. Arrange, cut-side down, in a single layer in the baking dish.

3 Mix together the cream, sugar, vanilla essence, cinnamon, nutmeg and ginger and pour over the pears.

4 Bake for 30–35 minutes, basting from time to time, until the pears are tender and browned on top and the cream is thick and bubbly. Cool slightly before serving.

Prunes Poached in Red Wine

Serve this simple dessert on its own, or with crème fraîche or vanilla ice cream.

INGREDIENTS

Serves 8–10

1 unwaxed orange

1 unwaxed lemon

750ml/1¼ pints/3 cups fruity red wine

50g/2oz/¼ cup caster sugar, or to taste

1 cinnamon stick

pinch of freshly grated nutmeg

2 or 3 cloves

5ml/1 tsp black peppercorns

1 bay leaf

900g/2lb large stoned prunes, soaked in cold water

strips of orange rind, to decorate

cream, to serve

1 Using a vegetable peeler, peel two or three strips of rind from both the orange and lemon. Squeeze the juice from both and put in a large saucepan.

2 Add the wine, sugar, spices, peppercorns, bay leaf, strips of rind to the pan and 475ml/16fl oz/ 2 cups of water.

3 Bring to the boil over a medium heat, stirring occasionally to dissolve the sugar. Drain the prunes and add to the saucepan, reduce the heat to low and simmer, covered, for 10–15 minutes until the prunes are tender. Remove from the heat and set aside until cool.

4 Using a slotted spoon, transfer the prunes to a serving dish. Return the cooking liquid to a medium-high heat and bring to the boil. Boil for 5–10 minutes until slightly reduced and syrupy, then pour or strain over the prunes. Cool, then chill before serving with cream, decorated with strips of orange rind, if you like.

Apple Strudel

This Austrian pudding is tradition-ally made with paper-thin layers of buttered strudel pastry, filled with spiced apples and nuts. Ready-made filo pastry makes an easy substitute.

INGREDIENTS

Serves 4–6

75g/3oz/¾ cup hazelnuts, chopped
    and roasted

30ml/2 tbsp nibbed almonds, roasted

50g/2oz/4 tbsp demerara sugar

2.5ml/½ tsp ground cinnamon

grated rind and juice of ½ lemon

2 large Bramley cooking apples, peeled,
    cored and chopped

50g/2oz/⅓ cup sultanas

4 large sheet filo pastry

50g/2oz/4 tbsp unsalted butter, melted

icing sugar, for dusting

cream, custard or yogurt, to serve

1 Preheat the oven to 190°C/ 375°F/Gas 5. In a bowl mix together the hazelnuts, almonds, sugar, cinnamon, lemon rind and juice, apples and sultanas. Set aside.

2 Lay one sheet of filo pastry on a clean dish towel and brush with melted butter. Lay a second sheet on top and brush again with melted butter. Repeat with the remaining two sheets.

3 Spread the fruit and nut mixture over the pastry, leaving a 7.5cm/3in border at the shorter ends. Fold the ends in over the filling. Roll up from one long edge, using the dish towel.

4 Transfer the strudel to a greased baking sheet, placing it seam side down. Brush with butter and bake for 30–35 minutes, until golden and crisp. Dust with icing sugar and serve hot with cream, custard or yogurt.

Chocolate Fruit Fondue

Fondues originated in Switzerland and this sweet treat is the perfect ending to any meal.

INGREDIENTS

Serves 6–8

16 fresh strawberries

4 rings fresh pineapple, cut into wedges

2 small nectarines, stoned and cut
    into wedges

1 kiwi fruit, halved and thickly sliced

small bunch of black seedless grapes

2 bananas, chopped

1 small eating apple, cored and cut
    into wedges

lemon juice, for brushing

225g/8oz plain chocolate

15g/½oz/1 tbsp butter

150ml/¼ pint/⅔ cup single cream

45ml/3 tbsp Irish cream liqueur

15ml/1 tbsp pistachio nuts, chopped

1 Arrange the fruit on a serving platter and brush the banana and apple pieces with a little lemon juice. Cover and place in the fridge until ready to serve.

2 Place the chocolate, butter, cream and liqueur in a bowl over a pan of simmering water. Stir until melted and completely smooth.

3 Pour the mixture into a warmed serving bowl; sprinkle with pistachios. Guests help themselves by skewering fruits on to forks and dipping in the hot sauce.

Crêpes Suzette

This is one of the best-known French desserts and is easy to do at home. You can make the crêpes in advance, then you will be able to put the dish together quickly at the last minute.

INGREDIENTS

Serves 6

115g/4oz/1 cup plain flour

1.5ml/¼ tsp salt

25g/1oz/2 tbsp caster sugar

2 eggs, lightly beaten

250ml/8fl oz/1 cup milk

30ml/2 tbsp orange flower water or
   orange liqueur (optional)

25g/1oz/2 tbsp unsalted butter, melted,
   plus more for frying

For the orange sauce

75g/3oz/6 tbsp unsalted butter

50g/2oz/¼ cup caster sugar

grated rind and juice of 1 large
   unwaxed orange

grated rind and juice of 1 unwaxed lemon

150ml/¼ pint/⅔ cup fresh orange juice

60ml/4 tbsp orange liqueur, plus more for
   flaming (optional)

brandy, for flaming (optional)

orange segments, to decorate

1 In a medium bowl, sift together the flour, salt and sugar. Make a well in the centre and pour in the beaten eggs. Using a whisk, beat the eggs, bringing in a little flour until it is all incorporated. Slowly whisk in the milk and 60ml/4 tbsp water to make a smooth batter.

2 Whisk in the orange flower water or liqueur, if using, then strain the batter into a large jug and set aside for 20–30 minutes. If the batter thickens, add a little milk or water to thin.

3 Heat an 18–20cm/7–8in crêpe pan over a medium heat. Stir the melted butter into the crêpe batter. Brush the hot pan with a little extra melted butter and pour in about 30ml/2 tbsp of batter. Quickly tilt and rotate the pan to cover the base with a thin layer of batter. Cook for about 1 minute until the top is set and the base is golden. With a palette knife, carefully turn over the crêpe and cook for 20–30 seconds, just to set. Tip out on to a plate.

4 Continue cooking the crêpes, stirring the batter occasionally and brushing the pan with a little melted butter as and when necessary. Place a sheet of clear film between each crêpe as they are stacked to prevent sticking.

5 To make the sauce, melt the butter in a large frying pan over a medium-low heat, then stir in the sugar, orange and lemon rind and juice, the additional orange juice and the orange liqueur, if using.

6 Place a crêpe in the pan browned-side down, swirling gently to coat with the sauce. Fold it in half, then in half again to form a triangle and push to the side of the pan. Continue heating and folding the crêpes until all are warm and covered with the sauce.

7 To flame the crêpes, heat 30–45ml/2–3 tbsp each of orange liqueur and brandy in a small saucepan over a medium heat. Remove the pan from the heat, carefully ignite the liquid with a match then gently pour over the crêpes. Scatter over the orange segments and serve at once.

Spiced Mexican Fritters

Hot, sweet and spicy fritters are popular in both Spain and Mexico for either breakfast or a snack.

INGREDIENTS

Makes 16 (serves 4)

175g/6oz/1 cup raspberries

45ml/3 tbsp icing sugar

45ml/3 tbsp orange juice

For the fritters

50g/2oz/4 tbsp butter

65g/2½oz/⅔ cup plain flour, sifted

2 eggs, lightly beaten

15ml/1 tbsp ground almonds

corn oil, for frying

15ml/1 tbsp icing sugar and 2.5ml/½ tsp
   ground cinnamon, for dusting

8 fresh raspberries, to decorate

1 Mash the raspberries with the icing sugar, push through a sieve into a bowl to remove all the seeds. Stir in the orange juice and chill until ready to serve.

2 To make the fritters, place the butter and 150ml/¼ pint/⅔ cup water in a saucepan and heat gently until the butter has melted. Bring to the boil and, when boiling, add the sifted flour all at once and turn off the heat.

3 Beat until the mixture leaves the sides of the pan and forms a ball. Cool slightly then beat in the eggs a little at a time, then add the almonds.

4 Spoon the mixture into a piping bag fitted with a large star nozzle. Half-fill a saucepan or deep-fat fryer with the oil and heat to 190°C/375°F.

5 Pipe about four 5cm/2in lengths at a time into the hot oil, cutting off the raw mixture with a knife as you go. Deep-fry for about 3–4 minutes, turning occasionally, until puffed up and golden. Drain on kitchen paper and keep warm in the oven while frying the remainder.

6 When you have fried all the mixture, dust the hot fritters with icing sugar and cinnamon. Serve three or four per person on serving plates drizzled with a little of the raspberry sauce, dust again with sieved icing sugar and decorate with fresh raspberries.

Thai Fried Bananas

A very simple and quick Thai pudding – bananas fried in butter, brown sugar and lime juice, and sprinkled with toasted coconut.

INGREDIENTS

Serves 4

40g/1½oz/3 tbsp butter

4 large slightly under-ripe bananas

15ml/1 tbsp desiccated coconut

60ml/4 tbsp soft light brown sugar

60ml/4 tbsp lime juice

2 fresh lime slices, to decorate

thick and creamy natural yogurt, to serve

1 Heat the butter in a large frying pan or wok and fry the bananas for 1–2 minutes on each side, or until they are lightly golden in colour.

2 Meanwhile, dry-fry the coconut in a small frying pan until lightly browned, and reserve.

3 Sprinkle the sugar into the pan with the bananas, add the lime juice and cook, stirring until dissolved. Arrange bananas on a serving dish. Sprinkle the coconut over the bananas, decorate with lime slices and serve with the thick and creamy yogurt.

Apple and Lemon Risotto with Poached Plums

Although it's entirely possible to cook this by the conventional risotto method – that is by adding the liquid gradually – it makes more sense to cook the rice with the milk in the same way as for a rice pudding.

INGREDIENTS

Serves 4

1 cooking apple

15g/½ oz/1 tbsp butter

175g/6oz/scant 1 cup risotto rice

600ml/1 pint/2½ cups creamy milk

about 50g/2oz/¼ cup caster sugar

1.5ml/¼ tsp ground cinnamon

30ml/2 tsp lemon juice

45ml/3 tbsp double cream

grated rind of 1 lemon, to decorate

For the poached plums

50g/2oz/¼ cup light brown
   muscovado sugar

200ml/7fl oz/scant 1 cup apple juice

3 star anise

cinnamon stick

6 plums, halved and sliced

1 Peel and core the apple and cut it into large chunks. Put the chunks in a large, non-stick pan and add the butter. Heat gently until the butter melts.

2 Add the rice and milk and stir well to mix. Bring to the boil over a medium heat, then simmer very gently for 20–25 minutes, stirring occasionally.

3 To make the poached plums, dissolve the sugar in 150ml/¼ pint/⅔ cup apple juice in a pan. Add the spices and bring to the boil. Boil for 2 minutes. Add the plums and simmer for 2 minutes. Set aside until ready to serve.

4 Stir the sugar, cinnamon and lemon juice into the risotto. Cook for 2 minutes, stirring all the time, then stir in the cream. Taste and add more sugar if necessary. Decorate with the lemon rind and serve hot with the poached plums.

Chocolate Risotto

If you've never tasted a sweet risotto, there's a treat in store. Chocolate risotto is delectable, and children of all ages love it.

INGREDIENTS

Serves 4–6

175g/6oz/scant 1 cup risotto rice
600ml/1 pint/2½ cups creamy milk
75g/3oz plain chocolate, broken into pieces
25g/1oz/2 tbsp butter
about 50g/2oz/¼ cup caster sugar
pinch of ground cinnamon
60ml/4 tbsp double cream
fresh raspberries and chocolate caraque,
    to decorate
chocolate sauce, to serve

1 Put the rice in a non-stick pan. Pour in the milk and bring to the boil over a low heat. Reduce the heat to the lowest setting and simmer for 20 minutes, stirring.

2 Stir in the chocolate, butter and sugar. Cook, stirring all the time over a very gentle heat for 1–2 minutes, until the chocolate has melted.

3 Remove the pan from the heat and stir in the ground cinnamon and double cream. Cover the pan and leave to stand for a few minutes.

4 Spoon the risotto into individual dishes or dessert plates, and decorate with fresh raspberries and chocolate caraque. Serve with chocolate sauce.

Caramel Rice Pudding

This rice pudding is delicious served with crunchy fresh fruit.

INGREDIENTS

Serves 4

15g/½ oz/1 tbsp butter

50g/2oz/¼ cup short grain (pudding) rice

75ml/5 tbsp demerara sugar

400g/14oz can evaporated milk made up
   to 600ml/1 pint/2½ cups with water

2 fresh baby pineapples

2 figs

1 crisp eating apple

10ml/2 tsp lemon juice

salt

1 Preheat the oven to 150°C/
300°F/Gas 2. Grease a soufflé
dish lightly with a little butter. Put
the rice in a sieve and wash it well
under cold running water. Drain
well and put into the soufflé dish.

2 Add 30ml/2 tbsp of the sugar
to the dish, with a pinch of
salt. Pour over the diluted
evaporated milk and stir gently.

3 Dot the surface of the rice
with butter. Bake for 2 hours,
then leave to cool for 30 minutes.

4 Meanwhile, quarter the
pineapple and the figs. Cut the
apple into segments and toss in the
lemon juice. Preheat the grill.

5 Sprinkle the remaining sugar
evenly over the rice. Grill for
5 minutes or until the sugar has
caramelized. Leave the rice to
stand for 5 minutes to allow the
caramel to harden, then serve
warm with the fresh fruit.

Orange Rice Pudding

In Morocco, as in Spain, Greece and Italy, thick, creamy rice puddings are very popular, especially when sweetened with honey and flavoured with orange.

INGREDIENTS

Serves 4

50g/2oz/generous ¼ cup short grain
   (pudding) rice
600ml/1 pint/2½ cups milk
finely grated rind of ½ small orange
30–45ml/2–3 tbsp clear honey
150ml/¼ pint/⅔ cup double cream
15ml/1 tbsp chopped pistachios,
   toasted (optional)
grated orange rind, to garnish

1 Mix the rice with the milk and orange rind in a saucepan. Pour in the honey and stir well.

2 Bring to the boil, then lower the heat, cover and simmer very gently for about 1¼ hours, stirring frequently.

3 Remove the lid and continue cooking and stirring for 15–20 minutes, until the rice is creamy.

4 Pour in the cream, stirring constantly, then simmer for 5–8 minutes more. Spoon the rice pudding into warmed individual bowls. Sprinkle with the pistachios, if wished, garnish with the orange rind and serve hot.

Cold Puddings & Desserts

❖

Boodles Orange Fool

This fool became the speciality of Boodles Club, a gentlemen's club in London's St James's.

INGREDIENTS

Serves 4

4 trifle sponge cakes, cubed

300ml/½ pint/1¼ cups double cream

30–60ml/2–4 tbsp caster sugar

grated rind and juice of 2 oranges

grated rind and juice of 1 lemon

orange and lemon slices and rind,
    to decorate

1 Line the base and halfway up the sides of a large glass serving bowl or china dish with the cubed trifle sponge cakes.

2 Whip the cream with the sugar until it starts to thicken, then gradually whip in the fruit juices, adding the fruit rinds once most of the juices have been incorporated.

3 Carefully pour the cream mixture into the bowl or dish, taking care not to dislodge the sponge. Cover and chill for 3–4 hours. Serve decorated with orange and lemon slices and rind.

Apricot and Orange Jelly

A light and refreshing dessert for a summer's day.

INGREDIENTS

Serves 4

350g/12oz well-flavoured fresh ripe
    apricots, stoned

50–75g/2–3oz/about ⅓ cup
    granulated sugar

about 300ml/½ pint/1¼ cups freshly
    squeezed orange juice

15ml/1 tbsp powdered gelatine

single cream, to serve

finely chopped candied orange peel,
    to decorate

1 Heat the apricots, sugar and 120ml/4fl oz/½ cup of the orange juice, stirring until the sugar has dissolved. Simmer gently until the apricots are tender.

2 Press the apricot mixture through a nylon sieve into a small measuring jug using a spoon.

3 Pour 45ml/3 tbsp of the orange juice into a small heatproof bowl, sprinkle over the gelatine and leave for about 5 minutes, until softened.

4 Place the bowl over a saucepan of hot water and heat until the gelatine has dissolved. Slowly pour into the apricot mixture, stirring all the time. Make up to 600ml/ 1 pint/2½ cups with the remaining orange juice.

5 Pour the apricot mixture into four individual dishes and chill until set. To serve, pour a thin layer of cream over the surface, and decorate with candied orange peel.

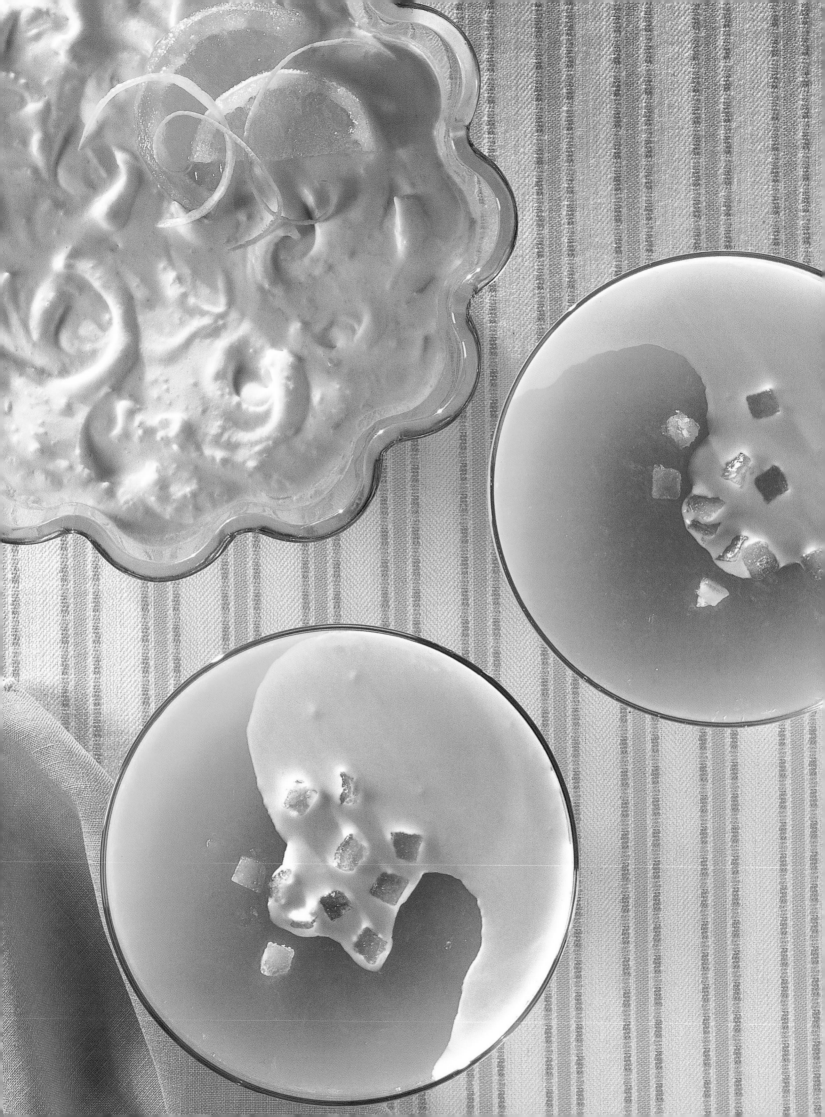

Peach Melba

The story goes that one of the great French chefs, Auguste Escoffier, created this dessert in honour of the opera singer Nellie Melba, now forever enshrined in culinary, if not musical, history.

Serves 6

50g/2oz/¼ cup caster sugar

1 vanilla pod, split lengthways

3 large peaches

For the sauce

450g/1lb/2⅔ cups fresh or frozen
   raspberries

15ml/1 tbsp lemon juice

25–40g/1–1½oz/2–3 tbsp caster sugar

30–45ml/2–3 tbsp raspberry liqueur
   (optional)

vanilla ice cream, to serve

mint leaves and fresh raspberries, to
   decorate (optional)

1 In a saucepan large enough to hold the peach halves in a single layer, combine 1 litre/ 1¾ pints/4 cups of water with the sugar and vanilla pod. Bring to the boil over a medium heat, stirring occasionally to dissolve the sugar.

2 Cut the peaches in half and twist the halves to separate them. Using a small teaspoon, remove the peach stones. Add the peach halves to the poaching syrup, cut-sides down, adding more water, if needed, to cover the fruit. Press a piece of grease-proof paper against the surface, reduce the heat to medium-low, then cover and simmer for 12–15 minutes until tender – the time will depend on the ripeness of the fruit. Remove the pan from the heat and leave the peaches to cool in the syrup.

3 Remove the peaches from the syrup and peel off the skins. Place on several thicknesses of kitchen paper to drain (reserve the syrup for another use), then cover and chill.

4 Put the raspberries, lemon juice and sugar in a blender or food processor fitted with the metal blade. Process for 1 minute, scraping down the sides once. Press through a fine sieve into a small bowl, then stir in the raspberry liqueur, if using, and put in the fridge to chill.

5 To serve, place a peach half, cut-side up, on a dessert plate, fill with a scoop of vanilla ice cream and spoon the raspberry sauce over the ice cream. Decorate with mint leaves and a few fresh raspberries, if using.

Gooseberry and Elderflower Cream

When elderflowers are in season, instead of using the cordial, cook two to three elderflower heads with the gooseberries.

INGREDIENTS

Serves 4

500g/1¼lb gooseberries, topped and
    tailed
300ml/½ pint/1¼ cups double cream
about 115g/4oz/1 cup icing sugar, to taste
30ml/2 tbsp elderflower cordial or orange
    flower water (optional)
mint sprigs, to decorate
almond biscuits, to serve

2 Beat the cream until soft peaks form, then fold in half the gooseberries. Sweeten and add elderflower cordial or orange flower water, if using. Sweeten the remaining gooseberries.

3 Layer the cream mixture and the crushed gooseberries in four dessert dishes or tall glasses, then cover and chill. Decorate with mint sprigs and serve accompanied by almond biscuits.

1 Place the gooseberries in a heavy saucepan, cover and cook over a low heat, shaking the pan occasionally, until the gooseberries are tender. Tip the gooseberries into a bowl, crush them, then leave to cool completely.

COOK'S TIP

If preferred, the cooked gooseberries can be puréed and sieved. An equivalent quantity of real custard can replace the cream.

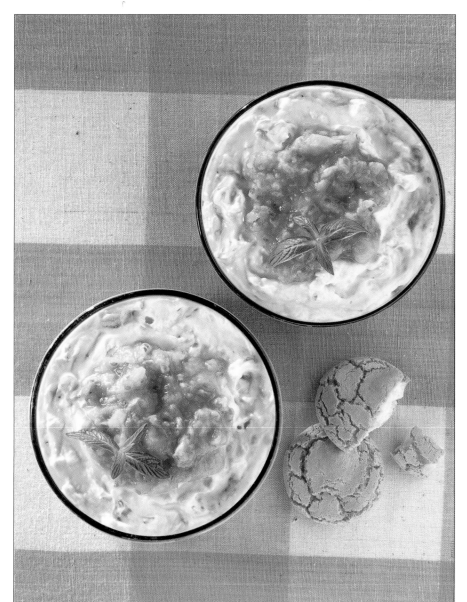

Apricots with Orange Cream

Mascarpone is a very rich cream cheese made from thick Lombardy cream. It is delicious flavoured with orange as a topping for these poached, chilled apricots.

Serves 4

450g/1lb/2 cups ready-to-eat dried
    apricots
strip of lemon peel
1 cinnamon stick
45ml/3 tbsp caster sugar
150ml/¼ pint/⅔ cup sweet dessert wine
    (such as Muscat de Beaumes de Venise)
115g/4oz/½ cup mascarpone cheese
45ml/3 tbsp orange juice
pinch of ground cinnamon and fresh mint
    sprig, to decorate

1 Place the apricots, lemon peel, cinnamon stick and 15ml/ 1 tbsp of the sugar in a pan and cover with 450ml/¼ pint/1⅞ cups cold water. Bring to the boil, cover and simmer gently for 25 minutes, until the fruit is tender.

2 Remove from the heat and stir in the dessert wine. Leave until cold, then chill for at least 3–4 hours or overnight.

3 Mix together the mascarpone cheese, orange juice and the remaining sugar in a bowl and beat well until smooth, then chill.

4 Just before serving remove the cinnamon stick and lemon peel and serve with a spoonful of the orange cream sprinkled with cinnamon and decorated with a sprig of fresh mint.

Rhubarb and Orange Fool

Perhaps this traditional English pudding got its name because it is so easy to make that even a "fool" can attempt it.

Serves 4

30ml/2 tbsp orange juice
5ml/1 tsp finely shredded orange rind
1kg/2lb (about 10–12 stems) rhubarb,
    chopped
15ml/1 tbsp redcurrant jelly
45ml/3 tbsp caster sugar
150g/5oz/⅔ cup ready-to-serve thick and
    creamy custard
150ml/¼ pint/⅔ cup double cream,
    whipped
sweet biscuits, to serve

1 Place the orange juice and rind, the rhubarb, redcurrant jelly and sugar in a saucepan. Cover and simmer gently for about 8 minutes, stirring occasionally, until the rhubarb is just tender but not mushy.

2 Remove the pan from the heat, transfer the rhubarb to a bowl and leave to cool completely.

3 Drain the cooled rhubarb to remove some of the liquid. Reserve a few pieces of the rhubarb and a little orange rind for decoration. Purée the remaining rhubarb in a food processor or blender, or push through a sieve.

4 Stir the custard into the purée, then fold in the whipped cream. Spoon the fool into individual bowls, cover and chill. Just before serving, top with the reserved fruit and rind. Serve with crisp, sweet biscuits.

Cherry Syllabub

This recipe follows the style of the earliest syllabubs from the sixteenth and seventeenth centuries, producing a frothy, creamy layer over a liquid one.

INGREDIENTS

Serves 4

225g/8oz ripe dark cherries, stoned and chopped
30ml/2 tbsp kirsch
2 egg whites
75g/3oz/scant ½ cup caster sugar
30ml/2 tbsp lemon juice
150ml/¼ pint/⅔ cup sweet white wine
300ml/½ pint/1¼ cups double cream

1 Divide the chopped cherries among six tall dessert glasses and sprinkle over the kirsch.

2 In a clean bowl, whisk the egg whites until stiff. Gently fold in the sugar, lemon juice and wine.

3 In a separate bowl (but using the same whisk), lightly beat the cream, then fold into the egg white mixture.

4 Spoon the cream mixture over the cherries and chill overnight.

Rose Petal Cream

This is an old-fashioned junket which is set with rennet – don't move it while it is setting, otherwise it will separate.

INGREDIENTS

Serves 4

600ml/1 pint/2½ cups milk
45ml/3 tbsp caster sugar
several drops triple-strength rosewater
10ml/2 tsp rennet
60ml/4 tbsp double cream
sugared rose petals, to decorate (optional)

1 Gently heat the milk and 30ml/2 tbsp of the sugar, stirring continuously, until the sugar has melted and the temperature reaches 36.9° C/98.4°F, or the milk feels lukewarm.

2 Stir rosewater to taste into the milk, then remove the pan from the heat before stirring in the rennet.

3 Pour the milk into a serving dish and leave undisturbed for 2–3 hours, until the junket has set.

4 Stir the remaining sugar into the cream, then carefully spoon over the junket. Decorate with sugared rose petals, if wished.

COOK'S TIP

Only use rose petals taken from bushes which have not been sprayed with chemicals of any kind.

Creole Ambrosia

A refreshing cold fruity pudding that can be made at any time of the year.

INGREDIENTS

Serves 6

6 oranges

1 coconut

25g/1oz/2 tbsp caster sugar

1 Peel the oranges removing all white pith, then slice thinly, picking out seeds with the point of a knife. Do this on a plate to catch the juice.

2 Pierce the "eyes" of the coconut and pour away the milk, then crack open the coconut with a hammer. (This is best done outside on a stone surface.)

COOK'S TIP

Mangoes instead of oranges make the dessert more exotic but less authentically Creole.

3 Peel the coconut with a sharp knife, then grate half the flesh coarsely, either on a hand grater or on the grating blade of a blender or food processor.

4 Layer the coconut and orange slices in a glass bowl, starting and finishing with the coconut. After each orange layer, sprinkle on a little sugar and pour over some of the reserved orange juice.

5 Let the dessert stand for 2 hours before serving, either at room temperature or, in hot weather, keep it refrigerated.

Chocolate and Chestnut Pots

Prepared in advance, these are the perfect ending for a dinner party. Remove them from the fridge about 30 minutes before serving, to allow them to "ripen".

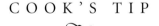

INGREDIENTS

Serves 6

250g/9oz plain chocolate

60ml/4 tbsp Madeira

25g/1oz/2 tbsp butter, diced

2 eggs, separated

225g/8oz/scant 1 cup unsweetened
   chestnut purée

crème fraîche or whipped double cream,
   to decorate

1 Make a few chocolate curls for decoration, then break the rest of the chocolate into squares and melt it with the Madeira in a saucepan over a gentle heat. Remove from the heat and add the butter, a few pieces at a time, stirring until melted and smooth.

COOK'S TIP

∿

If Madeira is not available, use brandy or rum instead. These chocolate pots can be frozen successfully for up to 2 months.

2 Beat the egg yolks quickly into the mixture, then beat in the chestnut purée, mixing until smooth.

3 Whisk the egg whites in a clean, grease-free bowl until stiff. Stir about 15ml/1 tbsp of the whites into the chestnut mixture to lighten it, then fold in the rest smoothly and evenly.

4 Spoon the mixture into six small ramekin dishes and chill until set. Serve the pots topped with a generous spoonful of crème fraîche or whipped double cream and decorated with the plain chocolate curls.

Coffee, Vanilla and Chocolate Stripe

This looks really special served in elegant wine glasses and tastes appropriately exquisite.

INGREDIENTS

Serves 6

285g/10½oz/1½ cups caster sugar

90ml/6 tbsp cornflour

900ml/1½ pints/3¾ cups milk

3 egg yolks

75g/3oz/6 tbsp unsalted butter, at room temperature

20ml/generous 1 tbsp instant coffee powder

10ml/2 tsp vanilla essence

30ml/2 tbsp cocoa powder

whipped cream, to serve

1 To make the coffee layer, place 90g/3½oz/½ cup of the sugar and 30ml/2 tbsp of the cornflour in a heavy-based saucepan. Gradually add one-third of the milk, whisking until well blended. Over a medium heat, whisk in one of the egg yolks and bring to the boil, whisking. Boil for 1 minute.

2 Remove the pan from the heat. Stir in 25g/1oz/2 tbsp of the butter and the instant coffee powder. Set aside in the pan to cool slightly.

3 Divide the coffee mixture among six wine glasses. Smooth the tops before the mixture sets.

4 Wipe any dribbles on the insides and outsides of the glasses with damp kitchen paper.

5 To make the vanilla layer, place half of the remaining sugar and cornflour in a heavy-based saucepan. Whisk in 300ml/ ½ pint/1¼ cups of the milk. Over a medium heat, whisk in another egg yolk and bring to the boil, whisking. Boil for 1 minute.

6 Remove the pan from the heat and stir in 25g/1oz/2 tbsp of the butter and the vanilla. Leave to cool slightly, then spoon into the glasses on top of the coffee layer. Smooth the tops and wipe the glasses with kitchen paper.

7 To make the chocolate layer, place the remaining sugar and cornflour in a heavy-based saucepan. Gradually whisk in the remaining milk and continue whisking until blended. Over a medium heat, whisk in the last egg yolk and bring to the boil, whisking constantly. Boil for 1 minute. Remove from the heat, stir in the remaining butter and the cocoa. Leave to cool slightly, then spoon into the glasses on top of the vanilla layer. Chill until set.

8 Pipe swirls of whipped cream on top of each dessert just before serving.

COOK'S TIP

For a special occasion, prepare the vanilla layer using a fresh vanilla pod. Choose a plump, supple pod and split it down the centre with a sharp knife. Add to the mixture with the milk and discard the pod before spooning the mixture into the glasses. The flavour will be more pronounced and the pudding will have pretty brown speckles from the vanilla seeds.

Chocolate Hazelnut Galettes

Chocolate rounds sandwiched with fromage frais. If only all sandwiches looked and tasted this good.

INGREDIENTS

Serves 4

175g/6oz plain chocolate, broken into
    squares
45ml/3 tbsp single cream
30ml/2 tbsp flaked hazelnuts
115g/4oz white chocolate, broken into
    squares
175g/6oz/¾ cup fromage frais (8% fat)
15ml/1 tbsp dry sherry
60ml/4 tbsp finely chopped hazelnuts,
    toasted
physalis (Cape gooseberries), dipped in
    white chocolate, to decorate

1 Melt the plain chocolate in a heatproof bowl over hot water, then remove from the heat and stir in the cream.

2 Draw 12 x 7.5cm/3in circles on sheets of non-stick baking paper. Turn the paper over and spread the plain chocolate over each marked circle, covering in a thin, even layer. Scatter flaked hazelnuts over four of the circles, then leave to set.

3 Melt the white chocolate in a heatproof bowl over hot water, then stir in the fromage frais and dry sherry. Fold in the chopped, toasted hazelnuts. Leave to cool until the mixture holds its shape.

4 Remove the chocolate rounds carefully from the paper and sandwich them together in stacks of three, spooning the hazelnut cream between each layer and using the hazelnut-covered rounds on top. Chill before serving.

5 To serve, place the galettes on individual plates and decorate with chocolate-dipped physalis.

COOK'S TIP
~
The chocolate could be spread over heart shapes instead, for a special Valentine's Day dessert.

Double Chocolate Snowball

This is an ideal party dessert as it can be prepared at least one day ahead and decorated on the day.

INGREDIENTS

Serves 12–14

350g/12oz plain chocolate, chopped

285g/10½oz/1½ cups caster sugar

275g/10oz/1¼ cups unsalted butter, cut
 into small pieces

8 eggs

50ml/2fl oz/¼ cup orange-flavoured
 liqueur or brandy (optional)

cocoa for dusting

For the white chocolate cream

200g/7oz fine quality white chocolate,
 broken into pieces

475ml/16fl oz/2 cups double or whipping
 cream

30ml/2 tbsp orange-flavour liqueur
 (optional)

1 Preheat the oven to 180°C/
350°F/Gas 4. Line a 1.75 litre/
3 pint/1½ quart round ovenproof
bowl with aluminium foil,
smoothing the sides. In a bowl
over a pan of simmering water,
melt the plain chocolate. Add the
sugar and stir until it dissolves.
Strain into a medium bowl. With
an electric mixer at low speed, beat
in the butter, then the eggs, one at
a time, beating well after each
addition. Stir in the liqueur or
brandy, if using, and pour into the
prepared bowl. Tap gently to
release any large air bubbles.

2 Bake for 1¼–1½ hours until
the surface is firm and slightly
risen, but cracked. The centre will
still be wobbly: this will set on
cooling. Remove to a rack to cool
to room temperature. Cover with a
plate, then cover completely with
clear film or foil and chill
overnight. To unmould, remove
plate and film or foil and invert
mould on to a plate; shake firmly
to release. Peel off foil. Cover until
ready to decorate.

3 Process the white chocolate in
a blender or food processor
until fine crumbs form. In a small
saucepan, heat 120ml/4fl oz/½ cup
of the cream until just beginning
to simmer. With the food
processor running, pour cream
through the feed tube and process
until the chocolate is completely
melted. Strain into a medium bowl
and cool to room temperature,
stirring occasionally.

4 Beat the remaining cream
until soft peaks form, add
the liqueur, if using, and beat for
30 seconds or until the cream just
holds its shape. Fold a spoonful of
cream into the chocolate then fold
in remaining cream. Spoon into
an icing bag fitted with a star tip
and pipe rosettes over the surface.
If you wish, dust with cocoa.

White Chocolate Parfait

Everything you could wish for in a dessert; white and dark chocolate in one mouth-watering slice.

Serves 10

225g/8oz white chocolate, chopped
600ml/1 pint/2½ cups whipping cream
120ml/4fl oz/½ cup milk
10 egg yolks
15ml/1 tbsp caster sugar
25g/1oz/scant ½ cup desiccated coconut
120ml/4fl oz/½ cup canned sweetened
 coconut milk
150g/5oz/1¼ cups unsalted
 macadamia nuts

For the chocolate icing
225g/8oz plain chocolate
75g/3oz/6 tbsp butter
20ml/generous 1 tbsp golden syrup
175ml/6fl oz/¾ cup whipping cream
curls of fresh coconut, to decorate

1 Line the base and sides of a 1.4 litre/2⅓ pint/6 cup terrine mould (25 x 10cm/10 x 4in) with clear film.

2 Place the chopped white chocolate and 50ml/2fl oz/ ½ cup of the cream in the top of a double boiler or in a heatproof bowl set over hot water. Stir until melted and smooth. Set aside.

3 Put 250ml/8fl oz/1 cup of the cream and the milk in a pan and bring to boiling point.

4 Meanwhile, whisk the egg yolks and caster sugar together in a large bowl, until thick and pale.

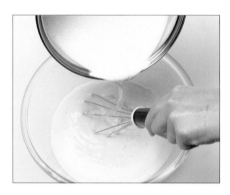

5 Add the hot cream mixture to the yolks, beating constantly. Pour back into the saucepan and cook over a low heat for 2–3 minutes, until thickened. Stir constantly and do not boil. Remove the pan from the heat.

6 Add the melted chocolate, desiccated coconut and coconut milk, then stir well and leave to cool.

7 Whip the remaining cream until thick, then fold into the chocolate and coconut mixture.

8 Put 475ml/16fl oz/2 cups of the parfait mixture in the prepared mould and spread evenly. Cover and freeze for about 2 hours, until just firm. Cover the remaining mixture and chill.

9 Scatter the macadamia nuts evenly over the frozen parfait. Pour in the remaining parfait mixture. Cover the terrine and freeze for 6–8 hours or overnight, until the parfait is firm.

10 To make the icing, melt the chocolate with the butter and syrup in the top of a double boiler set over hot water. Stir occasionally.

11 Heat the cream in a saucepan, until just simmering, then stir into the chocolate mixture. Remove the pan from the heat and leave to cool until lukewarm.

12 To turn out the parfait, wrap the terrine in a hot towel and set it upside-down on a plate. Lift off the terrine mould, then peel off the clear film. Place the parfait on a rack over a baking sheet and pour the chocolate icing evenly over the top. Working quickly, smooth the icing down the sides with a palette knife. Leave to set slightly, then freeze for a further 3–4 hours. Cut into slices using a knife dipped in hot water. Serve, decorated with curls of fresh coconut.

White Chocolate Mousse with Dark Sauce

Creamy vanilla-flavoured white chocolate mousse is served with a dark rum and chocolate sauce.

INGREDIENTS

Serves 6–8

200g/7oz white chocolate, broken into squares
2 eggs, separated
60ml/4 tbsp caster sugar
300ml/½ pint/1¼ cups double cream
1 sachet powdered gelatine or alternative
150ml/¼ pint/⅔ cup Greek-style yogurt
10ml/2 tsp vanilla essence

For the sauce
50g/2oz plain chocolate, broken into squares
30ml/2 tbsp dark rum
60ml/4 tbsp single cream

1 Line a 1 litre/1¾ pint/4 cup loaf tin with non-stick baking paper or clear film. Melt the chocolate in a heatproof bowl over hot water, then remove from the heat.

2 Whisk the egg yolks and sugar in a bowl until pale and thick, then beat in the melted chocolate.

3 Heat the cream in a small saucepan until almost boiling, then remove from the heat. Sprinkle the powdered gelatine over, stirring gently until until it is completely dissolved.

4 Then pour on to the chocolate mixture, whisking vigorously to mix until smooth.

5 Whisk the yogurt and vanilla essence into the mixture. In a clean, grease-free bowl, whisk the egg whites until stiff, then fold them into the mixture. Tip into the prepared loaf tin, level the surface and chill until set.

6 Make the sauce. Melt the chocolate with the rum and cream in a heatproof bowl over barely simmering water, stirring occasionally, then leave to cool.

7 When the mousse is set, remove it from the tin with the aid of the paper or clear film. Serve in thick slices with the cooled chocolate sauce poured around.

COOK'S TIP

Make sure the gelatine is completely dissolved in the cream before adding to the other ingredients.

Fluffy Banana and Pineapple Mousse

This light, low-fat mousse looks very impressive but is really very easy to make, especially with a food processor. To make it even simpler, use a 1 litre/1¾ pint/4 cup serving dish which will hold all the mixture without a paper "collar".

INGREDIENTS

Serves 6

2 ripe bananas

225g/8oz/1 cup cottage cheese

425g/15oz can pineapple chunks or pieces in juice

15ml/1 tbsp/1 sachet powdered gelatine, or alternative

2 egg whites

1 Tie a double band of non-stick baking paper around a 600ml/ 1 pint/2½ cup soufflé dish, to come 5cm/2in above the rim.

2 Peel and chop one banana and place it in a blender or food processor with the cottage cheese. Process them until smooth.

3 Drain the pineapple, reserving the juice, and reserve a few pieces or chunks for decoration. Add the rest to the mixture in the blender or food processor and process for a few seconds until finely chopped.

4 Dissolve the gelatine in 60ml/ 4 tbsp of the reserved pineapple juice. Stir the gelatine quickly into the fruit mixture.

5 Whisk the egg whites until they hold soft peaks and fold them into the mixture. Tip the mousse mixture into the prepared dish, smooth the surface and chill, until set.

6 When the mousse is set, carefully remove the paper collar and decorate with the reserved banana and pineapple.

Portuguese Rice Pudding

This pudding is popular all over Portugal, and if you visit you're likely to find it on most menus. Traditionally it is served cold, but is actually delicious warm as well.

INGREDIENTS

Serves 4–6

175g/6oz/scant 1 cup short grain
    (pudding) rice

600ml/1 pint/2½ cups creamy milk

2 or 3 strips pared lemon rind

65g/2½ oz/5 tbsp butter, in pieces

115g/4oz/½ cup caster sugar

4 egg yolks

salt

ground cinnamon, for dusting

lemon wedges, to serve

1 Cook the rice in plenty of lightly salted water for about 5 minutes, by which time it will have lost its brittleness.

2 Drain well, then return to the clean pan. Add the milk, lemon rind and butter. Bring to the boil over a moderately low heat, then cover, reduce the heat to the lowest setting and simmer for about 20 minutes or until the rice is thick and creamy.

3 Remove the pan from the heat and allow the rice to cool a little. Remove and discard the lemon rind, then stir in the sugar and the egg yolks. Mix well.

4 Divide among four to six serving bowls and dust with ground cinnamon. Serve cold, with lemon wedges for squeezing.

Rice Conde Sundae

Cooking rice pudding on top of the hob instead of in the oven gives it a light, creamy texture, especially if you remember to stir it frequently. It is particularly good served cold with a topping of fruit and toasted nuts or a trickle of hot chocolate sauce.

INGREDIENTS

Serves 4

50g/2oz/generous ¼ cup short grain (pudding) rice

5ml/1 tsp vanilla essence

2.5ml/½ tsp ground cinnamon

45ml/3 tbsp granulated sugar

600ml/1 pint/2½ cups milk

For the topping

soft berry fruits such as strawberries, raspberries and cherries

chocolate sauce and flaked toasted almonds (optional)

1 Mix the rice, vanilla essence, cinnamon and sugar in a saucepan. Pour in the milk. Bring to the boil, stirring constantly, then reduce the heat so that the mixture barely simmers.

2 Cook the rice over a low heat for 30–40 minutes, stirring frequently. Add extra milk to the rice if it begins to dry out.

3 When the grains are soft, remove the pan from the heat. Allow the rice to cool, stirring occasionally, then chill.

4 Before serving, stir the rice pudding and spoon it into four sundae dishes. Top with fresh fruits, and with chocolate sauce and almonds, if using.

VARIATION

For a special occasion, use single cream instead of milk, and glaze the fruit with a little melted redcurrant jelly. (Add a splash of port if you like.)

Cherries Jubilee

Fresh cherries are wonderful cooked lightly to serve hot over ice cream. Children will love this dessert.

INGREDIENTS

Serves 4

450g/1lb red or black cherries

115g/4oz/generous ½ cup granulated sugar

pared rind of 1 lemon

15ml/1 tbsp arrowroot

60ml/4 tbsp Kirsch

vanilla ice cream, to serve

COOK'S TIP

If you don't have a cherry stoner, simply push the stones through with a skewer. Remember to save the juice to use in the recipe.

1 Stone the cherries over a pan to catch the juice. Drop the stones into the pan as you work.

2 Add the sugar, lemon rind and 300ml/½ pint/1¼ cups water to the pan. Stir over a low heat until the sugar dissolves, then bring to the boil and simmer for 10 minutes. Strain the syrup, then return to the pan. Add the cherries and cook for 3–4 minutes.

3 Blend the arrowroot to a paste with 15ml/1 tbsp cold water and stir into the cherries, after removing them from the heat.

4 Return the pan to the heat and bring to the boil, stirring all the time. Cook the sauce for a minute or two, stirring until it is thick and smooth. Heat the Kirsch in a ladle over a flame, ignite and pour over the cherries. Spoon the cherries and hot sauce over scoops of ice cream and serve at once.

Apricots in Marsala

Make sure the apricots are completely covered by the syrup so that they don't discolour.

INGREDIENTS

Serves 4

12 apricots

50g/2oz/4 tbsp caster sugar

300ml/½ pint/1¼ cups Marsala

2 strips pared orange rind

1 vanilla pod, split

150ml/¼ pint/⅔ cup double or whipping cream

15ml/1 tbsp icing sugar

1.5ml/¼ tsp ground cinnamon

150ml/¼ pint/⅔ cup Greek-style yogurt

1 Halve and stone the apricots, then place in a bowl of boiling water for about 30 seconds. Drain well, then slip off their skins.

2 Place the caster sugar, Marsala, orange rind, vanilla pod and 250ml/8fl oz/1 cup water in a pan. Heat gently until the sugar dissolves. Bring to the boil, without stirring, then simmer for 2–3 minutes.

3 Add the apricot halves to the pan and poach for 5–6 minutes, or until just tender. Using a slotted spoon, transfer the apricots to a serving dish.

4 Boil the syrup rapidly until reduced by half, then pour over the apricots and leave to cool. Cover and chill. Remove the orange rind and vanilla pod.

5 Whip the cream with the icing sugar and cinnamon until it forms soft peaks. Gently fold in the yogurt. Spoon into a serving bowl and chill. Serve with the apricots.

Poached Pears in Red Wine

This makes a very pretty dessert, as the pears take on a red blush from the wine.

INGREDIENTS

Serves 4

1 bottle red wine

150g/5oz/¾ cup caster sugar

45ml/3 tbsp honey

juice of ½ lemon

1 cinnamon stick

1 vanilla pod, split open lengthways

5cm/2in piece of orange rind

1 clove

1 black peppercorn

4 firm, ripe pears

whipped cream or soured cream,
  to serve

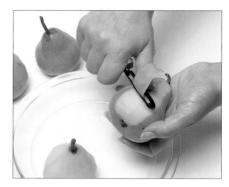

1 Place the wine, sugar, honey, lemon juice, cinnamon stick, vanilla pod, orange rind, clove and peppercorn in a saucepan just large enough to hold the pears standing upright. Heat gently, stirring occasionally until the sugar has completely dissolved.

2 Meanwhile, peel the pears, leaving the stem intact. Take a thin slice off the base of each pear so that it will stand square and upright in the pan.

3 Place the pears in the wine mixture, then simmer, uncovered, for 20–35 minutes depending on size and ripeness, until the pears are just tender; be careful not to overcook.

4 Carefully transfer the pears to a bowl using a slotted spoon. Continue to boil the poaching liquid until reduced by about half. Leave to cool, then strain the cooled liquid over the pears and chill for at least 3 hours.

5 Place the pears in four individual serving dishes and spoon over a little of the red wine syrup. Serve with whipped cream or soured cream.

Coffee Crêpes with Peaches and Cream

Juicy golden peaches and cream conjure up the sweet taste of summer. Here they are delicious as the filling for these coffee crêpes.

INGREDIENTS

Serves 6

75g/3oz/⅔ cup plain flour

25g/1oz/¼ cup buckwheat flour

1.5ml/¼ tsp salt

1 egg, beaten

200ml/7fl oz/scant 1 cup milk

15g/½oz/1 tbsp butter, melted

100ml/3½ oz/scant ½ cup strong coffee

sunflower oil, for frying

For the filling

6 ripe peaches

300ml/½ pint/1¼ cups double cream

15ml/1 tbsp Amaretto liqueur

225g/8oz/1 cup mascarpone

65g/2½oz/generous ¼ cup caster sugar

30ml/2 tbsp icing sugar, for dusting

1 Sift the flours and salt into a bowl. Make a well and add the egg, half the milk and the melted butter. Beat into the flour until smooth, then beat in the remaining milk and coffee.

2 Heat a drizzle of oil in a 15–20cm/6–8in crêpe pan. Pour in just enough batter to thinly cover the base of the pan. Cook for 2–3 minutes, until the underneath is golden brown, then flip over and cook the other side.

3 Slide the crêpe out of the pan on to a plate. Continue making crêpes until all the mixture is used, stacking and interleaving with greaseproof paper. Keep the crêpes warm while you make the filling.

4 To make the filling, halve the peaches and remove the stones. Cut into thick slices. Whip the cream and Amaretto liqueur until they form into soft peaks. Beat the mascarpone with the sugar until smooth. Beat 30ml/2 tbsp of the cream into the mascarpone, then fold in the remainder.

5 Spoon a little of the Amaretto cream on to one half of each pancake and top with peach slices. Gently fold the pancake over and dust with icing sugar. Serve at once while still warm.

Fruit Kebabs with Mango and Yogurt Sauce

These mixed fresh fruit kebabs make an attractive and healthy dessert.

INGREDIENTS

Serves 4

½ pineapple, peeled, cored and cubed

2 kiwi fruit, peeled and cubed

175g/6oz/1½ cups strawberries, hulled
   and cut in half, if large

½ mango, peeled, stoned and cubed

For the sauce

120ml/4fl oz/½ cup fresh mango purée,
   from 1–1½ peeled and pitted mangoes

120ml/4fl oz/½ cup thick plain yogurt

5ml/1 tsp caster sugar

few drops vanilla essence

15ml/1 tbsp finely chopped
   mint leaves

1 To make the sauce, beat together the mango purée, yogurt, sugar and vanilla with an electric mixer.

2 Stir in the chopped mint. Cover the sauce and place in the fridge until required.

3 Thread the prepared fruit on to twelve 15cm/6in wooden skewers, alternating the pineapple, kiwi fruit, strawberries and mango cubes.

4 Arrange the kebabs on a large serving tray with the mango and yogurt sauce in the centre.

Tropical Fruits in Cinnamon Syrup

An exotic glazed fruit salad, a simply prepared but satisfying end to any meal.

INGREDIENTS

Serves 6

450g/1lb/2¼ cups caster sugar

1 cinnamon stick

1 large or 2 medium paw paws (about
   675g/1½lb), peeled, seeded and cut
   lengthways into thin pieces

1 large or 2 medium mangoes (about
   675g/1½lb), peeled, stoned and cut
   lengthways into thin pieces

1 large or 2 small star fruit (about
   225g/8oz), thinly sliced

yogurt or crème fraîche, to serve

1 Sprinkle one-third of the sugar over the base of a large saucepan. Add the cinnamon stick and half the paw paw, mango and star fruit pieces.

2 Sprinkle half of the remaining sugar over the fruit pieces in the pan. Add all the remaining fruit and sprinkle with the rest of the sugar.

3 Cover the pan and cook the fruit over a medium-low heat for 35–45 minutes, until the sugar melts completely. Shake the pan occasionally, but do not stir or the fruit will collapse.

4 Uncover the pan and simmer until the fruit begins to appear translucent, about 10 minutes. Remove the pan from the heat and leave to cool.

5 Transfer the fruit and syrup to a bowl, cover and chill overnight. Serve with yogurt or crème fraîche.

Greek Fig and Honey Pudding

A quick and easy pudding made from fresh or canned figs topped with thick and creamy Greek-style yogurt, drizzled with honey and sprinkled with pistachio nuts.

INGREDIENTS

Serves 4

4 fresh or canned figs

2 x 225g/8oz tubs/2 cups Greek-style
   strained yogurt

60ml/4 tbsp clear honey

30ml/2 tbsp chopped pistachio nuts

1 Chop the figs and place in the bottom of four stemmed wine glasses or deep, individual dessert bowls.

2 Top each glass or bowl of figs with half a tub (½ cup) of the Greek-style yogurt. Chill until ready to serve.

3 Just before serving drizzle 15ml/1 tbsp of honey over each one and sprinkle with the pistachio nuts.

COOK'S TIP
∽
Try specialist honeys made from, clover, acacia or thyme.

Russian Fruit Compote

This fruit pudding is traditionally called "Kissel" and is made from the thickened juice of stewed red or blackcurrants. This recipe uses the whole fruit with an added dash of blackberry liqueur.

INGREDIENTS

Serves 4

225g/8oz/2 cups red or blackcurrants or a
   mixture of both

225g/8oz/1⅓ cups raspberries

50g/2oz/4 tbsp caster sugar

25ml/1½ tbsp arrowroot

15–30ml/1–2 tbsp Crème de Mûre

Greek-style yogurt, to serve

COOK'S TIP
∽
Use Crème de Cassis instead of Crème de Mûre.

1 Place the red or blackcurrants, raspberries and sugar in a pan with 150ml/¼ pint/⅔ cup of water. Cover the pan and cook gently over a low heat for 12–15 minutes, until the fruit is soft.

2 Blend the arrowroot with a little water in a bowl and stir into the fruit. Bring back to the boil, stirring until thickened.

3 Remove from the heat and cool slightly, then gently stir in the Crème de Mûre.

4 Pour into four serving bowls and leave until cold, then chill. Serve topped with spoonfuls of Greek-style yogurt.

Floating Islands

Originally these oval-shaped meringues were poached in milk and this was then used to make the rich custard sauce.

INGREDIENTS

Serves 4–6

1 vanilla pod
600ml/1 pint/2½ cups milk
8 egg yolks
50g/2oz/¼ cup granulated sugar

For the meringues

4 size 1 egg whites
1.5ml/¼ tsp cream of tartar
225g/8oz/1¼ cups caster sugar

For the caramel

150g/5oz/¾ cup granulated sugar

1 Split the vanilla pod lengthways and scrape the seeds into a saucepan. Add the milk and bring just to the boil over a medium heat, stirring frequently. Cover and set aside for 15–20 minutes.

2 In a medium bowl, whisk the egg yolks and sugar for 2–3 minutes until thick and creamy. Whisk in the hot milk and return the mixture to the saucepan. With a wooden spoon, stir over a medium-low heat until the sauce begins to thicken and coat the back of the spoon (do not allow to boil). Immediately strain into a chilled bowl, allow to cool, stirring occasionally and then chill.

3 Half-fill a large wide frying pan or saucepan with water and bring just to simmering point. In a clean, grease-free bowl, whisk the egg whites until frothy. Add the cream of tartar and continue whisking until they form soft peaks. Sprinkle over the caster sugar, about 30ml/2 tbsp at a time, and whisk until the whites are stiff and glossy.

4 Using two tablespoons, form egg-shaped meringues and slide them into the water (you may need to work in batches). Poach them for 2–3 minutes, turning once until just firm. Using a large slotted spoon, transfer the cooked meringues to a baking sheet lined with kitchen paper to drain.

5 Pour the cold custard into individual serving dishes and arrange the meringues on top.

6 To make the caramel, put the sugar into a small saucepan with 45ml/3 tbsp of water to moisten. Bring to the boil over a high heat, swirling the pan to dissolve the sugar. Boil, without stirring, until the syrup turns a dark caramel colour. Immediately drizzle the caramel over the meringues and custard sauce in a zig-zag pattern. Serve cold. (The caramel will soften if made too far ahead.)

Chestnut Pudding

This is an Italian speciality, made during the months of October and November, when fresh sweet chestnuts are gathered.

INGREDIENTS

Serves 4–5

450g/1lb fresh sweet chestnuts

300ml/½ pint/1¼ cups milk

115g/4oz/½ cup caster sugar

2 eggs, separated, at room temperature

25g/1oz/¼ cup unsweetened
   cocoa powder

2.5ml/½ tsp pure vanilla essence

50g/2oz/½ cup icing sugar, sifted

fresh whipped cream, to garnish

marrons glacés, to garnish

1 Cut a cross in the side of the chestnuts, and drop them into a pan of boiling water. Cook for 5–6 minutes. Remove with a slotted spoon, and peel while still warm.

2 Place the peeled chestnuts in a heavy or non-stick saucepan with the milk and half of the caster sugar. Cook over low heat, stirring occasionally, until soft. Remove from the heat and allow to cool. Press the contents of the pan through a strainer.

3 Preheat the oven to 180°C/ 350°F/Gas 4. Beat the egg yolks with the remaining caster sugar until the mixture is pale yellow and fluffy. Beat in the cocoa powder and the vanilla.

4 In a separate bowl, whisk the egg whites with a wire whisk or electric beater until they form soft peaks. Gradually beat in the sifted icing sugar and continue beating until the mixture forms stiff peaks.

5 Fold the chestnut and egg yolk mixtures together. Fold in the egg whites. Turn the mixture into one large or several individual buttered pudding moulds. Place on a baking sheet, and bake in the oven for 12–20 minutes, depending on the size. Remove from the oven, and allow to cool for 10 minutes before unmoulding. Serve garnished with whipped cream and marrons glacés.

Bitter Chocolate Mousse

This is the quintessential French dessert – easy to prepare ahead, rich and extremely delicious. Use the darkest chocolate you can find for the most authentic and intense chocolate flavour.

INGREDIENTS

Serves 8

225g/8oz plain chocolate, chopped

30ml/2 tbsp orange liqueur or brandy

25g/1oz/2 tbsp unsalted butter, cut into small pieces

4 eggs, separated

90ml/6 tbsp whipping cream

1.5ml/¼ tsp cream of tartar

45ml/3 tbsp caster sugar

crème fraîche or soured cream and chocolate curls, to decorate

1 Place the chocolate and 60ml/ 4 tbsp of water in a heavy saucepan. Melt over a low heat, stirring until smooth. Remove the pan from the heat and whisk in the liqueur and butter.

2 With an electric mixer, beat the egg yolks for 2–3 minutes until thick and creamy, then slowly beat into the melted chocolate until well blended. Set aside.

3 Whip the cream until soft peaks form and stir a spoonful into the chocolate to lighten it. Fold in the remaining cream.

4 In a clean, grease-free bowl, using an electric mixer, beat the egg whites until frothy. Add the cream of tartar and continue beating until they form soft peaks. Gradually sprinkle over the sugar and continue beating until the whites are stiff and glossy.

5 Using a rubber spatula or large metal spoon, stir quarter of the egg whites into the chocolate mixture, then gently fold in the remaining whites, cutting down to the bottom, along the sides and up to the top in a semicircular motion until they are just combined. (Don't worry about a few white streaks.) Gently spoon into a 2 litre/3½ pint/8 cup dish or into eight individual dishes. Chill for at least 2 hours until set and chilled.

6 Spoon a little crème fraîche or soured cream over the mousse and decorate with chocolate curls.

Brazilian Coffee Bananas

Rich, lavish and sinful-looking, this dessert takes only about two minutes to make!

INGREDIENTS

Serves 4

4 small ripe bananas

15ml/1 tbsp instant coffee granules or powder

30ml/2 tbsp dark muscovado sugar

250g/9oz/1⅛ cups Greek-style yogurt

15ml/1 tbsp toasted flaked almonds

1 Peel and slice one banana and mash the remaining three with a fork.

2 Dissolve the coffee in 15ml/ 1 tbsp of hot water and stir into the mashed bananas.

3 Spoon a little of the mashed banana mixture into four serving dishes and sprinkle with sugar. Top with a spoonful of yogurt, then repeat until all the ingredients are used up.

4 Swirl the last layer of yogurt for a marbled effect. Finish with a few banana slices and flaked almonds. Serve cold. Best eaten within about an hour of making.

VARIATION

For a special occasion, add a dash of dark rum or brandy to the bananas for extra richness.

Cakes
&
Gâteaux

•✦•

Raspberry Meringue Gâteau

A rich, hazelnut meringue sandwiched with whipped cream and raspberries makes an irresistible dessert for a special occasion.

INGREDIENTS

Serves 6

4 egg whites

225g/8oz/1 cup caster sugar

a few drops of vanilla essence

5ml/1 tsp distilled malt vinegar

115g/4oz/1 cup roasted and chopped
    hazelnuts, ground

300ml/½ pint/1¼ cups double cream

350g/12oz/2 cups raspberries

icing sugar, for dusting

raspberries and mint sprigs,
    to decorate

For the sauce

225g/8oz/1⅓ cups raspberries

45–60ml/3–4 tbsp icing sugar, sifted

15ml/1 tbsp orange liqueur

1 Preheat the oven to 180°C/
350°F/Gas 4. Grease two
20cm/8in sandwich tins and line
the bases with greaseproof paper.

2 Whisk the egg whites in a large
bowl until they hold stiff
peaks, then gradually whisk in the
caster sugar a tablespoon at a time,
whisking well after each addition.

3 Continue whisking the
meringue mixture for a
minute of two until very stiff, then
fold in the vanilla essence, vinegar
and ground hazelnuts.

4 Divide the meringue mixture
between the prepared
sandwich tins and spread level.
Bake for 50–60 minutes, until crisp.
Remove the meringues from the
tins and leave them to cool on a
wire rack.

5 While the meringues are
cooling, make the sauce.
Process the raspberries with the
icing sugar and orange liqueur in a
blender or food processor, then
press the purée through a fine
nylon sieve to remove any pips.
Chill the sauce until ready to serve.

6 Whip the cream until it forms
soft peaks, then gently fold in
the raspberries. Sandwich the
meringue rounds together with the
raspberry cream.

7 Dust the top of the gâteau with
icing sugar. Decorate with
mint sprigs and serve with the
raspberry sauce.

VARIATION

Fresh redcurrants make a good
alternative to raspberries. Pick over
the fruit, then pull each sprig
gently through the prongs of a fork
to release the redcurrants. Add
them to the whipped cream with a
little icing sugar, to taste.

COOK'S TIP

You can buy roasted chopped
hazelnuts in supermarkets.
Otherwise toast whole hazelnuts
under the grill and rub off the
flaky skins using a clean dish
towel. To chop finely, process in
a blender or food processor for a
few moments.

Chocolate Layer Cake

The cake layers can be made ahead, wrapped and frozen for future use. Always defrost cakes completely before icing.

INGREDIENTS

Serves 10–12
unsweetened cocoa for dusting
225g/8oz can cooked whole beetroot,
    drained and juice reserved
115g/4oz/½ cup unsalted butter, softened
500g/1¼lb/2½ cups light brown sugar,
    firmly packed
3 eggs
15ml/1 tbsp vanilla essence
75g/3oz unsweetened chocolate, melted
275g/10oz/2¼ cups plain flour
10ml/2 tsp baking powder
2.5ml/½ tsp salt
120ml/4fl oz/½ cup buttermilk
chocolate curls (optional)

For the chocolate ganache frosting
475ml/16fl oz/2 cups whipping or
    double cream
500g/1¼lb fine quality, bittersweet or
    semi-sweet chocolate, chopped
15ml/1 tbsp vanilla essence

1 Preheat oven to 180°C/350°F/ Gas 4. Grease two 23cm/9in cake tins and dust bottom and sides with cocoa. Grate beetroot and add to beet juice. With electric mixer, beat the butter, brown sugar, eggs and vanilla until pale and fluffy (3–5 minutes). Reduce speed and beat in chocolate.

2 In a bowl, sift flour, baking powder and salt. With mixer on low speed, alternately beat in flour mixture in fourths and buttermilk in thirds. Add beets and juice and beat for 1 minute. Divide between tins and bake for 30–35 minutes or until a cake tester inserted in the centre comes out clean. Cool for 10 minutes, then unmould and cool completely.

3 To make the frosting, in a heavy-based saucepan over medium heat, heat cream until it just begins to boil, stirring occasionally to prevent it from scorching.

4 Remove from heat and stir in chocolate, stirring constantly until melted and smooth. Stir in vanilla. Strain into a bowl and refrigerate, stirring every 10 minutes, until spreadable, about 1 hour.

5 Assemble the cake. Place one layer on a serving plate and spread with one-third of the ganache. Turn cake layer bottom side up and spread remaining ganache over top and side of cake. If using, top with the chocolate curls. Allow ganache to set for 20–30 minutes, then refrigerate before serving.

Spiced Date and Walnut Cake

A classic flavour combination, which makes a very easy low fat, high-fibre cake.

INGREDIENTS

Makes 1 cake

300g/11oz/2¾ cups wholemeal self-raising flour

10ml/2 tsp mixed spice

150g/5oz/1 cup chopped dates

50g/2oz/½ cup chopped walnuts

60ml/4 tbsp sunflower oil

115g/4oz/½ cup dark muscovado sugar

300ml/½ pint/1¼ cups skimmed milk

walnut halves, to decorate

1 Preheat the oven to 180°C/ 350°F/Gas 4. Grease and then line a 900g/2lb loaf tin with greaseproof paper.

2 Sift together the flour and spice, adding back any bran from the sieve. Stir in the dates and walnuts.

3 Mix the oil, sugar and milk, then stir evenly into the dry ingredients. Spoon into the prepared tin and arrange the walnut halves on top.

4 Bake the cake in the oven for about 45–50 minutes, or until golden brown and firm. Turn out the cake, remove the lining paper and leave to cool on a wire rack.

VARIATION

Pecan nuts can be used in place of the walnuts in this cake.

Banana Orange Loaf

For the best banana flavour and a really good, moist texture, make sure the bananas are very ripe.

INGREDIENTS

Makes 1 loaf

90g/3½oz/generous ¾ cup wholemeal plain flour

90g/3½oz/generous ¾ cup plain flour

5ml/1 tsp baking powder

5ml/1 tsp ground mixed spice

45ml/3 tbsp flaked hazelnuts, toasted

2 large ripe bananas

1 egg

30ml/2 tbsp sunflower oil

30ml/2 tbsp clear honey

finely grated rind and juice of 1 small orange

4 orange slices, halved

10ml/2 tsp icing sugar

1 Preheat the oven to 180°C/ 350°F/Gas 4. Brush a 1 litre/ 1¾ pint/4 cup loaf tin with sunflower oil and line the base with non-stick baking paper.

2 Sift the flours with the baking powder and spice into a bowl.

3 Stir the hazelnuts into the dry ingredients. Peel and mash the bananas. Beat in the egg, oil, honey and the orange rind and juice. Stir evenly into the dry ingredients.

4 Spoon into the prepared tin and smooth the top. Bake for 40–45 minutes, or until firm and golden brown. Turn out and cool on a wire rack.

5 Sprinkle the orange slices with the icing sugar and grill until golden. Use to decorate the cake.

COOK'S TIP

If you plan to keep the loaf for more than two or three days, omit the orange slices. Brush the cake with honey and sprinkle with flaked hazelnuts.

Banana Ginger Parkin

Parkin improves with keeping. Store it in a covered container for up to two months.

Makes 12 squares

200g/7oz/1¾ cups plain flour

10ml/2 tsp bicarbonate of soda

10ml/2 tsp ground ginger

150g/5oz/1¼ cups medium oatmeal

60ml/4 tbsp dark muscovado sugar

75g/3oz/6 tbsp sunflower margarine

150g/5oz/⅔ cup golden syrup

1 egg, beaten

3 ripe bananas, mashed

75g/3oz/¾ cup icing sugar

stem ginger, to decorate

1 Preheat the oven to 160°C/325°F/Gas 3. Grease and line an 18 x 28cm/7 x 11in cake tin.

2 Sift together the flour, bicarbonate of soda and ginger, then stir in the oatmeal. Melt the sugar, margarine and syrup in a saucepan, then stir into the flour mixture. Beat in the egg and mashed bananas.

3 Spoon into the tin and bake for about 1 hour, or until firm to the touch. Allow to cool in the tin, then turn out and cut into even-sized squares.

4 Sift the icing sugar into a bowl and stir in just enough water to make a smooth, runny icing. Drizzle the icing over each square and top with pieces of stem ginger, if you like.

COOK'S TIP

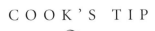

This is a nutritious cake, ideal for packed lunches as it doesn't break up too easily.

Greek Honey and Lemon Cake

The semolina in this recipe gives the cake an excellent texture.

INGREDIENTS

Makes 16 slices

40g/1½oz/3 tbsp sunflower margarine

60ml/4 tbsp clear honey

finely grated rind and juice of 1 lemon

150ml/¼ pint/⅔ cup skimmed milk

150g/5oz/1¼ cups plain flour

7.5ml/1½ tsp baking powder

2.5ml/½ tsp grated nutmeg

50g/2oz/⅓ cup semolina

2 egg whites

10ml/2 tsp sesame seeds

1 Preheat the oven to 200°C/ 400°F/Gas 6. Lightly oil a 19cm/7½in square deep cake tin and line the base with non-stick baking paper.

2 Place the margarine and 45ml/3 tbsp of the honey in a saucepan and heat gently until melted. Reserve 15ml/1 tbsp lemon juice, then stir in the rest with the lemon rind and milk.

3 Stir together the flour, baking powder and nutmeg, then beat in with the semolina. Whisk the egg whites until they form soft peaks, then fold evenly into the semolina mixture.

4 Spoon into the tin and sprinkle with sesame seeds. Bake for 25–30 minutes, until golden brown.

5 Mix the reserved honey and lemon juice and drizzle over the cake while warm. Cool in the tin, then cut into fingers to serve.

Strawberry Roulade

An attractive and delicious cake, perfect for a family supper.

INGREDIENTS

Serves 6

4 egg whites

115g/4oz/scant ⅔ cup golden caster sugar

75g/3oz/⅔ cup plain flour, sifted

30ml/2 tbsp orange juice

caster sugar, for sprinkling

115g/4oz/1 cup strawberries, chopped

150g/5oz/¾ cup low-fat fromage frais

strawberries, to decorate

1 Preheat the oven to 200°C/ 400°F/Gas 6. Oil a 23 x 33cm/ 9 x 13in Swiss roll tin and line with non-stick baking paper.

2 Place the egg whites in a large clean bowl and whisk until they form soft peaks. Gradually whisk in the sugar. Fold in half of the sifted flour, then fold in the rest with the orange juice.

3 Spoon the mixture into the prepared tin, spreading evenly. Bake for 15–18 minutes, or until it is golden brown and firm to the touch.

4 Meanwhile, spread out a sheet of non-stick baking paper and sprinkle with caster sugar. Turn out the cake on to this and remove the lining paper. Roll up the sponge loosely from one short side, with the paper inside. Cool.

5 Unroll and remove the paper. Stir the strawberries into the fromage frais and spread over the sponge. Roll up and serve decorated with strawberries.

Classic Cheesecake

You can decorate this with fruit and serve it with cream, if you like, but it tastes delicious just as it is.

INGREDIENTS

Serves 8

25g/1oz/½ cup digestive biscuit crumbs

900g/2lb cream cheese

250g/9oz/1¼ cups caster sugar

grated rind of 1 lemon

45ml/3 tbsp fresh lemon juice

5ml/1 tsp vanilla essence

4 eggs, at room temperature

1 Preheat the oven to 160°C/ 325°F/Gas 3. Grease a 23cm/8in springform cake tin. Place on a round of foil 13cm/5in larger than the diameter of the pan. Press it up the sides to seal tightly.

2 Sprinkle the crumbs in the base of the pan. Press to form an even layer.

3 With an electric mixer, beat the cream cheese until smooth. Add the sugar, lemon rind and juice and vanilla essence, and beat until blended. Beat in the eggs, one at a time. Beat just enough to blend thoroughly.

4 Pour into the prepared tin. Set the tin in a larger baking tray and place in the oven. Pour enough hot water in the outer tray to come 2.5cm/1in up the side of the tin.

5 Bake until the top of the cake is golden brown, about 1½ hours. Let cool in the tin.

6 Run a knife around the edge to loosen, then remove the rim of the tin. Chill for at least 4 hours before serving.

Chocolate Cheesecake

This popular variation of the classic dessert is made with a cinnamon and chocolate base.

INGREDIENTS

Serves 10–12

175g/6oz plain chocolate squares

115g/4oz bitter chocolate squares

1.15kg/2½lb cream cheese, at room temperature

200g/7oz/1 cup caster sugar

10ml/2 tsp vanilla essence

4 eggs, at room temperature

175ml/6fl oz/¾ cup sour cream

For the base

75g/3oz/1½ cups chocolate wafer crumbs

75g/3oz/6 tbsp butter, melted

2.5ml/½ tsp ground cinnamon

1 Preheat the oven to 180°C/350°F/Gas 4. Grease a 23cm/9in springform cake tin.

2 For the base, mix the chocolate wafer crumbs with the butter and cinnamon. Press evenly in the bottom of the tin.

3 Melt the plain and bitter chocolate in the top of a double boiler, or in a heatproof bowl set over hot water. Set aside.

4 With an electric mixer, beat the cream cheese until smooth, then beat in the sugar and vanilla essence. Add the eggs, one at a time, scraping the bowl with a spatula when necessary.

5 Add the sour cream. Stir in the melted chocolate.

6 Pour into the tin. Bake for 1 hour. Let cool in the tin; remove rim. Chill before serving.

Blueberry-hazelnut Cheesecake

The base for this cheesecake is made with ground hazelnuts – a tasty and unusual alternative to a biscuit base.

Serves 6–8

350g/12oz blueberries

15ml/1 tbsp clear honey

75g/3oz/6 tbsp granulated sugar

juice of 1 lemon

175g/6oz/¾ cup cream cheese, at room
    temperature

1 egg

5ml/1 tsp hazelnut liqueur (optional)

120ml/4fl oz/½ cup whipping cream

For the base

175g/6oz/1⅔ cups ground hazelnuts

75g/3oz/⅔ cup plain flour

pinch of salt

50g/2oz/4 tbsp butter, at room
    temperature

65g/2½oz/⅓ cup light brown sugar,
    firmly packed

1 egg yolk

1 For the base, put the hazelnuts in a large bowl. Sift in the flour and salt, and stir to mix. Set aside.

2 Beat the butter with the brown sugar until light and fluffy. Beat in the egg yolk. Gradually fold in the nut mixture, in three batches, until well combined.

3 Press the dough into a greased 23cm/9in pie tin, spreading it evenly against the sides. Form a rim around the top edge that is slightly thicker than the sides. Cover and chill for at least 30 minutes.

4 Preheat the oven to 180°C/ 350°F/Gas 4. Meanwhile, for the topping, combine the blueberries, honey, 15ml/1 tbsp of the granulated sugar and 5ml/1 tsp lemon juice in a heavy saucepan. Cook the mixture over low heat, stirring occasionally, until the berries have given off some liquid but still retain their shape, 5–7 minutes. Remove from the heat and set aside.

5 Place the pastry base in the oven and bake for 15 minutes. Remove and let cool while making the filling.

6 Beat together the cream cheese and remaining granulated sugar until light and fluffy. Add the egg, 15ml/1 tbsp lemon juice, the liqueur, if using, and the cream and beat until thoroughly blended.

7 Pour the cheese mixture into the pastry base and spread evenly. Bake until just set, 20–25 minutes.

8 Let the cheesecake cool completely on a wire rack, then cover and chill for at least 1 hour.

9 Spread the blueberry mixture evenly over the top of the cheesecake. Serve at cool room temperature.

COOK'S TIP

The cheesecake can be prepared 1 day in advance, but add the fruit shortly before serving.

Sponge Cake with Fruit and Cream

Called Génoise, this is the French cake used as the base for both simple and elaborate creations. You could simply dust it with icing sugar, or layer it with seasonal fruits to serve as a seasonal dessert.

INGREDIENTS

Serves 6

115g/4oz/1 cup plain flour

pinch of salt

4 eggs, at room temperature

115g/4oz/scant ⅔ cup caster sugar

2.5ml/½ tsp vanilla essence

50g/2oz/4 tbsp butter, melted or clarified and cooled

For the filling

450g/1lb fresh strawberries or raspberries

30–60ml/2–4 tbsp caster sugar

475ml/16fl oz/2 cups whipping cream

5ml/1 tsp vanilla essence

1 Preheat the oven to 180°C/350°F/Gas 4. Lightly butter a 23cm/9in springform tin or deep cake tin. Line the base with non-stick baking paper, and dust lightly with flour. Sift the flour and salt together twice.

2 Half-fill a medium saucepan with hot water and set over a low heat (do not allow the water to boil). Put the eggs in a heatproof bowl which just fits into the pan without touching the water. Using an electric mixer, beat the eggs at medium-high speed, gradually adding the sugar, for 8–10 minutes until the mixture is very thick and pale and leaves a ribbon trail when the beaters are lifted. Remove the bowl from the pan, add the vanilla essence and continue beating until the mixture is cool.

3 Fold in the flour mixture in three batches, using a balloon whisk or metal spoon. Before the third addition of flour, stir a large spoonful of the mixture into the melted or clarified butter to lighten it, then fold the butter into the remaining mixture with the last addition of flour. Work quickly, but gently, so the mixture does not deflate. Pour into the prepared tin, smoothing the top so the sides are slightly higher than the centre.

4 Bake in the oven for about 25–30 minutes until the top of the cake springs back when touched and the edge begins to shrink away from the sides of the tin. Place the cake in its tin on a wire rack to cool for 5–10 minutes, then invert the cake on to the rack to cool completely. Peel off the baking paper.

5 To make the filling, slice the strawberries, place in a bowl, sprinkle with 15–30ml/1–2 tbsp of the sugar and set aside. Beat the cream with 15–30ml/1–2 tbsp of the sugar and the vanilla essence until it holds soft peaks.

6 To assemble the cake (up to 4 hours before serving), split the cake horizontally, using a serrated knife. Place the top, cut side up, on a serving plate. Spread with a third of the cream and cover with an even layer of sliced strawberries.

7 Place the bottom half of the cake, cut side down, on top of the filling and press lightly. Spread the remaining cream over the top and sides of the cake. Chill until ready to serve. Serve the remaining strawberries with the cake.

Devil's Food Cake with Orange Frosting

Chocolate and orange are the ultimate combination. Can you resist the temptation?

INGREDIENTS

Serves 8–10

50g/2oz/½ cup unsweetened cocoa powder

175g/6oz/¾ cup butter, at room temperature

350g/12oz/1½ cups dark brown sugar, firmly packed

3 eggs, at room temperature

225g/8oz/2 cups plain flour

25ml/1½ tsp baking soda

1.5ml/¼ tsp baking powder

175ml/6fl oz/¾ cup sour cream

orange rind strips, for decoration

For the frosting

285g/10½oz/1½ cups granulated sugar

2 egg whites

60ml/4 tbsp frozen orange juice concentrate

15ml/1 tbsp fresh lemon juice

grated rind of 1 orange

1 Preheat the oven to 180°C/ 350°F/Gas 4. Line two 23cm/9in cake tins with greaseproof paper and grease. In a bowl, mix the cocoa and 175ml/ 6fl oz/¾ cup of boiling water until smooth. Set aside.

2 With an electric mixer, cream the butter and sugar until light and fluffy. Add the eggs, one at a time, beating well.

3 When the cocoa mixture is cooked to lukewarm, stir into the butter mixture.

4 Sift together the flour, baking soda and baking powder twice. Fold into the cocoa mixture in three batches, alternating with the sour cream.

5 Pour into the tins. Bake until the cakes pull away from the tin, 30–35 minutes. Stand for 15 minutes before unmoulding.

6 Thinly slice the orange rind strips. Blanch in boiling water for 1 minute.

7 For the frosting, place all the ingredients in the top of a double boiler or in a bowl set over hot water. With an electric mixer, beat until the mixture holds soft peaks. Continue beating off the heat until thick enough to spread.

8 Sandwich the cake with frosting, then spread over the top and sides. Arrange the rind on top.

Black Forest Gâteau

This light chocolate sponge, moistened with Kirsch and layered with cherries and cream, is still one of the most popular of all the chocolate gâteaux.

INGREDIENTS

Serves 8–10

6 eggs

200g/7oz/scant 1 cup caster sugar

5ml/1 tsp vanilla essence

50g/2oz/½ cup plain flour

50g/2oz/½ cup cocoa powder

115g/4oz/½ cup unsalted
   butter, melted

For the filling and topping

60ml/4 tbsp Kirsch

600ml/1 pint/2½ cups double or
   whipping cream

30ml/2 tbsp icing sugar

2.5ml/½ tsp vanilla essence

675g/1½lb jar stoned morello
   cherries, drained

To decorate

icing sugar, for dusting

grated chocolate

chocolate curls

fresh or drained canned
   morello cherries

1 Preheat the oven to 180°C/ 350°F/Gas 4. Grease three 19cm/7½in sandwich cake tins and line the base of each with non-stick baking paper. Whisk the eggs with the sugar and vanilla essence in a large bowl until pale and very thick – the mixture should hold a firm trail when the whisk is lifted.

2 Sift the flour and cocoa over the mixture and fold in lightly and evenly. Stir in the melted butter. Divide the mixture among the prepared cake tins, smoothing them level.

3 Bake for 15–18 minutes, until risen and springy to the touch. Leave to cool in the tins for about 5 minutes, then turn out on to wire racks and leave to cool completely.

4 Prick each layer all over with a skewer or fork, then sprinkle with Kirsch. Whip the cream in a bowl until it starts to thicken, then beat in the icing sugar and vanilla essence until the mixture begins to hold its shape.

5 To assemble, spread one cake layer with a thick layer of flavoured cream and top with a quarter of the cherries. Spread a second cake layer with cream and cherries, then place it on top of the first layer. Top with the final layer.

6 Spread the remaining cream all over the cake. Dust a plate with icing sugar; position the cake. Press grated chocolate over the sides and decorate with the chocolate curls and cherries.

Angel Food Cake

This cake is beautifully light. The secret? Sifting the flour over and over again to let plenty of air into it.

INGREDIENTS

Serves 12–14

115g/4oz/1 cup sifted cake flour

285g/10½oz/1½ cups caster sugar

300ml/½ pint/1¼ cups egg whites (about 10–11 eggs)

6.5ml/1¼ tsp cream of tartar

1.5ml/¼ tsp salt

5ml/1 tsp vanilla essence

1.5ml/¼ tsp almond essence

icing sugar, for dusting

1 Preheat the oven to 160°C/ 325°F/Gas 3. Sift the flour before measuring, then sift it four times with 90g/3½oz/½ cup of the sugar. Transfer to a bowl.

2 With an electric mixer, beat the egg whites until foamy. Sift over the cream of tartar and salt and continue to beat until they hold soft peaks when the beaters are lifted.

3 Add the remaining sugar in three batches, beating well after each addition. Stir in the vanilla and almond essence.

4 Add the flour mixture, ½ cup at a time, and fold in gently with a large metal spoon after each addition.

5 Transfer to an ungreased 25cm/10in straight-sided ring mould and bake until delicately browned on top, about 1 hour.

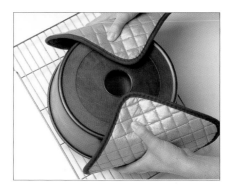

6 Turn the ring mould upside down on to a cake rack and let cool for 1 hour. If the cake does not unmould, run a spatula around the edge to loosen it. Invert on to a serving plate.

7 When cool, lay a star-shaped template on top of the cake, sift with icing sugar, and lift off.

Chocolate and Cherry Polenta Cake

Polenta and almonds add an unusual nutty texture to this delicious dessert.

INGREDIENTS

Serves 8

50g/2oz/⅓ cup quick-cook polenta

200g/7oz plain chocolate, broken into
squares

5 eggs, separated

175g/6oz/¾ cup caster sugar

115g/4oz/1 cup ground almonds

60ml/4 tbsp plain flour

finely grated rind of 1 orange

115g/4oz/½ cup glacé cherries, halved

icing sugar, for dusting

1 Place the polenta in a heatproof bowl and pour over just enough boiling water to cover, about 120ml/4fl oz/½ cup. Stir well, then cover the bowl and leave to stand for about 30 minutes, until the polenta has absorbed all the excess moisture.

2 Preheat the oven to 190°C/ 375°F/Gas 5. Grease a deep 22cm/8½in round cake tin and line the base with non-stick baking paper. Melt the chocolate in a heatproof bowl over hot water.

3 Whisk the egg yolks with the sugar in a bowl until thick and pale. Beat in the chocolate, then fold in the polenta, ground almonds, flour and orange rind.

4 Whisk the egg whites in a clean bowl until stiff. Stir 15ml/1 tbsp of the whites into the chocolate mixture, then fold in the rest. Finally, fold in the cherries.

5 Scrape the mixture into the prepared tin and bake for 45–55 minutes or until well risen and firm to the touch. Cool on a rack. Dust with icing sugar to serve.

Lemon Coconut Layer Cake

The flavours of lemon and coconut complement each other beautifully in this light dessert cake.

Serves 8–10

175g/6oz/1½ cups plain flour

pinch of salt

7 eggs

350g/12oz/1¾ cups granulated sugar

15ml/1 tbsp grated orange rind

grated rind of 1½ lemons

juice of 1 lemon

65g/2½oz/scant 1 cup desiccated coconut

15ml/1 tbsp cornflour

40g/1½oz/3 tbsp butter

For the frosting

75g/3oz/6 tbsp unsalted butter, at room
    temperature

175g/6oz/1½ cups icing sugar

grated rind of 1½ lemons

30ml/2 tbsp fresh lemon juice

200g/7oz/2½ cups desiccated coconut

1 Preheat the oven to 180°C/ 350°F/Gas 4. Line three 20cm/8in cake tins with baking parchment and grease. In a bowl, sift together the flour and salt and set aside.

2 Place six of the eggs in a large heatproof bowl set over hot water. With an electric mixer, beat until frothy. Gradually beat in 225g/8oz/generous 1 cup of the granulated sugar until the mixture doubles in volume and is thick enough to leave a ribbon trail when the beaters are lifted, which takes about 10 minutes.

3 Remove the bowl from the hot water. Fold in the orange rind, half the grated lemon rind and 15ml/1 tbsp of the lemon juice until blended. Fold in the coconut.

4 Sift over the flour mixture in three batches, gently folding in thoroughly after each addition.

5 Divide the mixture between the prepared tins.

6 Bake until the cakes pull away from the sides of the tin, 20–25 minutes. Leave to stand for 5 minutes, then turn out and transfer to a cooling rack.

7 In a bowl, blend the cornflour with a little cold water to dissolve. Whisk in the remaining egg until just blended. Set aside.

8 In a saucepan, combine the remaining lemon rind and juice, the remaining sugar, butter and 120ml/4fl oz/½ cup of water.

9 Over a moderate heat, bring the mixture to the boil. Whisk in the egg and cornflour, and return to the boil. Whisk continuously until thick, about 5 minutes. Remove from the heat and pour into a bowl. Cover with baking parchment and set aside until cool.

10 For the frosting, cream the butter and icing sugar until smooth. Stir in the lemon rind and enough lemon juice to obtain a thick, spreadable consistency.

11 Sandwich the three cake layers with the lemon custard mixture. Spread the frosting over the top and sides. Cover the cake with the coconut, pressing it in gently.

Carrot Cake with Maple Butter Frosting

A good, quick dessert cake for a family supper.

INGREDIENTS

Serves 12

450g/1lb carrots, peeled
175g/6oz/1½ cups plain flour
10ml/2 tsp baking powder
2.5ml/½ tsp baking soda
5ml/1 tsp salt
10ml/2 tsp ground cinnamon
4 eggs
10ml/2 tsp vanilla essence
225g/8oz/1 cup dark brown sugar,
　　firmly packed
90g/3½oz/½ cup granulated sugar
300ml/½ pint/1¼ cups sunflower oil
115g/4oz/1 cup walnuts,
　　finely chopped
65g/2½oz/½ cup raisins
walnut halves, for decorating
　　(optional)

For the frosting
75g/3oz/6 tbsp unsalted butter, at room
　　temperature
375g/12oz/3 cups icing sugar
50ml/2fl oz/¼ cup maple syrup

1 Preheat the oven to 180°C/
350°F/Gas 4. Line a 28 x 20cm/
11 x 8in rectangular cake tin with
non-stick baking paper and grease.
Grate the carrots and set aside.

2 Sift the flour, baking powder,
baking soda, salt and
cinnamon into a bowl. Set aside.

3 With an electric mixer, beat
the eggs until blended. Add the
vanilla, sugars and oil and beat
well to incorporate.

4 Add the carrots, walnuts and
raisins to the mixture, and
fold in thoroughly.

5 Pour the batter into the
prepared tin and bake until the
cake springs back when touched
lightly, 40–45 minutes. Let stand
10 minutes, then unmould and
transfer to a rack.

6 For the frosting, cream the
butter with half the sugar until
soft. Add the syrup, then beat in
the remaining sugar until blended.

7 Spread the frosting over the
top of the cake. Using a metal
spatula, make decorative ridges in
the frosting. Cut into squares.
Decorate with walnut halves.

Black and White Pound Cake

A good cake for packed lunches and picnics as it cuts into neat slices with no messy filling, or serve with custard for dessert.

INGREDIENTS

Serves 16

115g/4oz plain chocolate, broken
   into squares
350g/12oz/3 cups plain flour
5ml/1 tsp baking powder
450g/1lb/2 cups butter, at room
   temperature
650g/1lb 7oz/3⅓ cups sugar
15ml/1 tbsp vanilla essence
10 eggs, at room temperature
icing sugar, for dusting

1 Preheat the oven to 180°C/
350°F/Gas 4. Line the bottom of a 25cm/10in straight-sided ring mould with non-stick baking paper and grease. Dust with flour spread evenly with a brush.

2 Melt the chocolate in the top of a double boiler, or in a heatproof bowl set over a pan of hot water. Stir occasionally. Set aside.

3 In a bowl, sift together the flour and baking powder. In another bowl, cream the butter, sugar and vanilla essence with an electric mixer until light and fluffy. Add the eggs, two at a time, then gradually incorporate the flour mixture on low speed.

4 Spoon half of the batter into the prepared pan.

COOK'S TIP

This is also known as Marbled Cake because of its distinctive appearance.

5 Stir the chocolate into the remaining batter, then spoon into the pan. With a metal spatula, swirl the two batters to create a marbled effect.

6 Bake until a cake tester inserted in the centre comes out clean, about 1¾ hours. Cover with foil halfway through baking. Let stand 15 minutes, then unmould and transfer to a cooling rack. To serve, dust with icing sugar.

Chocolate Mousse Strawberry Layer Cake

The strawberries used in this cake can be replaced by raspberries or blackberries and the appropriate flavour liqueur.

INGREDIENTS

Serves 10

115g/4oz fine quality white chocolate, chopped

120ml/4fl oz/½ cup whipping or double cream

120ml/4fl oz/½ cup milk

15ml/1 tbsp rum or vanilla essence

115g/4oz/½ cup unsalted butter, softened

175g/6oz/generous ¾ cup granulated sugar

3 eggs

275g/10oz/2½ cups plain flour

5ml/1 tsp baking powder

pinch of salt

675g/1½lb fresh strawberries, sliced, plus extra for decoration

750ml/1¼ pints/3 cups whipping cream

30ml/2 tbsp rum or strawberry-flavour liqueur

For the white chocolate mousse

250g/9oz fine quality white chocolate, chopped

350ml/12fl oz/1½ cups whipping or double cream

30ml/2 tbsp rum or strawberry-flavour liqueur

1 Preheat oven to 180°C/350°F/ Gas 4. Grease and flour two 23 x 5cm/9 x 2in cake tins. Line the base of the tins with non-stick baking paper. Melt chocolate and cream in a double boiler over a low heat, stirring until smooth. Stir in milk and rum or vanilla essence; set aside to cool.

2 In a large bowl with an electric mixer, beat the butter and sugar until light and creamy. Add the eggs one at a time, beating well.

3 In a small bowl, stir together the flour, baking powder and salt. Alternately add flour and melted chocolate to the eggs in batches, just until blended. Pour the batter evenly into the tins.

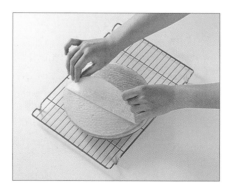

4 Bake for 20–25 minutes until a cake tester inserted in centre comes out clean. Cool on a wire rack for 10 minutes. Turn cakes out on to wire rack, peel off paper and cool completely.

5 Prepare the mousse. In a medium saucepan over low heat, melt the chocolate and cream until smooth, stirring frequently. Stir in rum or strawberry-flavour liqueur and pour into a bowl. Chill until just set. With a wire whisk, whip lightly until mixture has a "mousse" consistency.

6 Slice both cake layers in half crossways. Sandwich the four layers together with the mousse and strawberries.

7 Whip the cream with the rum or strawberry-flavour liqueur until firm peaks form. Spread half over top and sides of cake. Spoon remaining cream into a decorating bag with a star tip and pipe scrolls on top. Garnish with remaining strawberries.

Death by Chocolate

One of the richest chocolate cakes ever, so serve in thin slices.

Serves 16–20

225g/8oz plain dark chocolate, broken
   into squares
115g/4oz/½ cup unsalted butter
150ml/¼ pint/⅔ cup milk
225g/8oz/1¼ cups light muscovado sugar
10ml/2 tsp vanilla essence
2 eggs, separated
150ml/¼ pint/⅔ cup soured cream
225g/8oz/2 cups self-raising flour
5ml/1 tsp baking powder

For the filling
60ml/4 tbsp seedless raspberry jam
60ml/4 tbsp brandy
400g/14oz plain dark chocolate, broken
   into squares
200g/7oz/scant 1 cup unsalted butter

For the topping
250ml/8fl oz/1 cup double cream
225g/8oz plain dark chocolate, broken
   into squares
plain and white chocolate curls,
   to decorate
chocolate-dipped physalis (Cape
   gooseberries), to decorate (optional)

1 Preheat the oven to 180°C/350°F/ Gas 4. Grease and base-line a deep 23cm/9in springform cake tin. Place chocolate, butter and milk in a saucepan. Heat gently until smooth. Remove from heat, beat in sugar and vanilla, then cool.

2 Beat the egg yolks and cream in a bowl, then beat into the chocolate mixture. Sift the flour and baking powder over the surface and fold in. Whisk the egg whites in a grease-free bowl until stiff; fold into the mixture.

3 Scrape into the prepared tin and bake for 45–55 minutes, or until firm to the touch. Cool in the tin for 15 minutes, then invert to a wire rack to cool.

4 Slice the cold cake across the middle to make three even layers. In a small saucepan, warm the jam with 15ml/1 tbsp of the brandy, then brush over two of the layers. Heat the remaining brandy in a saucepan with the chocolate and butter, stirring, until smooth. Cool until beginning to thicken.

5 Spread the bottom layer of the cake with half the chocolate filling, taking care not to disturb the jam. Top with a second layer, jam side up, and spread with the remaining filling. Top with the final layer and press lightly. Leave to set.

6 To make the topping, heat the cream and chocolate together in a saucepan over a low heat, stirring frequently until the chocolate has melted. Pour into a bowl, leave to cool, then whisk until the mixture begins to hold its shape.

7 Spread the top and sides of the cake with the chocolate ganache. Decorate with plain and white chocolate curls and, if liked, chocolate-dipped physalis (Cape gooseberries).

Simple Chocolate Cake

An easy, everyday chocolate cake which can be filled with butter-cream, or with a rich chocolate ganache for a special occasion.

INGREDIENTS

Serves 6–8

115g/4oz plain chocolate, broken
   into squares
45ml/3 tbsp milk
150g/5oz/⅔ cup unsalted butter or
   margarine, softened
150g/5oz/scant 1 cup light
   muscovado sugar
3 eggs
200g/7oz/1¾ cups self-raising flour
15ml/1 tbsp cocoa powder

For the buttercream
75g/3oz/6 tbsp unsalted butter or
   margarine, softened
175g/6oz/1½ cups icing sugar
15ml/1 tbsp cocoa powder
2.5ml/½ tsp vanilla essence
icing sugar and cocoa powder,
   for dusting

1 Preheat the oven to 180°C/350°F/Gas 4. Grease two 18cm/7in round sandwich cake tins and line the base of each with non-stick baking paper. Melt the chocolate with the milk in a heatproof bowl set over a pan of simmering water.

2 Cream the butter or margarine with the sugar in a mixing bowl until pale and fluffy. Add the eggs one at a time, beating well after each addition. Stir in the chocolate mixture until it is well combined.

3 Sift the flour and cocoa over the mixture and fold in with a metal spoon until evenly mixed. Scrape into the prepared tins, smooth level and bake for 35–40 minutes or until well risen and firm. Turn out on wire racks and leave to cool.

4 To make the buttercream, beat the butter or margarine, icing sugar, cocoa powder and vanilla essence together in a bowl until the mixture is smooth.

5 Sandwich the cake layers together with the buttercream. Dust with a mixture of icing sugar and cocoa just before serving.

Pineapple Upside-down Cake

This is a perennial favourite to serve in winter or summer.

INGREDIENTS

Serves 8

115g/4oz/½ cup butter

225g/8oz/1 cup dark brown sugar, firmly packed

450g/16oz can pineapple slices, drained

4 eggs, separated

grated rind of 1 lemon

pinch of salt

90g/3½oz/½ cup granulated sugar

85g/3¼oz/¾ cup plain flour

5ml/1 tsp baking powder

1 Preheat the oven to 180°C/350°F/Gas 4. Melt the butter in an ovenproof cast-iron frying pan, about 25cm/10in in diameter. Remove 15ml/1 tbsp of the melted butter and set aside.

2 Add the brown sugar to the frying pan and stir until blended. Place the drained pineapple slices on top in one layer. Set aside.

3 In a bowl, whisk together the egg yolks, reserved butter and lemon rind until smooth and well blended. Set aside.

4 With an electric mixer, beat the egg whites with the salt until stiff. Fold in the granulated sugar, 30ml/2 tbsp at a time. Fold in the egg yolk mixture.

5 Sift the flour and baking powder together. Fold into the egg mixture in three batches.

6 Pour the batter over the pineapple and smooth level.

7 Bake until a cake tester inserted in the centre comes out clean, about 30 minutes.

8 While still hot, place a serving plate on top of the frying pan, bottom-side up. Holding them together with oven gloves, flip over. Serve hot or cold.

Raspberry and White Chocolate Cheesecake

Raspberries and white chocolate are an irresistible combination, especially when teamed with rich mascarpone on a crunchy ginger and pecan nut base.

Serves 8

50g/2oz/4 tbsp unsalted butter

225g/8oz/2⅓ cups ginger nut biscuits, crushed

50g/2oz/½ cup chopped pecan nuts or walnuts

For the filling

275g/10oz/1¼ cups mascarpone cheese

175g/6oz/¾ cup fromage frais

2 eggs, beaten

45ml/3 tbsp caster sugar

250g/9oz white chocolate, broken into squares

225g/8oz/1⅓ cups fresh or frozen raspberries

For the topping

115g/4oz/½ cup mascarpone cheese

75g/3oz/⅓ cup fromage frais

white chocolate curls and raspberries, to decorate

1 Preheat the oven to 150°C/ 300°F/Gas 2. Melt the butter in a saucepan, then stir in the crushed biscuits and nuts. Press into the base of a 23cm/9in spring-form cake tin.

2 Make the filling. Beat the mascarpone and fromage frais in a bowl, then beat in the eggs and caster sugar until evenly mixed.

3 Melt the white chocolate gently in a heatproof bowl over hot water.

4 Stir the chocolate into the cheese mixture with the raspberries.

5 Tip into the prepared tin and spread evenly, then bake for about 1 hour or until just set. Switch off the oven, but do not remove the cheesecake. Leave it until cold and completely set.

6 Release the tin and lift the cheesecake on to a plate. Make the topping by mixing the mascarpone and fromage frais in a bowl and spread over the cheesecake. Decorate with chocolate curls and raspberries.

Marbled Swiss Roll

The combination of light chocolate sponge and walnut chocolate buttercream is simply sensational.

INGREDIENTS

Serves 6–8

90g/3½oz/scant 1 cup plain flour

15ml/1 tbsp cocoa powder

25g/1oz plain chocolate, grated

25g/1oz white chocolate, grated

3 eggs

115g/4oz/generous ½ cup caster sugar

For the filling

75g/3oz/6 tbsp unsalted butter or
   margarine, softened

175g/6oz/1½ cups icing sugar

15ml/1 tbsp cocoa powder

2.5ml/½ tsp vanilla essence

45ml/3 tbsp chopped walnuts

plain and white chocolate curls, to
   decorate (optional)

1 Preheat the oven to 200°C/ 400°F/Gas 6. Grease a 30 x 20cm/12 x 8in Swiss roll tin and line with non-stick baking paper. Sift half the flour with the cocoa into bowl. Stir in the grated plain chocolate. Sift the remaining flour into another bowl; stir in the grated white chocolate.

2 Whisk the eggs and sugar in a heatproof bowl; set over a saucepan of hot water until it holds its shape when the whisk is lifted.

3 Remove the bowl from the heat and tip half the mixture into a separate bowl. Fold the white chocolate mixture into one portion, then fold the plain chocolate mixture into the other. Stir 15ml/1 tbsp boiling water into each half to soften the mixtures.

4 Place alternate spoonfuls of mixture in the prepared tin and swirl lightly together for a marbled effect. Bake for about 12–15 minutes, or until firm. Turn out on to a sheet of non-stick baking paper.

5 Trim the edges to neaten and cover with a damp, clean dish towel. Cool.

6 For the filling, beat the butter or margarine, icing sugar, cocoa powder and vanilla essence together in a bowl until smooth, then mix in the walnuts.

7 Uncover the sponge, lift off the baking paper and spread the surface with the buttercream. Roll up carefully from a long side and place on a serving plate. Decorate with plain and white chocolate curls, if wished.

Sachertorte

This glorious gâteau was created in Vienna in 1832 by Franz Sacher, a chef in the royal household.

INGREDIENTS

Serves 10–12

225g/8oz plain dark chocolate, broken into squares
150g/5oz/⅔ cup unsalted butter, softened
115g/4oz/generous ½ cup caster sugar
8 eggs, separated
115g/4oz/1 cup plain flour

For the glaze
225g/8oz/scant 1 cup apricot jam
15ml/1 tbsp lemon juice

For the icing
225g/8oz plain dark chocolate, broken into squares
200g/7oz/1 cup caster sugar
15ml/1 tbsp golden syrup
250ml/8fl oz/1 cup double cream
5ml/1 tsp vanilla essence
plain chocolate curls, to decorate

1 Preheat the oven to 180°C/ 350°F/Gas 4. Grease a 23cm/9in round springform cake tin and line with non-stick baking paper. Melt the chocolate in a heatproof bowl over hot water, then remove from the heat.

2 Cream the butter with the sugar in a mixing bowl until pale and fluffy, then add the egg yolks, one at a time, beating after each addition. Beat in the melted chocolate, then sift the flour over the mixture and fold it in evenly.

3 Whisk the egg whites in a clean, grease-free bowl until stiff, then stir about a quarter of the whites into the chocolate mixture to lighten it. Fold in the remaining whites.

4 Tip the mixture into the prepared cake tin and smooth level. Place in the oven and bake for about 50–55 minutes, or until firm. Turn out carefully on to a wire rack to cool.

5 Heat the apricot jam with the lemon juice in a small saucepan until melted, then strain through a sieve into a bowl. Once the cake is cold, slice in half across the middle to make two equal-size layers.

6 Brush the top and sides of each layer with the apricot glaze, then sandwich them together. Place on a wire rack.

7 Mix the icing ingredients in a heavy saucepan. Heat gently, stirring until thick. Simmer for 3–4 minutes, without stirring, until the mixture registers 95°C/200°F on a sugar thermometer. Pour quickly over the cake and spread evenly. Leave to set, then decorate with chocolate curls.

Australian Hazelnut Pavlova

Meringue topped with fresh fruit and cream – perfect for summer dinner parties.

Serves 4–6

3 egg whites

175g/6oz/generous ¾ cup caster sugar

5ml/1 tsp cornflour

5ml/1 tsp white wine vinegar

40g/1½oz/5 tbsp chopped roasted
    hazelnuts

250ml/8fl oz/1 cup double cream

15ml/1 tbsp orange juice

30ml/2 tbsp natural thick and
    creamy yogurt

2 ripe nectarines, stoned and sliced

225g/8oz/1⅓ cups raspberries

15–30ml/1–2 tbsp redcurrant
    jelly, warmed

1 Preheat the oven to 140°C/
275°F/Gas 1. Lightly grease a
baking sheet. Draw a 20cm/8in
circle on a sheet of baking
parchment. Place pencil-side down
on the baking sheet.

2 Place the egg whites in a large,
clean, grease-free bowl and
whisk with an electric mixer until
stiff. Whisk in the sugar 15ml/
1 tbsp at a time, whisking well after
each addition.

3 Add the cornflour, vinegar and
hazelnuts and fold in carefully
with a large metal spoon.

4 Spoon the meringue on to the
marked circle and spread out,
making a dip in the centre.

5 Bake for about 1¼–1½ hours,
until crisp. Leave to cool, then
transfer to a serving platter.

6 Whip the cream and orange
juice until just thick, stir in the
yogurt and spoon on to the
meringue. Top with the fruit and
drizzle over the redcurrant jelly.
Serve immediately.

Pastries
&
Pies

❖

Chocolate Almond Meringue Pie

This dream dessert combines three very popular flavours: velvety chocolate filling on a light orange pastry case, topped with fluffy white meringue.

Serves 6

175g/6oz/1½ cups plain flour

50g/2oz/⅓ cup ground rice

150g/5oz/⅔ cup unsalted butter

finely grated rind of 1 orange

1 egg yolk

flaked almonds and melted plain dark
    chocolate, to decorate

For the filling

150g/5oz plain dark chocolate, broken
    into squares

50g/2oz/4 tbsp unsalted butter, softened

75g/3oz/⅓ cup caster sugar

10ml/2 tsp cornflour

4 egg yolks

75g/3oz/¾ cup ground almonds

For the meringue

3 egg whites

150g/5oz/¾ cup caster sugar

1 Sift the flour and ground rice into a bowl. Rub in the butter until the mixture resembles breadcrumbs. Stir in the orange rind. Add the egg yolk; bring the dough together. Roll out and use to line a 23cm/9in round flan tin. Chill for 30 minutes.

2 Preheat the oven to 190°C/375°F/Gas 5. Prick the pastry base all over with a fork, cover with greaseproof paper weighed down with baking beans and bake blind for 10 minutes. Remove the pastry case; take out the baking beans and paper.

3 Make the filling. Melt the chocolate in a heatproof bowl over hot water. Cream the butter with the sugar in a bowl, then beat in the cornflour and egg yolks. Fold in the almonds, then the chocolate. Spread in the pastry case. Bake for a further 10 minutes.

4 Make the meringue. Whisk the egg whites until stiff, then gradually add half the caster sugar. Fold in remaining sugar.

5 Spoon the meringue over the chocolate filling, lifting if up with the back of the spoon to form peaks. Reduce the oven temperature to 180°C/350°F/Gas 4 and bake the pie for 15–20 minutes or until the topping is pale gold. Serve warm, scattered with almonds and drizzled with melted chocolate.

Red Berry Tart with Lemon Cream Filling

This flan is best filled just before serving so the pastry remains mouth-wateringly crisp. Select red berry fruits such as strawberries, raspberries or redcurrants.

INGREDIENTS

Serves 6–8

150g/5oz/1¼ cups plain flour

25g/1oz/¼ cup cornflour

40g/1½oz/5 tbsp icing sugar

90g/3½oz/7 tbsp butter

5ml/1 tsp vanilla essence

2 egg yolks, beaten

sprig of mint, to decorate

For the filling

200g/7oz/scant 1 cup cream cheese

45ml/3 tbsp lemon curd

grated rind and juice of 1 lemon

icing sugar, to sweeten (optional)

225g/8oz/2 cups mixed red berry fruits

45ml/3 tbsp redcurrant jelly

1 Sift the flour, cornflour and icing sugar together, then rub in the butter until the mixture resembles breadcrumbs.

2 Beat the vanilla into the egg yolks, then mix into the crumbs to make a firm dough, adding cold water if necessary.

3 Roll out the pastry and line a 23cm/9in round flan tin. Prick the base of the flan with a fork and allow it to rest in the fridge for 30 minutes.

4 Preheat the oven to 200°C/400°F/Gas 6. Line the flan with greaseproof paper and baking beans. Place the tin on a baking sheet and bake for 20 minutes, removing the paper and beans for the last 5 minutes. When cooked, cool and remove the pastry case from the flan tin.

5 Cream the cheese, lemon curd and lemon rind and juice, adding icing sugar to sweeten, if you wish. Spread the mixture into the base of the flan.

6 Top the flan with the fruits. Gently warm the redcurrant jelly and trickle it over the fruits just before serving the flan decorated with a sprig of mint.

VARIATION

There are all sorts of delightful variations to this recipe. For instance, leave out the redcurrant jelly and sprinkle lightly with icing sugar or decorate with fresh strawberry leaves. Alternatively, top with sliced kiwi fruits or bananas slices sprinkled with lemon juice.

Peach and Blueberry Pie

The unusual combination of fruits in this pie looks especially good with a lattice pastry topping.

Serves 8

225g/8oz/2 cups plain flour

pinch of salt

10ml/2 tsp sugar

150g/5oz/10 tbsp cold butter
  or margarine

1 egg yolk

30ml/2 tbsp milk, to glaze

For the filling

450g/1lb fresh peaches, peeled, stoned
  and sliced

275g/10oz/2 cups fresh blueberries

150g/5oz/¾ cup caster sugar

30ml/2 tbsp fresh lemon juice

40g/1½oz/⅓ cup plain flour

large pinch of grated nutmeg

25g/1oz/2 tbsp butter or margarine, cut
  into tiny pieces

1 To make the pastry, sift the flour, salt and sugar into a bowl. Rub the butter or margarine into the dry ingredients as quickly as possible until the mixture resembles coarse breadcrumbs.

2 Mix the egg yolk with 50ml/2fl oz/¼ cup of iced water and sprinkle over the flour mixture. Combine with a fork until the dough holds together. If the dough is too crumbly, add a little more water, 15ml/1 tbsp at a time. Gather the dough into a ball and flatten into a round. Place in a sealed polythene bag and chill for at least 20 minutes.

3 Roll out two-thirds of the pastry between two sheets of greaseproof paper to a thickness of about 3mm/⅛in. Use to line a 23cm/9in pie dish.

4 Trim the pastry all around, leaving a 1cm/½in overhang. Fold the overhang under to form the edge. Using a fork, press the edge to the rim of the pie dish.

5 Gather the trimmings and remaining pastry into a ball, and roll out to a thickness of about 5mm/¼in. Using a pastry wheel or sharp knife, cut into long, 1cm/½in wide strips. Chill both the pastry case and the strips of pastry for 20 minutes. Meanwhile, preheat the oven to 200°C/400°F/Gas 6.

6 Line the pastry case with greaseproof paper and fill with dried beans. Bake for 7–10 minutes, until the pastry is just set. Remove from the oven and carefully lift out the paper with the beans. Prick the base of the pastry case with a fork, then return to the oven and bake for a further 5 minutes. Leave to cool slightly before filling. Leave the oven on.

7 For the filling, place the peach slices and blueberries in a bowl and stir in the sugar, lemon juice, flour and nutmeg. Spoon the fruit mixture into the pastry case. Dot the top with the pieces of butter or margarine.

8 Weave a lattice top with the chilled pastry strips, pressing the ends to the edge of the baked pastry case. Brush the strips with the milk.

9 Bake the pie for 15 minutes. Reduce the oven temperature to 180°C/350°F/Gas 4, and continue baking for another 30 minutes, until the filling is tender and bubbling and the pastry lattice is golden. If the pastry becomes too brown, cover loosely with a piece of foil. Serve the pie warm or at room temperature.

COOK'S TIP

Don't over-chill the pastry strips. If they become too firm, they may crack and break as you weave them into a lattice.

Rhubarb Pie

Use a biscuit cutter to cut out decorative pastry shapes and make this pie extra special.

INGREDIENTS

Serves 6
175g/6oz/1½ cups plain flour
2.5ml/½ tsp salt
10ml/2 tsp caster sugar
75g/3oz/6 tbsp cold butter or margarine
30ml/2 tbsp single cream
single or double cream, to serve

For the filling
1kg/2¼lb fresh rhubarb, cut into
   2.5cm/1in slices
30ml/2 tbsp cornflour
1 egg
275g/10oz/1½ cups caster sugar
15ml/1 tbsp grated orange rind

1 To make the pastry, sift the flour, salt and sugar into a bowl. Using a pastry blender or two knives, cut the butter or margarine into the dry ingredients as quickly as possible until the mixture resembles breadcrumbs.

2 Sprinkle the flour mixture with about 50ml/2fl oz/¼ cup of iced water and mix until the dough just holds together. If the dough is too crumbly, add a little more water, 15ml/1 tbsp at a time.

3 Gather the dough into a ball, flatten into a round, place in a polythene bag and put in the fridge for 20 minutes.

4 Roll out the pastry between two sheets of greaseproof paper to a 3mm/⅛in thickness. Use to line a 23cm/9in pie dish or tin. Trim all around, leaving a 1cm/½in overhang. Fold the overhang under the edge and flute. Chill the case and trimmings for 30 minutes.

5 To make the filling, put the rhubarb in a bowl, sprinkle with the cornflour and toss to coat.

6 Preheat the oven to 220°C/ 425°F/Gas 7. Beat the egg with the sugar in a bowl until thoroughly blended, then mix in the orange rind.

7 Stir the sugar mixture into the rhubarb and mix well together, then spoon the fruit into the prepared pastry case.

8 Roll out the pastry trimmings. Stamp out decorative shapes with a biscuit cutter.

9 Arrange the pastry shapes on top of the pie. Brush the shapes and the edge of the pastry case with cream.

10 Bake the pie for 30 minutes. Reduce the oven temperature to 160°C/325°F/Gas 3 and continue baking for a further 15–20 minutes, until the pastry is golden brown and the rhubarb is tender. Serve the pie hot with cream.

Chocolate Pecan Torte

This torte uses finely ground nuts instead of flour. Toast then cool the nuts before grinding finely in a blender or food processor. Do not over-grind the nuts, as the oils will form a paste.

INGREDIENTS

Serves 16

200g/7oz bittersweet or plain chocolate, chopped

150g/5oz/10 tbsp unsalted butter, cut into pieces

4 eggs

90g/3½oz/½ cup caster sugar

10ml/2 tsp vanilla essence

115g/4oz/1 cup ground pecans

10ml/2 tsp ground cinnamon

24 toasted pecan halves to decorate (optional)

For the chocolate honey glaze

115g/4oz bittersweet or semi-sweet chocolate, chopped

60g/2oz/¼ cup unsalted butter, cut into pieces

30ml/2 tbsp clear honey

pinch of ground cinnamon

1 Preheat oven to 180°C/350°F/ Gas 4. Grease a 20 x 5cm/ 8 x 2in springform tin; line with baking paper then grease the paper. Wrap bottom and side of tin with foil to prevent water seeping in. In a saucepan over a low heat, melt the chocolate and butter, stirring until smooth. Remove from the heat. In a mixing bowl with the electric mixer, beat the eggs, sugar and vanilla essence until frothy, 1–2 minutes. Stir in the melted chocolate, ground nuts and cinnamon. Pour into the prepared tin.

2 Place the foil-wrapped tin in a large roasting tin and pour boiling water into the roasting tin, to come 2cm/¾in up the side of the springform tin. Bake for 25–30 minutes until the edge of the cake is set, but centre is soft. Remove from the water bath and remove foil. Cool on a rack.

3 Prepare glaze. In a small saucepan over low heat, melt the chocolate, butter, honey and cinnamon, stirring until smooth; remove from the heat. Carefully dip toasted pecan halves halfway into glaze and place on a non-stick baking paper-lined baking sheet until it is set.

4 Remove side from springform tin and invert the cake on to wire rack. Remove the tin bottom and paper, so the bottom of the cake is now the top. Pour the thickened glaze over cake, tilting rack slightly to spread glaze. Use a metal palette knife to smooth the sides. Arrange the glazed nuts around outside edge of the torte and allow the glaze to set.

Key Lime Pie

Key limes come from Florida but if they are not available, ordinary limes will do just as well.

INGREDIENTS

Serves 8

3 large egg yolks

400g/14oz can sweetened condensed milk

15ml/1 tbsp grated Key lime rind

120ml/4fl oz/½ cup fresh Key lime juice

green food colouring (optional)

120ml/4fl oz/½ cup whipping cream

For the crust

1¼ cups digestive biscuit crumbs

75ml/5 tbsp butter or margarine, melted

1 Preheat the oven to 180°C/ 350°F/Gas 4. For the crust, place the biscuit crumbs in a bowl and add the butter or margarine. Mix to combine.

2 Press the crumbs evenly over the bottom and sides of a 23cm/9in pie dish or tin. Bake for 8 minutes. Let cool.

3 Beat the yolks until thick. Beat in the milk, lime rind and juice, and colouring, if using. Pour into the prebaked pie crust and refrigerate until set, about 4 hours. To serve, whip the cream. Pipe a lattice pattern on top, or spoon dollops around the edge.

Fruit Tartlets

The chocolate pastry cases make a dramatic base to these tartlets.

INGREDIENTS

Makes 8

215g/7½oz/¾ cup redcurrant or grape jelly

15ml/1 tbsp fresh lemon juice

175ml/6fl oz/¾ cup whipping cream

675g/1½lb fresh fruit, such as strawberries, raspberries, kiwi fruit, peaches, grapes or blueberries, peeled and sliced as necessary

For the pastry

150g/5oz/⅔ cup cold butter, cut in pieces

65g/2½oz/⅓ cup dark brown sugar, firmly packed

45ml/3 tbsp unsweetened cocoa powder

175g/6oz/1½ cups plain flour

1 egg white

1 For the pastry, combine the butter, brown sugar and cocoa over low heat. When the butter is melted, remove from the heat and sift over the flour. Stir, then add just enough egg white to bind the mixture. Gather into a ball, wrap in greaseproof paper, and chill for at least 30 minutes.

2 Preheat the oven to 180°C/ 350°F/Gas 4. Grease eight 7.5cm/3in tartlet tins. Roll out the dough between two sheets of greaseproof paper and stamp out eight 10cm/4in rounds with a fluted cutter.

3 Line the tartlet tins with dough. Prick the bottoms. Chill for 15 minutes.

4 Bake until firm, 20–25 minutes. Leave to cool, then remove from the tins.

5 Melt the jelly with the lemon juice. Brush a thin layer in the bottom of the tartlets. Whip the cream and spread a thin layer in the tartlet shells. Arrange the fruit on top. Brush evenly with the glaze and serve.

Cherry Pie

The woven lattice is the perfect finishing touch, although you can cheat and use a lattice pastry roller if you prefer.

INGREDIENTS

Serves 8

900g/2lb fresh Morello cherries, stoned, or 2 x 450g /1lb cans or jars, drained and stoned
65g/2½oz/generous ¾ cup caster sugar
25g/1oz/¼ cup plain flour
25ml/1½ tbsp fresh lemon juice
1.5ml/¼ tsp almond essence
25g/1oz/2 tbsp butter or margarine

For the pastry

225g/8oz/2 cups plain flour
5ml/1 tsp salt
175g/6oz/¾ cup lard or vegetable fat

1 For the pastry, sift the flour and salt into a mixing bowl. Using a pastry blender, cut in the fat until the mixture resembles coarse breadcrumbs.

2 Sprinkle in 60–75ml/4–5 tbsp iced water, a tablespoon at a time, tossing lightly with your fingertips or a fork until the pastry forms a ball.

3 Preheat the oven to 220°C/425°F/Gas 7. Divide the pastry in half and shape each half into a ball. On a lightly floured surface, roll out one of the balls to a circle about 30cm/12in in diameter.

4 Use it to line a 23cm/9in pie tin, easing the pastry in and being careful not to stretch it. With scissors, trim off excess pastry, leaving a 1cm/½in overhang around the pie tin.

5 Roll out the remaining pastry to 3mm/⅛in thick. Cut out eleven strips 1cm/½in wide.

6 In a mixing bowl, combine the cherries, sugar, flour, lemon juice and almond essence. Spoon the mixture into the pastry case and dot the top with the butter or margarine.

7 To make the lattice, place five of the pastry strips evenly across the filling. Fold every other strip back. Lay the first strip across in the opposite direction. Continue in this pattern, folding back every other strip each time you add a cross strip.

8 Trim the ends of the lattice strips even with the case overhang. Press together so that the edge rests on the pie-tin rim. With your thumbs, flute the edge. Chill for 15 minutes.

9 Bake the pie for 30 minutes, covering the edge of the pastry case with foil, if necessary, to prevent over-browning. Let cool, in the tin, on a wire rack.

Mince Pies with Orange Cinnamon Pastry

Home-made mince pies are so much nicer than shop bought, especially with this tasty pastry.

INGREDIENTS

Makes 18

225g/8oz/2 cups plain flour

40g/1½oz icing sugar

10ml/2 tsp ground cinnamon

150g/5oz/10 tbsp butter

grated rind of 1 orange

225g/8oz/⅔ cup mincemeat

1 beaten egg, to glaze

icing sugar, to dust

1 Sift together the flour, icing sugar and cinnamon then rub in the butter until it forms crumbs. (This can be done in a food processor.) Stir in the grated orange rind.

2 Mix to a firm dough with about 60ml/4 tbsp ice cold water. Knead lightly, then roll out to a 5mm/¼in thickness.

3 Using a 6cm/2½in round cutter, cut out 18 circles, re-rolling as necessary. Then cut out 18 smaller 5cm/2in circles.

4 Line two bun tins with the 18 larger circles – they will fill one and a half tins. Spoon a small spoonful of mincemeat into each pastry case and top with the smaller pastry circles, pressing the edges lightly together to seal.

5 Glaze the tops of the pies with egg and leave to rest in the fridge for 30 minutes. Preheat the oven to 200°C/400°F/Gas 6.

6 Bake the pies for 15– 20 minutes until they are golden brown. Remove them to wire racks to cool. Serve just warm, dusted with icing sugar.

Apple-cranberry Lattice Pie

Use fresh or frozen cranberries for this classic American pie.

INGREDIENTS

Serves 8

grated rind of 1 orange

45ml/3 tbsp fresh orange juice

2 large, tart cooking apples

115g/4oz/1 cup cranberries

65g/2½oz/½ cup raisins

25g/1oz/¼ cup walnuts, chopped

225g/8oz/1 cup granulated sugar

115g/4oz/½ cup dark brown sugar

15ml/1 tbsp quick-cooking tapioca

For the pastry

225g/8oz/2 cups plain flour

2.5ml/½ tsp salt

90ml/6 tbsp cold butter, cut in pieces

60ml/4 tbsp cold lard, cut in pieces

15ml/1 tbsp granulated sugar,
  for sprinkling

1 For the pastry, sift the flour and salt into a bowl. Add the butter and lard and rub in until the mixture resembles coarse crumbs. With a fork, stir in just enough iced water to bind the dough. Gather into two equal balls, wrap in greaseproof paper, and chill for at least 20 minutes.

2 Put the orange rind and juice into a mixing bowl. Peel and core the apples and grate them into the bowl. Stir in the cranberries, raisins, walnuts, granulated sugar, brown sugar and tapioca.

3 Place a baking sheet in the oven and preheat to 200°C/400°F/Gas 6.

4 On a lightly floured surface, roll out one ball of dough about 3mm/⅛in thick. Transfer to a 23cm/9in pie tin and trim the edge. Spoon the cranberry and apple mixture into the shell.

5 Roll out the remaining dough to a circle about 28cm/11in in diameter. With a serrated pastry wheel, cut the dough into ten strips, 2cm/¾in wide. Place five strips horizontally across the top of the tart at 1-inch intervals. Weave in six vertical strips. Trim the edges. Sprinkle the top with 15ml/1 tbsp of sugar.

6 Bake for 20 minutes. Reduce the heat to 180°C/350°F/Gas 4 and bake until the crust is golden and the filling is bubbling, about 15 minutes more.

Lemon Meringue Pie

Serve this exactly as it is, hot, warm or cold. It doesn't need any accompaniment.

Serves 8

grated rind and juice of 1 large lemon
200g/7oz/1 cup caster sugar
25g/1oz/2 tbsp butter
45ml/3 tbsp cornflour
3 eggs, separated
pinch of salt
.75ml/⅛ tsp cream of tartar

For the pastry
115g/4oz/1 cup plain flour
2.5ml/½ tsp salt
65g/2½oz/⅓ cup cold lard, cut in pieces

1 For the pastry, sift the flour and salt into a bowl. Add the lard and cut in with a pastry blender until the mixture resembles coarse crumbs. With a fork, stir in just enough iced water to bind the dough (about 30ml/ 2 tbsp). Gather the dough into a ball.

2 On a lightly floured surface, roll out the dough to 3mm/⅛in thick. Transfer to a 23cm/9in pie tin and trim the edge to leave a 1cm/½in overhang.

3 Fold the overhang under and crimp the edge. Chill the pie shell in the fridge for at least 20 minutes. Preheat the oven to 200°C/400°F/Gas 6.

4 Prick the dough all over with a fork. Line with greaseproof paper and fill with baking beans. Bake for 12 minutes. Remove the paper and beans and continue baking until golden, about 6–8 minutes more.

5 In a saucepan, combine the lemon rind and juice, 90g/ 3½oz/½ cup of the sugar, butter and 250ml/8fl oz/1 cup of water. Bring the mixture to the boil.

6 Meanwhile, in a mixing bowl, dissolve the cornflour in 15ml/1 tbsp of cold water. Add the egg yolks.

7 Add the egg yolks to the lemon mixture and return to the boil, whisking continuously until the mixture thickens, about 5 minutes.

8 Cover the surface with grease-proof paper to prevent a skin forming and let cool.

9 For the meringue, using an electric mixer beat the egg whites with the salt and cream of tartar until they hold stiff peaks. Add the remaining sugar and beat until glossy.

10 Spoon the lemon mixture into the pie shell and spread level. Spoon the meringue on top, smoothing it up to the edge of the crust to seal. Bake until golden, 12–15 minutes.

Chocolate Chiffon Pie

This light and creamy dessert is as luxurious as its name suggests.

Serves 8

175g/6oz plain chocolate squares

25g/1oz square bitter chocolate

250ml/8fl oz/1 cup milk

15ml/1 tbsp gelatine, or alternative

130g/4½oz/⅔ cup granulated sugar

2 size 1 eggs, separated

5ml/1 tsp vanilla essence

350ml/12fl oz/1½ cups whipping cream

pinch of salt

whipped cream and chocolate curls,
    to decorate

For the crust

75g/3oz/1½ cups digestive biscuit crumbs

75g/3oz/6 tbsp butter, melted

1 Place a baking sheet in the oven and preheat to 180°C/350°F/Gas 4. For the crust, mix the digestive biscuit crumbs and butter in a bowl. Press the crumbs evenly over the bottom and sides of a 23cm/9in pie tin. Bake for 8 minutes. Let cool.

2 Chop the chocolate, then grind in a food processor or blender. Set aside.

3 Place the milk in the top of a double boiler or in a heatproof bowl. Sprinkle over the gelatine. Let stand 5 minutes to soften.

4 Set the top of the double boiler or heatproof bowl over hot water. Add 50g/2oz/⅓ cup of the sugar, the chocolate and egg yolks. Stir until dissolved. Add the vanilla essence.

5 Set the top of the double boiler in a bowl of ice and stir until the mixture reaches room temperature. Remove from the ice and set aside.

6 Whip the cream lightly. Set aside. With an electric mixer, beat the egg whites and salt until they hold soft peaks. Add the remaining sugar and beat only enough to blend.

7 Fold a dollop of egg whites into the chocolate mixture, then pour back into the whites and gently fold in.

8 Fold in the whipped cream and pour into the pastry shell. Put in the freezer until just set, about 5 minutes. If the centre sinks, fill with any remaining mixture. Chill for 3–4 hours. Decorate with whipped cream and chocolate curls. Serve cold.

Coconut Cream Pie

Once you have made the pastry, the delicious filling can be put together in moments.

Serves 8

200g/7oz/2½ cups shredded coconut

115g/4oz/⅔ cup caster sugar

60ml/4 tbsp cornflour

pinch of salt

600ml/1 pint/2½ cups milk

50ml/2fl oz/¼ cup whipping cream

2 egg yolks

25g/1oz/2 tbsp unsalted butter

10ml/2 tsp vanilla essence

For the pastry

115g/4oz/1 cup plain flour

1.5ml/¼ tsp salt

40g/1½oz/3 tbsp cold butter, cut in pieces

25g/1oz/2 tbsp cold lard

1 For the pastry, sift the flour and salt into a bowl. Add the butter and lard and cut in with a pastry blender or two knives until the mixture resembles coarse breadcrumbs.

2 With a fork, stir in just enough iced water to bind the dough (30–45ml/2–3 tbsp). Gather into a ball, wrap in greaseproof paper and chill for at least 20 minutes.

3 Preheat the oven to 220°C/ 425°F/Gas 7. Roll out the dough 3mm/⅛in thick. Transfer to a 23cm/9in flan tin. Trim and flute the edges. Prick the bottom. Line with greaseproof paper and fill with baking beans. Bake for 10–12 minutes. Remove the paper and beans, reduce the heat to 180°C/350°F/Gas 4 and bake until brown, about10–15 minutes more.

4 Spread 75g/3oz/1 cup of the coconut on a baking sheet and toast in the oven until golden, 6–8 minutes, stirring often. Set aside for decorating.

5 Put the sugar, cornflour and salt in a saucepan. In a bowl, whisk together the milk, cream and egg yolks. Add the egg mixture to the saucepan.

6 Cook over low heat, stirring constantly, until the mixture comes to the boil. Boil for 1 minute, then remove from the heat. Add the butter, vanilla essence and remaining coconut.

7 Pour into the prebaked pastry case. When the filling is cool, sprinkle toasted coconut in a ring in the centre.

Peach Tart with Almond Cream

The almond cream filling should be baked until it is just turning brown. Take care not to overbake it or the delicate flavours will be spoilt.

Serves 8–10

4 large ripe peaches

115g/4oz/⅔ cup blanched almonds

30ml/2 tbsp plain flour

90g/3½oz/7 tbsp unsalted butter, at room temperature

130g/4½oz/scant ¾ cup granulated sugar

1 egg

1 egg yolk

2.5ml/½ tsp vanilla essence, or 10ml/ 2 tsp rum

For the pastry

150g/5oz/1¼ cups flour

4ml/¾ tsp salt

90g/3½oz/7 tbsp cold unsalted butter, cut in pieces

1 egg yolk

1 For the pastry, sift the flour and salt into a bowl.

2 Add the butter and cut in with a pastry blender until the mixture resembles coarse crumbs. With a fork, stir in the egg yolk and just enough iced water (30–45ml/ 2–3 tbsp) to bind the dough. Gather into a ball, wrap in grease-proof paper and chill for at least 20 minutes. Place a baking sheet in the oven and preheat to 200°C/400°F/Gas 6.

3 On a lightly floured surface, roll out the pastry 3mm/⅛in thick. Transfer to a 25cm/10in flan tin. Trim the edge, prick the bottom and chill.

4 Score the bottoms of the peaches. Drop the peaches, one at a time, into boiling water. Leave for 20 seconds, then dip in cold water. Peel off the skins using a sharp knife.

5 Grind the almonds finely with the flour in a food processor, blender or nut grinder. With an electric mixer, cream the butter and 90g/3½oz/½ cup of the sugar until light and fluffy. Gradually beat in the egg and yolk. Stir in the almonds and vanilla or rum. Spread in the pastry shell.

6 Halve the peaches and remove the stones. Cut crosswise in thin slices and arrange on top of the almond cream like the spokes of a wheel; keep the slices of each peach-half together. Fan them out by pressing down gently at a slight angle.

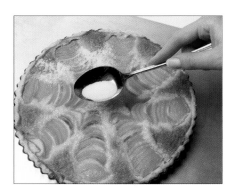

7 Bake until the pastry begins to brown, 10–15 minutes. Lower the heat to 180°C/350°F/Gas 4 and continue baking until the almond cream sets, about 15 minutes more. Ten minutes before the end of the cooking time, sprinkle with the remaining sugar.

VARIATION

For a Nectarine and Apricot Tart with Almond Cream, replace the peaches with nectarines, prepared and arranged the same way. Peel and chop three fresh apricots. Fill the spaces between the fanned-out nectarines with chopped apricots. Bake as above.

Raspberry Tart

This glazed fruit tart really does taste as good as it looks.

Serves 8

4 egg yolks

65g/2½ oz/⅓ cup granulated sugar

45ml/3 tbsp plain flour

300ml/½ pint/1¼ cups milk

pinch of salt

2.5ml/½ tsp vanilla essence

450g/1lb fresh raspberries

75ml/5 tbsp grape or redcurrant jelly

15ml/1 tbsp fresh orange juice

For the pastry

150g/5oz/1¼ cups plain flour

2.5ml/½ tsp baking powder

1.5ml/¼ tsp salt

15ml/1 tbsp sugar

grated rind of ½ orange

90ml/6 tbsp cold butter, cut in pieces

1 egg yolk

45–60ml/3–4 tbsp whipping cream

1 For the pastry, sift the flour, baking powder and salt into a bowl. Stir in the sugar and orange rind. Add the butter and mix until the mixture resembles coarse crumbs. With a fork, stir in the egg yolk and just enough cream to bind the dough. Gather into a ball, wrap in greaseproof paper and chill.

2 For the custard filling, beat the egg yolks and sugar until thick and lemon-coloured. Gradually stir in the flour.

3 In a saucepan, bring the milk and salt just to the boil, and remove from the heat. Whisk into the egg yolk mixture, return to the pan, and continue whisking over moderately high heat until just bubbling. Cook for 3 minutes to thicken. Transfer immediately to a bowl. Stir in the vanilla to blend.

4 Cover with greaseproof paper to prevent a skin from forming.

5 Preheat the oven to 200°C/ 400°F/Gas 6. On a lightly floured surface, roll out the dough about 3mm/⅛in thick, transfer to a 25cm/10in flan tin and trim the edge. Prick the bottom all over with a fork and line with greaseproof paper. Fill with baking beans and bake for 15 minutes. Remove the paper and baking beans. Continue baking until golden, 6–8 minutes more. Let cool.

6 Spread an even layer of the pastry cream filling in the tart shell and arrange the raspberries on top. Melt the jelly and orange juice in a pan over a low heat and brush on top to glaze.

Kiwi Ricotta Cheese Tart

*It is well worth taking your time
arranging the kiwi fruit topping in
neat rows for this exotic and
impressive-looking tart.*

INGREDIENTS

Serves 8

50g/2oz/½ cup blanched almonds

90g/3½oz/½ cup plus 15ml/1 tbsp
   caster sugar

900g/2lb/4 cups ricotta cheese

250ml/8fl oz/1 cup whipping cream

1 egg

3 egg yolks

15ml/1 tbsp plain flour

pinch of salt

30ml/2 tbsp rum

grated rind of 1 lemon

40ml/2½ tbsp lemon juice

50ml/2fl oz/¼ cup clear honey

5 kiwi fruit

For the pastry

150g/5oz/1¼ cups plain flour

15ml/1 tbsp granulated sugar

2.5ml/½ tsp salt

2.5ml/½ tsp baking powder

75g/3oz/6 tbsp cold butter, cut in pieces

1 egg yolk

45–60ml/3–4 tbsp whipping cream

1 For the pastry, sift the flour, sugar, salt and baking powder into a bowl. Cut in the butter until the mixture resembles coarse crumbs. Mix the egg yolk and cream. Stir in just enough to bind the dough.

2 Transfer to a lightly floured surface, flatten slightly, wrap in greaseproof paper and chill for 30 minutes. Preheat the oven to 220°C/425°F/Gas 7.

3 On a lightly floured surface, roll out the dough 3mm/⅛in thick and transfer to a 23cm/9in springform tin. Crimp the edge.

4 Prick the bottom of the dough all over with a fork. Line with greaseproof paper and fill with baking beans. Bake for 10 minutes. Remove the paper and beans and bake until golden, 6–8 minutes more. Let cool. Reduce the heat to 180°C/350°F/Gas 4.

5 Grind the almonds finely with 15ml/1 tbsp of the sugar in a food processor or blender.

6 With an electric mixer, beat the ricotta until creamy. Add the cream, egg, yolks, remaining sugar, flour, salt, rum, lemon rind and 30ml/2 tbsp of the lemon juice. Beat to combine.

7 Stir in the ground almonds until well blended.

8 Pour into the shell and bake until golden, about 1 hour. Let cool, then chill, loosely covered, for 2–3 hours. Unmould and place on a serving plate.

9 Combine the honey and remaining lemon juice for the glaze. Set aside.

10 Peel the kiwis. Halve them lengthwise, then cut crosswise into 5mm/¼in slices. Arrange the slices in rows across the top of the tart. Just before serving, brush with the glaze.

Lemon and Orange Tart

Refreshing citrus fruits in a crisp, nutty pastry case.

INGREDIENTS

Serves 8–10

115g/4oz/1 cup plain flour, sifted

115g/4oz/1 cup wholemeal flour

25g/1oz/3 tbsp ground hazelnuts

25g/1oz/3 tbsp icing sugar, sifted

pinch of salt

115g/4oz/½ cup unsalted butter

60ml/4 tbsp lemon curd

300ml/½ pint/1¼ cups whipped cream or
     fromage frais

4 oranges, peeled and thinly sliced

1 Place the flours, hazelnuts, sugar, salt and butter in a food processor and process in short bursts until the mixture resembles breadcrumbs. Add 30–45ml/ 2–3 tbsp cold water and process until the dough comes together.

2 Turn out on to a lightly floured surface and knead gently until smooth. Roll out and line a 25cm/10in flan tin. Ease the pastry gently into the corners without stretching it. Chill for 20 minutes. Preheat the oven to 190°C/375°F/Gas 5.

3 Line the pastry with grease-proof paper and fill with baking beans. Bake blind for 15 minutes, remove the paper and beans and continue for a further 5–10 minutes, until the pastry is crisp. Allow to cool.

4 Whisk the lemon curd into the cream or fromage frais and spread over the base of the pastry. Arrange the orange slices on top and serve at room temperature.

Chocolate Pear Tart

Serve slices of this drizzled with single cream or with a scoop of vanilla ice cream for a special treat.

INGREDIENTS

Serves 8

115g/4oz plain chocolate, grated

3 large firm, ripe pears

1 egg

1 egg yolk

120ml/4fl oz/½ cup single cream

2.5ml/½ tsp vanilla essence

45ml/3 tbsp caster sugar

For the pastry

115g/4oz/1 cup plain flour

pinch of salt

30ml/2 tbsp caster sugar

115g/4oz/½ cup cold unsalted butter, cut
   into pieces

1 egg yolk

15ml/1 tbsp fresh lemon juice

1 For the pastry, sift the flour and salt into a bowl. Add the sugar and butter. Cut in with a pastry blender until the mixture resembles coarse crumbs. With a fork, stir in the egg yolk and lemon juice until the mixture forms a dough. Gather into a ball, wrap in greaseproof paper, and chill for at least 20 minutes.

2 Place a baking sheet in the oven and preheat to 200°C/400°F/Gas 6. On a lightly floured surface, roll out the dough to 3mm/⅛in thick and trim the edge. Transfer to a 25cm/10in flan tin.

3 Sprinkle the bottom of the tart shell with the grated chocolate.

4 Peel, halve and core the pears. Cut in thin slices crosswise, then fan them out slightly.

5 Transfer the pear halves to the tart with the help of a metal spatula and arrange on top of the chocolate to resemble the spokes of a wheel.

6 Whisk together the egg and egg yolk, cream and vanilla essence. Ladle over the pears, then sprinkle with sugar.

7 Bake for 10 minutes. Reduce the heat to 180°C/350°F/Gas 4 and cook until the custard is set and the pears begin to caramelize, about 20 minutes more. Serve at room temperature.

Tarte au Citron

You can find this classic lemon tart in bistros all over France.

INGREDIENTS

Serves 8–10

350g/12oz shortcrust or sweet shortcrust pastry

grated rind of 2 or 3 lemons

150ml/¼ pint/⅔ cup freshly squeezed lemon juice

90g/3½oz/½ cup caster sugar

60ml/4 tbsp crème fraîche or double cream

4 eggs, plus 3 egg yolks

icing sugar, for dusting

1 Preheat the oven to 190°C/ 375°F/Gas 5. Roll out the pastry thinly and use to line a 23cm/9in flan tin. Prick the base of the pastry.

2 Line the pastry case with foil and fill with baking beans. Bake for about 15 minutes until the edges are set and dry. Remove the foil and beans and continue baking for a further 5–7 minutes until golden.

3 Place the lemon rind, juice and sugar in a bowl. Beat until combined and then gradually add the crème fraîche or double cream and beat until well blended.

4 Beat in the eggs, one at a time, then beat in the egg yolks and pour the filling into the pastry case. Bake for 15–20 minutes, until the filling is set. If the pastry begins to brown too much, cover the edges with foil. Leave to cool. Dust with a little icing sugar before serving.

Treacle Tart

Quite a filling tart, this, so best served after a light main course.

INGREDIENTS

Serves 4–6
175ml/6fl oz/¾ cup golden syrup
75g/3oz/1½ cups fresh white breadcrumbs
grated rind of 1 lemon
30ml/2 tbsp fresh lemon juice

For the pastry
150g/5oz/1¼ cups flour
2.5ml/½ tsp salt
75g/3oz/6 tbsp cold butter, cut in pieces
75g/3oz/3 tbsp cold margarine, cut
   in pieces

1 For the pastry, combine the flour and salt in a bowl. Add the butter and margarine and cut in with a pastry blender until the mixture resembles coarse crumbs.

2 With a fork, stir in just enough iced water (about 45–60ml/ 3–4 tbsp) to bind the dough. Gather into a ball, wrap in grease-proof paper, and chill for at least 20 minutes.

3 On a lightly floured surface, roll out the dough 3mm/⅛in thick. Transfer to a 20cm/8in flan tin and trim off the overhang. Chill for at least 20 minutes. Reserve the trimmings for the lattice top.

4 Place a baking sheet above the centre of the oven and heat to 200°C/400°F/Gas 6.

5 In a saucepan, warm the syrup until thin and runny.

6 Remove from the heat and stir in the breadcrumbs and lemon rind. Let sit for 10 minutes so the bread can absorb the syrup. Add more breadcrumbs if the mixture is thin. Stir in the lemon juice and spread evenly in the pastry shell.

7 Roll out the pastry trimmings and cut into 10–12 thin strips.

8 Lay half the strips on the filling, then carefully arrange the remaining strips to form a lattice pattern.

9 Place on the hot sheet and bake for 10 minutes. Lower the heat to 190°C/375°F/Gas 5. Bake until golden, about 15 minutes more. Serve warm or cold.

Rich Chocolate-berry Tart

Use any berries you like to top this exotic tart.

INGREDIENTS

Serves 10

115g/4oz/½ cup unsalted butter, softened

90g/3½oz/½ cup caster sugar

2.5ml/½ tsp salt

15ml/1 tbsp vanilla essence

50g/2oz/½ cup unsweetened cocoa

215g/7½oz/1¾ cups plain flour

450g/1lb fresh berries for topping

For the chocolate ganache filling

475ml/16fl oz/2 cups double cream

150g/5oz/½ cup seedless blackberry preserve

225g/8oz plain chocolate, chopped

25g/1oz/2 tbsp unsalted butter

For the blackberry sauce

225g/8oz fresh or frozen blackberries or raspberries

15ml/1 tbsp lemon juice

25g/1oz/2 tbsp caster sugar

30ml/2 tbsp blackberry liqueur

1 Prepare the pastry. Place the butter, sugar, salt and vanilla in a food processor and process until creamy. Add cocoa and process for 1 minute. Add flour all at once and process for 10–15 seconds, until just blended. Place a piece of clear film on work surface. Turn out dough on to clear film. Use clear film to help shape dough into flat disc and wrap tightly. Chill for 1 hour.

2 Lightly grease a 23cm/9in tart tin with removable base. Roll out dough between two sheets of clear film to a 28cm/11in round, about 5 mm/¼in thick. Peel off top sheet of clear film and invert dough into prepared tin. Ease dough into tin. Remove clear film.

3 With floured fingers, press dough on to base and side of tin, then roll rolling pin over edge of tin to cut off any excess dough. Prick base of dough with fork. Chill for 1 hour. Preheat oven to 180°C/350°F/Gas 4. Line tart shell with foil or baking paper; fill with dry beans or rice. Bake for 10 minutes; lift out foil with beans and bake for 5 minutes more, until just set (pastry may look underdone on the bottom, but will dry out). Remove to wire rack to cool completely.

4 Prepare filling. In a medium saucepan over medium heat, bring cream and blackberry preserve to the boil. Remove from heat and add chocolate, stirring until smooth. Stir in butter and strain into cooled tart, smoothing top. Cool tart completely.

5 Prepare sauce. In a food processor combine blackberries, lemon juice and sugar and process until smooth. Strain into a small bowl and add blackberry-flavour liqueur. If sauce is too thick, thin with a little water.

6 To serve, remove tart from tin. Place on serving plate and arrange the berries on the top of the tart. With a pastry brush, brush berries with a little of the blackberry sauce to glaze lightly. Serve remaining sauce separately.

Bakewell Tart

Although the pastry base makes this a tart, the original recipe describes it as a pudding.

INGREDIENTS

Serves 4

225g/8oz ready-made puff pastry

30ml/2 tbsp raspberry or apricot jam

2 eggs

2 egg yolks

115g/4oz/generous ½ cup caster sugar

115g/4oz/½ cup butter, melted

50g/2oz/½ cup ground almonds

few drops of almond essence

icing sugar, for sifting

1 Preheat the oven to 200°C/ 400°F/Gas 6. Roll out the pastry on a lightly floured surface and use it to line an 18cm/7in pie plate or loose-based flan tin. Spread the jam over the bottom of the pastry case.

> ### COOK'S TIP
> ~
> Since this pastry case isn't baked blind first, place a baking sheet in the oven while it preheats, then place the flan tin on the hot sheet. This will ensure that the bottom of the pastry case cooks right through.

2 Whisk the eggs, egg yolks and sugar together in a large bowl until thick and pale.

3 Gently stir the butter, ground almonds and almond essence into the mixture.

4 Pour the mixture into the pastry case and bake for 30 minutes, until the filling is just set and browned. Sift icing sugar over the top before serving the tart hot, warm or cold.

VARIATION

Ground hazelnuts are increasingly available and make an interesting change to the almonds in this tart. If you are going to grind shelled hazelnuts yourself, first roast them in the oven for 10–15 minutes to bring out their flavour then rub in a dish towel to remove skins.

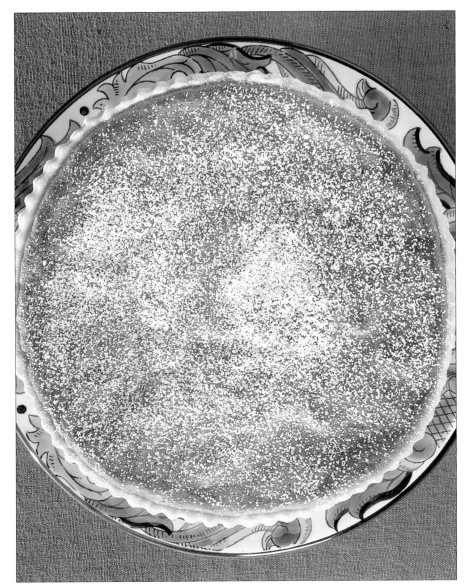

Apple Pie

Delicious on its own, or with a dollop of double cream or ice cream.

Serves 8

900g/2lb tart cooking apples

30ml/2 tbsp plain flour

90g/3½oz/½ cup sugar

25ml/1½ tbsp fresh lemon juice

2.5ml/½ tsp ground cinnamon

2.5ml/½ tsp ground allspice

1.5ml/¼ tsp ground ginger

1.5ml/¼ tsp grated nutmeg

1.5ml/¼ tsp salt

50g/2oz/4 tbsp butter, diced

For the pastry

225g/8oz/2 cups plain flour

5ml/1 tsp salt

75g/3oz/6 tbsp cold butter, cut in pieces

50g/2oz/4 tbsp cold lard, cut in pieces

1 For the pastry, sift the flour and salt into a bowl.

2 Add the butter and lard and cut in with a pastry blender or rub between your fingertips until the mixture resembles coarse crumbs. With a fork, stir in just enough iced water to bind the dough (60–120ml/4–8 tbsp).

3 Gather into two balls, wrap in greaseproof paper and chill for 20 minutes.

4 On a lightly floured surface, roll out one dough ball to 3mm/⅛in thick. Transfer to a 23cm/9in pie tin and trim the edge. Place a baking sheet in the centre of the oven and preheat to 220°C/425°F/Gas 7.

5 Peel, core and slice the apples into a bowl. Toss with the flour, sugar, lemon juice, spices and salt. Spoon into pie shell; dot with butter.

6 Roll out the remaining dough. Place on top of the pie and trim to leave a 2cm/¾in overhang. Fold the overhang under the bottom dough and press to seal. Crimp the edge.

7 Roll out the scraps and cut out leaf shapes and roll balls. Arrange on top of the pie. Cut steam vents.

8 Bake for 10 minutes. Reduce the heat to 180°C/350°F/Gas 4 and bake until golden, 40–45 minutes more. If the pie browns too quickly, protect with foil.

Mississippi Pecan Pie

This fabulous dessert started life in the United States but has become an international favourite.

Serves 6–8

For the pastry

115g/4oz/1 cup plain flour

50g/2oz/4 tbsp butter, cubed

25g/1oz/2 tbsp caster sugar

1 egg yolk

For the filling

175g/6oz/½ cup golden syrup

50g/2oz/⅓ cup dark muscovado sugar

50g/2oz/4 tbsp butter

3 eggs, lightly beaten

2.5ml/½ tsp vanilla essence

150g/5oz/1¼ cups pecan nuts

fresh cream or ice cream, to serve

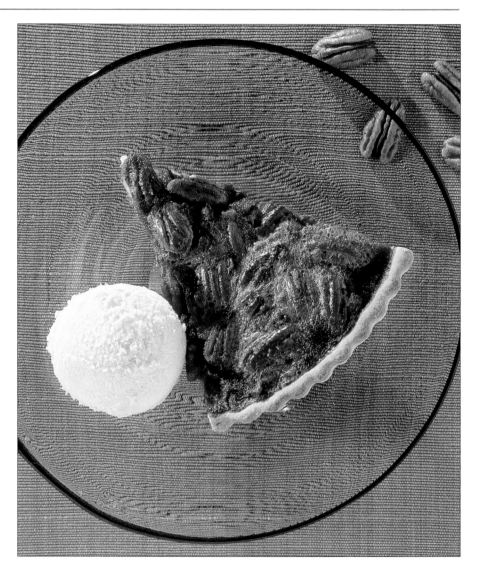

1 Place the flour in a bowl and add the butter. Rub in the butter with your fingertips until the mixture resembles bread-crumbs, then stir in the sugar, egg yolk and about 30ml/2 tbsp cold water. Mix to a dough and knead lightly on a floured surface until smooth and free of lumps.

2 Roll out the pastry and use to line a 20cm/8in loose-based fluted flan tin. Prick the base, then line with greaseproof paper and fill with baking beans. Chill for 30 minutes. Preheat the oven to 200°C/400°F/Gas 6.

3 Bake the pastry case for 10 minutes. Remove the paper and beans and bake for 5 minutes. Reduce the oven temperature to 180°C/350°F/Gas 4.

4 Meanwhile, heat the syrup, sugar and butter in a pan until the sugar dissolves. Remove from the heat and cool slightly. Whisk in the eggs and vanilla essence and stir in the pecans.

5 Pour into the pastry case and bake for 35–40 minutes, until the filling is set. Serve with cream or ice cream.

Boston Banoffee Pie

There are many variations of this American treat; this one is easy to make and tastes wonderful.

INGREDIENTS

Serves 6–8

150g/5oz/1¼ cups plain flour

225g/8oz/1 cup butter

50g/2oz/4 tbsp caster sugar

½ x 405g/14oz can skimmed, sweetened condensed milk

115g/4oz/⅔ cup soft light brown sugar

30ml/2 tbsp golden syrup

2 small bananas, sliced

a little lemon juice

whipped cream, to decorate

5ml/1 tsp grated plain chocolate

1 Preheat the oven to 160°C/ 325°F/Gas 3. Place the flour and 115g/4oz/½ cup of the butter in a food processor and blend until crumbed (or rub in with your fingertips). Stir in the caster sugar.

2 Squeeze the mixture together until it forms a dough. Press into the base of a 20cm/8in loose-based fluted flan tin. Bake for 25–30 minutes.

3 Place the remaining 115g/4oz/½ cup of butter with the condensed milk, brown sugar and golden syrup in a large non-stick saucepan and heat gently, stirring, until the butter has melted and the sugar has dissolved.

4 Bring to a gentle boil and cook for 7 minutes, stirring all the time (to prevent burning), until the mixture thickens and turns a light caramel colour. Pour on to the cooked pastry base and leave until cold.

5 Sprinkle the bananas with lemon juice and arrange in overlapping circles on top of the caramel filling, leaving a gap in the centre. Pipe a swirl of whipped cream in the centre and sprinkle with the grated chocolate.

Chocolate Profiteroles

This mouth-watering dessert is served in cafés throughout France. Sometimes the profiteroles are filled with whipped cream instead of ice cream, but they are always drizzled with chocolate sauce.

Serves 4–6

275g/10oz plain chocolate

750ml/1¼ pints/3 cups vanilla ice cream

For the profiteroles

110g/3¾oz/¾ cup plain flour

1.5ml/¼ tsp salt

pinch of freshly grated nutmeg

75g/3oz/6 tbsp unsalted butter, cut into
    6 pieces

3 eggs

1 Preheat the oven to 200°C/400°F/Gas 6 and butter a baking sheet.

2 To make the profiteroles, sift together the flour, salt and nutmeg. In a medium saucepan, bring the butter and 175ml/6fl oz/¾ cup of water to the boil. Remove from the heat and add the dry ingredients all at once. Beat with a wooden spoon for about 1 minute until well blended and the mixture starts to pull away from the sides of the pan, then set the pan over a low heat and cook the mixture for about 2 minutes, beating constantly. Remove from the heat.

3 Beat one egg in a small bowl and set aside. Add the remaining eggs, one at a time, to the flour mixture, beating well. Add the beaten egg gradually until the dough is smooth and shiny; it should fall slowly when dropped from a spoon.

4 Using a tablespoon, drop the dough on to the baking sheet in 12 mounds. Bake for 25–30 minutes until the pastry is well risen and browned. Turn off the oven and leave the puffs to cool with the oven door open.

5 To make the sauce, place the chocolate and 120ml/4fl oz/½ cup of warm water in a double boiler or in a bowl and melt, stirring occasionally over a pan of hot water.

6 Split the profiteroles in half and put a small scoop of ice cream in each. Arrange on a serving platter. Pour the sauce over the top and serve at once.

Pear and Almond Cream Tart

This tart is equally successful made with other kinds of fruit, and some variation can be seen in almost every good French pâtisserie. Try making it with nectarines, peaches, apricots or apples.

INGREDIENTS

Serves 6

350g/12oz shortcrust or sweet shortcrust pastry

3 firm pears

lemon juice

15ml/1 tbsp peach brandy or water

60ml/4 tbsp peach preserve, strained

For the almond cream filling

115g/4oz/¾ cup blanched whole almonds

50g/2oz/¼ cup caster sugar

65g/2½oz/5 tbsp butter

1 egg, plus 1 egg white

few drops almond essence

1 Roll out the pastry thinly and use to line a 23cm/9in flan tin. Chill the pastry case while you make the filling. Put the almonds and sugar in a food processor and pulse until finely ground; they should not be pasty. Add the butter and process until creamy, then add the egg, egg white and almond essence and mix well.

2 Place a baking sheet in the oven and preheat to 190°C/ 375°F/Gas 5. Peel the pears, halve them, remove the cores and rub with lemon juice.

3 Put the pear halves cut-side down on a board and slice thinly crossways, keeping the slices together.

4 Pour the almond cream filling into the pastry case. Slide a palette knife under one pear half and press the top with your fingers to fan out the slices. Transfer to the tart, placing the fruit on the filling like spokes of a wheel. If you like, remove a few slices from each half before arranging and use to fill in any gaps in the centre.

5 Place on the baking sheet and bake for 50–55 minutes until the filling is set and well browned. Cool on a rack.

6 Meanwhile, heat the brandy or water and the preserve in a small saucepan, then brush over the top of the hot tart to glaze. Serve the tart warm.

Greek Chocolate Mousse Tartlets

The combination of white chocolate and Greek-style yogurt makes an irresistibly light, but not too sweet, filling for these little tarts.

INGREDIENTS

Serves 6
175g/6oz/1½ cups plain flour
30ml/2 tbsp cocoa powder
30ml/2 tbsp icing sugar
115g/4oz/½ cup butter
melted dark chocolate, to decorate

For the filling
200g/7oz white chocolate, broken
    into squares
120ml/4fl oz/½ cup milk
10ml/2 tsp powdered gelatine
30ml/2 tbsp caster sugar
5ml/1 tsp vanilla essence
2 eggs, separated
250g/9oz/generous 1 cup Greek-
    style yogurt

1 Preheat the oven to 190°C/ 375°F/Gas 5. Sift the flour, cocoa and icing sugar into a large bowl.

2 Place the butter in a pan with 60ml/4 tbsp water and heat gently until just melted. Cool, then stir into the flour to make a smooth dough. Chill until firm.

3 Roll out the pastry and line six deep 10cm/4in loose-based flan tins.

4 Prick the base of each pastry case all over with a fork, cover with greaseproof paper weighed down with baking beans and bake blind for 10 minutes. Remove the baking beans and paper, return to the oven and bake a further 15 minutes, or until the pastry is firm. Leave to cool in the tins.

5 Make the filling. Melt the chocolate in a heatproof bowl over hot water. Pour the milk into a saucepan, sprinkle over the gelatine and heat gently, stirring, until the gelatine has dissolved completely. Remove from the heat and stir in the chocolate.

6 Whisk the sugar, vanilla essence and egg yolks in a large bowl, then beat in the chocolate mixture. Beat in the yogurt until evenly mixed.

7 Whisk the egg whites in a clean, grease-free bowl until stiff, then fold into the mixture. Divide among the pastry cases and leave to set.

8 Drizzle the melted white chocolate over the tartlets to decorate.

Tarte Tatin

This upside-down apple tart was first made by two sisters who served it in their restaurant in the Loire Valley in France.

INGREDIENTS

Serves 8–10

225g/8oz puff or shortcrust pastry
10–12 large Golden Delicious apples
lemon juice
115g/4oz/½ cup butter, cut into pieces
90g/3½oz/½ cup caster sugar
1.5ml/½ tsp ground cinnamon
crème fraîche or whipped cream, to serve

1 On a lightly floured surface, roll out the pastry into a 28cm/11in round less than 5mm/¼in thick. Transfer to a lightly floured baking sheet and chill.

2 Peel the apples, cut them in half lengthwise and core. Sprinkle them generously with lemon juice.

3 Preheat the oven to 230°C/ 450°F/Gas 8. In a 25cm/10in tarte tatin tin, cook the butter, sugar and cinnamon over medium heat until the butter has melted and sugar dissolved, stirring occasionally. Continue cooking for 6–8 minutes, until the mixture turns a medium caramel colour, then remove the pan from the heat and arrange the apple halves, standing on their edges, in the tin, fitting them in tightly since they shrink during cooking.

4 Return the apple-filled tin to the heat and bring to a simmer over a medium heat for 20–25 minutes until the apples are tender and coloured. Remove the tin from the heat and cool slightly.

5 Place the pastry on top of the apple-filled pan and tuck the edges of the pastry inside the edge of the tin around the apples.

6 Pierce the pastry in two or three places, then bake for 25–30 minutes until the pastry is golden and the filling is bubbling. Let the tart cool in the tin for 10–15 minutes.

7 To serve, run a sharp knife around edge of the tin to loosen the pastry. Cover with a serving plate and, holding them tightly, carefully invert the tin and plate together (do this over the sink in case any caramel drips). Lift off the tin and loosen any apples that stick with a spatula. Serve the tart warm with cream.

Jam Tart

Jam tarts are popular in Italy where they are traditionally decorated with pastry strips.

INGREDIENTS

Serves 6–8

200g/7oz/1¾ cups plain flour

pinch of salt

50g/2oz/¼ cup granulated sugar

115g/4oz/½ cup butter or
   margarine, chilled

1 egg

1.5ml/¼ tsp grated lemon rind

350g/12oz/1¼ cups fruit jam, such as
   raspberry, apricot or strawberry

1 egg, lightly beaten with 30ml/2 tbsp
   whipping cream, for glazing

1 Make the pastry by placing the flour, salt and sugar in a mixing bowl. Using a pastry blender or two knives, cut the butter or margarine into the dry ingredients as quickly as possible until the mixture resembles coarse crumbs.

2 Beat the egg with the lemon rind in a cup, and pour it over the flour mixture. Combine with a fork until the dough holds together. If it is too crumbly, mix in 15–30ml/1–2 tbsp of water.

3 Gather the dough into two balls, one slightly larger than the other, and flatten into discs. Wrap in greaseproof or waxed paper, and put in the fridge for at least 40 minutes.

4 Lightly grease a shallow 23cm/9in tart or pie tin, preferably with a removable bottom. Roll out the larger disc of pastry on a lightly floured surface to a thickness of about 3mm/⅛in.

5 Roll the pastry around the rolling pin and transfer to the prepared tin. Trim the edges evenly with a small knife. Prick the bottom with a fork. Chill for at least 30 minutes.

6 Preheat the oven to 190°C/ 375°F/Gas 5. Spread the jam thickly and evenly over the base of the pastry. Roll out the remaining pastry.

7 Cut the pastry into strips about 1cm/¼in wide using a ruler as a guide. Arrange them over the jam in a lattice pattern. Trim the edges of the strips even with the edge of the tin, pressing them lightly on to the pastry shell. Brush the pastry with the egg and cream glaze. Bake for about 35 minutes, or until the pastry is golden brown. Cool before serving.

American Spiced Pumpkin Pie

The unofficial national dish of the United States.

Serves 4–6

175g/6oz/1½ cups plain flour

pinch of salt

75g/3oz/6 tbsp unsalted butter

15ml/1 tbsp caster sugar

450g/1lb/4 cups peeled fresh pumpkin, cubed, or 400g/14oz/2 cups canned pumpkin, drained

115g/4oz/½ cup soft light brown sugar

1.5ml/¼ tsp salt

1.5ml/¼ ground allspice

2.5ml/½ tsp ground cinnamon

2.5ml/½ tsp ground ginger

2 eggs, lightly beaten

120ml/4fl oz/½ cup double cream

whipped cream, to serve

1 Place the flour in a bowl with the salt and butter and rub with your fingertips until the mixture resembles breadcrumbs (or use a food processor).

2 Stir in the sugar and add about 30-45ml/2-3 tbsp water and mix to a soft dough. Knead the dough lightly on a floured surface. Flatten out into a round, wrap in a polythene bag and chill for 1 hour.

3 Preheat the oven to 200°C/400°F/Gas 6 with a baking sheet inside. If you are using raw pumpkin for the pie, steam for 15 minutes until quite tender, then leave to cool completely. Purée the steamed or canned pumpkin in a food processor or blender until it is very smooth.

4 Roll out the pastry quite thinly and use to line a 24cm/9½in (measured across the top) x 2.5cm/1in deep pie tin. Trim off any excess pastry and reserve for the decoration. Prick the base of the pastry case with a fork.

5 Cut as many leaf shapes as you can from the excess pastry and make vein markings with the back of a knife on each. Brush the edge of the pastry with water and stick the leaves all round the edge. Chill.

6 In a large bowl mix together the pumpkin purée, sugar, salt, spices, eggs and cream and pour into the prepared pastry case. Smooth the top with a knife.

7 Place on the preheated baking sheet and bake for 15 minutes. Then reduce the temperature to 180°C/350°F/Gas 4 and cook for a further 30 minutes, or until the filling is set and the pastry golden. Serve the pie warm with a generous dollop of whipped cream.

Custards, Soufflés & Whips

◆ ✦ ◆

Coffee Coeur à la Crème

These pretty heart-shaped creams, speckled with espresso-roasted coffee beans, are served with a fruit sauce.

INGREDIENTS

Serves 6

25g/1oz/generous ¼ cup espresso-roasted
   coffee beans
225g/8oz/1 cup ricotta or curd cheese
300ml/½ pint/1¼ cups crème fraîche
25g/1oz/2 tbsp caster sugar
finely grated rind of ½ orange
2 egg whites

For the red fruit coulis
175g/6oz/1 cup raspberries
30ml/2 tbsp icing sugar, sifted
115g/4oz/⅔ cup small strawberries (or
   wild ones, if available), halved

1 Preheat the oven to 180°C/
350°F/Gas 4. Spread the coffee
beans on to a baking sheet and
toast for 10 minutes. Cool, put in a
large plastic bag and crush with a
rolling pin.

2 Rinse 12 pieces of muslin in
cold water and squeeze dry. Use
to line six coeur à la crème moulds
with a double layer, allowing the
muslin to overhang the edges.

3 Press the ricotta or curd cheese
through a fine sieve into a
bowl. Stir the crème fraîche, sugar,
orange rind and crushed roasted
coffee beans together. Add to the
cheese and mix well.

4 Whisk the egg whites until stiff
and fold into the mixture.
Spoon into the prepared moulds,
then bring the muslin up and over
the filling. Drain and chill in the
fridge overnight.

5 To make the red fruit coulis,
put the raspberries and icing
sugar in a food processor and blend
until smooth. Push through a fine
sieve to remove the pips. Stir in the
strawberries. Chill until you are
ready to serve.

6 Unmould the hearts on to
individual serving plates and
carefully remove the muslin. Spoon
the coulis over before serving.

Tiramisù

The name of this classic dessert translates as "pick me up", and is said to derive from the fact that it is so good that it literally makes you swoon when you eat it.

INGREDIENTS

Serves 4

225g/8oz/1 cup mascarpone

25g/1oz/¼ cup icing sugar, sifted

150ml/¼ pint/⅔ cup strong coffee, chilled

300ml/½ pint/1¼ cups double cream

45ml/3 tbsp coffee liqueur such as Tia Maria, Kahlúa or Toussaint

115g/4oz Savoiardi (sponge finger) biscuits

50g/2oz bittersweet or plain chocolate, coarsely grated

cocoa powder, for dusting

1 Lightly grease and line a 900g/2lb loaf tin with clear film. In a large bowl, beat the mascarpone and icing sugar for 1 minute. Stir in 30ml/2 tbsp of the chilled coffee. Mix thoroughly.

2 Whip the cream and 15ml/1 tbsp of the liqueur to soft peaks. Stir a spoonful into the mascarpone, then fold in the rest. Spoon half the mixture into the tin and smooth the top.

COOK'S TIP

This dish also works well with a single layer of Savoiardi biscuits.

3 Put the remaining strong brewed coffee and liqueur in a shallow dish just wider than the Savoiardi biscuits. Using half the biscuits, dip one side of each biscuit into the coffee mixture, then arrange on top of the mascarpone mixture in a single layer.

4 Spoon the rest of the mascarpone mixture over the biscuit layer and smooth the top.

5 Dip the remaining biscuits in the coffee, arrange on top, and drizzle over any remaining coffee mixture. Cover with clear film and chill for 4 hours. Turn the tiramisù out of the tin and sprinkle with grated chocolate and cocoa powder; serve cut into slices.

Hot Chocolate Zabaglione

This is a delicious chocolate-flavoured variation of the classic Italian dessert.

INGREDIENTS

Serves 6

6 egg yolks

150g/5oz/¾ cup caster sugar

45ml/3 tbsp cocoa powder

200ml/7fl oz/⅞ cup Marsala

cocoa powder or icing sugar,
   for dusting

almond biscuits, to serve

1 Half fill a medium saucepan with water and bring to simmering point.

2 Place the egg yolks and sugar in a heatproof bowl and whisk until the mixture is pale and all the sugar has dissolved.

3 Add the cocoa and Marsala, then place the bowl over the simmering water. Whisk until the consistency of the mixture is smooth, thick and foamy.

4 Pour quickly into tall heatproof glasses, dust lightly with cocoa or icing sugar and serve immediately with almond biscuits.

Crème Caramel

Crème caramel, or crème renversée, is one of the most popular French desserts and is wonderful when freshly made. This is a slightly lighter modern version of the traditional recipe.

INGREDIENTS

Serves 6–8

250g/9oz/1¼ cups granulated sugar
60ml/4 tbsp water
1 vanilla pod or 10ml/2 tsp vanilla essence
400ml/14fl oz/1⅔ cups milk
250ml/8fl oz/1 cup whipping cream
5 large eggs
2 egg yolks

1 Put 175g/6oz/⅞ cup of the sugar in a small heavy saucepan with 60ml/4 tbsp of water to moisten. Bring to the boil over a high heat, swirling the pan to dissolve the sugar. Boil, without stirring, until the syrup turns a dark caramel colour (this will take about 4–5 minutes).

2 Immediately pour the caramel into a 1 litre/1¾ pint/4 cup soufflé dish. Holding the dish with oven gloves, quickly swirl the dish to coat the base and sides with the caramel and set aside. (The caramel will harden quickly as it cools.) Place the dish in a small roasting tin.

3 Preheat the oven to 160°C/ 325°F/Gas 3. With a small sharp knife, carefully split the vanilla pod lengthways and scrape the black seeds into a medium saucepan. Add the milk and cream and bring just to the boil over a medium-high heat, stirring frequently. Remove the pan from the heat, cover and set aside for 15–20 minutes.

4 In a bowl, whisk the eggs and egg yolks with the remaining sugar for 2–3 minutes until smooth and creamy. Whisk in the hot milk and carefully strain the mixture into the caramel-lined dish. Cover with foil.

5 Place the dish in a roasting tin and pour in enough boiling water to come halfway up the sides of the dish. Bake the custard for 40–45 minutes until just set and a knife inserted about 5cm/2in from the edge comes out clean. Remove from the roasting tin and cool for at least 30 minutes, then chill overnight.

6 To turn out, carefully run a sharp knife around the edge of the dish to loosen the custard. Cover the dish with a serving plate and, holding them tightly, invert the dish and plate together. Gently lift one edge of the dish, allowing the caramel to run over the sides, then slowly lift off the dish.

Classic Coffee Crème Caramel

These lightly set coffee custards are served in a pool of caramel sauce. For a richer flavour, make them with half single cream, half milk.

INGREDIENTS

Serves 6
600ml/1 pint/2½ cups milk
45ml/3 tbsp ground coffee
50g/2oz/¼ cup caster sugar
4 eggs
4 egg yolks
spun sugar, to decorate (optional)

For the caramel sauce
150g/5oz/¾ cup caster sugar
60ml/4 tbsp water

1 Preheat the oven to 160°C/ 325°F/Gas 3. To make the sauce, heat the sugar with the water in a heavy-based pan until it has dissolved.

2 Bring to the boil and boil rapidly until the syrup turns a rich golden brown. Quickly pour the hot syrup into six warmed 150ml/¼ pint/⅔ cup ramekins.

3 To make the coffee custard, heat the milk until almost boiling. Pour over the ground coffee and leave to infuse for about 5 minutes. Strain through a fine sieve into a jug.

4 In a bowl, whisk the caster sugar, eggs and yolks until light and creamy. Whisk the coffee-flavoured milk into the egg mixture. Pour into the ramekins.

5 Put the ramekins in a roasting tin and add hot water to come two-thirds of the way up the dishes. Bake for 30–35 minutes until just set. Remove the custards from the heat and cool, then chill for 3 hours. To serve, invert on to plates and decorate if you wish.

COOK'S TIP

To make spun sugar, gently heat 75g/3oz/scant ½ cup caster sugar, 5ml/1 tsp liquid glucose and 30ml/2 tbsp water in a heavy-based pan until the sugar dissolves. Boil the syrup to 160°C/325°F, then dip the base of the pan into cold water. Place greaseproof paper on the work surface and, holding two forks together, dip them in the syrup and flick rapidly back and forth over an oiled rolling pin.

Crème Brûlée

This dessert actually originated in Cambridge, but has become associated with France and is widely eaten there. Add a little liqueur, if you like, but it is equally delicious without it.

INGREDIENTS

Serves 6

1 vanilla pod

1 litre/1¾ pints/4 cups double cream

6 egg yolks

90g/3½oz/½ cup caster sugar

30ml/2 tbsp almond or orange liqueur
  (optional)

75g/3oz/⅓ cup soft light brown sugar

1 Preheat the oven to 150°C/300°F/Gas 2. Place six 120ml/4fl oz/½ cup ramekins in a roasting tin and set aside.

2 With a small sharp knife, split the vanilla pod lengthways and scrape the black seeds into a medium saucepan. Add the cream and bring just to the boil over a medium heat, stirring. Remove from the heat and cover. Set aside for 15–20 minutes.

3 In a bowl, whisk the egg yolks, caster sugar and liqueur, if using, until well blended. Whisk in the hot cream and strain into a large jug. Divide the custard equally among the ramekins.

4 Pour enough boiling water into the roasting tin to come halfway up the sides of the ramekins. Cover the tin with foil and bake for about 30 minutes until the custards are just set. Remove from the tin and leave to cool. Return to the dry roasting tin and chill.

5 Preheat the grill. Sprinkle the sugar evenly over the surface of each custard and grill for 30–60 seconds until the sugar melts and caramelizes. (Do not let the sugar burn or the custard curdle.) Place in the fridge to set the crust and chill completely before serving.

COOK'S TIP

To test if the custards are ready, push the point of a knife into centre of one – if it comes out clean, the custards are cooked.

Coffee Cardamom Zabaglione

This warm Italian dessert is usually made with Italian Marsala wine. In this recipe coffee liqueur is used with freshly crushed cardamom.

INGREDIENTS

Serves 4

4 cardamom pods
8 egg yolks
50g/2oz/4 tbsp golden caster sugar
30ml/2 tbsp strong brewed coffee
50ml/2fl oz/¼ cup coffee liqueur such as
    Tia Maria, Kahlúa or Toussaint
a few crushed roasted coffee beans,
    to decorate

1 Peel away the pale green outer husks from the cardamom pods and remove the black seeds. Crush these to a fine powder using a pestle and mortar.

2 Put the egg yolks, caster sugar and cardamom in a bowl and whisk until pale and creamy.

3 Gradually whisk the coffee and the liqueur into the egg yolk mixture until evenly combined.

4 Place the bowl over a saucepan of near-boiling water and continue whisking for about 10 minutes.

5 Continue whisking until the mixture is very thick and fluffy and has doubled in volume, making sure the water doesn't boil – if it does the mixture will curdle. Remove the bowl from the heat and carefully pour the zabaglione into four warmed glasses or dishes. Sprinkle with a few crushed roasted coffee beans and serve at once.

Petits Pots de Cappuccino

These rich coffee custards, with a cream topping and a light dusting of drinking chocolate, look wonderful presented in fine china coffee cups.

INGREDIENTS

Serves 6–8

75g/3oz/1 cup roasted coffee beans

300ml/½ pint/1¼ cups milk

300ml/½ pint/1¼ cups single cream

1 whole egg and 4 egg yolks

50g/2oz/4 tbsp caster sugar

2.5ml/½ tsp vanilla extract

For the topping

120ml/4fl oz/½ cup whipping cream

45ml/3 tbsp iced water

10ml/2 tsp drinking chocolate

1 Preheat the oven to 160°C/ 325°F/ Gas 3. Put the coffee beans in a pan over a low heat for 3 minutes, shaking frequently.

2 Pour the milk and cream over the beans. Heat until almost boiling; cover and infuse for 30 minutes. Whisk the egg and yolks, sugar and vanilla together. Return the milk to boiling and pour through a sieve on to the egg mixture. Discard the beans.

3 Pour the mixture into eight 75ml/5 tbsp coffee cups or six 120ml/4fl oz/½ cup ramekins. Cover each with a piece of foil.

4 Put the coffee cups or ramekins in a roasting tin with hot water reaching about two-thirds of the way up the sides of the dishes. Bake for 30–35 minutes, or until lightly set. Leave to cool. Chill in the fridge for at least 2 hours.

5 Whisk the whipping cream and iced water until thick and frothy and spoon on top of the custards. Dust with drinking chocolate before serving.

Almost Instant Banana Pudding

Banana and ginger make a great combination in this very fast dessert.

Serves 6–8

4 thick slices ginger cake

6 bananas

30ml/2 tbsp lemon juice

300ml/½ pint/1¼ cups whipping cream or
   fromage frais

60ml/4 tbsp fruit juice

30–45ml/3–4 tbsp soft brown sugar

1 Break up the cake into chunks and arrange in an ovenproof dish. Slice the bananas and toss in the lemon juice.

2 Whip the cream and, when firm, gently whip in the juice. (If using fromage frais, just gently stir in the juice.) Fold in the bananas and spoon the mixture over the ginger cake.

3 Top with the soft brown sugar and place under a hot grill for 2–3 minutes to caramelize. Chill to set firm again if you wish, or serve when required.

Ginger and Orange Crème Brûlée

This is a useful way of cheating at crème brûlée! Most people would never know unless you overchill the custard, or keep it more than a day, but there's little risk of that!

Serves 4–5

2 eggs, plus 2 egg yolks

300ml/½ pint/1¼ cups single cream

30ml/2 tbsp caster sugar

5ml/1 tsp powdered gelatine or alternative
   finely grated rind and juice of ½ orange

1 large piece stem ginger, finely chopped

45–60ml/3–4 tbsp icing or caster sugar
   orange segments and sprig of mint,
   to decorate

1 Whisk the eggs and yolks together until pale. Bring the cream and sugar to the boil, remove from the heat and sprinkle on the gelatine. Stir until the gelatine has dissolved and then pour the cream mixture on to the eggs, whisking all the time.

2 Add the orange rind, a little juice to taste, and the chopped ginger to the mixture.

3 Pour into four or five ramekins and chill until set.

4 Some time before serving, sprinkle the sugar generously over the top of the custard and put under a very hot grill. Watch closely for the couple of moments it takes for the tops to caramelize. Allow to cool before serving. Decorate with a few segments of orange and a sprig of mint.

C O O K ' S   T I P

~

For a milder ginger flavour, just add up to 5ml/1 tsp ground ginger instead of the stem ginger.

Chocolate Mandarin Trifle

Trifle is always a tempting treat, but when a rich chocolate and mascarpone custard is combined with amaretto and mandarin oranges, it becomes irresistible.

INGREDIENTS

Serves 6–8

4 trifle sponges

14 amaretti biscuits

60ml/4 tbsp Amaretto di Saronno or
    sweet sherry

8 mandarin oranges

For the custard

200g/7oz plain chocolate, broken
    into squares

30ml/2 tbsp cornflour or
    custard powder

30ml/2 tbsp caster sugar

2 egg yolks

200ml/7fl oz/⅞ cup milk

250g/9oz/generous 1 cup
mascarpone cheese

For the topping

250g/9oz/generous 1 cup
    fromage frais

chocolate shapes

mandarin slices

1 Break up the trifle sponges and place them in a large glass serving dish. Crumble the amaretti biscuits over and then sprinkle with amaretto or sweet sherry.

2 Squeeze the juice from two of the mandarins and sprinkle into the dish. Segment the rest and put in the dish.

3 Make the custard. Melt the chocolate in a heatproof bowl over hot water. In a separate bowl, mix the cornflour or custard powder, sugar and egg yolks to a smooth paste.

4 Heat the milk in a small saucepan until almost boiling, then pour in a steady stream on to the egg yolk mixture, stirring constantly. Return to the clean pan and stir over a low heat until the custard has thickened slightly and is smooth.

5 Stir the mascarpone until melted, then add the melted chocolate, mixing it thoroughly. Spread evenly over the trifle, cool, then chill until set.

6 To finish, spread the fromage frais over the custard, then decorate with chocolate shapes and the remaining mandarin slices just before serving.

COOK'S TIP

Always use the best chocolate which has a high percentage of cocoa solids, and take care not to overheat the chocolate when melting as it will lose its gloss and look "grainy".

Tangerine Trifle

An unusual variation on a traditional trifle – of course, you can add a little alcohol if you wish.

INGREDIENTS

Serves 4

5 trifle sponges, halved lengthways

30ml/2 tbsp apricot jam

15–20 ratafia biscuits

142g/4¾oz packet tangerine jelly

300g/11oz can mandarin oranges, drained, reserving juice

600ml/1 pint/2½ cups ready-made (or home-made) custard

whipped cream and shreds of orange rind, to decorate

caster sugar, for sprinkling

1 Spread the halved sponge cakes with apricot jam and arrange in the base of a deep serving bowl or glass dish. Sprinkle over the ratafia biscuits.

2 Break up the jelly into a heatproof measuring jug, add the juice from the canned mandarins and dissolve in a pan of hot water or in the microwave. Stir until the liquid clears.

3 Make up to 600ml/1 pint/ 2½ cups with ice cold water, stir well and leave to cool for up to 30 minutes. Scatter the mandarin oranges over the cakes and ratafias.

4 Pour the jelly over the mandarin oranges, cake and ratafias and chill for 1 hour.

5 When the jelly has set, pour the custard smoothly over the top and chill again.

6 When ready to serve, pipe the whipped cream over the custard. Wash the orange rind shreds, sprinkle them with caster sugar and use to decorate the trifle.

Raspberry Trifle

Use fresh or frozen raspberries for this ever-popular dessert.

Serves 6 or more

175g/6oz trifle sponges, or 2.5cm/1in
  cubes of plain Victoria sponge or
  coarsely crumbled sponge fingers
60ml/4 tbsp medium sherry
115g/4oz raspberry jam
275g/10oz/1⅔ cups raspberries
450ml/¾ pint/scant 2 cups custard,
  flavoured with 30ml/2 tbsp medium or
  sweet sherry
300ml/½ pint/1¼ cups sweetened
  whipped cream
toasted flaked almonds and mint leaves,
  to decorate

1 Spread half of the sponges,
  cake cubes or sponge fingers
over the bottom of a large serving
bowl. (A glass bowl is best for
presentation.)

2 Sprinkle half of the sherry over
  the cake to moisten it. Spoon
over half of the jam, dotting it
evenly over the cake cubes.

3 Reserve a few raspberries for
  decoration. Make a layer of
half of the remaining raspberries
on top.

4 Pour over half of the custard,
  covering the fruit and cake.
Repeat the layers of moistened
cake, jam, fruit and custard. Cover
and chill for at least 2 hours.

5 Before serving, spoon the
  sweetened whipped cream
evenly over the top. To decorate,
sprinkle with toasted flaked
almonds and arrange the reserved
raspberries and the mint leaves
on the top.

VARIATION

You can use other ripe summer
fruit in the trifle, such as apricots,
peaches, nectarines and
strawberries, with different jams
and fruit liqueurs to suit.

Coconut and Coffee Trifle

Dark coffee sponge, laced with liqueur, coconut custard and a coffee cream topping makes a rich dessert.

Serves 6–8
For the coffee sponge
45ml/3 tbsp strong-flavoured
   ground coffee
45ml/3 tbsp near-boiling water
2 eggs
50g/2oz/¼ cup soft dark brown sugar
40g/1½oz/⅓ cup self-raising flour, sifted
25ml/1½ tbsp hazelnut or sunflower oil

For the coconut custard
400ml/14fl oz/1⅔ cup canned coconut milk
3 eggs
40g/1½oz/3 tbsp caster sugar
10ml/2 tsp cornflour

For the filling and topping
2 medium bananas
60ml/4 tbsp coffee liqueur, such as
   Tia Maria
300ml/½ pint/1¼ cups double cream
30ml/2 tbsp icing sugar, sifted
ribbons of fresh coconut, to decorate

1 Preheat the oven to 160°C/325°F/Gas 3. Oil and line an 18cm/7in square tin with grease-proof paper.

2 Put the ground coffee in a small bowl. Pour the hot water over and leave to infuse for 4 minutes. Strain the coffee, discarding the grounds.

3 Whisk the eggs and soft dark brown sugar in a large bowl until the whisk leaves a trail when lifted from the mixture.

4 Gently fold in the flour, 15ml/1 tbsp of the coffee and the oil. Spoon the mixture into the tin and bake for 20 minutes. Turn out on a rack, remove the paper and cool.

5 To make the coconut custard, heat the coconut milk in a saucepan until it is almost boiling.

6 Whisk the eggs, sugar and cornflour until frothy, then whisk in the hot coconut milk. Add to the pan and heat gently, stirring for 1–2 minutes, until the custard thickens. Set aside to cool.

7 Cut the coffee sponge into 5cm/2in squares and arrange in a large glass bowl. Slice the bananas and arrange on the sponge. Drizzle the coffee liqueur on top. Pour the custard over and leave until cold.

8 Whip the cream with the remaining coffee and icing sugar until soft peaks form. Spoon the cream over the custard. Cover and chill for several hours. Sprinkle with ribbons of fresh coconut.

COOK'S TIP

If fresh coconut is not available, use shredded coconut and toast until pale golden.

Jamaican Fruit Trifle

This trifle is actually based on a Caribbean fool that consists of fruit stirred into thick vanilla-flavoured cream. This version is much less rich, redressing the balance with plenty of fruit, and with crème fraîche replacing some of the cream.

INGREDIENTS

Serves 8

1 large sweet pineapple, peeled and cored, about 350g/12oz

300ml/½ pint/1¼ cups double cream

200ml/7fl oz/scant 1 cup crème fraîche

60ml/4 tbsp icing sugar, sifted

10ml/2 tsp pure vanilla essence

30ml/2 tbsp white or coconut rum

3 papayas, peeled, seeded and chopped

3 mangoes, peeled, stoned and chopped

thinly pared rind and juice of 1 lime

25g/1oz/⅓ cup coarsely shredded or flaked coconut, toasted

1 Cut the pineapple into large chunks, place in a food processor or blender and process briefly until chopped. Tip into a sieve placed over a bowl and leave for 5 minutes to drain the juices from the fruit.

2 Whip the double cream to soft peaks. Fold in the crème fraîche, icing sugar, vanilla essence and rum.

3 Fold the drained chopped pineapple into the cream mixture. Place the chopped papayas and mangoes in a large bowl and pour over the lime juice. Gently stir the fruit mixture to combine the ingredients. Shred the pared lime rind.

4 Divide the fruit mixture and the pineapple cream among eight dessert plates. Decorate with the lime shreds, toasted coconut and a few small pineapple leaves, if you like, and serve at once.

Grilled Pineapple with Rum Custard

Freshly ground black pepper may seem an unusual ingredient to put with pineapple, until you realise that peppercorns are the fruit of a tropical vine. If the idea does not appeal, leave out the pepper.

INGREDIENTS

Serves 4

1 ripe pineapple

25g/1oz/2tbsp butter

fresh strawberries, sliced, to serve

a few pineapple leaves, to decorate

For the sauce

1 egg

2 egg yolks

30ml/2 tbsp caster sugar

30ml/2 tbsp dark rum

2.5ml/½ tsp freshly ground black pepper

1 Remove the top and bottom from the pineapple with a serrated knife. Pare away the outer skin from top to bottom, remove the core and cut into slices.

2 Preheat a moderate grill. Dot the pineapple slices with butter and grill for about 5 minutes.

3 To make the sauce, place all the ingredients in a bowl. Set over a saucepan of simmering water and whisk with a hand-held mixer for about 3–4 minutes or until foamy and cooked. Scatter the strawberries over the pineapple, decorate with a few pineapple leaves and serve with the sauce.

COOK'S TIP
~

The sweetest pineapples are picked and exported when ripe. Contrary to popular belief, pineapples do not ripen well after picking. Choose fruit that smells sweet and yields to firm pressure from your thumbs.

Banana and Passion Fruit Whip

This very easy and quickly prepared dessert is delicious served with crisp shortcake or ginger biscuits.

Serves 4

2 ripe bananas

2 passion fruit

90ml/6 tbsp fromage frais

150ml/¼ pint/⅔ cup double cream

10ml/2 tsp clear honey

shortcake or ginger biscuits, to serve

1 Peel the bananas, then mash them with a fork in a bowl to a smooth purée.

2 Halve the passion fruit and scoop out the pulp. Mix the pulp with the bananas and fromage frais. In a separate bowl, whip the cream with the honey until it forms soft peaks.

3 Carefully fold the cream and honey mixture into the fruit mixture. Spoon the whip into individual glass dishes and serve immediately with shortcake or ginger biscuits.

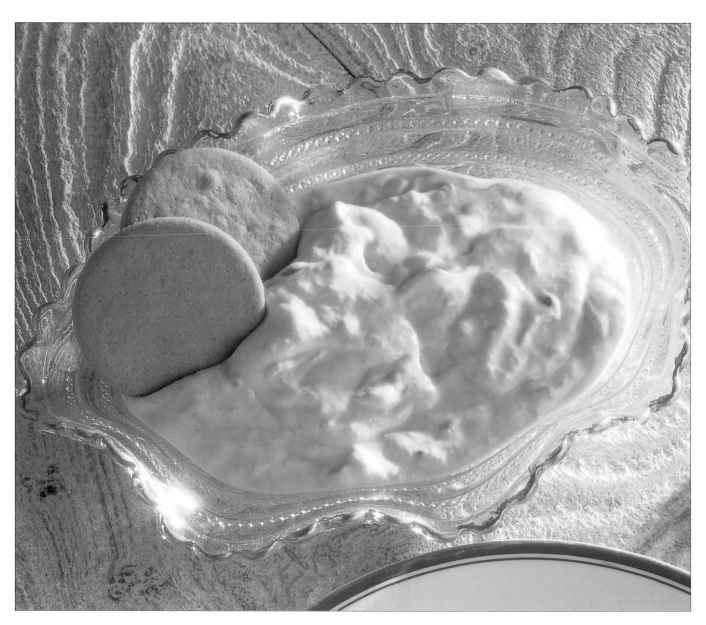

Cappuccino Coffee Cups

Coffee-lovers will love this one – and it tastes rich and creamy, even though it's very light.

INGREDIENTS

Serves 4

2 eggs

215g/7.7oz carton evaporated semi-
   skimmed milk

25ml/1½ tbsp instant coffee granules
   or powder

30ml/2 tbsp caster sugar

10ml/2 tsp powdered gelatine,
   or alternative

60ml/4 tbsp light crème fraîche

cocoa powder or ground cinnamon,
   to decorate

1 Separate one egg and reserve the white. Beat the yolk with the whole of the remaining egg.

2 Put the evaporated milk, coffee granules, sugar and beaten eggs in a pan; whisk until evenly combined.

3 Put the pan over a low heat and stir constantly until the mixture is hot, but not boiling. Cook, stirring constantly, without boiling, until the mixture is slightly thickened and smooth.

4 Remove the pan from the heat. Sprinkle the gelatine over the pan and whisk until the gelatine has completely dissolved.

5 Spoon the coffee custard into four individual dishes or glasses and chill them until set.

6 Whisk the reserved egg white until stiff. Whisk in the crème fraîche and then spoon the mixture over the desserts. Sprinkle with cocoa or cinnamon and serve.

VARIATION

Greek-style yogurt can be used instead of the crème fraîche, if you prefer.

Vermont Baked Maple Custard

Try to find pure maple syrup for this custard as it will really enhance the flavour.

COOK'S TIP

Baking delicate mixtures such as custards in a water bath helps protect them from uneven heating which could make them rubbery.

INGREDIENTS

Serves 6

3 eggs

120ml/4fl oz/½ cup maple syrup

600ml/1 pint/2½ cups milk

pinch of salt

pinch of grated nutmeg

1 Preheat the oven to 180°C/350°F/Gas 4. Combine all the ingredients in a large bowl and mix together thoroughly.

2 Set individual custard cups or ramekins in a roasting tin half filled with hot water. Pour the custard mixture into the cups. Bake until the custards are set, 45 minutes–1 hour. Test by inserting the blade of a knife in the centre: it should come out clean. Serve warm or chilled.

Mocha Cream Pots

The name of this rich baked custard, a classic French dessert, comes from the baking cups, called pots de crème. *The addition of coffee gives the dessert an exotic touch.*

INGREDIENTS

Serves 8

15ml/1 tbsp instant coffee powder

475ml/16fl oz/2 cups milk

75g/3oz/⅓ cup caster sugar

225g/8oz plain chocolate, chopped

10ml/2 tsp vanilla essence

30ml/2 tbsp coffee liqueur (optional)

7 egg yolks

whipped cream and crystallized mimosa balls, to decorate (optional)

1 Preheat the oven to 160°C/ 325°F/Gas 3. Place eight 120ml/4fl oz/½ cup *pots de crème* cups or ramekins in a roasting tin.

2 Put the instant coffee into a saucepan and stir in the milk, then add the sugar and set the pan over a medium-high heat. Bring to the boil, stirring constantly, until both the coffee and sugar have dissolved.

3 Remove the pan from the heat and add the chocolate. Stir until the chocolate has melted and the sauce is smooth. Stir in the vanilla essence and coffee liqueur, if using, until evenly combined.

4 In a bowl, whisk the egg yolks to blend them lightly. Slowly whisk in the chocolate mixture until well blended, then strain the mixture into a large jug and divide equally among the cups or ramekins. Place them in a roasting tin and pour in enough boiling water to come halfway up the sides of the cups or ramekins. Cover the tin with foil.

5 Bake for 30–35 minutes until the custard is just set and a knife inserted into a custard comes out clean. Remove the cups or ramekins from the roasting tin and allow to cool. Place on a baking sheet, cover and chill completely. Decorate with the whipped cream and crystallized mimosa balls, if using.

Plum and Custard Creams

If you were reluctantly raised on stewed plums and custard, this sophisticated version, prettily layered in a glass, will bring a smile to your lips.

INGREDIENTS

Serves 6

675g/1½lb red plums, stoned and sliced

grated rind and juice of 1 orange

50g/2oz/¼ cup caster sugar

400g/14oz carton ready-made
 custard sauce

300ml/½ pint/1¼ cups double cream

30ml/2 tbsp water

15ml/1 tbsp powdered gelatine

1 egg white

plum slices and fresh mint sprigs,
 to decorate

1 Put the plums in a saucepan with the orange rind and juice and caster sugar. Heat, stirring constantly, until the sugar has dissolved. Cook the plums until tender. Allow to cool slightly, then process the plums to a smooth purée. Pass through a sieve into a bowl and cool.

2 Put the custard and half the cream in a saucepan, and heat until boiling. Pour the water into a heatproof bowl and sprinkle the gelatine on top; set aside for 5 minutes. Whisk the soaked gelatine into the hot custard until dissolved and allow to cool.

3 Whip the remaining cream and fold it into the custard mixture. In a grease-free bowl, whisk the egg white to form soft peaks and fold into the custard. Leave aside until just setting.

4 Quickly spoon alternate spoonfuls of the custard and plum purée into six tall dessert glasses. Marble the mixtures together. Chill for 2–3 hours or until the custard has set. Decorate each dessert with plum slices and fresh mint sprigs before serving.

Amaretto Soufflé

A mouth-watering soufflé with more than a hint of Amaretto liqueur.

INGREDIENTS

Serves 6

6 amaretti biscuits, coarsely crushed

90ml/4 tbsp Amaretto liqueur

4 eggs, separated, plus 1 egg white

130g/3½oz/½ cup caster sugar

30ml/2 tbsp plain flour

250ml/8fl oz/1 cup milk

pinch of cream of tartar (if needed)

icing sugar, for dusting

1 Preheat the oven to 200°C/400°F/Gas 6. Butter a 1.5 litre/2½ pint/6¼ cup soufflé dish and sprinkle it with a little of the caster sugar.

2 Put the biscuits in a bowl. Sprinkle them with 30ml/2 tbsp of the Amaretto liqueur and set aside.

3 In another bowl, carefully mix together the four egg yolks, 30ml/2 tbsp of the sugar and all of flour.

4 Heat the milk just to the boil in a heavy saucepan. Gradually add the hot milk to the egg mixture, stirring.

5 Pour the mixture back into the pan. Set over a low heat and simmer gently for 3–4 minutes or until thickened, stirring occasionally.

6 Add the remaining Amaretto liqueur. Remove from the heat.

7 In a scrupulously clean, grease-free bowl, whisk the five egg whites until they will hold soft peaks. (If not using a copper bowl, add the cream of tartar as soon as the whites are frothy.) Add the remaining sugar and continue whisking until stiff.

8 Add about one-quarter of the whites to the liqueur mixture and stir in with a rubber spatula. Add the remaining whites and fold in gently.

9 Spoon half of the mixture into the prepared soufflé dish. Cover with a layer of the moistened amaretti biscuits, then spoon the remaining soufflé mixture on top.

10 Bake for 20 minutes or until the soufflé is risen and lightly browned. Sprinkle with sifted icing sugar and serve immediately.

Hot Quince Soufflés

These delicious fruits are more often picked than purchased, as they are seldom found in shops or markets. You can use pears instead.

Serves 6

2 quinces, peeled and cored
60ml/4 tbsp water
115g/4oz/½ cup caster sugar
5 egg whites
melted butter, for greasing
icing sugar, for dusting

For the pastry cream
250ml/8fl oz/1 cup milk
1 vanilla pod
3 egg yolks
75g/3oz/⅓ cup caster sugar
25g/1oz/¼ cup plain flour
15ml/1 tbsp Poire William liqueur

1 Cut the quinces into cubes. Place in a saucepan with the water. Stir in half the sugar and bring to the boil. Lower the heat, cover and simmer until tender. Remove the lid and boil until the liquid has almost evaporated.

2 Cool slightly, then purée the fruit in a blender or food processor. Press through a sieve into a bowl and set aside.

3 Make the pastry cream. Pour the milk into a small saucepan. Add the vanilla pod and bring to the boil over a low heat. Meanwhile, beat the egg yolks, caster sugar and flour in a bowl until smooth.

4 Gradually strain the hot milk on to the yolks, whisking frequently until the mixture is smooth and free of lumps.

5 Discard the vanilla pod. Return the mixture to a clean pan and heat gently, stirring until thickened. Cook for a further 2 minutes, whisking constantly, to ensure that the sauce is quite smooth and the flour is cooked.

6 Remove the pan from the heat and stir in the quince purée and liqueur. Cover the surface of the pastry cream with clear film to prevent it from forming a skin. Allow to cool slightly, while you prepare the ramekins.

7 Preheat the oven to 220ºC/ 425ºF/Gas 7. Place a baking sheet in the oven to heat. Butter six ramekins and sprinkle the insides with caster sugar. In a grease-free bowl, whisk the egg whites to stiff peaks. Slowly whisk in the remaining caster sugar, then carefully fold the egg whites into the pastry cream.

8 Divide the mixture among the prepared ramekins and level the surfaces. Carefully run a sharp knife around the sides of the ramekins, then place them on the hot baking sheet and bake for 8–10 minutes, until the tops of the soufflés are well risen and golden. Generously dust the tops with icing sugar and serve the soufflés at once.

COOK'S TIP
~
Kirsch, made from cherries, is a good alternative to Poire William.

Lemon Soufflé with Blackberries

The simple fresh taste of cold lemon mousse combines well with rich blackberry sauce, and the colour contrast looks wonderful, too. Blueberries or raspberries make equally delicious alternatives to blackberries.

INGREDIENTS

Serves 6

grated rind of 1 lemon and juice of
  2 lemons
15ml/1 tbsp/1 sachet powdered gelatine
5 size 4 eggs, separated
150g/5oz/¾ cup caster sugar
few drops vanilla essence
400ml/14fl oz/1⅔ cups whipping cream

For the sauce

175g/6oz/¾ cup blackberries (fresh or
  frozen)
30–45ml/2–3 tbsp caster sugar
few fresh blackberries and blackberry
  leaves, to decorate

1 Place the lemon juice in a small pan and heat through. Sprinkle on the gelatine and leave to dissolve or heat further until clear. Allow to cool.

2 Put the lemon rind, egg yolks, sugar and vanilla into a large bowl and whisk until the mixture is very thick, pale and creamy.

3 Whisk the egg whites until stiff and almost peaky. Whip the cream until stiff.

4 Stir the gelatine mixture into the yolks, then fold in the whipped cream and lastly the egg whites. Turn into a 1.5 litre/ 2½ pint/6 cup soufflé dish and freeze for about 2 hours.

5 To make the sauce, place the blackberries in a pan with the sugar and cook for 4–6 minutes, until the juices begin to run and all the sugar has dissolved. Pass through a sieve to remove the seeds, then chill.

6 When the soufflé is almost frozen, but still spoonable, scoop or spoon out on to individual plates and serve with the blackberry sauce, decorated with fresh blackberries and blackberry leaves.

Apple Soufflé Omelette

Apples sautéed until they are slightly caramelized make a delicious autumn filling – you could use fresh raspberries or strawberries when they are in seeason.

INGREDIENTS

Serves 2

4 eggs, separated
30ml/2 tbsp single cream
15ml/1 tbsp caster sugar
15g/½oz/1 tbsp butter
icing sugar, for dredging

For the filling

1 eating apple, peeled, cored and sliced
25g/1oz/2 tbsp butter
30ml/2 tbsp soft light brown sugar
45ml/3 tbsp single cream

1 To make the filling, sauté the apple slices in the butter and sugar until just tender. Stir in the cream and keep warm, while making the omelette.

2 Place the egg yolks in a bowl with the cream and sugar and beat well. Whisk the egg whites until they form stiff peaks, then fold into the yolk mixture.

3 Melt the butter in a large heavy-based frying pan, pour in the soufflé mixture and spread evenly. Cook for 1 minute until golden underneath, then cover the pan handle with foil and place under a hot grill to brown the top.

4 Slide the omelette on to a plate, add the apple mixture, then fold over. Sift the icing sugar over thickly, then mark in a criss-cross pattern with a hot metal skewer. Serve immediately.

Hot Mocha Rum Soufflés

Serve these superb soufflés as soon as they are cooked for a fantastic finale to a dinner party.

INGREDIENTS

Serves 6
25g/1oz/2 tbsp unsalted butter, melted
65g/2½ oz/generous ½ cup cocoa powder
75g/3oz/generous ⅓ cup caster sugar
60ml/4 tbsp strong black coffee
30ml/2 tbsp dark rum
6 egg whites
icing sugar, for dusting

1 Preheat the oven with a baking sheet inside to 190°C/375°F/ Gas 5. Grease six 250ml/8fl oz/ 1 cup soufflé dishes with the melted butter.

2 Mix 15ml/1 tbsp of the cocoa with 15ml/1 tbsp of the caster sugar in a bowl. Tip the mixture into each of the dishes in turn, rotating them so that they are evenly coated.

3 Mix the remaining cocoa with the coffee and rum.

4 Whisk the egg whites in a clean, grease-free bowl until they form firm peaks. Whisk in the remaining caster sugar. Stir a generous spoonful of the whites into the cocoa mixture to lighten it, then gently fold in the remaining whites.

5 Spoon the mixture into the prepared dishes, smoothing the tops. Place on the hot baking sheet, and bake for 12–15 minutes or until well risen. Serve the soufflés immediately, lightly dusted with icing sugar.

COOK'S TIP

When serving the soufflés at the end of a dinner party, prepare them just before the meal is served. Pop in the oven as soon as the main course is finished and serve freshly baked.

Cold Mango Soufflés with Toasted Coconut

Fragrant, fresh mango is one of the most delicious exotic fruits around, whether it is simply served in slices or used as the basis for an ice cream or soufflé.

Makes 4

4 small mangoes, peeled, stoned and chopped

30ml/2 tbsp water

15ml/1 tbsp powdered gelatine

2 egg yolks

115g/4oz/½ cup caster sugar

120ml/4fl oz/½ cup milk

grated rind of 1 orange

300ml/½ pint/1¼ cups double cream

toasted flaked or coarsely shredded coconut, to decorate

1 Place a few pieces of mango in the base of four ramekins. Wrap a greased collar of non-stick baking paper around the outside of each ramekin so that it stands about 5cm/2in above the rim the dish. Tape to secure, then tie with string.

2 Pour the water into a small heatproof bowl and sprinkle the gelatine over it. Leave for 5 minutes. Place the bowl in a pan of hot water. Stir until the gelatine has dissolved.

3 Whisk the egg yolks, caster sugar and milk in another heatproof bowl. Place the bowl over a saucepan of simmering water and whisk until the mixture is thick and frothy. Remove from the heat and whisk continuously until the mixture cools. Whisk in the liquid gelatine.

4 Process the remaining mango pieces to a purée, then fold the purée into the egg yolk mixture with the orange rind. Set the mixture aside until it is starting to thicken.

5 Whip the double cream to form soft peaks. Reserve 60ml/4 tbsp and keep refrigerated. Fold the rest into the mango mixture. Spoon into the ramekins until the mixture is 2.5cm/1in above the rim of each dish. Chill for 3–4 hours.

6 Carefully remove the paper collars from the soufflés. Spoon a little of the reserved cream on top of each soufflé and decorate with the coconut before serving.

Chocolate Soufflé Crêpes

A non-stick pan is ideal as it does not need greasing between each crêpe. Serve two crêpes per person.

INGREDIENTS

Makes 12 crêpes
75g/3oz/⅔ cup plain flour
10g/¼oz/1 tbsp unsweetened cocoa
5ml/1 tsp caster sugar
pinch of salt
5ml/1 tsp ground cinnamon
2 eggs
175ml/6fl oz/¾ cup milk
5ml/1 tsp vanilla essence
50g/2oz/4 tbsp unsalted butter, melted
icing sugar, for dusting
raspberries, pineapple and mint sprigs,
    to decorate

For the pineapple syrup
½ medium pineapple, peeled, cored and
    finely chopped
30ml/2 tbsp natural maple syrup
5ml/1 tsp cornflour
½ cinnamon stick
30ml/2 tbsp rum

For the soufflé filling
250g/9oz semi-sweet or bittersweet
    chocolate
85ml/3fl oz/⅓ cup double cream
3 eggs, separated
25g/1oz/2 tbsp caster sugar

1 Prepare syrup. In a saucepan over medium heat, bring pineapple, 125ml/4fl oz/½ cup of water, maple syrup, cornflour and cinnamon stick to the boil. Simmer for 2–3 minutes until sauce thickens, whisking frequently. Remove from heat; discard cinnamon. Pour into a bowl, stir in rum and chill.

2 Prepare crêpes. In a bowl, sift flour, cocoa, sugar, salt and cinnamon. Stir to blend, then make a well in the centre. In a bowl, beat eggs, milk and vanilla and gradually add to the well, whisking in flour from the side to form a smooth batter. Stir in half the melted butter and pour batter into a jug. Allow to stand 1 hour.

3 Heat an 18–20cm/7–8in crêpe pan. Brush with butter. Stir the batter. Pour 45ml/3 tbsp batter into the pan; swirl pan quickly to cover bottom with a thin layer. Cook over medium-high heat for 1–2 minutes until bottom is golden. Turn over and cook for 30–45 seconds, then turn on to a plate. Stack crêpes between non-stick baking paper and set aside.

4 Prepare filling. In a small saucepan, over medium heat, melt chocolate and cream until smooth, stirring frequently.

5 In a bowl, beat yolks with half the sugar for 3–5 minutes, until light and creamy. Gradually beat in the chocolate mixture. Allow to cool. In a large bowl, beat egg whites until soft peaks form. Gradually beat in remaining sugar until stiff. Beat in a spoonful of egg whites to the chocolate mixture, then fold in remaining whites.

6 Preheat the oven to 200°C/400°F/Gas 6. Lay a crêpe on a plate. Spoon a little soufflé mixture on to crêpe, spreading it to the edge. Fold the bottom half over the soufflé mixture, then fold in half again to form a filled "triangle". Place on a buttered baking sheet. Repeat with remaining crêpes.

7 Brush the tops with melted butter and bake for 15–20 minutes until souffléd. Dust with icing sugar and garnish with raspberries, pineapple, mint and a spoonful of pineapple syrup.

Chocolate Soufflés

These are easy to make and can be prepared in advance – the filled dishes can wait for up to one hour before baking. For best results, use good quality Continental chocolate.

INGREDIENTS

Serves 6

175g/6oz plain chocolate, chopped
150g/5oz/⅔ cup unsalted butter, cut in small pieces
4 large eggs, separated
30ml/2 tbsp orange liqueur (optional)
1.5ml/¼ tsp cream of tartar
45ml/3 tbsp caster sugar
icing sugar, for dusting
sprigs of redcurrants and white chocolate roses, to decorate

For the white chocolate sauce
75g/3oz white chocolate, chopped
90ml/6 tbsp whipping cream
15–30ml/1–2 tbsp orange liqueur
grated rind of ½ orange

1 Generously butter six 150ml/ ¼ pint/⅓ cup ramekins. Sprinkle each with a little caster sugar and tap out any excess. Place the ramekins on a baking sheet.

2 In a heavy saucepan over a very low heat, melt the chocolate and butter, stirring until smooth. Remove from the heat and cool slightly, then beat in the egg yolks and orange liqueur, if using. Set aside, stirring occasionally.

3 Preheat the oven to 220°C/ 425°F/Gas 7. In a clean, grease-free bowl, whisk the egg whites slowly until frothy. Add the cream of tartar, increase the spreed and whisk until they form soft peaks. Gradually sprinkle over the sugar, 15ml/1 tbsp at a time, whisking until the whites are stiff and glossy.

4 Stir a third of the whites into the cooled chocolate mixture to lighten it, then pour the chocolate mixture over the remaining whites. Using a rubber spatula or large metal spoon, gently fold the sauce into the whites. (Don't worry about a few white streaks.) Spoon into the prepared dishes.

5 To make the white chocolate sauce, put the chopped white chocolate and the cream into a small saucepan. Place over a low heat and cook, stirring constantly until melted and smooth. Remove from the heat and stir in the liqueur and orange rind, then pour into a serving jug and keep warm.

6 Bake the soufflés for 10– 12 minutes until risen and set, but still slightly wobbly in the centre. Dust with icing sugar and decorate with a sprig of redcurrants and a white chocolate rose. Serve the sauce separately.

Iced Gin and Damson Soufflés

For an unforgettable taste sensation, use sloe gin for these delicious individual frozen soufflés.

INGREDIENTS

Makes 6

500g/1¼lb damsons

250ml/8fl oz/1 cup water

275g/10oz/1¼ cups caster sugar

30ml/2 tbsp gin or sloe gin

4 large egg whites

300ml/½ pint/1¼ cups double
   cream, whipped

fresh mint leaves, to decorate

1 Wrap collars of greased non-stick baking paper around the outside of six ramekins, so that they extend 5cm/2in above the rim. Tie in place with string.

2 Slice two damsons and reserve. Put the rest in a pan with half the water and 50g/2oz/¼ cup of the caster sugar. Cover and simmer for about 7 minutes, until the damsons are tender. Sieve the pulp into a bowl to remove all the stones and skin, stir in the gin and set aside.

3 Combine the remaining sugar and water in the clean pan and heat gently until the sugar has dissolved. Bring to the boil and cook the syrup until it registers 119ºC/238ºF on a sugar ther-mometer, or until a small amount of the mixture dropped into a cup of cold water can be moulded into a soft ball.

4 Whisk the egg whites in a grease-free bowl until they form stiff peaks. Still whisking, slowly pour in the hot syrup until the meringue mixture is stiff and glossy. Fold in the whipped cream and fruit purée.

5 Spoon the mixture into the dishes to come 2.5cm/1in above the rim. Freeze until firm. Remove from the freezer 10 minutes before serving. Remove the collars, then decorate each with damson slices and mint leaves.

Chilled Coffee and Praline Soufflé

A smooth coffee soufflé with a crushed praline topping that is spectacular and easy.

INGREDIENTS

Serves 6

150g/5oz/¾ cup caster sugar

75ml/5 tbsp water

150g/5oz/generous 1 cup blanched almonds, plus extra, for decoration

120ml/4fl oz/½ cup strong brewed coffee

15ml/1 tbsp powdered gelatine

3 eggs, separated

75g/3oz/scant ½ cup soft light brown sugar

15ml/1 tbsp coffee liqueur, such as Tia Maria

150ml/¼ pint/⅔ cup double cream

about 150ml/¼ pint/⅔ cup double cream, for decoration (optional)

1 Make a collar of greased non-stick paper, 5cm/2in deeper than a 900ml/1½ pint/3¾ cup soufflé dish. Wrap around the dish and tie in place with string. Refrigerate.

2 Oil a baking sheet. Heat the caster sugar with the water in a heavy-based pan until dissolved. Boil rapidly until pale golden. Add the almonds and boil until golden.

3 Pour on to the baking sheet and leave to set hard. Break into pieces, reserving 50g/2oz/½ cup, transfer the remainder to a plastic bag and crush with a rolling pin.

4 Pour half the coffee into a bowl; sprinkle over the gelatine and soak for 5 minutes, then place the bowl over hot water and stir until completely dissolved.

5 Over a pan of simmering water whisk the egg yolks, light brown sugar, remaining coffee and liqueur, until thick, then whisk in the gelatine.

6 Whip the cream until thick, then whisk the egg whites until stiff. Fold the praline into the cream, then fold into the coffee mixture. Finally, fold in the egg whites, half at a time.

7 Spoon into the soufflé dish and smooth the top; chill for at least 2 hours. Put in the freezer for 15–20 minutes before serving. Remove the paper collar by running a warmed palette knife between the soufflé and the paper. Whisk the cream, if using, and place large spoonfuls on top. Decorate with the reserved praline pieces and blanched almonds.

Twice-baked Mocha Soufflé

The perfect way to end a meal, these mini mocha soufflés can be made up to 3 hours ahead, then reheated just before you serve them.

INGREDIENTS

Serves 6

75g/3oz/6 tbsp unsalted butter, softened

90g/3½ oz bittersweet or plain chocolate, grated

30ml/2 tbsp ground coffee

400ml/14fl oz/1⅔ cups milk

40g/1½oz/⅓ cup plain flour, sifted

15g/½ oz/2 tbsp cocoa, sifted

3 eggs, separated

50g/2oz/¼ cup caster sugar

175ml/6fl oz/¾ cup creamy chocolate or coffee liqueur, such as Crème de Caçao, Sheridans

1 Preheat the oven to 200°C/ 400°F/ Gas 6. Brush six 150ml/ ¼ pint/ ⅔ cup dariole moulds or pudding basins with 25g/1oz/2 tbsp of the butter. Coat with 50g/2oz of the grated chocolate.

2 Put the coffee in a small bowl. Heat the milk until almost boiling and pour over the coffee. Infuse for 4 minutes and strain.

3 Melt the remaining butter in a pan. Stir in the flour and cocoa to make a roux. Cook for 1 minute, then add the coffee milk, stirring all the time to make a thick sauce. Simmer for 2 minutes. Remove from the heat and stir in the yolks.

4 Cool for 5 minutes, then stir in the chocolate. Whisk the egg whites until stiff, then gradually whisk in the sugar. Stir half into the sauce, then fold in the remainder.

5 Spoon the mixture into the dariole moulds and place them in a roasting tin. Pour in hot water to come two-thirds of the way up the sides of the tin.

6 Bake the soufflés for 15 minutes. Turn them out on to a baking tray and leave to cool.

7 Before serving, spoon 15ml/ 1 tbsp chocolate or coffee liqueur over each pudding and reheat in the oven for 6–7 minutes. Serve the puddings on individual plates with the remaining liqueur poured over them.

Lemon Soufflé with Caramelized Almonds

This attractive and refreshing dessert soufflé is light and luscious, with a deliciously crunchy caramelized nut topping.

Serves 6

oil, for greasing

grated rind and juice of 3 large lemons

5 large eggs, separated

115g/4oz/½ cup caster sugar

25ml/1½ tbsp powdered gelatine

450ml/¾ pint/scant 2 cups
   double cream

For the decoration

75g/3oz/¾ cup flaked almonds

75g/3oz/¾ cup icing sugar

3 physalis (Cape gooseberries)

1 Make the soufflé collar. Cut a strip of non-stick baking paper to fit around a 900ml/1½ pint/ 3¾ cup soufflé dish and extending 7.5cm/3in above the rim. Fit the strip around the dish, tape, then tie it around the top of the dish with string. Brush the inside of the paper lightly with oil.

2 Put the lemon rind and egg yolks in a bowl. Add 75g/3oz/ 6 tbsp of the caster sugar and whisk until light and creamy.

3 Place the lemon juice in a bowl and sprinkle the gelatine over it. Soak for 5 minutes, then place the bowl over a pan of simmering water. Stir until the gelatine has dissolved. Cool, then stir the gelatine into the egg yolk mixture. In a separate bowl, lightly whip the cream to soft peaks. Fold into the egg yolk mixture and set aside.

4 Whisk the egg whites in a grease-free bowl until stiff. Gradually whisk in the caster sugar, then lightly fold the whites into the yolk mixture. Pour into the prepared dish, smooth the surface and chill for 4–5 hours.

5 Preheat the grill. Lightly oil a baking sheet and scatter the almonds and sifted icing sugar over it. Grill until the sugar has caramelized and the nuts are golden. Allow to cool, then remove from the tray and break into pieces.

6 Carefully peel the paper off the soufflé and decorate with the caramelized almonds and physalis.

Fruit Salads, Ices & Sorbets

✦ ✦ ✦

Frudités with Honey Dip

A colourful and tasty variation on the popular savoury crudités. Quick to prepare from ingredients to hand, it's ideal for impromptu entertaining.

INGREDIENTS

Serves 4

225g/8oz/1 cup Greek-style yogurt

45ml/3 tbsp clear honey

selection of fresh fruit for dipping such as apples, pears, tangerines, grapes, figs, cherries, strawberries and kiwi fruit

1 Place the yogurt in a dish, beat until smooth, then partially stir in the honey, leaving a little marbled effect.

2 Cut the various fruits into wedges or bite-sized pieces or leave whole.

3 Arrange the fruits on a platter with the bowl of dip in the centre. Serve chilled.

COOK'S TIP

Sprinkle the apple and pear wedges with lemon juice to prevent discolouring.

Watermelon, Ginger and Grapefruit Salad

This pretty, pink combination is very light and refreshing for any summer meal.

INGREDIENTS

Serves 4

500g/1lb/2 cups diced watermelon flesh

2 ruby or pink grapefruit

2 pieces stem ginger in syrup

30ml/2 tbsp stem ginger syrup

whipped cream, to serve

1 Remove any seeds from the watermelon and cut into bite-sized chunks.

2 Using a small sharp knife, cut away all the peel and white pith from the grapefruit and carefully lift out the segments, catching any juice in a bowl.

COOK'S TIP

Toss the fruits gently – grapefruit segments will break up easily and the appearance of the dish will be spoiled.

3 Finely chop the stem ginger and place in a serving bowl with the melon cubes and grapefruit segments, adding the reserved juice.

4 Spoon over the ginger syrup and toss the fruits lightly to give them an equal coating. Chill before serving with a bowl of whipped cream.

Fruits of the Forest with Chocolate Creams

Colourful berries make a fantastic accompaniment to a delightfully creamy white chocolate mousse.

Serves 4

75g/3oz white cooking chocolate, in squares
150ml/¼ pint/⅔ cup double cream
30ml/2 tbsp crème fraîche
1 egg, separated
5ml/1 tsp powdered gelatine
30ml/2 tbsp cold water
a few drops of pure vanilla essence
115g/4oz/1 cup small strawberries, sliced
75g/3oz/½ cup raspberries
75g/3oz/¾ cup blueberries
45ml/3 tbsp caster sugar
75ml/5 tbsp white coconut rum
strawberry leaves, to decorate (optional)

1 Melt the chocolate in a heatproof bowl set over a pan of hot water. Heat the cream in a separate pan until almost boiling, then stir into the chocolate with the crème fraîche. Cool slightly, then beat in the egg yolk.

2 Sprinkle the gelatine over the cold water in another heatproof bowl and set aside for a few minutes to swell.

3 Set the bowl in a pan of hot water until the gelatine has dissolved completely. Stir the dissolved gelatine into the chocolate mixture and add the vanilla essence. Set aside until starting to thicken and set.

4 Oil four dariole moulds or small soufflé dishes and line the base of each with non-stick baking paper.

5 In a grease-free bowl, whisk the egg white to soft peaks, then fold into the chocolate mixture.

6 Spoon the mixture into the prepared moulds or soufflé dishes, then level the surface of each and chill for 2–3 hours or until firm.

7 Meanwhile, place the fruits in a bowl. Add the caster sugar and coconut rum and stir gently to mix. Cover and chill until required.

8 Ease the chocolate cream away from the rims of the moulds or dishes and turn out on to dessert plates. Spoon the fruits around the outside. Decorate with the strawberry leaves, if you like, then serve immediately.

Fruit Salad with Passion Fruit Dressing

Passion fruit juice makes a superb dressing for any fruit, but really brings out the flavour of exotic varieties in particular.

INGREDIENTS

Serves 6

1 mango

1 papaya

2 kiwi fruit

coconut or vanilla ice cream,
  to serve

For the dressing

3 passion fruit

thinly pared rind and juice of 1 lime

5ml/1 tsp hazelnut or walnut oil

15ml/1 tbsp clear honey

1 Peel the mango, cut it into three slices, then cut the flesh into chunks and place it in a large bowl. Peel the papaya and cut it in half. Scoop out the seeds, then chop the flesh.

2 Cut both ends off each kiwi fruit, then stand them on a board. Using a small sharp knife, cut off the skin from top to bottom. Cut each kiwi fruit in half lengthways, then cut into thick slices. Combine all the fruit in a large bowl.

3 Cut each passion fruit in half and scoop the seeds into a sieve, over a bowl. Press well to extract all the juices. Lightly whisk the remaining dressing ingredients into the juice, then pour over the fruit. Mix gently and chill for 1 hour before serving with coconut or vanilla ice cream.

Iced Pear Terrine with Chocolate Sauce

This terrine, based on a classic French dessert, makes a refreshing and impressive end to any meal.

INGREDIENTS

Serves 8

1.5kg/3–3½lb ripe Williams pears
juice of 1 lemon
115g/4oz/½ cup caster sugar
10 whole cloves
90ml/6 tbsp water
julienne strips of orange rind, to decorate

For the sauce
200g/7oz plain chocolate
60ml/4 tbsp hot strong black coffee
200ml/7fl oz/scant 1 cup double cream
30ml/2 tbsp Calvados or brandy

1 Peel, core and slice the pears. Put in a pan with the lemon juice, sugar, cloves and water. Cover and simmer for 10 minutes. Remove the cloves and cool.

2 Process the pears and juice in a processor or blender until smooth. Pour into a freezerproof bowl, cover and freeze until firm.

3 Meanwhile, line a 900g/2lb loaf tin with clear film, allowing plenty of overlap. Spoon the frozen pear purée into a food processor or blender. Process until smooth. Pour into the prepared tin, cover and freeze until firm.

4 Break the chocolate into a large heatproof bowl and place over a saucepan of hot water. When the chocolate has melted, stir in the coffee until smooth. Gradually stir in the cream and then the Calvados or brandy. Set the sauce aside.

5 20 minutes before serving, remove the tin from the freezer. Invert the terrine on to a plate, lift off the clear film and place in the fridge to soften slightly. To serve, warm the sauce over hot water. Place a slice of terrine on each dessert plate and spoon over some sauce. Decorate with julienne strips of orange rind.

Chocolate Sorbet with Red Fruits

The chill that thrills – that's chocolate sorbet. For a really fine texture, it helps to have an ice cream maker, which churns the mixture as it freezes, but you can make it by hand quite easily.

INGREDIENTS

Serves 6

475ml/16fl oz/2 cups water
45ml/3 tbsp clear honey
115g/4oz/½ cup caster sugar
75g/3oz/¾ cup cocoa powder
50g/2oz plain dark chocolate, broken into squares
400g/14oz soft fruits, such as raspberries, redcurrants or strawberries

1 Place the water, honey, sugar and cocoa in a saucepan. Heat gently, stirring occasionally, until the sugar has completely dissolved.

2 Remove from the heat, add the chocolate and stir until melted. Leave to cool.

3 Tip into an ice cream maker and churn until frozen. Alternatively, pour into a freezer-proof container, freeze until slushy, whisk until smooth, then freeze again. Whisk for a second time before the mixture hardens.

4 Remove from the freezer 10–15 minutes before serving, so that the sorbet softens slightly. Serve in scoops, with a mixture of berries, or with just one variety.

COOK'S TIP

This sorbet looks attractive if served in small oval scoops – simply scoop out the sorbet with one tablespoon, then use another to smooth it off and transfer it to the plate.

Lemon Sorbet

This is probably the most classic sorbet of all. It is refreshingly tangy and yet deliciously smooth.

INGREDIENTS

Serves 6

200g/7oz/1 cup caster sugar

300ml/¹/₂ pint/1¹/₄ cups water

4 lemons, well scrubbed

1 egg white

sugared lemon rind to decorate

1 Put the sugar and water into a saucepan and bring to the boil, stirring occasionally, until the sugar has just dissolved.

2 Using a swivel vegetable peeler, pare the rind thinly from two of the lemons so that it falls straight into the pan. Simmer for 2 minutes without stirring, then take the pan off the heat, leave to cool, then chill.

COOK'S TIP

Cut one third off the top of the lemon and retain as a lid. Squeeze the juice out of the larger portion. Remove any membrane and use the shell as a ready-made container. Scoop or pipe sorbet into the shell, top with the lid and add lemon leaves or small bay leaves.

3 Squeeze the juice from the lemons and add to the syrup. Strain the syrup and lemon juice and churn in an ice cream maker until thick. Alternatively, freeze and whisk as in the previous recipe.

4 In a small bowl, whisk the egg white lightly with a fork.

5 Using an ice cream maker, add the egg white to the mixture and continue to churn for 10–15 minutes until firm enough to scoop.

6 Scoop into bowls or glasses and decorate with sugared lemon rind to serve.

Mango Sorbet

A light and refreshing dessert that's surprisingly easy to make.

INGREDIENTS

Serves 6
150g/5oz/¾ cup caster sugar
a large strip of orange rind
1 large mango, peeled, stoned and cubed
60ml/4 tbsp orange juice
mint sprigs, to decorate

1 Combine the sugar, orange rind and 175ml/6fl oz/¾ cup of water in a saucepan. Bring to the boil, stirring to dissolve the sugar. Leave the syrup to cool.

2 Purée the mango cubes with the orange juice in a blender or food processor. There should be about 475ml/16fl oz/2 cups of purée.

3 Add the purée to the cooled sugar syrup and mix well. Strain, then chill.

4 When cold, tip into a freezer container and freeze until firm around the edges.

5 Spoon the semi-frozen mixture into the food processor and process until smooth. Return to the freezer and freeze until solid. Allow the sorbet to soften slightly at room temperature for 15–20 minutes before serving, decorated with mint sprigs.

VARIATIONS

For Banana Sorbet: peel and cube 4–5 large bananas. Purée with 30ml/2 tbsp lemon juice to make 475ml/16fl oz/2 cups. If liked, replace the orange rind in the sugar syrup with 2–3 whole cloves, or omit the rind.

For Paw Paw Sorbet: peel, seed and cube 675g/1½lb paw paw. Purée with 45ml/3 tbsp lime juice to make 475ml/16fl oz/2 cups. Replace the orange rind with lime rind.

For Passion Fruit Sorbet: halve 16 or more passion fruit and scoop out the seeds and pulp (there should be about 475ml/16fl oz/2 cups). Work in a blender or food processor until the seeds are like coarse pepper. Omit the orange juice and rind. Add the passion fruit to the sugar syrup, then press through a wire sieve before freezing.

Lime Sherbet

This light, refreshing sherbet is a good dessert to serve after a substantial main course.

Serves 4

250g/9oz/1¼ cups granulated sugar
grated rind of 1 lime
175ml/6fl oz/¾ cup freshly squeezed
    lime juice
15–30ml/1–2 tbsp fresh lemon juice
icing sugar, to taste
slivers of lime rind, to decorate

1 In a small heavy saucepan, dissolve the granulated sugar in 600ml/1 pint/2½ cups of water, without stirring, over medium heat. When the sugar has dissolved, boil for 5-6 minutes. Remove from the heat and let cool.

2 Combine the cooled sugar syrup and lime rind and juice in a measuring jug or bowl. Stir well. Taste and adjust the flavour by adding lemon juice or some icing sugar, if necessary. Do not over-sweeten.

3 Freeze the mixture in an ice cream maker, following the manufacturer's instructions.

4 If you do not have an ice cream maker, pour the mixture into a metal or plastic freezer container and freeze until softly set, for about 3 hours.

5 Remove from the container and chop roughly into 7.5cm/3in pieces. Place in a food processor and process until smooth. Return the mixture to the freezer container and freeze again until set. Repeat this freezing and chopping process two or three times, until a smooth consistency is obtained.

6 Serve in scoops decorated with slivers of lime rind.

COOK'S TIP

If using an ice cream maker for these sherbets, check the manufacturer's instructions to find out the freezing capacity. If necessary, halve the recipe quantities.

Ruby Orange Sherbet in Ginger Baskets

This superb frozen dessert is perfect for people without ice cream makers who can't be bothered with the freezing and stirring that home-made ices normally require. It is also ideal for serving at a special dinner party as both the sherbet and ginger baskets can be made in advance, leaving you to simply assemble the dessert between courses.

INGREDIENTS

Serves 6

grated rind and juice of 2 blood oranges

175g/6oz/1½ cups icing sugar

300ml/½ pint/1¼ cups double cream

200g/7oz/scant 1 cup Greek-style
    natural yogurt

blood orange segments, to
    decorate (optional)

For the ginger baskets

25g/1oz/2 tbsp unsalted butter

15ml/1 tbsp golden syrup

30ml/2 tbsp caster sugar

1.5ml/¼ tsp ground ginger

15ml/1 tbsp finely chopped mixed
    citrus peel

15ml/1 tbsp plain flour

1 Place the orange rind and juice in a bowl. Sift the icing sugar over the top and set aside for 30 minutes, then stir until smooth.

2 Whisk the double cream in a large bowl until the mixture forms soft peaks, then carefully fold in the yogurt.

3 Gently stir in the orange juice, then pour into a freezerproof container. Cover, freeze until firm.

4 Make the baskets. Preheat the oven to 180ºC/350ºF/Gas 4. Place the butter, syrup and sugar in a heavy-based saucepan and heat gently until melted.

5 Add the ground ginger, mixed citrus peel and flour and stir until the mixture is smooth.

COOK'S TIP

It is essential to have the greased tins or cups ready and to work quickly. If the biscuits firm up before you have made them all, a few seconds in the oven will soften them.

6 Lightly grease two baking sheets. Drop three portions of the ginger dough on to each baking sheet, using about 10ml/2 tsp of the mixture at a time; space well apart. Spread each one to a 5cm/2in circle, then bake for 12–14 minutes until dark golden.

7 Remove the biscuits from the oven and allow to stand on the baking sheets for 1 minute to firm slightly. Lift off with a fish slice and drape over six greased mini pudding tins or upturned cups; flatten the top (which will become the base) and flute the edges to form a basket shape.

8 When cool, lift the baskets off the tins or cups and place on individual dessert plates. Arrange scoops of the frozen sherbet in each basket. Decorate each portion with a few orange segments, if you like.

Apple and Cider Water Ice

This very English combination has a subtle apple flavour with just a hint of cider. As the apple purée is very pale, almost white, add a few drops of green food colouring to echo the pale green skin of the Granny Smith apples.

INGREDIENTS

Serves 6

500g/1¼lb Granny Smith apples
150g/5oz/¾ cup caster sugar
300ml/½ pint/1¼ cups water
250ml/8fl oz/1 cup strong dry cider
few drops of green food colouring
   (optional)
strips of thinly pared lime rind,
   to decorate

1 Quarter, core and roughly chop the apples. Put them into a saucepan. Add the caster sugar and half the water. Cover and simmer for 10 minutes or until the apples are soft.

COOK'S TIP

Add the food colouring gradually, making the mixture a little darker than you would like the finished sorbet to be as freezing lightens the colour slightly.

2 Press the mixture through a sieve placed over a bowl. Discard the apple skins and seeds. Stir the cider and the remaining water into the apple purée and add a little colouring, if you like.

3 If making by hand, pour the mixture into a shallow plastic container and freeze for 6 hours, beating with a fork once or twice to break up the ice crystals. If you have an ice cream maker, churn the mixture until it is firm enough to scoop.

4 Scoop into the water ice into dishes and decorate with twists of thinly pared lime rind.

Gooseberry and Clotted Cream Ice Cream

The delicious, slightly tart flavour of gooseberries goes particularly well with melt-in-the-mouth meringues.

Serves 4–6

500g/1¼lb/4 cups gooseberries, topped and tailed

60ml/4 tbsp water

75g/3oz/6 tbsp caster sugar

150ml/¼ pint/⅔ cup whipping cream

a few drops of green food colouring (optional)

120ml/4fl oz/½ cup clotted cream

fresh mint sprigs, to decorate

meringues, to serve

1 Put the gooseberries in a saucepan and add the water and sugar. Cover and simmer for 10 minutes or until soft.

2 Tip into a food processor or blender and process to a smooth purée. Press through a sieve placed over a bowl. Cool, then chill.

3 Chill the purée in a plastic tub or similar container. Whip the cream until it is thick but still falls from a spoon. Fold into the purée with the green food colouring, if using. Freeze for 2 hours, then beat with a fork, electric mixer or in a food processor, to break up. Return to the freezer for 2 hours.

4 If making by hand, beat the ice cream again, then fold in the clotted cream. Freeze for 2–3 hours. If using an ice cream maker, mix the chilled purée with the whipping cream, add a few drops of green food colouring, if using, and churn until thickened and semi-frozen. Add the clotted cream and continue to churn until thick enough to scoop.

5 To serve, scoop the ice cream into dishes or small plates, decorate with fresh mint sprigs and add a few small meringues to each serving.

Banana and Toffee Ice Cream

The addition of sweetened condensed milk helps to bring out the natural flavour of the bananas and, surprisingly, the ice cream is not excessively sweet.

Serves 4–6

3 ripe bananas

juice of 1 lemon

370g/12½oz can sweetened condensed milk

150ml/¼ pint/⅔ cup whipping cream

150g/5oz toffees

chopped toffees, to decorate

1 Process the bananas to a purée in a food processor or blender, then add the lemon juice and process briefly to mix. Scrape the purée into a plastic tub or similar freezerproof container.

2 Pour in the condensed milk, stirring with a metal spoon, then add the cream. Mix well, cover and freeze for 4 hours or until mushy.

3 Unwrap the toffees and chop them finely, using a sharp knife. If this proves difficult, put them in a double plastic bag and hit them with a rolling pin.

4 Beat the semi-frozen ice cream with a fork or electric mixer to break up the ice crystals, then stir in the toffees. Return the ice cream to the freezer for 3–5 hours or until firm. Scoop on to a plate or into a bowl and decorate with chopped toffees. Serve at once.

COOK'S TIP

To reduce the initial freezing time, start chilling the mixture in a stainless steel roasting tin, transferring to a plastic tub only after adding the toffees. If you are making this ice cream for small children, you may prefer to leave the toffees out or use chopped chocolate instead.

Strawberry Semi-freddo

Serve this quick strawberry and ricotta dessert semi-frozen to enjoy the flavour at its best.

Serves 4–6

250g/9oz/generous 2 cups strawberries
115g/4oz/scant ½ cup strawberry jam
250g/9oz/generous 1 cup ricotta
   cheese
200g/7oz/scant 1 cup Greek yogurt
5ml/1 tsp natural vanilla essence
40g/1½oz/3 tbsp caster sugar
extra strawberries and mint or lemon
   balm, to decorate

1 Put the strawberries in a bowl and mash them with a fork until broken into small pieces but not completely puréed. Stir in the strawberry jam. Drain off any whey from the ricotta.

2 Tip the ricotta into a bowl and stir in the Greek yogurt, natural vanilla essence and sugar. Using a dessertspoon, gently fold the mashed strawberries into the ricotta mixture until rippled.

3 Spoon into individual freezerproof dishes and freeze for at least 2 hours until almost solid. Alternatively, freeze until completely solid, then transfer the ice cream to the fridge for about 45 minutes to soften before serving. Serve in small bowls with extra strawberries and decorated with mint or lemon balm.

COOK'S TIP
~
Don't mash the strawberries too much or they'll become too liquid. Freeze in a large freezer container if you don't have suitable small dishes. Transfer to the fridge to thaw slightly, then scoop into glasses.

Mango and Passion Fruit Gelato

Fresh and fruity, this tropical ice cream has a delicate perfume. Passion fruit tend to vary in size. If you can locate the large ones, four will be plenty for this dish.

INGREDIENTS

Serves 4

4 large mangoes

grated rind and juice of 1 lime

50g/2oz/¼ cup caster sugar

**300ml/½ pint/1¼ cups whipping
    cream**

4–6 passion fruit

1 Cut a thick slice from either side of the stone on each unpeeled mango. Make criss-cross cuts in the flesh, cutting down as far as the skin.

2 Turn the slices inside out so that the pieces of mango stand proud of the skin, then scoop them into a food processor or blender.

3 Process the mango flesh until smooth, then add the grated lime rind, lime juice and caster sugar and process briefly.

4 If making by hand, whip the cream until it is just thick but will still fall from a spoon. Fold in the puréed mango and lime mixture, then pour into a plastic tub or similar freezerproof container. Freeze for 4 hours until semi-frozen. If using an ice cream maker, churn the fruit mixture for 10–15 minutes, then add the cream and continue to churn until the mixture is thick but still too soft to scoop. Scrape it into a plastic tub.

5 Cut the passion fruit in half and scoop the seeds and pulp into the ice cream mixture, mix well and freeze for 2 hours until firm enough to scoop.

Fresh Strawberry Ice Cream

You can make the ice cream by hand if you freeze it for several hours, whisking it every hour or so, but the texture won't be as good.

INGREDIENTS

Serves 6

300ml/½ pint/1¼ cups creamy milk

1 vanilla pod

3 large egg yolks

225g/8oz/1½–2 cups strawberries

juice of ½ lemon

75g/3oz/¾ cup icing sugar

300ml/½ pint/1¼ cups double cream

sliced strawberries, to serve

3 Meanwhile, purée the strawberries with the lemon juice in a food processor or blender. Press the strawberry purée through a sieve into a bowl. Stir in the icing sugar and set aside. In a separate bowl whip the cream until it forms soft peaks.

4 Gently fold the cream into the custard with the strawberry purée. Pour the mixture into an ice cream maker. Churn for 20–30 minutes, or until the mixture holds its shape. Transfer the ice cream to a freezerproof container, cover and freeze until firm. Soften briefly before serving decorated with sliced strawberries.

1 Put the milk and vanilla pod into a pan and slowly bring to the boil. Remove from the heat and leave for 20 minutes. Strain the warm milk into a bowl containing the egg yolks and whisk well.

2 Return the mixture to a clean pan and heat, stirring constantly, until the custard just coats the back of the spoon. Pour into a clean bowl, cover with clear film and set aside to cool.

Chocolate Ice Cream

Use good quality plain or cooking chocolate for the best flavour.

Makes about 850ml/1½ pints/3¾ cups

750ml/1¼ pints/3 cups milk

10cm/4in piece of vanilla pod

4 egg yolks

225g/8oz cooking chocolate, melted

150g/5oz/¾ cup granulated sugar

1 To make the custard, heat the milk with the vanilla pod in a small saucepan. Remove from the heat as soon as small bubbles start to form. Do not boil.

2 Beat the egg yolks with a wire whisk or electric beater. Gradually incorporate the sugar, and continue beating for about 5 minutes until the mixture is pale yellow. Strain the milk. Slowly add it to the egg mixture drop by drop.

3 Pour the mixture into a double boiler with the melted chocolate. Stir over moderate heat until the water in the pan is boiling, and the custard thickens enough to lightly coat the back of a spoon. Remove from the heat and allow to cool.

4 Freeze in an ice cream maker, or if you do not have an ice cream maker, pour the mixture into a metal or plastic freezer container and freeze until set, about 3 hours. Remove from the container and chop roughly into 7.5cm/3in pieces. Place in the bowl of a food processor and process until smooth. Return to the freezer container, and freeze again until firm. Repeat the freezing-chopping process 2 or 3 times, until a smooth consistency is reached.

Buttermilk Vanilla Ice Cream

Enriched with just a little double cream, this unusual ice cream tastes far more luxurious than it really is.

INGREDIENTS

Serves 6

250ml/8fl oz/1 cup buttermilk

60ml/4 tbsp double cream

1 vanilla pod or 2.5ml/½ tsp vanilla
   essence

2 eggs

30ml/2 tbsp clear honey

fresh fruit purée, to serve

1 Place the buttermilk and cream in a pan with the vanilla pod, if using, and heat gently over a low heat until the mixture is almost boiling. Remove the vanilla pod.

2 Place the eggs in a bowl over a pan of hot water and whisk until they are pale and thick. Add the heated buttermilk in a thin stream, while whisking hard. Continue whisking over the hot water until the mixture has thickened slightly.

COOK'S TIP
❧

This basic vanilla ice cream can be used as a base for other flavours: stir in puréed fruit, citrus ring or coffee.

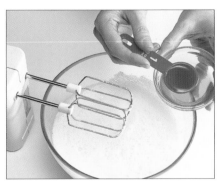

3 Whisk in the honey and vanilla essence, if using. Spoon the mixture into a freezer-proof container and freeze until firm.

4 Spoon the firm ice cream on to a sheet of non-stick baking paper. Roll it up in the paper to form a cylinder and freeze again until firm. Serve the ice cream on plates in slices.

Frozen Strawberry Mousse Cake

Children love this pretty dessert – it tastes just like an ice cream.

INGREDIENTS

Serves 4–6

425g/15oz can strawberries in syrup

15ml/1 tbsp/1 sachet powdered gelatine

6 trifle sponge cakes

45ml/3 tbsp strawberry jam

200ml/7fl oz/⅞ cup crème fraîche

200ml/7fl oz/⅞ cup whipped cream, to decorate

1 Strain the syrup from the strawberries into a large heatproof bowl. Sprinkle over the gelatine and stir well. Stand the bowl in a pan of hot water and stir until the gelatine has dissolved.

2 Leave to cool, then chill for just under 1 hour, until beginning to set. Meanwhile, cut the sponge cakes in half lengthways and spread the cut surfaces with the strawberry jam.

3 Carefully whisk the crème fraîche into the strawberry jelly, then whisk in the canned strawberries. Line a deep, 20cm/8in loose-based cake tin with non-stick baking paper.

4 Pour half the strawberry mousse mixture into the tin, arrange the sponge cakes over the surface, and then spoon over the remaining mousse mixture, pushing down any sponge cakes which rise up.

5 Freeze for 1–2 hours until firm. Remove the cake from the tin and carefully peel away the lining paper. Transfer to a serving plate. Decorate the mousse with whirls of whipped cream and a few strawberry leaves and a fresh strawberry, if you have them.

Hazelnut Ice Cream

*This popular flavour goes very well
served with scoops of chocolate and
vanilla ice creams.*

INGREDIENTS

Serves 4–6

75g/3oz/½ cup hazelnuts

75g/3oz/6 tbsp granulated sugar

475ml/16fl oz/2 cups milk

10cm/4in piece of vanilla pod

4 egg yolks

1 Spread the hazelnuts on a
baking tray and place under a
grill for about 5 minutes, shaking
the pan frequently to turn the nuts
over. Remove from the heat and
allow to cool slightly. Place the
nuts on a clean dish towel, and rub
them with a cloth to remove their
dark outer skin. Chop very finely
or grind in a food processor with
30ml/2 tbsp of the sugar.

2 Make the custard. Heat the
milk with the vanilla pod in a
small saucepan. Remove from the
heat as soon as small bubbles start
to form on the surface.

3 Beat the egg yolks with a wire
whisk or an electric beater.
Gradually add the remaining sugar
and continue beating until the
mixture turns a pale yellow.
Discard the vanilla pod and,
stirring constantly, very gradually
add the milk, pouring it through
a strainer.

4 Pour the mixture into a double
boiler, or into a bowl placed
over a pan of simmering water.
Add the chopped nuts. Stir over a
moderate heat until the water in
the pan is boiling, and the custard
thickens enough to lightly coat the
back of a spoon. Remove from the
heat and allow to cool.

5 Freeze in an ice cream maker,
or transfer the mixture to a
freezerproof container and freeze
for 5–6 hours. During the freezing
time beat twice with a fork, electric
whisk or in a food processor until
a smooth consistency has been
reached. Serve in scoops.

Coffee Ice Cream with Caramelized Pecans

Coffee and sweetened nuts make a mouth-watering combination.

INGREDIENTS

Serves 4–6

For the ice cream

300ml/10fl oz/1¼ cups milk

1 tbsp demerara sugar

25g/1oz/6 tbsp finely ground coffee or
    1 tbsp instant coffee granules

1 egg plus 2 yolks

300ml/10fl oz/1¼ cups double cream

1 tbsp caster sugar

For the pecans

115g/4oz/1 cup pecan halves

50g/2oz/4 tbsp soft dark brown sugar

1 Heat the milk and demerara sugar in a small pan to boiling point. Remove from the heat and sprinkle on the coffee. Leave to stand for 2 minutes, then stir, cover and allow to cool.

2 In a heatproof bowl, beat the egg and extra yolks until the mixture is thick and pale.

COOK'S TIP

You can give good-quality bought ice cream a fillip with the same nutty garnish.

3 Strain the coffee mixture into a clean pan, heat to boiling point, then pour on to the eggs in a steady stream, beating hard.

4 Set the bowl over a pan of gently simmering water and stir until it thickens. Cool, then chill in the fridge.

5 Whip the cream with the caster sugar. Fold it into the coffee custard and freeze in a covered container. Beat twice at hourly intervals, then leave to freeze firm.

6 To caramelize the nuts, preheat the oven to 180°C/350°F/Gas 4. Spread the nuts on a baking sheet in a single layer. Put them into the oven for 10–15 minutes to toast until they release their fragrance.

7 On the top of the stove, dissolve the brown sugar in 2 tbsp water in a heavy-based pan, shaking it about over a low heat until the sugar dissolves completely and the syrup clears.

8 When the syrup begins to bubble, tip in the toasted pecans and cook for a minute or two over a medium heat until the syrup coats and clings to the nuts.

9 Spread the nuts on a lightly oiled baking sheet, separating them with the tip of a knife, and leave to cool. Store when cold in an airtight tin if they are not to be eaten on the same day.

10 Transfer the ice cream from the freezer to the fridge 30 minutes before scooping it into portions and serving with caramelized pecans.

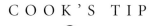

Brown Bread Ice Cream

Delicious on its own and irresistible served with this blackcurrant coulis, brown bread ice cream is a classic that has never lost its popularity.

INGREDIENTS

Serves 6

50g/2oz/½ cup roasted and chopped
    hazelnuts, ground
75g/3oz/1¼ cups wholemeal
    breadcrumbs
4 tbsp soft brown sugar
3 egg whites
115g/4oz/½ cup caster sugar
300ml/½ pint/1¼ cups double cream
few drops of vanilla extract

For the sauce

225g/8oz/2 cups blackcurrants
75g/3oz/6 tbsp caster sugar
15ml/1 tbsp creme de cassis
fresh mint to decorate

1 Combine the hazelnuts and breadcrumbs on a baking sheet, then sprinkle over the raw sugar. Place under a medium grill and toast, stirring, until the mixture is crisp and evenly browned. Leave to cool.

2 Whisk the egg whites in a bowl until stiff, then gradually whisk in the caster sugar until thick and glossy. Whip the cream until it forms soft peaks and fold into the meringue with the breadcrumb mixture and vanilla extract.

3 Spoon the mixture into a 1.25 litre/2 pint/5 cup loaf tin. Smooth the top level, then cover and freeze for several hours or until firm.

4 Meanwhile, make the sauce. Strip the blackcurrants from their stalks using a fork and put them in a small bowl with the sugar. Toss gently to mix and leave for 30 minutes.

5 Purée the blackcurrants in a blender or food processor, then press through a nylon sieve until smooth. Add the crème de cassis and chill well.

6 To serve, turn out the ice cream on to a plate and cut into slices. Arrange each slice on a serving plate, spoon over a little sauce and decorate with fresh mint sprigs.

Indian Ice Cream (Kulfi)

Kulfi-wallahs (ice cream vendors) have always made kulfi, and continue to this day, without using modern freezers. Try this method – it works extremely well in an ordinary freezer. You will need to start making kulfi the day before you want to serve it.

INGREDIENTS

Serves 4–6

3 x 400ml/14fl oz cans evaporated milk

3 egg whites, whisked until peaks form

350g/12oz/3 cups icing sugar

5ml/1 tsp cardamom powder

15ml/1 tbsp rose water

175g/6oz/1½ cups pistachios, chopped

75g/3oz/generous ½ cup sultanas

75g/3oz/¾ cup sliced almonds

25g/1oz/2 tbsp glacé cherries, halved

1 Remove the labels from the cans of evaporated milk and lay the cans down in a pan with a tight-fitting cover. Fill the pan with water to reach three-quarters up the cans. Bring to the boil, cover and simmer for 20 minutes. When cool, remove and chill the cans in the fridge for 24 hours.

2 Open the cans and empty the milk into a large, chilled bowl. Whisk until it doubles in quantity, then fold in the whisked egg whites and icing sugar.

3 Gently fold in the remaining ingredients, seal the bowl with cling film and leave in the freezer for 1 hour.

4 Remove the ice cream from the freezer and mix well with a fork. Transfer to a freezer container and return to the freezer for a final setting. Remove from the freezer 10 minutes before serving in scoops.

Turkish Delight Ice Cream

Not strictly a traditional Middle Eastern recipe, but a delicious way of using Turkish Delight. Scatter with rose petals, if you have them.

Serves 6

4 egg yolks
115g/4oz/½ cup caster sugar
300ml/½ pint/1¼ cups milk
300ml/½ pint/1¼ cups double cream
15ml/1 tbsp rose water
175g/6oz rose flavoured Turkish
  Delight, chopped

1 Beat the egg yolks and sugar together until pale and thick. In a pan, bring the milk to the boil. Add to the yolks and sugar, stirring, then return to the pan.

2 Continue stirring over a low heat until the custard is thick enough to coat the back of a spoon. Do not boil, or it will curdle. Leave to cool, then stir in the cream and rose water.

3 Put the Turkish Delight in a pan with 30–45ml/2–3tbsp water. Heat gently, until almost melted, but with just a few small lumps. Remove from the heat and stir into the cool custard mixture.

4 Leave the mixture to cool completely, then pour into a shallow freezer container. Freeze for 3 hours until just frozen all over. Transfer the mixture into a mixing bowl.

5 Using a whisk, beat the mixture until smooth, return to the freezer container and freeze for 2 hours more. Repeat the beating process, then return to the freezer for about 3 hours, or until firm. Remove the ice cream from the freezer 20–25 minutes before serving. Serve with thin almond biscuits or meringues.

Pineapple Ice Cream

Tropically flavoured, this ice cream can be made at any time of the year, but it is particularly good when made with fresh pineapple.

INGREDIENTS

Serves 8–10

8 eggs, separated

115g/4oz/½ cup caster sugar

2.5ml/½ tsp vanilla essence

600ml/1 pint/2½ cups whipping cream

60ml/4 tbsp icing sugar

425g/15oz can pineapple chunks

75g/3oz/¼ cup pistachio nuts, chopped

wafer biscuits to serve

1 Place the egg yolks in a bowl, add the caster sugar and vanilla essence and beat until thick and pale yellow.

2 In a separate bowl, whip the cream and icing sugar to soft peaks. Add to the egg yolk mixture.

3 Whisk the egg whites in a separate large bowl until they are firm and hold stiff peaks. Gently fold the egg whites into the cream mixture and blend well.

COOK'S TIP
~

Use a small fresh pineapple when available. Remove the rough skin and core, then chop into chunks.

4 Cut the pineapple into very small pieces, add the pistachio nuts and stir into the cream mixture, mixing well with a spoon.

5 Pour the mixture into an ice cream container and place in the freezer for a few hours until it is set and firm, stirring it once or twice during the freezing time.

6 Cut into thick slices and serve in a pretty glass dish decorated with wafer biscuits.

Coconut Ice Cream

An easy-to-make ice cream that is quite heavenly and will be loved by all for its fresh tropical taste.

INGREDIENTS

Serves 8

400g/14oz can evaporated milk

400g/14oz can condensed milk

400g/14oz can coconut milk

freshly grated nutmeg

5ml/1 tsp almond essence

lemon balm sprigs, lime slices and
    shredded coconut, to decorate

1 Mix together the evaporated, condensed and coconut milks in a freezerproof bowl and stir in the nutmeg and almond essence.

2 Put in the freezer and chill for an hour or two until the mixture is semi-frozen.

3 Remove from the freezer and whisk the mixture with a hand or electric whisk until it is fluffy and almost doubled in volume.

4 Pour into a freezer container, then cover and freeze until firm. Before serving, allow the ice cream to soften slightly at room temperature. Decorate with a sprig of lemon balm, lime slices and shredded coconut.

Cinnamon and Coffee Swirl Ice Cream

Light ice cream subtly spiced with cinnamon and rippled with a sweet coffee syrup.

INGREDIENTS

Serves 6

300ml/½ pint/1¼ cups single cream
1 cinnamon stick
4 egg yolks
150g/5oz/¾ cup caster sugar
300ml/½ pint/1¼ cups double cream

For the coffee syrup
45ml/3 tbsp ground coffee
45ml/3 tbsp near-boiling water
90g/3½oz/½ cup caster sugar
50ml/2fl oz/¼ cup water

1 Slowly bring to the boil the cream and cinnamon stick. Turn off the heat, cover and infuse for 30 minutes. Bring back to the boil and remove the cinnamon.

2 Whisk the yolks and sugar until light. Pour the hot cream over the egg mixture, whisking. Return to the pan and stir over low heat for 1–2 minutes, until it thickens. Allow the mixture to cool.

3 Whip the double cream until peaks form and fold into the custard. Pour into a container and freeze for 3 hours.

4 Meanwhile, put the coffee in a bowl and pour the hot water over. Leave to infuse for 4 minutes, then strain through a sieve. Discard the coffee grounds.

5 Gently heat the sugar and cold water in a pan until completely dissolved. Bring to the boil and gently simmer for 5 minutes. Cool, then stir in the coffee.

6 Turn the ice cream into a chilled bowl and briefly whisk to break down the ice crystals.

7 Spoon a third back into the container and drizzle over some coffee syrup. Repeat until it is all used.

8 Drag a skewer through the mixture a few times to achieve a marbled effect. Freeze for 4 hours, or until solid. Allow to soften slightly before serving.

Mint Ice Cream

This ice cream is best served slightly softened at room temperature, so take it out of the freezer 20 minutes before you want to serve it. For a special occasion, this looks spectacular served in an ice bowl.

INGREDIENTS

Serves 8

8 egg yolks

75g/3oz/6 tbsp caster sugar

600ml/1 pint/2½ cups single cream

1 vanilla pod

60ml/4 tbsp chopped fresh mint

2 Pour the cream into a separate saucepan and add the vanilla pod. On a medium heat gently bring the cream just to the boil.

5 Gently heat the mixture until the custard thickens enough to coat the back of a wooden spoon. Leave to cool.

1 Place the egg yolks and sugar in a bowl and beat, using a hand-held electric beater or a balloon whisk, until it is pale and slightly thick. Transfer the mixture to a saucepan.

3 Remove the vanilla pod and pour the hot cream on to the egg mixture, whisking briskly.

4 Continue whisking to ensure the eggs are thoroughly mixed into the cream.

6 Stir in the mint and place in an ice cream maker to churn and freeze (about 3–4 hours). If you don't have an ice cream maker, freeze the ice cream until mushy and then whisk it well again, to break down the ice crystals. Freeze for another 3 hours until it is softly frozen and whisk again. Finally, freeze the ice cream until hard, preferably overnight.

COOK'S TIP

To make an ice bowl, place a few ice cubes in the bottom of a freezerproof bowl, adding a few sprigs of the herb for decoration. Place a smaller bowl inside, to give a gap of 1cm/½ in, level and secure with tape. Fill the gap with cooled boiled water and freeze until solid. To unmould, pour a little hot water into the inner bowl, then dip briefly in hot water to release the ice bowl.

VARIATION

For an equally refreshing alternative use lemon balm, borage or rose geranium instead of mint. Gather enough sprigs of the chosen herb to make 4 tbsp of chopped herb and use in the recipe in exactly the same way.

Rocky Road Ice Cream

For chills and thrills, there's nothing to beat this classic sweet ice cream. A perennial favourite, packed with flavour and contrasting textures.

INGREDIENTS

Serves 6

115g/4oz plain chocolate broken
    into squares
150ml/¼ pint/⅔ cup milk
300ml/½ pint/1¼ cups double cream
115g/4oz/½ cup marshmallows,
    chopped
50g/2oz/¼ cup glace cherries,
    chopped
50g/2oz/1 cup crumbled shortbread
    biscuits
30ml/2 tbsp chopped walnuts

1 Melt the chocolate in the milk in a saucepan over a gentle heat, stirring from time to time. Leave to cool.

2 Whip the cream in a bowl until it just holds it shape. Beat in the chocolate mixture.

3 Tip the chocolate cream mixture into an ice cream maker and churn until thick and almost frozen. Alternatively, pour into a container suitable for use in the freezer, freeze until ice crystals form around the edges, then whisk until completely smooth.

4 Stir the marshmallows, cherries, crushed biscuits and nuts into the iced mixture, then return to the freezer and freeze until firm.

5 Allow the ice cream to soften at room temperature for 15–20 minutes before serving in scoops.

COOK'S TIP

For a quick version, simply stir the flavourings into bought soft-scoop chocolate ice cream and freeze until firm.

Brandied Fruit and Rice Ice Cream

Based on a favourite Victorian rice ice cream, this rich dessert combines spicy rice pudding with a creamy egg custard flecked with brandy-soaked fruits. The mixture is then frozen until it is just firm enough to serve in scoops.

INGREDIENTS

Serves 4–6

50g/2oz/¹/₄ cup ready-to-eat
   stoned prunes
50g/2oz/¹/₄ cup ready-to-eat dried apricots
50g/2oz/¹/₄ cup glacé cherries
30ml/2 tbsp brandy
150ml/¹/₄ pint/²/₃ cup single cream

For the rice mixture

40g/1¹/₂oz/generous ¹/₄ cup pudding rice
450ml/³/₄ pint/scant 2 cups full-
   cream milk
1 cinnamon stick, halved, plus extra
   cinnamon sticks, to decorate
4 cloves

For the custard

4 egg yolks
75g/3oz/6 tbsp caster sugar
5ml/1 tsp cornflour
300ml/¹/₂ pint/1¹/₄ cups full-cream milk

1 Chop the prunes, apricots and glacé cherries finely and put them in a bowl. Pour over the brandy. Cover and leave to soak for 3 hours or overnight if possible.

2 Put the rice, milk and whole spices in a saucepan. Bring to the boil, then simmer gently for 30 minutes, stirring occasionally, until most of the milk has been absorbed. Lift out the spices and leave the rice to cool.

3 Whisk the egg yolks, sugar and cornflower in a bowl until thick and creamy. Heat the milk in a heavy-based pan, then gradually pour it on the yolks, whisking constantly. Pour back into the pan and cook, stirring until the custard thickens. Leave to cool, then chill.

4 Mix the chilled custard, rice and single cream together. Pour into a plastic container or similar freezerproof container and freeze for 4–5 hours, until mushy. Beat the ice cream lightly with a fork to break up the ice crystals.

5 Fold in the fruits, then freeze for 2–3 hours until firm enough to scoop.

6 Scoop the ice cream into individual dishes and decorate with cinnamon sticks.

COOK'S TIP

As the brandy-soaked fruits are so soft, it is better to remove the ice cream from the ice cream maker, fold in the fruits and then freeze the mixture in a tub until firm enough to scoop.

Praline Ice Cream in Baskets

Praline, a delicious crunchy caramel and nut mixture, is a very popular flavouring in France – it can be made with almonds or hazelnuts or a mixture of the two, if you prefer.

INGREDIENTS

Serves 6–8

55g/2oz/½ cup blanched almonds
   or hazelnuts
175g/6oz/⅞ cup caster sugar
60ml/4 tbsp water
250ml/8fl oz/1 cup double cream
6 egg yolks
500ml/16fl oz/2 cups milk

For the biscuit baskets

70g/2½oz/½ cup whole blanched almonds,
   lightly toasted
100g/3½oz/½ cup caster sugar
40g/1½oz/3 tbsp unsalted
   butter, softened
2 egg whites
2.5ml/½ tsp almond essence
35g/1¼oz/¼ cup plain flour, sifted

1 Lightly brush a baking sheet with oil. Put the nuts in a saucepan with 75g/3oz/⅓ cup of the sugar and the water. Bring to the boil over a high heat, swirling the pan to dissolve the sugar, then boil, without stirring, for 4–5 minutes until the syrup and nuts begin to pop. Immediately pour on to the baking sheet (do not touch the hot caramel). Set aside to cool completely then break into pieces.

2 Finely grind the praline in a food processor, using the metal blade. Or, put in a strong polythene bag and crush with a rolling pin.

3 Pour the cream into a cold bowl and set aside. In another bowl whisk the egg yolks and remaining sugar until thick and creamy. Meanwhile, bring the milk just to a simmer over a medium heat, then whisk into the eggs and return the mixture to the saucepan.

4 With a wooden spoon, stir over a low heat for 3–4 minutes until the sauce thickens and coats the back of the spoon, then strain the custard into the bowl of cream. Cool, then chill until cold. Stir in the praline and freeze in an ice cream maker, or in the freezer, beating once or twice until smooth.

5 Preheat the oven to 200°C/ 400°F/Gas 6. Butter two baking sheets. To make the baskets, put the almonds and 30ml/2 tbsp of the sugar in a food processor and finely grind with the metal blade. Beat the butter until creamy.

6 Add the remaining sugar to the butter and beat until light and fluffy, then gradually beat in the egg whites and the almond essence. Sift the flour over the butter mixture, fold in, then fold in the ground almond mixture.

7 Drop tablespoons of mixture about 20cm/8in apart on to the prepared baking sheets. With the back of a wet spoon, spread into paper-thin rounds 10cm/4in across.

8 Bake the biscuits, for 4–5 minutes until the edges are golden and the centres are still pale. Transfer to a wire rack and, working quickly, loosen the edge of a hot biscuit and carefully transfer to an upturned drinking glass or ramekin, pressing gently over the base to form a fluted basket shape. If the biscuits become too crisp to shape, soften them in the oven for 15–30 seconds. Repeat with the remaining biscuits. Set aside to cool completely before transferring to a wire rack.

9 To serve, leave the ice cream to soften at room temperature for 5–10 minutes. Place the baskets on dessert plates and fill with scoops of the ice cream.

Black Forest Sundae

Here is a truly indulgent variation on the classic Black Forest gâteau, but this one is spectacularly served in a sundae glass.

Serves 4

400g/14oz can stoned black cherries
   in syrup
15ml/1 tbsp cornflour
45ml/3 tbsp kirsch
15ml/1 tbsp icing sugar
150ml/¼ pint/ ⅔ cup whipping cream
600ml/1 pint/2½ cups chocolate
   ice cream
115g/4oz ready-made chocolate cake
8 fresh cherries, to decorate
vanilla ice cream, to serve

2 Over a medium heat, bring the syrup in the saucepan to the boil. Add the cornflour and syrup mixture, stirring until it is well blended, and then simmer briefly to thicken, stirring continuously.

5 Place a spoonful of cherries in the bottom of four sundae glasses. Add a layer of ice cream, then chocolate cake, whipped cream and more cherries, continue until the glasses are full.

1 Strain all but 30ml/2tbsp of the cherry syrup into a saucepan. Measure the cornflour into a small bowl with the remaining syrup and mix together until smooth and creamy.

3 Add the cherries, stir in the kirsch and then spread on to a metal tray to cool.

6 To finish the sundaes add a piece of chocolate cake, two scoops of ice cream and another spoonful of cream. Place in the freezer for 5–10 minutes, to firm the ice cream, and serve decorated with fresh cherries.

4 Sift the icing sugar over the cream, fold in and then whip until the mixture is thick and holds its shape.

COOK'S TIP

Bottled black cherries often have a better flavour than canned, especially if the stones are left in. You don't need to remove the stones – but do remember to tell your guests.

Ice Cream Strawberry Shortcake

This pudding is an American classic, and couldn't be easier to make. Fresh juicy strawberries, store-bought flan cases and rich vanilla ice cream are all you need to create an irresistible feast of a dessert.

Serves 4

3x15cm/6in sponge flan cases or
   shortbreads
1.2 litres/2 pints/5 cups vanilla or
   strawberry ice cream
675g/1½lb hulled fresh strawberries
icing sugar, for dusting

1 If using store-bought flan cases, trim the raised edges level with the base, using a serrated knife or bread knife.

2 Start with the flan case, or shortbread, and place one-third of the ice cream and the strawberries on top. Spread them evenly to make a level base. Add another layer of flan case or short-bread and another third of the ice cream and the strawberries. Then the final layer of flan or shortbread.

3 Arrange the remaining ice cream on top and finish with the strawberries. Chill in the freezer before serving dusted with icing sugar.

COOK'S TIP

Don't worry if the shortbread falls apart when you cut into it. Messy cakes are best. Ice Cream Strawberry Shortbread can be assembled up to 1 hour in advance and kept in the freezer without spoiling the fruit.

Chocolate Mint Ice Cream Pie

This colourful dessert uses ready-made ice cream and it looks and tastes really professional.

Serves 8

85g/3oz plain chocolate chips
45g/1½oz butter or margarine
55g/2oz crisped rice cereal
1 litre/1¼pt mint-chocolate-chip ice cream
85g/3oz plain chocolate

1 In a heatproof bowl set over a pan of barely simmering water, melt the chocolate chips and the butter or margarine.

2 Remove the bowl from the heat and gradually stir in the cereal. Let it cool for 5 minutes.

3 Line a 23cm/9in pie tin with foil and place a round of greaseproof paper over the foil in the bottom of the tin. Press the chocolate and cereal mixture over the bottom and around the sides of the lined tin, forming a rim. Refrigerate until set hard.

4 Carefully remove the cereal base from the tin and peel off the foil and greaseproof paper. Return the base to the pie tin.

5 Remove the ice cream from the freezer and allow to soften for 10 minutes.

6 Spread the ice cream evenly in the crust then freeze for about 1 hour until firm.

7 For the decoration, use the heat of your hands to soften the chocolate slightly. Draw the blade of a swivel-headed vegetable peeler along the smooth surface of the chocolate to shave off short, wide curls. Refrigerate the curls until needed.

8 Just before serving, scatter the chocolate curls over the ice cream to cover the surface.

Pistachio and Nougat Torte

Pistachios, nougat, honey and rosewater make a perfect blend of flavours in this quick and easy iced torte.

Serves 6–8

75g/3oz/¾ cup pistachios

150g/5oz nougat

300ml/½ pint/1¼ cups whipping cream

90ml/6 tbsp clear honey

30ml/2tbsp rosewater

250g/9oz/generous 1 cup fromage frais

8 trifle sponges

icing sugar, for dusting

fresh raspberries, poached apricots or cherries, to serve (optional)

1 Soak the pistachios in boiling water for 2 minutes. Drain them thoroughly, then rub them between pieces of kitchen paper to remove the skins. Peel off any skins that remain, then chop the pistachios roughly.

2 Using a small sharp knife or scissors, cut the nougat into small pieces.

3 Pour the cream into a bowl, add the honey and rosewater and whip until it is just beginning to hold its shape. Stir in the fromage frais, chopped pistachios and nougat.

4 Slice the trifle sponges horizontally into three very thin layers.

5 Line a 15–17cm/6–6½in square loose-based cake tin with greaseproof paper or clear film. Arrange a layer of sponge on the bottom of the tin, trimming the pieces to fit.

6 Pack the pistachio and nougat filling into the tin and level the surface. Cover with the remaining sponges, then cover with clear film and freeze overnight.

7 To serve, invert the torte on to a serving plate and dust with icing sugar. Serve with fresh raspberries, poached apricots or cherries, if you like.

Coffee and Chocolate Bombe

This impressive dessert is known in Italy as zuccotto, *meaning pumpkin. A wide-based pudding basin gives the most authentic shape, but it will taste delicious whatever shape it is.*

INGREDIENTS

Serves 6-8

175ml/6fl oz/¾ cup sweet Marsala

15-18 savoiardi (Italian sponge fingers)

75g/3oz amaretti biscuits

about 475ml/ 16fl oz/2 cups coffee ice
   cream, softened

about 475ml/ 16fl oz/2 cups vanilla ice
   cream, softened

50g/2oz bittersweet or plain
   chocolate, grated

chocolate curls and sifted cocoa powder or
   icing sugar, to decorate

1 Line a 1 litre/1¾ pint/4 cup pudding basin with a large piece of damp muslin. Pour the Marsala into a shallow dish and dip a sponge finger, turning it quickly to saturate it. Place against the side of the basin, sugared-side out. Repeat with the remaining sponge fingers, to line the basin.

2 Fill the base and any gaps around the side with any trimmings of sponge fingers cut to fit. Chill for about 30 minutes.

3 Put the amaretti biscuits in a large bowl and crush them with a large rolling pin. Add the coffee ice cream and any remaining Marsala and beat until mixed. Spoon the mixture into the sponge-finger-lined basin.

4 Press the ice cream against the sponge to form an even layer with a hollow. Freeze for 2 hours.

5 Put the vanilla ice cream and grated chocolate in a bowl and beat together until evenly mixed. Spoon into the hollow in the centre of the mould. Smooth the top, then cover with the overhanging muslin. Place in the freezer overnight.

6 To serve, run a palette knife between the muslin and the basin, then unfold the top of the muslin. Place a chilled serving plate on top of the bombe, then invert them so that the bombe is upside down on the plate. Carefully peel off the muslin. Decorate the bombe with the chocolate curls, then sift cocoa powder or icing sugar over. Serve at once.

Maple Coffee and Pistachio Bombes

Real maple syrup tastes infinitely better than the synthetic varieties and is well worth searching for.

INGREDIENTS

Serves 6

For the pistachio ice cream
50g/2oz/¼ cup caster sugar
50ml/2fl oz/¼ cup water
175g/6oz can evaporated milk, chilled
50g/2oz/½ cup shelled and skinned
    pistachio nuts, finely chopped
drop of green food colouring
    (optional)
200ml/7fl oz/scant 1 cup
    whipping cream

For the maple coffee centres
30ml/2 tbsp ground coffee
150ml/¼ pint/⅔ cup single cream
50ml/2fl oz/¼ cup maple syrup
2 egg yolks
5ml/1 tsp cornflour
150ml/¼ pint/⅔ cup
    whipping cream

1 Put six 175ml/6fl oz/¾ cup mini pudding basins or dariole moulds into the freezer to chill. Put the sugar and water in a heavy-based saucepan and heat gently until dissolved. Bring to the boil and simmer for 3 minutes. Cool.

2 Stir in the evaporated milk, nuts and colouring, if using. Lightly whip the cream to soft peaks and blend into the mixture.

3 Pour into a freezerproof container and freeze for at least 2 hours. Whisk the ice cream until smooth, then freeze for a further 2 hours or until frozen, but not completely solid.

4 Put the ground coffee in a jug. Heat the single cream to near-boiling , pour over the coffee and infuse for 4 minutes. Whisk the maple syrup, egg yolks and cornflour together. Strain the hot coffee cream over the egg mixture, whisking continuously. Return to the pan and cook gently for 1–2 minutes, until the custard thickens. Leave to cool, stirring occasionally.

5 Meanwhile, line the moulds right up to the rim with an even thickness of the ice cream. Freeze until the ice cream is firm.

6 Beat the cream to soft peaks, and fold into the custard. Spoon into the middle of the moulds. Cover and freeze for 2 hours. Serve immediately.

Iced Coffee and Nut Meringue

This impressive frozen dessert may seem difficult, but is actually very easy to prepare.

INGREDIENTS

Serves 8–10

100g/3½oz/scant 1 cup hazelnuts, toasted

275g/ 10oz/1⅓ cups caster sugar

5 egg whites

pinch of cream of tartar

1 litre/1¾ pints/4 cups coffee ice cream

For the chocolate cream

500ml/17fl oz/2 cups whipping cream

30ml/2 tbsp coffee liqueur

275g/10oz plain chocolate, melted and
cooled

white chocolate curls and fresh
raspberries, to decorate

3 Leave the ice cream to soften for 15–20 minutes and then beat until smooth. Spread half the ice cream over one meringue layer, and continue layering ice cream and meringue, finishing with the last meringue layer on top. Press down gently, then wrap and freeze for at least 4 hours until firm.

4 To make the chocolate cream, beat the whipping cream until soft peaks form. Quickly fold in the liqueur and melted chocolate. Unwrap the frozen meringue and spread the chocolate cream over the top and sides, return to the freezer, rewrapping when firm. To serve, soften slightly before slicing.

1 Preheat the oven to 180°C/ 350°F/Gas 4. Line three baking sheets with non-stick baking paper. Using a plate as a guide, mark a 20cm/8in circle on each and turn the paper over. Process the hazelnuts in a food processor until roughly chopped. Add a third of the sugar and process again until finely ground.

2 Whisk the egg whites until frothy, add the cream of tartar and whisk until they form soft peaks. Spoon the mixture on to the paper and spread within the marked circles. Bake for 1 hour until firm and dry. Leave to cool in a turned off oven. Peel off the paper.

Iced Praline Torte

Make this elaborate torte several days ahead, decorate it and return it to the freezer until you are nearly ready to serve it. Allow the torte to stand at room temperature for an hour before serving, or leave it in the refrigerator overnight to soften.

INGREDIENTS

Serves 8

115g/4oz/1 cup almonds or hazelnuts
115g/4oz/8 tbsp caster sugar
115g/4oz/⅔ cup raisins
90ml/6 tbsp rum or brandy
115g/4oz dark chocolate, broken
   into squares
30ml/2 tbsp milk
450ml/¾ pint/1⅞ cups double cream
30ml/2 tbsp strong black coffee
16 sponge-finger biscuits

To finish

150ml/¼ pint/⅔ cup double cream
50g/2oz/½ cup flaked almonds, toasted
15g/½oz dark chocolate, melted

1 To make the praline, have ready an oiled cake tin or baking sheet. Put the nuts into a heavy-based pan with the sugar and heat gently until the sugar melts. Swirl the pan to coat the nuts in the hot sugar. Cook slowly until the nuts brown and the sugar caramelizes. Transfer the nuts quickly to the tin or tray and leave them to cool completely. Break them up and grind them to a fine powder in a blender or food processor.

2 Soak the raisins in 45ml/3 tbsp of the rum or brandy for an hour (or better still overnight), so they soften and absorb the rum. Melt the chocolate with the milk in a bowl over a pan of hot, but not boiling water. Remove and allow to cool. Lightly grease a 1.2 litre/ 2 pint/5 cup loaf tin and line it with greaseproof paper.

3 Whisk the cream in a bowl until it holds soft peaks. Whisk in the cold chocolate. Then fold in the praline and the soaked raisins, with any liquid.

4 Mix the coffee and remaining rum or brandy in a shallow dish. Dip in the sponge-fingers and arrange half in a layer over the base of the prepared loaf tin.

5 Cover with the chocolate mixture and add another layer of soaked sponge-fingers. Leave in the freezer overnight.

6 Whip the double cream for the topping. Dip the tin briefly into warm water to loosen it and turn the torte out on to a serving plate. Cover with the whipped cream, sprinkle the top with toasted flaked almonds and drizzle the melted chocolate over the top. Return the torte to the freezer until it is needed.

COOK'S TIP

Make the praline in advance and store it in an airtight jar until needed.

Chocolate Fudge Sundaes

*They look impressive, taste fantastic
and only take minutes to make.*

INGREDIENTS

Serves 4

4 scoops each vanilla and coffee ice cream
2 small ripe bananas, sliced
whipped cream
toasted flaked almonds

For the sauce

50g/2oz/¼ cup soft light brown sugar
120ml/4fl oz/½ cup golden syrup
45ml/3 tbsp strong black coffee
5ml/1 tsp ground cinnamon
150g/5oz plain chocolate, chopped
85ml/3fl oz/⅓ cup whipping cream
45ml/3 tbsp coffee liqueur (optional)

1 To make the sauce, place the sugar, syrup, coffee and cinnamon in a heavy-based saucepan. Bring to the boil, then boil for about 5 minutes, stirring the mixture constantly.

2 Turn off the heat and stir in the chocolate. When melted and smooth, stir in the cream and liqueur, if using. Leave the sauce to cool slightly. If made ahead, reheat the sauce gently until just warm.

3 Fill four glasses with one scoop of vanilla and another of coffee ice cream.

4 Scatter the sliced bananas over the ice cream. Pour the warm fudge sauce over the bananas, then top each sundae with a generous swirl of whipped cream. Sprinkle toasted almonds over the cream and serve at once.

VARIATION

Ring the changes by choosing other flavours of ice cream such as strawberry, toffee or chocolate. In the summer, substitute raspberries or strawberries for the bananas, and scatter chopped roasted hazelnuts on top in place of the flaked almonds.

Frosted Raspberry and Coffee Terrine

A white chocolate and raspberry layer and contrasting smooth coffee layer, which is jewelled with whole raspberries, makes this attractive dessert doubly delicious.

INGREDIENTS

Serves 6–8

30ml/2 tbsp flavoured ground coffee

250ml/8fl oz/1 cup milk

4 eggs, separated

50g/2oz/¼ cup caster sugar

30ml/2 tbsp cornflour

150ml/¼ pint/⅔ cup double cream

150g/5oz white chocolate,
   roughly chopped

115g/4oz/⅔ cup raspberries

shavings of white chocolate and cocoa
   powder, to decorate

1 Line a 1.5 litre/2½ pint/6¼ cup loaf tin with clear film and chill. Put the ground coffee in a jug. Heat 100ml/3½ fl oz/scant ½ cup of the milk to near boiling point and pour over the coffee.

2 Blend the egg yolks, sugar and cornflour in a pan and whisk in the remaining milk and cream. Bring to the boil, stirring, until the mixture has thickened.

3 Divide the mixture between two bowls and add the white chocolate to one, stirring until melted. Strain the coffee through a fine sieve into the other bowl and mix. Cool, stirring occasionally.

4 Whisk two egg whites until stiff and fold into the coffee custard. Spoon into the tin and freeze for 30 minutes. Whisk the remaining whites and fold into the the chocolate mixture with the fruit.

5 Spoon into the tin and level. Freeze for 4 hours. Turn out on to a flat serving plate and peel off the film. Cover with chocolate shavings and dust with cocoa powder before serving.

Café Glace

A perfect finish to a summer meal, this delicious dessert is not only very quick and easy to prepare in advance, it needs only minutes to finish and serve. This must be the ultimate no-fuss dessert that looks as good as it tastes.

INGREDIENTS

Serves 4–6

600ml/1 pint/2½ cups water

30-45ml/2-3 tbsp instant dried coffee

15ml/1 tbsp sugar

600ml/1 pint/2½ cups milk

ice cubes

vanilla ice cream

4-6 chocolate flakes

8-12 crisp ice cream biscuits,
    to serve

1 Bring 120ml/4floz/½ cup of the water to the boil, then transfer to a small bowl and stir in the coffee. Add the sugar and stir to dissolve. Chill for 2 hours. Mix together the milk and remaining water in a large jug. Add the chilled coffee and stir well.

2 Pour the coffee mixture into long glasses until they are three quarters full. Add ice cubes and the ice cream to the top of each glass and decorate with the chocolate flakes. To serve, place the long glasses on plates with the ice cream biscuits to the side.

COOK'S TIP

You'll need to provide straws and long spoons for eating this dessert. Adjust the amount of coffee and sugar to suit your own taste.

Iced Mint and Chocolate Cooler

Many chocolate drinks are warm and comforting, but this one is really refreshing and ideal for a hot summer's day.

INGREDIENTS

Serves 4

60ml/4 tbsp drinking chocolate

400ml/14fl oz/1²⁄₃ cups chilled milk

150ml/¹⁄₄ pint/²⁄₃ cup natural yogurt

2.5ml/¹⁄₂ tsp peppermint essence

4 scoops chocolate ice cream

mint leaves and chocolate shapes
    to decorate

1 Place the drinking chocolate in a small saucepan and stir in 120ml/4fl oz/¹⁄₂ cup of the milk. Heat gently, stirring continuously, until almost boiling, then remove from the heat and leave to cool.

COOK'S TIP

~

Use cocoa powder instead of drinking chocolate if you prefer, but add sugar to taste.

2 Pour the cool chocolate milk into a large bowl or jug and whisk in the remaining milk, the yogurt and peppermint essence.

3 Pour the mixture into tall glasses and top each one with a scoop of ice cream. Decorate with mint leaves and chocolate shapes and serve immediately.

Blushing Pina Colada

This is good with or without the rum. Don't be tempted to put roughly crushed ice into the blender; it will not be smooth and will ruin the blades. Make sure you crush it well first.

INGREDIENTS

Serves 2

1 banana, peeled and sliced

1 thick slice pineapple, peeled

3 measures/70ml/4½ tbsp
   pineapple juice

1 scoop strawberry ice cream or sorbet

1 measures/22.5ml/1½ tbsp
   coconut milk

30ml/2 tbsp grenadine

wedges of pineapple and steamed
   maraschino cherries to decorate

1 Roughly chop the banana. Cut two small wedges from the pineapple for decoration and reserve. Cut up the remainder of the pineapple and place in the blender with the chopped banana. Place two large cocktail glasses in the refrigerator to chill.

VARIATION

For classic pina colada use vanilla ice cream and 1 measure white rum. For a passionate encounter, blend 2 scoops passion fruit sorbet and 15ml/1 tbsp coconut milk with a measure each of pineapple and apricot juice.

2 Add the pineapple juice to the blender and process until the mixture is a smooth paste.

3 Add the strawberry ice cream or sorbet, and the coconut milk plus a small scoop of finely crushed ice, and process until very smooth.

4 Take the chilled cocktail glasses and pour in the mixture, taking care not to splash the sides of the glass.

5 Pour the grenadine syrup slowly on top of the pina colada; it will filter through the drink in a dappled effect.

6 Decorate each glass with a wedge of pineapple and a stemmed cherry and serve immediately with drinking straws.

COOK'S TIP

To crush the ice, place ice cubes into a clean kitchen cloth or a heavy duty plastic bag. Wrap up the cloth or seal the plastic bag, making sure that the ice cubes are quite secure and cannot come out. Place on a firm surface and crush with a wooden rolling pin until the cubes are in tiny pieces.

Low-fat Desserts

All too often, desserts are the downfall of anyone trying to follow a low-fat diet. After a sensible starter and a main course of grilled fish or chicken and fresh vegetables, there's an almost irresistible temptation to award yourself a large portion of pudding. The good news is that you can. You don't have to give up lovely, luscious desserts – provided that you stick to the recipes in this section of the book. Here you will find low-fat versions of old favourites such as Bread Pudding, Fruit Crumble and Angel Cake, together with new and exotic ideas such as Papaya Baked with Ginger and Tropical Fruit Pancakes.

◆ ✦ ◆

Facts About Fats

We all know we need to cut down on the amount of fat we eat – it would be difficult to live in the developed world and be unaware of that fact – but before making changes in our diet, it may be helpful to find out a bit more about the fats that we eat: some types are believed to be less harmful than others.

Fats are essential for the proper functioning of the body. However, we need the right kind of fat and the right amount. The average Western diet contains far too much of the "wrong" type of fat – saturated fat – which leads to obesity, heart problems and strokes. The daily recommended maximum amount of calories that should come from fat is between 30% and 35%. Unfortunately, too many Westerners obtain well over 40% of their calories from fat, often in the form of sweet treats and desserts and pastries.

Fats in our food are made up of different types of fatty acids and glycerol. Fats may be saturated or unsaturated, with unsaturated fat further categorized as mono-unsaturated or polyunsaturated.

Saturated fats

To appreciate the difference between saturated and unsaturated fatty acids, it is necessary to understand a little about their molecular structure. Put very simply, fatty acids are made up of chains of carbon atoms. A common analogy is to a string of beads. Unlike beads, however, which are linked only to each other, the carbon atoms are also able to link up – or bond – with one or more other atoms. In a saturated fat, all these potential linkages have been

Left: A bottle of sunflower oil (left) contains mostly polyunsaturated fats (68%), while olive oil is made of up mainly mono-unsaturated fats (70%).

made: the carbon atoms are linked to each other and each is further linked to two hydrogen atoms. No further linkages are possible, and the fat is therefore said to be saturated.

Saturated fat is mainly found in foods of animal origin: meat and dairy products such as butter, which is solid at room temperature. However, there are also some saturated fats of vegetable origin, notably coconut oil and also palm oil which is the main vegetable oil used in hard margarines.

Unsaturated fats

Unsaturated fatty acids differ from saturated fatty acids in their structure – not all of the linkages or bonds are complete. Some of the carbon atoms are linked to only one hydrogen atom instead of the usual two, and some of the carbon atoms may be joined to each other by a double bond. Depending on how many double bonds there are, the fatty acid is described as mono-unsaturated (one double bond) or polyunsaturated (many double bonds). The different molecular structures need not concern us here – suffice it to say that unsaturated fats are generally more healthy than saturated fats.

Mono-unsaturated fats

These are found in foods such as olive oil, rapeseed oil, some nuts, oily fish and avocado pears. Mono-unsaturated fats are believed to be neutral, neither raising or lowering blood cholesterol levels. This, plus the lower saturated fat intake as well as the higher fruit and vegetable intake, which are high in antioxidants, could explain the low incidence of heart disease in the Mediterranean countries.

Above: Many common foods contain some fats. Cheese, butter, milk, cream and nuts – all of which are frequently used in desserts – should be strictly limited, unless fat free or very low fat.

Polyunsaturated fats

Polyunsaturated fat has two types. The first (omega 6) is found in vegetable and seed oils, such as sunflower or almond oil, and the second (omega 3) comes from oily fish, green leaves and some seed oils, including rapeseed or canola oil.

Polyunsaturated fats are liquid at room temperature. When vegetable oils are used in soft margarine, they have to be hardened artificially. During this process, the composition of some of the unsaturated fatty acids changes. In the body, these altered or "trans" fatty acids are treated like saturated fats, so, although an oil such as sunflower oil may be high in polyunsaturated fatty acids which lowers cholesterol levels, the same is not necessarily true of a margarine made from that oil.

Although unsaturated fats are healthier then saturated ones, most experts agree that what matters more is reducing our total intake of fat.

A Guide to Low-fat Dessert Ingredients

Watching your fat intake doesn't mean you have to forgo creamy puddings. A wide range of low-fat and virtually fat-free products are on sale in supermarkets, some of them backed by alluring advertising. Clever packaging can sometimes persuade the impulse buyer to make an unwise choice, however, so always check the statistical data printed on the label.

Low-fat spreads have become very popular. These have a high water content, so, while they are perfectly acceptable for spreading on bread and teabreads, they are not necessarily suitable for cooking. When baking puddings or making cakes, look for a spread with a fat content of around 40%. If substituting a reduced-fat spread for butter in a conventional recipe, be prepared to experiment a little, as the results will not necessarily be the same.

Try to avoid using saturated fats such as butter and hard margarine. Oils that are high in polyunsaturates, such as sunflower, corn or safflower, are the healthier option. Cakes and baked puddings made with oil are often excellent. If you must use margarine, choose a brand that is low in saturates and high in polyunsaturates.

Skimmed milk works well in batters and bakes, although you may get a better result using semi-skimmed.

Yogurt and fromage frais make excellent alternatives to cream, and when combined with honey, liqueur or other flavourings, they make delicious fillings or toppings for cheesecakes and fruit desserts. Many delectable desserts are based on soft cheeses. Cream cheese used to be the preferred option, but low-fat alternatives work just as well and are often easier to mix. If you're not familiar with it already, experiment with Quark, a virtually fat-free cheese that is very versatile.

Oils and low-fat spreads

Corn oil: A polyunsaturated oil, this has a slight flavour, so it is not as good as sunflower oil for baking. Fried foods should be avoided completely if you are trying to limit your fat intake, but if you must fry this is a good choice if used sparingly, as it can reach a high temperature without smoking.
Sunflower oil spread: High in polyunsaturates, this light, delicately flavoured oil is a good choice for puddings, as is safflower oil. Both can be used in cakes and bakes and are particularly good in muffins.
Sunflower light spread: Like reduced-fat butter, this contains about 38% fat, plus emulsified milk solids and water. The flavour is mild.
Olive oil reduced-fat spread: With a fat content of around 63%, this spread is richer than many low-fat spreads, but it has an excellent flavour. It can be used for cooking.

Left: A selection of cooking oils and low-fat spreads. Always check the packaging when buying low-fat spreads – if you are going to use them for cooking, they must have a fat content of about 40%.

Low-fat spread (rich buttermilk blend): This product is made with a high proportion of buttermilk, which is naturally low in fat. Low-fat spreads with a fat content of around 40% can be used for cooking: check the label.
Very low-fat spread: This contains about 20–30% fat and has a high water content; it is not suitable for cooking.

Low-fat milks

Buttermilk: This is the liquid that remains after cream has been churned into butter. Buttermilk produced in this way has a light flavour, similar to skimmed milk. Commercial buttermilk is made by adding a bacterial culture to skimmed milk. This gives it a slightly sharper taste than traditional buttermilk. It is very low in fat (0.5%).
Powdered skimmed milk: This is a useful, low-fat standby. You can make up as little or as much as you need. Always follow the instructions on the packet. Of itself, the powder has quite a high fat content, so if you use too much, the drink will not be the low-fat alternative you wanted.
Semi-skimmed milk: With a fat content of only 1.6%, this milk doesn't taste as rich as full-cream milk. It is favoured by many people for everyday use for precisely this reason. Semi-skimmed milk can be used in all recipes calling for full-cream milk.
Skimmed milk: This milk has had virtually all the fat removed, leaving 0.1%. It is ideal for those wishing to reduce their intake of fats.

Low-fat cream substitutes

Crème Fraîche: Look out for half-fat versions of this thick soured cream, where the normal fat content of 40% is

Above: Almost all dairy products now come in low-fat or reduced-fat versions.

reduced to 15%. Crème fraîche has a mild, lemony taste and is ideal as a dessert topping.
Greek yogurt: This thick, creamy yogurt is made from whole milk with a fat content of 9.1%. A low-fat version is also available.
Low-fat natural yogurt: With a fat content of only about 1%, low-fat natural yogurt is a gift to the dessert cook. Use it instead of cream in whips, as a topping or as an accompaniment. Drizzle a little honey on top if you like.

Low-fat cheeses

Cottage cheese: This low-fat cheese is also available in a half-fat form. Cottage cheese can be used instead of cream cheese in cheesecakes – press it through a sieve to remove the lumps.
Curd cheese: This low-fat soft cheese is generally made from skimmed or

semi-skimmed milk. A simple version can be made at home, using low-fat natural yogurt. Use curd cheese instead of cream cheese.
Edam: Hard cheeses are not widely used in desserts, except in some baked cheesecakes. If a recipe does call for grated hard cheese, however, this is a good choice as it is lower in fat than standards like Cheddar or Cheshire. If you prefer the taste of Cheddar, choose a half-fat version, where the fat will be reduced to 15%.
Fromage frais: This is a fresh, soft cheese with a very mild flavour. It is available in two grades: virtually fat-free (0.2% fat), and a more creamy variety (7.1% fat). Fromage frais is too soft to use on its own as a cheesecake filling, but it can be mixed with curd cheese.
Quark: Perfect for many different types of pudding, this soft white cheese is virtually fat-free. It is made from fermented skimmed milk.

Fat and Calorie Counts per 100g

The chart below lists both full-fat and low or reduced-fat typical dessert ingredients, so that you can see the savings at a glance if you choose the healthier option.

Ingredient	Fat (g)	Energy	Ingredient	Fat (g)	Energy
Oils and Spreads			Curd cheese	11.7	173 Kcals/723 kJ
Butter	81.7	737 Kcals/3031 kJ	Edam	25	333 Kcals/1382 kJ
Corn oil	99.9	899 Kcals/3696 kJ	Fromage frais (plain)	7.1	113 Kcals/469 kJ
Low-fat spread	40.5	390 Kcals/1605 kJ	Half-fat cheddar	15	261 Kcals/1091 kJ
Margarine	81.6	739 Kcals/3039 kJ	Quark	1.4	86 Kcals/360 kJ
Olive oil	99.9	899 Kcals/3696 kJ	Reduced-fat cottage cheese	1.4	78 Kcals/331 kJ
Olive oil reduced-fat spread	63	571 Kcals/2389 kJ	Very low-fat fromage frais	0.2	58 Kcals/247 kJ
Saffflower oil	99.9	899 Kcals/3696 kJ			
Sunflower oil	99.9	899 Kcals/3696 kJ	*Eggs*		
Sunflower light spread	38	357 Kcals/1494 kJ	about 2 (medium)	10.9	147 Kcals/615 kJ
Very low-fat spread	27	259 Kcals/1084 kJ	Egg white	trace	36 Kcals/153 kJ
			Egg yolk	30.5	339 Kcals/1402 kJ
Milk					
Buttermilk	0.5	37 Kcals/157 kJ	*Baking Products and Preserves*		
Semi-skimmed milk	1.6	46 Kcals/195 kJ	Chocolate (milk)	30.3	520 Kcals/2214 kJ
Skimmed milk	0.1	33 Kcals/140 kJ	Chocolate (plain)	29.2	510 Kcals/2157 kJ
Skimmed milk powder	0.6	348 Kcals/1482 kJ	Cocoa powder	21.7	359 Kcals/1496 kJ
Whole milk	3.9	66 Kcals/275 kJ	Fatless sponge cake	6.1	294 Kcals/1230 kJ
			Honey	0	288 Kcals/1229 kJ
Cream/Cream Substitutes			Sugar (white)	0	394 Kcals/1648 kJ
Crème fraîche	40	380 Kcals/1582 kJ			
Double cream	48	449 Kcals/1849 kJ	*Fruit and Nuts*		
Greek yogurt	9.1	115 Kcals/477 kJ	Almonds	55.8	612 Kcals/2534 kJ
Half-fat crème fraîche	15	166 Kcals/692 kJ	Apples (eating)	0.1	47 Kcals/199 kJ
Low-fat yogurt (plain)	0.8	56 Kcals/236 kJ	Bananas	0.3	95 Kcals/403 kJ
Reduced-fat Greek yogurt	5.0	80 Kcals/335 kJ	Brazil nuts	68.2	682 Kcals/2813 kJ
Single cream	19.1	198 Kcals/817 kJ	Dried mixed fruit	0.4	268 Kcals/1114 kJ
Whipping cream	39.3	373 Kcals/1539 kJ	Hazelnuts	63.5	650 Kcals/2685 kJ
			Oranges	0.1	37 Kcals/158 kJ
Cheeses			Peaches	0.1	33 Kcals/142 kJ
Cheddar	34.4	412 Kcals/1708 kJ	Peanut butter (smooth)	53.7	623 Kcals/2581 kJ
Cottage cheese (plain)	3.9	98 Kcals/413 kJ	Pears	0.1	40 Kcals/169 kJ
Cream cheese	47.7	439 Kcals/1807 kJ	Pine nuts	68.6	688 Kcals/2840 kJ

Information from *The Composition of Foods* (5th edition 1991) is reproduced with the permission of the Controller of Her Majesty's Stationery Office.

Making Desserts the Fat-free Way

To many people, dessert means lashings of cream, butter and chocolate. Nowadays, however, it is perfectly possible for a host to hoodwink guests into thinking they are having a luscious, creamy sweet, when all the while, the constituents are fat-free or low in fat.

Many ingredients are available in full-fat and reduced-fat or very low-fat forms. In every supermarket you will find a huge array of low-fat products, such as milk, cream, yogurt, hard and soft cheeses and fromage frais, reduced-fat sweet or chocolate biscuits; low-fat, half-fat or very low-fat spreads; as well as reduced-fat ready-made desserts. Some ingredients work better than others in cooking, but often a simple substitution will spell success. In a crumb crust, for instance, reduced-fat biscuits work just as well as digestives.

Some of the most delicious desserts are based upon fruit. Serve fresh or dried fruit in a salad or compote, and there's no need to introduce fats.

If you are making a baked or steamed pudding, or pan-frying fruit such as bananas or pineapple rings, you can get away with using the merest slick of polyunsaturated oil, especially if you use a non-stick pan. Alternatively, use spray oil: a one-second spray of sunflower oil (about 1ml) has 4.6 Kcals/18.8 kJ and just over half the fat of conventional cooking oil. Spray oil is particularly useful for lightly coating frying pans when making pancakes.

Right: This sumptuous pineapple and strawberry mallow meringue looks and tastes delicious even though it is very low in fat.

When seeking inspiration for the dessert course for that special dinner party, remember that there are plenty of ingredients that naturally contain very little fat. Rice, flour, porridge oats, bread and cornflakes can all be used to make puddings and toppings, and there's no fat in wine, sherry, sugar or honey, although you may wish to restrict these for other reasons! Meringues are among the most popular puddings – topped with fresh fruit and yogurt or fromage frais, they are irresistible to eat and look great.

Spices and essences add plenty of extra flavour and colour to desserts, while decorations like rose petals, mint leaves or curls of pared citrus rind improve the appearance and stimulate the appetite.

Low-fat spreads in cooking

Some low-fat spreads can safely be substituted for butter or margarine in baked puddings, but others are only suitable for spreading. The limiting factor is the amount of water in the product. Very low-fat spreads achieve levels of fat of around 20% by virtue of their high water content and cannot be melted successfully. Spreads with a fat content of around 40% are suitable for spreading and for some cooking methods. The information on the label will indicate its suitability.

Left: Fresh fruit can be used to make simply superb sweet dishes, and there's no need at all to add any fat.

When using low-fat spreads for cooking, the fat may behave slightly differently to full-fat products such as butter or margarine. Be prepared to experiment a little – the results may surprise you. Some recipes actually work better with low-fat ingredients. For example, choux pastry made with half- or low-fat spread is often slightly crisper and lighter in texture than traditional choux pastry. A cheesecake biscuit base made with melted half- or low-fat spread combined with crumbs from reduced-fat biscuits may be slightly softer in texture and less crisp than one made using melted butter, but it will still be very good.

Quick Tips for Fat-Free Cooking

• Use heavy-based or non-stick pans – that way you won't need as much fat for cooking.

• When baking low-fat or reduced-fat cakes, it is advisable to use good quality cookware that doesn't need greasing before use, or line the pan with non-stick paper and only grease very lightly before filling.

• Look out for non-stick coated fabric sheeting. This reusable material will not stick and is amazingly versatile. It can be cut to size and used to line cake tins, baking sheets or frying pans. Heat resistant to 290°C/550°F and microwave safe, it will last for up to 5 years.

• Bake fruit in a loosely sealed parcel of greaseproof paper, moistening it with wine, fruit juice or liqueur instead of butter before sealing the parcel.

• When grilling fruit, the naturally high moisture content means that it is often unnecessary to add fat. If the fruit looks a bit dry, brush lightly and sparingly with a polyunsaturated oil such as sunflower or corn oil.

• Fruit cooked in the microwave seldom needs additional fat; add spices for extra colour and flavour.

• Poach fresh or dried fruit in natural juice or syrup – there's no need to add any fat.

• Become an expert at cooking with filo pastry. Of itself, filo is extremely low in fat, and if you brush the sheets sparingly with melted low-fat spread, it can be used to make delicious puddings that will not significantly damage a low-fat diet and will replace other high-fat pastries.

• Avoid cooking with chocolate, which is high in fat. If you can't bear to abandon your favourite flavour, use reduced-fat cocoa powder instead.

• Get to know the full range of low- or reduced-fat products, including yogurt, crème fraîche and fromage frais. Low-fat yogurt can be used for making "creamy" sauces, but needs to be treated with a little more care as it can curdle when heated. Stabilize it by stirring in a little cornflour, mixed to a paste with water or skimmed milk.

• Use skimmed milk rather than whole milk in rice pudding, semolina pudding and batters.

Above: Many delicious desserts can be made in moments if you have a well-stocked storecupboard.

When heating low-fat spreads, never let them get too hot. Always use a heavy-based pan over a low heat to avoid the product burning, spitting or spoiling, and stir all the time. Half-fat or low-fat spreads cannot be used for shallow- or deep-frying, traditional pastry making, rich fruit cakes, shortbread and preserves such as lemon curd.

Baked goods, such as cakes, pies and pastries, made using reduced- or low-

fat spreads will not keep as well as cakes and teabreads made using butter; this is due to the lower fat content.

Fruit purées
One way of reducing the fat content of a recipe is to replace all or part of the fat with a fruit purée. This is particularly successful with breads, probably because the amount of fat is usually relatively small, and it also works well with some biscuits and bars, such as brownies.

To make a dried fruit purée for this purpose, roughly chop 115g/4oz/ ⅔ cup ready-to-eat dried fruit and put

it in a blender or food processor. Add 75ml/5 tbsp water and blend to a fairly smooth purée. Scrape into a bowl, cover and keep in the fridge for up to 3 days. When baking, simply substitute the same weight of this dried fruit purée for all or just some of the fat in the recipe. You may need to experiment a little to find the proportions that work best. If preferred, you can purée a single variety of dried fruit, such as prunes, apricots, peaches or apples, or substitute mashed fresh fruit, such as ripe bananas or lightly cooked apples. If you choose to purée fresh fruit, omit the water.

Useful Techniques

Cooked or prepared in the right way, delicious desserts like meringues, fruit-filled pancakes and jellies are actually very low in fat. Follow the simple techniques on these pages for certain success.

WHISKING EGG WHITES

1 Place the egg whites in a completely clean, grease-free bowl. If even a speck of egg yolk is present, you will not be able to beat the whites successfully. Use one half of the shell to remove any traces of yolk.

2 Use a balloon whisk in a wide bowl for the greatest volume (egg whites can increase their volume by about eight times), but an electric hand whisk will also do an efficient job. Purists swear that eggs whisked in a copper bowl give the greatest volume.

3 Whisk the whites until they are firm enough to hold either soft or stiff peaks when you lift the whisk – see individual recipes. For stiffly whisked whites, you should be able to hold the bowl upside down without their sliding out, but this is a risky test!

MAKING PANCAKES

1 Apply a light, even coat of spray oil to a 20cm/8in pancake pan, then heat it gently. Pour in about 45ml/ 3 tbsp of the batter, then quickly tilt the pan so that the batter spreads to cover the bottom thinly and evenly.

2 Cook the pancake for 30-45 seconds, until it has set. Carefully lift the edge with a palette knife; the base of the pancake should have browned lightly. Shake the pan to loosen the pancake, then turn it over with the palette knife or flip it with a quick twist of your wrist.

3 Cook the other side of the pancake for about 30 seconds, then slide the pancake out on to a plate. Make more pancakes in the same way, then spread them with your chosen filling before rolling them or folding them neatly into triangles.

DISSOLVING GELATINE

1 Powdered gelatine is very easy to use. For every 15ml/1 tbsp of gelatine in the recipe, place 45ml/3 tbsp of very hot water in a small bowl.

2 Holding the bowl steady, sprinkle the powdered gelatine lightly and evenly over the hot liquid. Always add the gelatine to the liquid; never the other way round.

3 Stir until the gelatine has dissolved completely and the liquid is clear, with no visible crystals. You may need to stand the bowl in a pan of hot water.

UNMOULDING A JELLY

1 Have ready a serving plate that has been rinsed with cold water. Shake it but leave it damp – this will make it easier to centre the jelly. Run the tip of a knife around the moulded mixture, to loosen it.

2 Dip the mould briefly into a bowl of hot water. One or two seconds is usually enough – if you leave it for too long, the mixture will start to melt around the edges. If the jelly is stuck, dip again. Several short dips are better than one long one.

3 Quickly invert the plate over the mould. Holding mould and plate together, turn both over. Shake firmly to dislodge the jelly; as soon as you feel it drop, lift off the mould. If it does not lift off, give it another shake.

QUICK TIPS FOR GELATINE

Some recipes require gelatine to be dissolved in a cold liquid, such as apple or orange juice. In this case, pour the liquid into a small heatproof bowl and sprinkle the gelatine on top. Leave until the liquid has absorbed the gelatine and looks spongy, then place the bowl over very hot water until the gelatine has dissolved completely. You could either use a *bain marie* or simply a pan full of boiling water.

Techniques for Tasty Toppings

Although whipped cream is taboo on a low-fat diet, there are some excellent alternatives. Whipped "cream" can be made from skimmed milk powder or yogurt, with very good results. Neither will hold the shape indefinitely, however, so use them as soon as possible after making. Strained yogurt and curd cheese are simple to make at home, and tend to be lower in fat than commercial varieties. Serve strained yogurt with puddings instead of cream, sweetening it with a little honey, if liked. Curd cheese can be used instead of soured cream, cream cheese or butter. Apricot glaze is very useful for brushing over a large variety of fresh fruit toppings. It gives the fruit a lovely shiny appearance.

LOW-FAT WHIPPED CREAM

INGREDIENTS

Makes 150ml/¼ pint/⅔ cup

2.5ml/½ tsp powdered gelatine

75ml/5 tbsp water

50g/2oz/¼ cup skimmed milk powder

15ml/1 tbsp caster sugar

15ml/1 tbsp lemon juice

1 Sprinkle the powdered gelatine over 15ml/1 tbsp cold water in a small bowl and leave to "sponge" for 5 minutes. Place the bowl over a pan of hot water and stir until dissolved. Leave to cool.

2 Whisk the milk powder, sugar, lemon juice and remaining water until frothy. Add the dissolved gelatine and whisk. Chill for 30 minutes.

3 Using an electric hand whisk, whisk the chilled mixture again until it holds its shape and is very thick and frothy. Serve within 30 minutes of making.

YOGURT PIPING CREAM

INGREDIENTS

Makes 450ml/¾ pint/scant 2 cups

10ml/2 tsp powdered gelatine

45ml/3 tbsp water

300ml/½ pint/1¼ cups strained yogurt

15ml/1 tbsp fructose

2.5ml/½ tsp vanilla essence

1 egg white

1 Sprinkle the gelatine over the water in a small bowl and leave to "sponge" for 5 minutes. Place the bowl over a saucepan of hot water and stir until dissolved. Leave to cool.

2 Mix together the yogurt, fructose and vanilla essence. Stir in the gelatine. Chill in the fridge for 30 minutes, or until just beginning to set around the edges.

3 Whisk the egg white until stiff, then carefully fold it into the yogurt mixture. Spoon into a piping bag fitted with a piping nozzle and use immediately.

STRAINED YOGURT AND SIMPLE CURD CHEESE

Makes 300ml/¹/₂ pint/1¹/₄ cups strained yogurt or 115g/4oz/¹/₂ cup curd cheese

600ml/1 pint/2¹/₂ cups low-fat yogurt

1 For strained yogurt, line a nylon or stainless steel sieve with a double layer of muslin. Put it over a bowl and carefully pour in the low-fat yogurt.

2 Leave to drain in the fridge for 3 hours, by which time it will have separated into thick strained yogurt and watery whey. Discard the whey.

3 For curd cheese, leave to drain in the fridge for 8 hours or overnight. Spoon the curd cheese into a serving bowl, cover and keep chilled.

APRICOT GLAZE

1 Place a few spoonfuls of apricot jam in a small pan and add a squeeze of lemon juice. Heat the jam, stirring until it has melted and is runny.

2 Set a wire sieve over a heatproof bowl. Pour the jam into the sieve, then stir it with a wooden spoon to help it go through the mesh.

3 Return the strained jam to the pan. Keep the glaze warm until needed, then brush it generously over the fresh fruit until evenly coated.

Decorating with Citrus Rind Shreds

Shredded citrus rind makes a very effective decoration for a low-fat dessert. Thinly pare the rind from an orange, lemon or lime, using a swivel vegetable peeler. Take care not to remove any of the white pith, which has a bitter flavour. Cut the strips of pared rind into very fine shreds with a sharp knife. Boil the shreds for a couple of minutes in water or sugar syrup to soften them.

Right: Shredded citrus rind adds extra colour and appeal to this simple jelly.

Hot Low-fat Puddings & Desserts

◆ ✦ ◆

Spiced Pear and Blueberry Parcels

This combination makes a delicious dessert for a summer's evening and can be cooked on a barbecue or in the oven.

INGREDIENTS

Serves 4

4 firm, ripe pears

30ml/2 tbsp lemon juice

15ml/1 tbsp low-fat spread, melted

150g/5oz/1¼ cups blueberries

60ml/4 tbsp light muscovado sugar

freshly ground black pepper

NUTRITIONAL NOTES
Per portion:

Energy	146Kcals/614kJ
Fat, total	1.8g
Saturated fat	0.37g
Cholesterol	0.2mg
Fibre	4g

2 Brush the foil squares with melted spread. Place two pear halves on each, cut side upwards. Gather the foil around them, to hold them level.

3 Mix the blueberries and sugar together and spoon them on top of the pears. Sprinkle with black pepper. Close the foil and barbecue for 20–25 minutes or bake in a hot oven.

1 Prepare the barbecue or preheat the oven to 200ºC/400ºF/Gas 6. Peel the pears thinly. Cut in half lengthways. Scoop out the core from each half. Brush the pears with lemon juice, to stop them browning. Cut four squares of double-thickness foil, each large enough to wrap a pear.

Fruit and Spice Bread Pudding

*An easy-to-make fruity dessert with a
hint of spice, this is delicious served
either hot or cold.*

2 Mix together the sultanas, apricots,
sugar and spice and sprinkle half the
fruit mixture over the bread in the dish.

3 Top with the remaining bread
triangles and then the fruit.

4 Beat the eggs, milk and lemon
rind together and pour over the
bread. Set aside for about 30 minutes,
to allow the bread to absorb some of
the liquid. Bake for 45–60 minutes,
until lightly set and golden brown.
Serve hot or cold.

INGREDIENTS

Serves 4

6 medium slices wholemeal bread

50g/2oz apricot or strawberry jam

low-fat spread, for greasing

50g/2oz/^{1}/3 cup sultanas

50g/2oz/^{1}/4 cup ready-to-eat dried
    apricots, chopped

50g/2oz/^{1}/3 cup soft light brown sugar

5ml/1 tsp ground mixed spice

2 eggs

600ml/1 pint/2^1/2 cups skimmed milk

finely grated rind of 1 lemon

1 Preheat the oven to 160ºC/325ºF/
Gas 3. Remove and discard the
crusts from the bread. Spread the
bread slices with jam and cut into small
triangles. Place half the bread triangles
in a lightly greased ovenproof dish.

NUTRITIONAL NOTES
Per portion:

Energy	305Kcals/1293kJ
Fat, total	4.51g
Saturated fat	1.27g
Cholesterol	99.3mg
Fibre	3.75g

Fruity Bread Pudding

A delicious family favourite from grandmother's kitchen, with a lighter, healthier touch for today.

NUTRITIONAL NOTES
Per portion:

Energy	190Kcals/800kJ
Fat, total	0.89g
Saturated fat	0.21g
Cholesterol	0.75mg
Fibre	1.8g

2 Remove the pan from the heat and stir in the bread cubes, spice and banana. Spoon the mixture into a shallow 1.2 litre/2 pint/5 cup ovenproof dish and pour over the milk.

3 Sprinkle with demerara sugar and bake for 25–30 minutes, until firm and golden brown. Serve hot or cold, with natural yogurt if you like.

INGREDIENTS

Serves 4

75g/3oz/1/2 cup mixed dried fruit

150ml/1/4 pint/2/3 cup unsweetened
  apple juice

115g/4oz/3–4 slices day-old brown or white
  bread, cubed

5ml/1 tsp mixed spice

1 large banana, sliced

150ml/1/4 pint/2/3 cup skimmed milk

15ml/1 tbsp demerara sugar

low-fat natural yogurt, to serve (optional)

1 Preheat the oven to 200ºC/400ºF/ Gas 6. In a small pan, bring the dried fruit and apple juice to the boil.

Baked Apples with Red Wine

Special-occasion baked apples include a delicious filling of sultanas soaked in spiced red wine.

INGREDIENTS

Serves 6

65g/2¹/2 oz/scant ¹/2 cup sultanas

350ml/12fl oz/1¹/2 cups red wine

pinch of grated nutmeg

pinch of ground cinnamon

50g/2oz/¹/4 cup granulated sugar

pinch of grated lemon rind

35ml/7 tsp low-fat spread

6 baking apples of even size

1 Put the sultanas in a small bowl and pour over the wine. Stir in the grated nutmeg, ground cinnamon, sugar and lemon rind. Cover and leave to stand for approximately 1 hour.

2 Preheat the oven to 190ºC/375ºF/ Gas 5. Use a little of the low-fat spread to grease a baking dish. Core the apples, without cutting right through to the bottom.

3 Divide the sultana mixture among the apples. Spoon in a little extra spiced wine. Arrange the apples in the prepared baking dish.

4 Pour the remaining wine around the apples. Top the filling in each apple with 5ml/1 tsp of the low-fat remaining spread. Bake for 40– 50 minutes, or until the apples are soft but not mushy. Serve hot or at room temperature.

NUTRITIONAL NOTES

Per portion:

Energy	187Kcals/784kJ
Fat, total	2.7g
Saturated fat	0.61g
Cholesterol	0.4mg
Fibre	2.6g

Baked Apples with Apricot Nut Filling

This is an interesting version of an old favourite. Omit the low-fat spread if you want to reduce the fat content further.

Serves 6

75g/3oz/¹/2 cup chopped dried apricots

20g/³/4 oz/3 tbsp chopped walnuts

5ml/1 tsp grated lemon rind

1.5ml/¹/4 tsp ground cinnamon

115g/4oz/²/3 cup soft light brown sugar

30ml/2 tbsp low-fat spread

6 Bramley or other cooking apples

3 Stand the apples in a baking dish just large enough to hold them comfortably side by side.

4 Melt the remaining spread and brush it over the apples. Bake for 40–45 minutes until tender. Serve hot.

1 Preheat the oven to 190ºC/375ºF/ Gas 5. In a bowl, combine the apricots, walnuts, lemon rind and cinnamon. Add the sugar and rub in two-thirds of the low-fat spread until thoroughly combined.

2 Core the apples, without cutting all the way through to the base. Peel the top third of each apple. With a small knife, widen the top of each cavity by about 4cm/1½ in for the filling. Spoon the filling into the apples.

NUTRITIONAL NOTES
Per portion:

Energy	263Kcals/1095kJ
Fat, total	4.9g
Saturated fat	0.89g
Cholesterol	0.3mg
Fibre	4.3g

Baked Apples in Honey and Lemon

A classic combination of flavours in a traditional family pudding. Serve warm, with skimmed-milk custard, if you like.

2 With a cannelle knife or a narrow bladed, sharp knife, cut lines through the apple skin at intervals. Stand the apples in an ovenproof dish.

3 Mix together the honey, lemon rind, juice and low-fat spread.

INGREDIENTS

Serves 4

4 Bramley or other cooking apples

15ml/1 tbsp clear honey

grated rind and juice of 1 lemon

15ml/1 tbsp low-fat spread

skimmed milk custard, to serve (optional)

NUTRITIONAL NOTES
Per portion:

Energy	78Kcals/326kJ
Fat, total	1.7g
Saturated fat	0.37g
Cholesterol	0.2mg
Fibre	2.4g

1 Preheat the oven to 180ºC/350ºF/ Gas 4. Remove the cores from the apples, taking care not to go right through the bottoms of the apples.

4 Spoon the mixture into the apples and cover the dish with foil or a lid. Bake for 40–45 minutes, or until the apples are tender. Serve with skimmed-milk custard, if you wish.

Date, Chocolate and Walnut Pudding

*Proper puddings are not totally taboo
when you're reducing your fat intake –
this one is just within the rules!*

2 Separate the whole egg and place the yolk in a heatproof bowl. Add vanilla essence and sugar. Place over a pan of hot water and whisk to thicken.

3 Sift the flour and cocoa into the mixture and fold in. Stir in the milk. Whisk the egg whites and fold in.

4 Spoon the mixture into the basin and bake for 40–45 minutes, until the pudding has risen well and is firm to the touch. Run a knife around the pudding then turn it out and serve hot.

INGREDIENTS

Serves 4

low-fat spread, for greasing

15g/1/2 oz/1 tbsp chopped walnuts

25g/1oz/2 tbsp chopped dates

1 egg plus 1 egg white

5ml/1 tsp pure vanilla essence

30ml/2 tbsp golden caster sugar

20g/3/4 oz/3 tbsp wholemeal flour

15ml/1 tbsp cocoa powder

30ml/2 tbsp skimmed milk

1 Preheat the oven to 180ºC/350ºF/ Gas 4. Grease a 1.2 litre/2 pint/ 5 cup pudding basin and place a small circle of greaseproof or non-stick baking paper in the base. Spoon in the walnuts and dates.

NUTRITIONAL NOTES
Per portion:

Energy	126Kcals/530kJ
Fat, total	4.9g
Saturated fat	1.15g
Cholesterol	48.3mg
Fibre	1.3g

Sultana and Couscous Puddings

Most couscous is the pre-cooked variety,
which hardly needs cooking, but check
the pack instructions first.

INGREDIENTS

Serves 4

50g/2oz/¹/3 cup sultanas

475ml/16fl oz/2 cups unsweetened
   apple juice

90g/3¹/2 oz/scant 1 cup couscous

2.5ml/¹/2 tsp mixed spice

skimmed milk custard, to serve (optional)

NUTRITIONAL NOTES
Per portion:

Energy	132Kcals/557kJ
Fat, total	0.4g
Saturated fat	0.09g
Cholesterol	0mg
Fibre	0.3g

1 Lightly grease four 250ml/8fl oz/
1 cup pudding basins. Place the
sultanas and apple juice in a pan.

2 Bring the apple juice to the boil,
then lower the heat and simmer
the mixture gently for 2–3 minutes, to
plump up the fruit. Place about half
the fruit in the bottom of the basins.

3 Add the couscous and mixed spice
to the pan and bring the liquid
back to the boil, stirring. Cover and
leave over a low heat for 8–10 minutes,
or until all the liquid has been absorbed.

4 Spoon the couscous into the
basins, spread it level, then cover
the basins tightly with foil. Place the
basins in a steamer over boiling water,
cover and steam for about 30 minutes.
Run a knife around the edges, turn the
puddings out carefully and serve hot,
with skimmed milk custard, if you like.

COOK'S TIP

These puddings can also be cooked
in the microwave. Use microwave-
safe basins or teacups, cover, and
cook on High for 8–10 minutes.

Blackberry Batter Pudding

Batter puddings are easy to make – this one has a juicy blackberry compote under a crunchy batter blanket.

INGREDIENTS

Serves 8

800g/1¾ lb/7 cups blackberries

250g/9oz/generous 1 cup
    granulated sugar

45ml/3 tbsp plain flour

grated rind of 1 lemon

1.5ml/¼ tsp grated nutmeg

For the topping

225g/8oz/2 cups plain flour

225g/8oz/1 cup granulated sugar

15ml/1 tbsp baking powder

pinch of salt

250ml/8fl oz/1 cup skimmed milk

75g/3oz/6 tbsp low-fat spread, melted

1 Preheat the oven to 180ºC/350ºF/ Gas 4. In a large mixing bowl, combine the blackberries with 225g/8oz/1 cup of the sugar. Add the flour and lemon rind. Using a large spoon, stir gently to blend. Transfer to a 2 litre/3½ pint/8 cup baking dish.

2 Make the topping. Sift the flour, sugar, baking powder and salt into a large bowl. Set aside. In a jug, combine the milk and melted low-fat spread.

3 Gradually stir the milk mixture into the dry ingredients and stir until the batter is just smooth.

4 Spoon the batter over the berries. Mix the remaining sugar with the nutmeg, then sprinkle the mixture over the pudding. Bake for about 50 minutes, until the topping is set. Serve hot.

NUTRITIONAL NOTES

Per portion:

Energy	427Kcals/1812kJ
Fat, total	4.5g
Saturated fat	1g
Cholesterol	1.2mg
Fibre	4.1g

Peach Cobbler

All the flavour of the traditional and popular pudding, with less fat than in a conventional cobbler.

INGREDIENTS

Serves 6

1.5kg/3–3½ lb/5 cups peaches, peeled
   and sliced
40g/1½ oz/3 tbsp sugar
30ml/2 tbsp peach brandy
15ml/1 tbsp fresh lemon juice
15ml/1 tbsp cornflour

For the topping
115g/4oz/1 cup plain flour
7.5ml/1½ tsp baking powder
1.5ml/¼ tsp salt
20g/¾oz/¼ cup ground almonds
65g/2½ oz sugar
30ml/2 tbsp low-fat spread
75ml/5 tbsp skimmed milk
1.5ml/¼ tsp almond essence
ice cream, to serve (optional)

3 Add the milk and almond essence. Stir until the mixture is combined.

4 Drop the almond mixture on to the peaches and sprinkle with the sugar.

5 Bake for 30–35 minutes until piping hot. The cobbler topping should be lightly browned. Serve hot, with ice cream, if you like.

NUTRITIONAL NOTES
Per portion:

Energy	393Kcals/1661kJ
Fat, total	4.4g
Saturated fat	0.68g
Cholesterol	0.6mg
Fibre	4g

1 Preheat the oven to 220ºC/425ºF/ Gas 7. In a bowl, toss the peaches with the sugar, peach brandy, lemon juice and cornflour. Spoon the peach mixture into a 2-quart baking dish.

2 Using a fine sieve, sift the flour, baking powder and salt into a mixing bowl. Add the ground almonds and 50g/2oz of the sugar. With 2 knives, cut in the spread until the mixture resembles coarse crumbs.

Apple Brown Betty

A traditional favourite, this tasty dessert is good served with low-fat yogurt or fromage frais.

INGREDIENTS

Serves 6

50g/2oz/1 cup fresh white breadcrumbs

low-fat spread, for greasing

175g/6oz/1 cup light brown sugar

2.5ml/½ tsp ground cinnamon

1.5ml/¼ tsp ground cloves

1.5ml/¼ tsp grated nutmeg

900g/2lb eating apples

juice of 1 lemon

30ml/2 tbsp low-fat spread

20g/¾ oz/3 tbsp finely chopped walnuts

1 Preheat the grill. Spread the bread-crumbs on a baking sheet and toast under the grill until golden, stirring so that they colour evenly. Set aside.

2 Preheat the oven to 190ºC/375ºF/Gas 5. Grease a 2 litre/3½ pint/8 cup baking dish. Mix the sugar with the cinnamon, cloves and nutmeg in a medium-sized mixing bowl.

3 Peel, core and slice the apples. Toss the slices with the lemon juice to prevent them from turning brown.

4 Sprinkle about 45ml/3 tbsp of the breadcrumbs over the bottom of the prepared dish. Cover with one-third of the apples and sprinkle one-third of the sugar-spice mixture on top.

5 Add another layer of breadcrumbs and dot with one-quarter of the spread. Repeat the layers two more times, ending with a layer of breadcrumbs. Sprinkle with the nuts, and dot with the remaining spread.

6 Bake for 35–40 minutes, until the apples are tender and the top is golden brown. Serve warm.

NUTRITIONAL NOTES

Per portion:

Energy	257Kcals/1073kJ
Fat, total	4.7g
Saturated fat	0.73g
Cholesterol	0.3mg
Fibre	2.9g

Blueberry Buckle

*This fruity dessert is an American spe-
ciality and can be served with low-fat
Greek yogurt, if you like.*

INGREDIENTS

Serves 8

low-fat spread, for greasing

225g/8oz/2 cups plain flour

10ml/2 tsp baking powder

2.5ml/^{1}/2 tsp salt

30ml/2 tbsp low-fat spread

175g/6oz/^{3}/4 cup granulated sugar

1 egg

2.5ml/^{1}/2 tsp pure vanilla essence

175ml/6fl oz/^{3}/4 cup skimmed milk

450g/1lb/4 cups fresh blueberries

low-fat Greek yogurt, to serve (optional)

For the topping

115g/4oz/^{2}/3 cup soft light brown sugar

50g/2oz/^{1}/2 cup plain flour

2.5ml/^{1}/2 tsp salt

2.5ml/^{1}/2 tsp ground allspice

45ml/3 tbsp low-fat spread

10ml/2 tsp skimmed milk

5ml/1 tsp pure vanilla essence

1 Preheat the oven to 190ºC/375ºF/
Gas 5. Grease a 23cm/9in round
gratin dish or shallow baking dish. Sift
the flour, baking powder and salt into
a bowl. Set aside.

2 Cream the low-fat spread and sugar.
Beat in the egg and vanilla essence.
Add the flour mix and milk alternately,
beginning and ending with flour.

3 Pour the mixture into the prepared
dish and sprinkle over the
blueberries.

4 Make the topping. Mix the brown
sugar, flour, salt and allspice in a
bowl. Rub in the spread until the
mixture resembles coarse crumbs.

NUTRITIONAL NOTES
Per portion:

Energy	338Kcals/1432kJ
Fat, total	4.9g
Saturated fat	1.14g
Cholesterol	25.1mg
Fibre	2.1g

5 Mix the milk and vanilla essence
together. Drizzle over the flour
mixture and mix with a fork. Sprinkle
the topping over the blueberries. Bake
for 45 minutes, or until an inserted
skewer comes out clean. Serve warm,
with low-fat Greek yogurt, if you like.

Apple and Walnut Crumble

Another American favourite, combining delicious apples with crunchy walnuts, for a simple, but tasty, dessert.

INGREDIENTS

Serves 6

low-fat spread, for greasing

900g/2lb eating apples, peeled and sliced

grated rind of 1/2 lemon

15ml/1 tbsp fresh lemon juice

115g/4oz/1/2 cup light brown sugar

75g/3oz/3/4 cup plain flour

1.5ml/1/4 tsp salt

1.5ml/1/4 tsp grated nutmeg

2.5ml/1/2 tsp ground cardamom

2.5ml/1/2 tsp ground cinnamon

30ml/2 tbsp low-fat spread

20g/3/4 oz/3 tbsp walnut pieces, chopped

1 Preheat the oven to 180ºC/350ºF/ Gas 4. Grease a 23cm/9in shallow baking dish. Toss the apples with the lemon rind and juice. Arrange them evenly in the bottom of the dish.

2 In a mixing bowl, combine the brown sugar, flour, salt, nutmeg, cardamom and cinnamon. Rub in the spread until the mixture resembles coarse crumbs. Mix in the walnuts.

3 Sprinkle the crumble mixture evenly over the apples. Cover with foil and bake for 30 minutes.

4 Remove the foil and continue baking for about 30 minutes more, until the apples are tender and the crumble topping is crisp. Serve warm.

NUTRITIONAL NOTES

Per portion:

Energy	240Kcals/1003kJ
Fat, total	4.7g
Saturated fat	0.76g
Cholesterol	0.3mg
Fibre	3.1g

Strawberry and Apple Crumble

A high-fibre, low-fat version of apple crumble. Fresh or frozen raspberries can be used instead of strawberries.

INGREDIENTS

Serves 4

450g/1lb cooking apples

150g/5oz/1¼ cups strawberries, hulled

30ml/2 tbsp caster sugar

2.5ml/½ tsp ground cinnamon

30ml/2 tbsp orange juice

low-fat custard or yogurt, to serve (optional)

For the crumble

45ml/3 tbsp plain wholemeal flour

50g/2oz/⅔ cup porridge oats

30ml/2 tbsp low-fat spread

1 Preheat the oven to 180ºC/350ºF/ Gas 4. Peel, core and cut the apples into approximately 5mm/¼in-size slices. Halve the strawberries.

2 Toss together the apples, strawberries, sugar, cinnamon and orange juice. Tip the mixture into a 1.2 litre/2 pint/5 cup ovenproof dish.

3 Make the crumble. Combine the flour and oats in a bowl and mix in the low-fat spread with a fork.

4 Sprinkle the crumble evenly over the fruit. Bake for 40–45 minutes, until golden brown and bubbling. Serve warm, with low-fat custard or yogurt, if you like.

NUTRITIONAL NOTES

Per portion:

Energy	173Kcals/729kJ
Fat, total	3.9g
Saturated fat	0.85g
Cholesterol	0.4mg
Fibre	3.5g

Blackberry Charlotte

This delicious classic pudding is the perfect reward for an afternoon's blackberry picking.

INGREDIENTS

Serves 4

30ml/2 tbsp low-fat spread

175g/6oz/3 cups fresh white breadcrumbs

50g/2oz/1/4 cup soft light brown sugar

60ml/4 tbsp golden syrup

finely grated rind and juice of 2 lemons

450g/1lb cooking apples

450g/1lb/4 cups blackberries

NUTRITIONAL NOTES
Per portion:

Energy	346Kcals/1462kJ
Fat, total	4.2g
Saturated fat	0.74g
Cholesterol	0.5mg
Fibre	6.3g

1 Preheat the oven to 180°C/350°F/ Gas 4. Melt the spread in a pan with the breadcrumbs. Sauté for 5–7 minutes, until the crumbs are golden and fairly crisp. Leave to cool slightly.

2 Heat the sugar, syrup, lemon rind and juice gently in a small saucepan. Add the crumbs and mix well.

3 With a sharp knife, cut the apples in quarters, peel them and remove the cores. Slice the wedges thinly.

4 Arrange a thin layer of blackberries in a baking dish. Top with a thin layer of crumbs, then a thin layer of apple, topping the fruit with another thin layer of crumbs. Repeat the process with another layer of blackberries, followed by another layer of crumbs.

5 Continue until you have used up all the ingredients, finishing with a layer of crumbs.

6 Bake for 30 minutes, until the crumbs are golden and the fruit is soft.

Peach Pudding

On chilly days, try this delicious hot fruit pudding with its tantalizing, feather-light sponge topping.

INGREDIENTS

Serves 4

400g/14oz can peach slices in natural juice

50g/2oz/¹/4 cup low-fat spread

40g/1¹/2oz/¹/4 cup soft light brown sugar

1 egg, beaten

65g/2¹/2oz/¹/2 cup plain wholemeal flour

50g/2oz/¹/2 cup plain flour

5ml/1 tsp baking powder

2.5ml/¹/2 tsp ground cinnamon

60ml/4 tbsp skimmed milk

2.5ml/¹/2 tsp vanilla essence

10ml/2 tsp icing sugar, for dusting

low-fat, ready-to-serve custard, to serve

NUTRITIONAL NOTES
Per portion:

Energy	255Kcals/1071kJ
Fat, total	6.78g
Saturated fat	1.57g
Cholesterol	0.5mg
Fibre	2.65g

1 Preheat the oven to 180°C/350°F/ Gas 4. Drain the peaches and put into a 1 litre/1³/4 pint/4 cup pie dish with 30ml/2 tbsp of the juice.

2 Put all the remaining ingredients, except the icing sugar, into a mixing bowl. Beat for 3–4 minutes, until thoroughly combined.

3 Spoon the sponge mixture over the peaches and level the top. Cook in the oven for 35–40 minutes, until springy to the touch. Lightly dust the top with icing sugar before serving hot with the custard.

Chunky Apple Bake

This filling, economical family pudding is a good way of using up bread that is a day or so old.

INGREDIENTS

INGREDIENTS

Serves 4

450g/1lb Bramley or other cooking apples

75g/3oz wholemeal bread, about 3 slices, without crusts

115g/4oz/1/2 cup low-fat cottage cheese

45ml/3 tbsp light muscovado sugar

200ml/7fl oz/scant 1 cup skimmed milk

5ml/1 tsp demerara sugar

1 Preheat the oven to 220ºC/425ºF/ Gas 7. Peel the apples, cut them in quarters and remove the cores.

VARIATION

You could experiment with other types of bread such as oat, rye or white. Pears could be used instead of apples.

NUTRITIONAL NOTES

Per portion:

Energy	158Kcals/669kJ
Fat, total	1g
Saturated fat	0.38g
Cholesterol	2.4mg
Fibre	2.3g

2 Using a sharp knife, roughly chop the apples into even-size pieces, about 1cm/1/2 in in width and depth.

3 Cut the bread into 1cm/1/2 in cubes. Do not use crusts as these will be too thick for the mixture.

4 Put the apples in a bowl and add the bread cubes, cottage cheese and muscovado sugar. Toss lightly and mix thoroughly.

5 Stir in the skimmed milk and then tip the mixture into a wide ovenproof dish. Sprinkle demerara sugar over the top of the mixture.

6 Bake for 30–35 minutes, or until the apple bake is golden brown and bubbling. Serve hot.

COOK'S TIP

You may need to adjust the amount of milk used, depending on the dryness of the bread; the more stale the bread, the more milk it will absorb. The texture should be very moist but not falling apart.

Apple Couscous Pudding

This unusual mixture makes a delicious family pudding with a rich fruity flavour, but virtually no fat.

INGREDIENTS

Serves 4

600ml/1 pint/2¹/₂ cups unsweetened apple juice

115g/4oz/²/₃ cup couscous

40g/1¹/₂oz/¹/₄ cup sultanas

2.5ml/¹/₂ tsp mixed spice

2 large Bramley or other cooking apples

30ml/2 tbsp demerara sugar

low-fat natural yogurt, to serve

NUTRITIONAL NOTES
Per portion:

Energy	194Kcals/815kJ
Fat, total	0.58g
Saturated fat	0.09g
Cholesterol	0mg
Fibre	0.75g

1 Preheat the oven to 200°C/400°F/ Gas 6. Bring to boil the apple juice, couscous, sultanas and spice in a pan, stirring. Lower heat, cover and simmer.

COOK'S TIP
~
Couscous is a pre-cooked wheat that is widely available in supermarkets.

2 Spoon half the couscous mix into a 1.2 litre/2 pint/5 cup ovenproof dish. Peel, core and slice the apples and arrange half the slices on top, then add the remaining couscous.

3 Arrange the remaining apple slices over the top and sprinkle with demerara sugar. Bake for 25–30 minutes or until golden brown. Serve while still hot, with low-fat yogurt.

Baked Fruit Compote

This marvellous medley of dried fruit looks good, tastes even better and is quick and easy to make.

Serves 6

115g/4oz/²/3 cup ready-to-eat dried figs

115g/4oz/¹/2 cup ready-to-eat
   dried apricots

50g/2oz/¹/2 cup ready-to-eat dried
   apple rings

50g/2oz/¹/4 cup ready-to-eat prunes

50g/2oz/¹/2 cup ready-to-eat dried pears

50g/2oz/¹/2 cup ready-to-eat dried peaches

300ml/¹/2 pint/1¹/4 cups unsweetened
   apple juice

300ml/¹/2 pint/1¹/4 cups unsweetened
   orange juice

6 cloves

1 cinnamon stick

a few toasted flaked almonds, to decorate

2 Mix together the unsweetened apple and orange juices and pour evenly over the fruit, thoroughly coating all the fruit with the apple and orange juices. Add the cloves and cinnamon stick and stir gently to mix.

3 Bake for about 30 minutes until the fruit mixture is hot, stirring once or twice during cooking. Set aside and soak for 20 minutes, then discard the cloves and cinnamon stick.

4 Spoon into serving bowls and serve warm or cold, decorated with toasted flaked almonds.

COOK'S TIP

Pineapple and orange or grape and apple juice can be used instead.

1 Preheat the oven to 180ºC/350ºF/ Gas 4. Place the figs, apricots, apple rings, prunes, pears and peaches in a shallow ovenproof dish and stir to mix.

NUTRITIONAL NOTES
Per portion:

Energy	174Kcals/744kJ
Fat, total	0.8g
Saturated fat	0.05g
Cholesterol	0mg
Fibre	5.16g

Kumquat Compote

Warm, spicy and full of sun-ripened ingredients, this is the perfect winter dessert to remind you of summer days.

2 Pare the orange rind and add to the pan. Peel and grate the ginger and add to the pan. Crush the cardamom pods and add the seeds to the mixture, with the cloves.

3 Reduce the heat, cover, and simmer gently for 30 minutes, until the fruit is tender, stirring occasionally.

4 Add the squeezed orange juice to the compote. Sweeten with the honey, sprinkle with the almonds and serve warm.

INGREDIENTS

Serves 4

200g/7oz/2 cups kumquats
200g/7oz/scant 1 cup dried apricots
30ml/2 tbsp sultanas
400ml/14fl oz/1²/3 cups water
1 orange
2.5cm/1in piece of fresh root ginger
4 cardamom pods
4 cloves
30ml/2 tbsp clear honey
15ml/1 tbsp flaked almonds, toasted

1 Wash the kumquats, and, if they are large, cut them in half. Place them in a pan with the apricots, sultanas and water. Bring to the boil.

NUTRITIONAL NOTES
Per portion:

Energy	198Kcals/833kJ
Fat, total	2.9g
Saturated fat	0.25g
Cholesterol	0mg
Fibre	6.9g

Russian Blackcurrant Pudding

This Russian pudding is traditionally made from the thickened juice of stewed red or blackcurrants.

INGREDIENTS

Serves 4

225g/8oz/2 cups red or blackcurrants or
  a mixture of both
225g/8oz/2 cups raspberries
150ml/¼ pint/⅔ cup water
50g/2oz/¼ cup caster sugar
25ml/1½ tbsp arrowroot
15ml/1 tbsp crème de mûre
low-fat Greek yogurt, to serve (optional)

1 Place the currants and raspberries, water and sugar in a pan. Cover the pan and cook over a low heat for 12–15 minutes, until the fruit is soft.

2 Blend the arrowroot to a paste with a little water in a small bowl and stir into the hot fruit mixture. Bring the fruit mixture back to the boil, stirring all the time until thickened and smooth.

3 Remove the pan from the heat and leave the fruit compote to cool slightly, then gently stir in the crème de mûre.

4 Pour the compote into four glass serving bowls and leave until cold, then chill until required. Serve solo or with low-fat Greek yogurt.

NUTRITIONAL NOTES

Per portion:

Energy	105Kcals/443kJ
Fat, total	0.2g
Saturated fat	0g
Cholesterol	0mg
Fibre	3.3g

COOK'S TIP

Crème de mûre is a blackberry liqueur available from large supermarkets – you could use crème de cassis instead, if you prefer.

Cornflake-topped Peach Bake

With a few store-cupboard ingredients, this golden, crisp-crusted pudding can be rustled up in next to no time.

INGREDIENTS

Serves 4

415g/14^1/2 oz can peach slices in juice

30ml/2 tbsp sultanas

1 cinnamon stick

strip of pared orange rind

30ml/2 tbsp low-fat spread

50g/2oz/1^1/2 cups cornflakes

10ml/2 tsp sesame seeds

1 Preheat the oven to 200ºC/400ºF/ Gas 6. Drain the peaches, reserving the juice in a saucepan. Arrange the peaches in a shallow ovenproof dish.

2 Bring to the boil the sultanas, cinnamon, orange rind and juice. Lower the heat and simmer, to reduce the liquid by half. Remove the rind and cinnamon and spoon over the peaches.

3 Melt the low-fat spread in a small pan, stir in the cornflakes and sesame seeds.

4 Spread the cornflake mixture over the fruit. Bake for 15–20 minutes, or until the topping is crisp and golden. Serve hot.

NUTRITIONAL NOTES

Per portion:

Energy	150Kcals/633kJ
Fat, total	4.6g
Saturated fat	1g
Cholesterol	0.5mg
Fibre	1.3g

Rhubarb Spiral Cobbler

The tangy taste of rhubarb combines perfectly with the ginger spice in this unusual Swiss roll.

3 Roll out the dough on a floured surface to a 25cm/10in square. Mix the orange rind, demerara sugar and ginger, then sprinkle this over the dough.

4 Roll up quite tightly, then cut into about 10 slices using a sharp knife. Arrange the slices over the rhubarb.

5 Bake for 20–25 minutes, or until the spirals are well risen and golden brown. Serve warm.

INGREDIENTS

Serves 4

675g/1¹/2 lb rhubarb, sliced

45ml/3 tbsp unsweetened orange juice

75g/3oz/6 tbsp caster sugar

200g/7oz/1³/4 cups self-raising flour

about 250ml/8fl oz/1 cup low-fat
  natural yogurt

grated rind of 1 orange

30ml/2 tbsp demerara sugar

5ml/1 tsp ground ginger

1 Preheat the oven to 200ºC/400ºF/ Gas 6. Mix the rhubarb, orange juice and 50g/2oz/4 tbsp of the caster sugar in a pan. Cover and cook over a low heat for 10 minutes or until tender. Tip into an ovenproof dish.

2 To make the topping, mix the flour and remaining caster sugar in a bowl, then stir in enough of the yogurt to bind to a soft dough.

NUTRITIONAL NOTES

Per portion:

Energy	320Kcals/1343kJ
Fat, total	1.2g
Saturated fat	0.34g
Cholesterol	2mg
Fibre	3.92g

COOK'S TIP

In the summer you could substitute halved plums, sliced nectarines or peaches for the rhubarb, if you prefer.

Plum, Apple and Banana Scone Pie

This is one of those simple, satisfying puddings that everyone enjoys. Serve hot or cold with low-fat natural yogurt.

INGREDIENTS

Serves 4

450g/1lb plums

1 Bramley or other cooking apple

1 large banana

150ml/¼ pint/⅔ cup water

115g/4oz/1 cup wholemeal flour, or half wholemeal and half plain flour

10ml/2 tsp baking powder

25g/1oz/3 tbsp raisins

about 60ml/4 tbsp soured milk or low-fat natural yogurt

low-fat natural yogurt, to serve (optional)

2 Mix the fruit in a saucepan. Pour in the water. Bring to simmering point and cook gently for 15 minutes or until the fruit is completely soft.

5 Transfer the scone dough to a lightly floured surface and divide it into 6–8 portions, then pat them into flattish scones.

1 Preheat the oven to 180ºC/350ºF/ Gas 4. Cut the plums in half and ease out the stones. Peel, core and chop the apple, then slice the banana.

3 Spoon the fruit mixture into a pie dish. Level the surface.

4 Mix the flour, baking powder and raisins in a bowl. Add the soured milk or low-fat natural yogurt and mix to a very soft dough.

6 Cover the plum and apple mixture with the scones. Bake the pie for 40 minutes until the scone topping is cooked through. Serve the pie hot with natural yogurt, or leave it until cold.

NUTRITIONAL NOTES
Per portion:

Energy	195Kcals/831kJ
Fat, total	1g
Saturated fat	0.2g
Cholesterol	0.6mg
Fibre	5.2g

COOK'S TIP

To prevent the banana discolouring before cooking, dip each slice in fresh lemon juice.

Griddle Cakes with Mulled Plums

*These light little pancakes, with their
rich, spicy plum sauce, can just as easily
be cooked on the hob as on the barbecue.*

INGREDIENTS

Serves 6

500g/1¼ lb red plums
90ml/6 tbsp light muscovado sugar
1 cinnamon stick
2 whole cloves
1 piece star anise
90ml/6 tbsp unsweetened apple juice
low-fat Greek yogurt or fromage frais,
    to serve (optional)

For the griddle cakes

50g/2oz/½ cup plain flour
10ml/2 tsp baking powder
pinch of salt
50g/2oz/½ cup fine cornmeal
30ml/2 tbsp light muscovado sugar
1 egg, beaten
300ml/½ pint/1¼ cups skimmed milk
15ml/1 tbsp corn oil

1 Halve, stone and quarter the
plums. Place them in a pan, with
the sugar, spices and apple juice.

COOK'S TIP
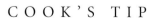
Use spray oil on the griddle if you
prefer, and cut the fat content
still further.

2 Place on a hot barbecue or hob
and bring to the boil. Lower heat,
cover and simmer gently for 8–10
minutes, stirring, until the plums are
soft. Remove the spices and keep warm.

3 For the griddle cakes, sift the flour,
baking powder and salt into a large
bowl and stir in the cornmeal and sugar.

4 Make a well in the centre and add
the egg; gradually beat in the milk.
Beat with a wooden spoon to a smooth
batter. Beat in 5ml/1 tsp of the oil.

5 Heat a griddle or a heavy frying-
pan on a hot barbecue or hob.
When it is very hot, brush with oil and
then drop tablespoons of batter on to
it. Cook the griddle cakes for about a
minute, until bubbles appear on the
surface and the underside is golden.

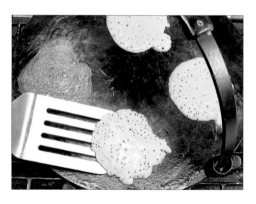

6 Turn the cakes over and cook the
other side for a further minute, or
until golden. Bake the other cakes.
Serve hot with the mulled plums. Add
a spoonful of low-fat Greek yogurt or
fromage frais, if you like.

NUTRITIONAL NOTES
Per portion:

Energy	159Kcals/669kJ
Fat, total	3.3g
Saturated fat	0.58g
Cholesterol	33.1mg
Fibre	1.7g

Barbecued Bananas with Spicy Vanilla Spread

Baked bananas are easy because they bake in their own skins and need no preparation at all.

2 Meanwhile, split the cardamom pods, remove the seeds and crush them lightly with a pestle and mortar.

3 Split the vanilla pod lengthways and scrape out the tiny seeds. Mix with the cardamom, orange rind, sugar brandy and spread, to make a paste.

4 Slit the skin of each banana, open out slightly and spoon in a little of the paste. Serve at once.

INGREDIENTS

Serves 4

4 bananas

6 green cardamom pods

1 vanilla pod

finely grated rind of 1 small orange

30ml/2 tbsp brandy

60ml/4 tbsp light muscovado sugar

45ml/3 tbsp low-fat spread

COOK'S TIP

If making this for children, use orange juice instead of the brandy or, if the fat content is no object, drizzle the cooked bananas with melted chocolate.

1 Place the bananas, in their skins, on the hot barbecue and leave for 6–8 minutes, turning occasionally, until they are turning brownish-black.

NUTRITIONAL NOTES
Per portion:

Energy	215Kcals/900kJ
Fat, total	4.9g
Saturated fat	1.22g
Cholesterol	0.7mg
Fibre	1.1g

Hot Spiced Bananas

Baking bananas in a rum and fruit syrup makes for a dessert with negligible fat and maximum flavour.

INGREDIENTS

Serves 6

low-fat spread, for greasing

6 ripe bananas

200g/7oz/generous 1 cup light brown sugar

250ml/8fl oz/1 cup unsweetened
   pineapple juice

120ml/4fl oz/1/2 cup dark rum

2 cinnamon sticks

12 whole cloves

NUTRITIONAL NOTES
Per portion:

Energy	290Kcals/1215kJ
Fat, total	0.3g
Saturated fat	0.11g
Cholesterol	0mg
Fibre	1.1g

1 Preheat the oven to 180ºC/350ºF/ Gas 4. Grease a 23cm/9in shallow baking dish.

2 Peel the bananas and cut them diagonally into 2.5cm/1in pieces. Arrange the banana pieces, to spread evenly over the bottom of the prepared baking dish.

3 Mix the sugar and pineapple juice in a saucepan. Heat gently until the sugar has dissolved, stirring. Add the rum, cinnamon and cloves. Bring to the boil, then remove from the heat.

4 Pour the hot pineapple and spice mixture over the bananas in the baking dish. Bake in the oven for 25–30 minutes until the bananas are tender. Serve while still hot.

Rum and Raisin Bananas

Choose almost-ripe bananas with evenly coloured skins, either all yellow or just green at the tips.

Serves 4

40g/1¹/2 oz/¹/4 cup seedless raisins

75ml/5 tbsp dark rum

15ml/1 tbsp low-fat spread

60ml/4 tbsp soft light brown sugar

4 ripe bananas, peeled and
   halved lengthways

1.5ml/¹/4 tsp grated nutmeg

1.5ml/¹/4 tsp ground cinnamon

15ml/1 tbsp slivered almonds, toasted

low-fat fromage frais or low-fat vanilla
   ice cream, to serve (optional)

1 Put the raisins in a bowl and pour over the rum. Leave them to soak for about 30 minutes until plump.

2 Melt the spread in a frying pan, add the sugar and stir until it has completely dissolved. Add the bananas and cook for a few minutes until tender, turning occasionally.

3 Sprinkle the spices over the bananas, then pour over the rum and raisins. Carefully set alight using a long-handled match; stir gently to mix.

4 Scatter over the slivered almonds and serve immediately with low-fat fromage frais or low-fat vanilla ice cream, if you like.

COOK'S TIP

For an accompaniment that won't add too much fat, make your own frozen yogurt by churning extra low-fat yogurt in an ice-cream maker.

NUTRITIONAL NOTES

Per portion:

Energy	263Kcals/1110kJ
Fat, total	4.1g
Saturated fat	0.51g
Cholesterol	0.2mg
Fibre	1.6g

Caribbean Bananas

Tender baked bananas in a rich and spicy sauce of ground allspice and ginger – a dessert for those with a sweet tooth!

INGREDIENTS

Serves 4

30ml/2 tbsp low-fat spread
8 firm ripe bananas
juice of 1 lime
75g/3oz/¹/2 cup soft dark brown sugar
5ml/1 tsp ground allspice
2.5ml/¹/2 tsp ground ginger
seeds from 6 cardamoms crushed
30ml/2 tbsp rum
pared lime rind, to decorate
low-fat crème fraîche, to serve (optional)

1 Preheat the oven to 200°C/400°F/ Gas 6. Use a little of the spread to grease a shallow baking dish large enough to hold the bananas snugly in a single layer.

2 Peel the bananas and cut them in half lengthways. Arrange the bananas in the dish and pour over the lime juice.

NUTRITIONAL NOTES
Per portion:

Energy	310Kcals/1306kJ
Fat, total	3.2g
Saturated fat	0.87g
Cholesterol	0.4mg
Fibre	2.2g

3 Mix the sugar, allspice, ginger and crushed cardamom seeds in a bowl. Scatter the mixture over the bananas. Dot with the remaining low-fat spread. Bake, basting once, for 15 minutes, or until the bananas are soft.

4 Remove the dish from the oven. Warm the rum in a small pan or metal soup ladle, pour it over the bananas and set it alight.

5 As soon as the flames die down, decorate the dessert with the pared lime rind. Serve while still hot and add a dollop of low-fat crème fraîche to each portion, if you like.

VARIATION

For a version that will appeal more to children, use orange juice instead of lime and leave out the rum.

Barbecued Pineapple Boats with Rum Glaze

Pineapple is even more full of flavour when barbecued or grilled; this spiced rum glaze turns it into a special dessert.

INGREDIENTS

Serves 4

1 medium pineapple, about 600g/1lb 6oz

30ml/2 tbsp dark muscovado sugar

5ml/1 tsp ground ginger

45ml/3 tbsp low-fat spread, melted

30ml/2 tbsp dark rum

COOK'S TIP

For an easier version, cut off the skin and then slice the whole pineapple into thick slices and cook as shown.

1 With a large, sharp knife, cut the pineapple lengthways into quarters. Cut out and discard the hard centre core from each quarter. Take care when handling the rough outer skin.

2 Cut between the flesh and skin, to release the flesh, but not cut the skin. Slice the flesh across, into chunks.

3 Push a bamboo skewer lengthways through each quarter and into the stalk, to hold the chunks in place.

4 Mix together the sugar, ginger, melted spread and rum and brush over the pineapple. Cook the quarters on a hot barbecue for 3–4 minutes; pour the remaining glaze over the top and serve.

NUTRITIONAL NOTES

Per portion:

Energy	155Kcals/646kJ
Fat, total	4.9g
Saturated fat	1.14g
Cholesterol	0.7mg
Fibre	1.8g

Grilled Nectarines with Amaretto

Amaretto, the sweet almond-flavoured liqueur from Italy, adds a touch of luxury to these low-fat grilled nectarines.

INGREDIENTS

Serves 4

6 ripe nectarines

30ml/2 tbsp clear honey

60ml/4 tbsp Amaretto

half-fat crème fraîche, to serve (optional)

NUTRITIONAL NOTES

Per portion:

Energy	150Kcals/627kJ
Fat, total	0.2g
Saturated fat	0g
Cholesterol	0mg
Fibre	2.7g

1 Cut the nectarines in half by running a small sharp knife down the side of each fruit from top to bottom, cutting right through to the stone. Gently ease the nectarine apart and remove the stone. Handle the fruit carefully as nectarines bruise easily.

2 Place the nectarines cut side up in an ovenproof dish and drizzle 2.5ml/½ tsp honey and 5ml/1 tsp Amaretto over each half. Preheat the grill until very hot and then grill the fruit until slightly charred. Serve with a little half-fat crème fraîche, if you like.

Nectarines with Marzipan and Yogurt

A luscious dessert that few can resist; marzipan and nectarines are a wonderful combination.

INGREDIENTS

Serves 4

4 firm, ripe nectarines or peaches

75g/3oz marzipan

75ml/5 tbsp low-fat Greek yogurt

3 amaretti biscuits, crushed

3 Spoon the low-fat Greek yogurt on top. Sprinkle the crushed amaretti biscuits over the yogurt.

4 Place the fruits on a hot barbecue or under a hot grill. Cook for 3–5 minutes, until the yogurt starts to melt.

NUTRITIONAL NOTES

Per portion:

Energy	176Kcals/737kJ
Fat, total	4.3g
Saturated fat	0.98g
Cholesterol	3.2mg
Fibre	2.3g

1 Cut the nectarines or peaches in half, removing the stones.

2 Cut the marzipan into eight pieces and press one piece into the stone cavity of each nectarine half. Preheat the grill, unless you are cooking on the barbecue.

COOK'S TIP

If the stone does not pull out easily when you halve the fruit, use a small, sharp knife to cut around it.

Spiced Nectarines with Fromage Frais

This easy dessert is good at any time of year – use canned peach halves if fresh nectarines are not available.

2 Arrange the fruit, cut-side upwards, in a wide flameproof dish or on a baking sheet.

3 Stir the sugar into the fromage frais. Using a teaspoon, spoon the mixture into the hollow of each half.

1 With a sharp knife cut the nectarines or peaches in half and remove the stones.

4 Sprinkle the fruit with the ground star anise or mixed spice. Place under a moderately hot grill for 6–8 minutes, or until the fruit is hot and bubbling. Serve warm.

INGREDIENTS

Serves 4

4 ripe nectarines or peaches

15ml/1 tbsp light muscovado sugar

115g/4oz/$^1/_2$ cup low-fat fromage frais

2.5ml/$^1/_2$ tsp ground star anise or
    mixed spice

NUTRITIONAL NOTES
Per portion:

Energy	108Kcals/450kJ
Fat, total	3.3g
Saturated fat	2g
Cholesterol	14.4mg
Fibre	1.5g

Barbecued Orange Parcels

This is one of the most delicious ways of rounding off a barbecue party. Serve on their own, or with low-fat fromage frais.

INGREDIENTS

Serves 4

30ml/2 tbsp low-fat spread, plus extra, melted, for brushing

4 oranges

30ml/2 tbsp maple syrup

30ml/2 tbsp Cointreau or Grand Marnier liqueur

low-fat fromage frais, to serve (optional)

1 Cut four double-thickness squares of foil, large enough to wrap the oranges. Melt about 10ml/2 tsp of the low-fat spread and brush it over the centre of each piece of foil.

NUTRITIONAL NOTES

Per portion:

Energy	127Kcals/532kJ
Fat, total	3.2g
Saturated fat	0.74g
Cholesterol	0.5mg
Fibre	2.7g

2 Remove some shreds of orange rind, for the decoration. Blanch and dry them and set aside. Peel the oranges, removing the white pith and peel and catching the juice in a bowl.

3 Slice the oranges crossways into thick slices. Reassemble, and place each orange on a square of foil.

4 Create a cup shape by tucking the foil up high around the oranges. This will keep them in shape, but leave the foil open at the top.

5 Mix together the reserved orange juice, maple syrup and liqueur and spoon the mixture over the oranges.

6 Add a dab of low-fat spread to each parcel and fold over the foil, to seal in the juices. Place the parcels on a hot barbecue for 10–12 minutes, until hot. Serve topped with shreds of orange rind and fromage frais, if you like.

COOK'S TIP

To make the orange shreds for the decoration, slice off several pieces of orange rind, taking care to avoid the bitter white pith, then cut them into thin matchsticks. Add to a small pan of boiling water, for 1 minute, then drain and dry on kitchen paper.

Apples and Raspberries in Rose Syrup

Inspiration for this dessert stems from the fact that the apple and the raspberry belong to the rose family.

INGREDIENTS

Serves 4

5ml/1 tsp rose pouchong tea

900ml/1¹/2 pints/3³/4 cups boiling water

5ml/1 tsp rose-water (optional)

50g/2oz/¹/4 cup granulated sugar

5ml/1 tsp lemon juice

5 dessert apples

175g/6oz/1¹/2 cups fresh raspberries

1 Warm a large tea pot. Add the rose pouchong tea, then pour on the boiling water, together with the rose-water, if using. Allow to stand and infuse for 4 minutes.

2 Measure the sugar and lemon juice into a stainless steel saucepan. Strain in the tea and stir to dissolve the sugar.

3 Peel and core the apples, then cut into quarters.

4 Poach the apples in the syrup for about 5 minutes.

5 Transfer the apples and syrup to a large metal tray and leave to cool to room temperature.

6 Pour the cooled apples and syrup into a bowl, add the raspberries and mix to combine. Spoon into individual dishes or bowls and serve while still warm.

NUTRITIONAL NOTES

Per portion:

Energy	125Kcals/526kJ
Fat, total	0.4g
Saturated fat	0g
Cholesterol	0mg
Fibre	3.6g

Papaya Baked with Ginger

*Ginger enhances the flavour of papaya
in this recipe, which takes no more than
ten minutes to prepare.*

INGREDIENTS

Serves 4

2 ripe papayas

2 pieces stem ginger in syrup, drained, plus
    15ml/1 tbsp syrup from the jar

8 dessert biscuits, coarsely crushed

45ml/3 tbsp raisins

shredded, finely pared rind and juice
    of 1 lime

15ml/1 tbsp light muscovado sugar

60ml/4 tbsp low-fat Greek yogurt, plus extra to
    serve (optional)

15ml/1 tbsp finely chopped unsalted
    pistachio nuts

COOK'S TIP

Don't overcook papaya or the flesh
will become very watery.

1 Preheat the oven to 200ºC/400ºF/
Gas 6. Cut the papayas in half and
scoop out their seeds. Place the halves
in a baking dish and set aside. Cut the
stem ginger into fine matchsticks.

2 Make the filling. Combine the
crushed biscuits, stem ginger matchsticks and raisins in a bowl. Make sure
they are all mixed well together.

3 Stir in the lime rind and juice,
then add the sugar and the yogurt.
Mix well.

4 Fill the papaya halves and drizzle
with the ginger syrup. Sprinkle
with the pistachios.

5 Bake for about 25 minutes or until
tender. Serve hot, with extra low-
fat Greek yogurt, if you like.

NUTRITIONAL NOTES

Per portion:

Energy	218Kcals/922kJ
Fat, total	4.2g
Saturated fat	1.23g
Cholesterol	6mg
Fibre	3.8g

Baked Peaches with Raspberry Sauce

*Pretty as a picture – that's the effect
when you serve these tasty stuffed
peaches to delighted dinner party guests.*

INGREDIENTS

Serves 6

30ml/2 tbsp low-fat spread

50g/2oz/¼ cup granulated sugar

1 egg, beaten

20g/¾oz/¼ cup ground almonds

6 ripe peaches

glossy leaves and plain or frosted raspberries,
    to decorate

For the sauce

225g/8oz/2 cups raspberries

15ml/1 tbsp icing sugar

NUTRITIONAL NOTES

Per portion:

Energy	137Kcals/576kJ
Fat, total	4.7g
Saturated fat	0.81g
Cholesterol	32.3mg
Fibre	2.8g

1 Preheat the oven to 180ºC/350ºF/
Gas 4. Beat the low-fat spread and
sugar together, then beat in the egg
and ground almonds.

2 Cut the peaches in half and
remove the stones. With a spoon,
scrape out some of the flesh from each
peach half, slightly enlarging the
hollow left by the stone. Save the
excess peach for the sauce.

3 Stand the peach halves on a baking
sheet, supporting them with
crumpled foil to keep them steady. Fill
each peach hollow with the almond
mixture. Bake for 30 minutes, or until
the almond filling is puffed and golden
and the peaches are very tender.

4 Meanwhile, process the raspberries,
icing sugar and the reserved peach
flesh in a food processor or blender,
until smooth. Press through a strainer
over a bowl to remove fibres and seeds.

5 Let the peaches cool slightly.
Spoon the sauce on each plate and
arrange two peach halves on top.
Decorate with the leaves and
raspberries and serve immediately.

COOK'S TIP

For a special occasion, stir about
15ml/1 tbsp framboise or peach
brandy into the raspberry sauce.

Stuffed Peaches with Almond Liqueur

Together amaretti biscuits and amaretto liqueur have an intense almond flavour, and make a natural partner for peaches.

INGREDIENTS

Serves 4

4 ripe but firm peaches

50g/2oz/¹/2 cup amaretti biscuits

30ml/2 tbsp low-fat spread

30ml/2 tbsp caster sugar

1 egg yolk

60ml/4 tbsp almond liqueur

low-fat spread, for greasing

250ml/8fl oz/1 cup dry white wine

8 tiny sprigs of fresh basil, to decorate

low-fat ice cream, to serve (optional)

1 Preheat the oven to 180°C/350°F/ Gas 4. Cut the peaches in half and remove the stones. With a spoon, scrape out some of the flesh from each peach half, slightly enlarging the hollow. Chop this flesh and set it aside.

2 Put the amaretti biscuits in a bowl and crush them finely with the end of a rolling pin.

3 Cream the low-fat spread and sugar together in a separate bowl until smooth. Stir in the reserved chopped peach flesh, the egg yolk and half the liqueur with the amaretti crumbs. Lightly grease a baking dish that is just large enough to hold the peach halves in a single layer.

NUTRITIONAL NOTES
Per portion:

Energy	232Kcals/971kJ
Fat, total	5g
Saturated fat	1.37g
Cholesterol	54.7mg
Fibre	1.9g

4 Stand the peaches in the dish and spoon the stuffing into them. Mix the remaining liqueur with the wine, pour over the peaches and bake for 25 minutes or until the peaches feel tender. Decorate with basil and serve at once, with low-fat ice cream, if you like.

Coconut Dumplings with Apricot Sauce

These delicate little dumplings are simple to make. The sharp flavour of the sauce offsets the creamy dumplings.

INGREDIENTS

Serves 4

75g/3oz/6 tbsp low-fat cottage cheese
1 egg white
15ml/1 tbsp low-fat spread
15ml/1 tbsp light muscovado sugar
30ml/2 tbsp self-raising wholemeal flour
finely grated rind of 1/2 lemon
15ml/1 tbsp desiccated coconut, toasted

For the sauce

225g/8oz can apricot halves in
    natural juice
15ml/1 tbsp lemon juice

1 Half-fill a steamer with boiling water and put it on to boil. If you do not own a steamer, place a heatproof plate or shallow dish over a pan of boiling water.

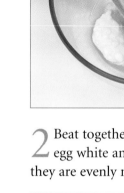

2 Beat together the cottage cheese, egg white and low-fat spread until they are evenly mixed.

3 Stir in the sugar, flour, lemon rind and coconut, mixing everything evenly to a fairly firm dough.

4 Place 8–12 spoonfuls of the mixture in the steamer or on the plate, leaving a space between them.

5 Cover the steamer or pan tightly with a lid or a plate and steam for about 10 minutes, until the dumplings have risen and are firm to the touch.

6 Meanwhile make the sauce. Purée the can of apricots and stir in the lemon juice. Pour into a small pan and heat until boiling, then serve with the dumplings. Sprinkle with extra coconut to serve, if you like and can afford the extra fat.

NUTRITIONAL NOTES
Per portion:

Energy	112Kcals/470kJ
Fat, total	4.3g
Saturated fat	2.56g
Cholesterol	1.2mg
Fibre	1.7g

COOK'S TIP

The mixture should be quite stiff; if it is not stiff enough to hold its shape, stir in a little more flour.

Pineapple Flambé

Flambéing means adding alcohol and then burning it off so that the flavour is not too overpowering.

INGREDIENTS

Serves 4

1 large, ripe pineapple, about 600g/1lb 6oz

30ml/2 tbsp low-fat spread

40g/1¹/2 oz/¹/4 cup soft light brown sugar

60ml/4 tbsp fresh orange juice

30ml/2 tbsp brandy or vodka

15g/¹/2 oz/1 tbsp slivered almonds, toasted

1 Cut away the top and base of the pineapple. Then cut down the sides, removing all the dark "eyes".

2 Cut the pineapple into thin slices. Using an apple corer, remove the hard, central core from each slice.

VARIATION

Try this with nectarines, peaches or cherries. Omit the almonds if you want to reduce the fat content a little.

3 Melt the spread in a frying pan, with the sugar. Add the orange juice. Stir until hot, then add as many pineapple slices as the pan will hold. Cook for 1–2 minutes, turning once. Remove each slice as it browns.

4 Return all the pineapple slices to the pan, heat briefly, then pour over the brandy or vodka and light with a long-handled match. Let the flames die down, then sprinkle with the almonds. Serve at once.

NUTRITIONAL NOTES

Per portion:

Energy	171Kcals/711kJ
Fat, total	5g
Saturated fat	0.62g
Cholesterol	0.4mg
Fibre	2.1g

Warm Pears in Cider

Serve these pears with low-fat Greek yogurt or fromage frais if you must, but they are very good on their own.

INGREDIENTS

Serves 4

1 lemon

50g/2oz/¼ cup caster sugar

a little grated nutmeg

250ml/8fl oz/1 cup sweet cider

4 firm, ripe pears

NUTRITIONAL NOTES

Per portion:

Energy	11Kcals/46kJ
Fat, total	0g
Saturated fat	0g
Cholesterol	0mg
Fibre	3.3g

1 Using a potato peeler remove the rind from the lemon in thin strips, leaving any white pith behind.

2 Squeeze the juice from the lemon and pour it into a saucepan. Add the lemon rind, sugar, grated nutmeg and cider and heat gently until the sugar has completely dissolved.

3 Peel the pears, leaving the stalks on if possible, and place in the pan of cider. Poach for 10–15 minutes until almost tender, turning them frequently.

4 Transfer the pears to individual serving dishes using a slotted spoon. Simmer the liquid over a high heat until it reduces slightly and becomes syrupy. Pour the warm syrup over the pears. Serve at once.

COOK'S TIP

To make sure that the pears are firm enough for this dish, buy them slightly under-ripe and then wait a day or more.

Fanned Poached Pears in Port Syrup

The perfect choice for autumn dining,
this simple dessert has a beautiful rich
colour and fantastic flavour.

INGREDIENTS

Serves 4

2 ripe, firm pears

pared rind of 1 lemon

175ml/6fl oz/³/4 cup ruby port

50g/2oz/¹/4 cup caster sugar

1 cinnamon stick

60ml/4 tbsp cold water

half-fat crème fraîche, to serve (optional)

To decorate

15ml/1 tbsp sliced hazelnuts, toasted

fresh mint, pear or rose leaves

NUTRITIONAL NOTES

Per portion:

Energy	173Kcals/725kJ
Fat	2.5g
Saturated fat	0.17g
Cholesterol	0mg
Fibre	1.9g

1 Peel the pears, cut them in half and remove the cores. Place the lemon rind, port, sugar, cinnamon stick and water in a shallow pan. Bring to the boil over a low heat. Add the pears, cover and poach for 5 minutes. Let the pears cool in the syrup.

2 When the pears are cold, transfer them to a bowl with a slotted spoon. Return the syrup to the heat. Boil rapidly until it has reduced to form a syrup. Remove the cinnamon stick and lemon rind and leave the syrup to cool.

3 To serve, place each pear half on a board, cut side down. Keeping it intact at the stalk end, slice lengthways. Carefully lift it off, using a palette knife, and place on a dessert plate. Press gently to fan out the pears. Spoon over the port syrup, top with a few hazelnuts and decorate with fresh mint, pear or rose leaves. Serve with half-fat crème fraîche, if you like.

Mulled Pears with Ginger and Brandy

The flavours improve with keeping, so you can mull the pears several days before you want to serve them.

INGREDIENTS

Serves 8

600ml/1 pint/2¹/₂ cups red wine

225g/8oz/1 cup caster sugar

1 cinnamon stick

6 cloves

finely grated rind of 1 orange

10ml/2 tsp grated fresh root ginger

8 even-sized firm pears, with stalks

15ml/1 tbsp brandy

25g/1oz/¹/₄ cup almonds or hazelnuts, toasted, to decorate

low-fat whipped cream, to serve (optional)

3 Gently remove the pears from the syrup with a slotted spoon, being very careful not to dislodge the stalks. Put the cooked pears in a serving bowl or individual bowls, if you prefer.

NUTRITIONAL NOTES
Per portion:

Energy	246Kcals/1038kJ
Fat, total	1.9g
Saturated fat	0.13g
Cholesterol	0mg
Fibre	3.5g

4 Boil the syrup until it thickens and reduces. Cool slightly, add the brandy and strain over the pears. Decorate with toasted nuts. Serve with whipped cream, if you like.

1 Put all the ingredients except the pears, brandy and nuts into a large pan and heat slowly until the sugar has dissolved. Simmer for 5 minutes.

2 Peel the pears, leaving the stalks on. Arrange them upright in the pan. Cover and simmer until tender, for 45–50 minutes, depending on size.

Poached Pears in Maple-yogurt Sauce

Poach the pears in advance, and have the cooled syrup ready to spoon on to the plates just before you serve.

Serves 6

6 firm dessert pears
15ml/1 tbsp lemon juice
250ml/8fl oz/1 cup sweet white wine
   or cider
thinly pared rind of 1 lemon
1 cinnamon stick
30ml/2 tbsp maple syrup
2.5ml/$^{1}/_{2}$ tsp arrowroot
150ml/$^{1}/_{4}$ pint/$^{2}/_{3}$ cup low-fat
   Greek yogurt

1 Peel the pears thinly, leaving them whole and with the stalks. Brush them with lemon juice, to prevent them from browning. Use a potato peeler or small knife to scoop out the core from the base of each pear.

2 Place them in a wide, heavy pan and add the wine or cider, with cold water to almost cover the pears.

3 Add the lemon rind and cinnamon stick and bring to the boil. Reduce the heat, cover and simmer gently for 30–40 minutes, or until tender. Turn the pears so that they cook evenly. Lift out carefully, draining them well.

4 Boil the liquid uncovered to reduce to about 120ml/4fl oz/$^{1}/_{2}$ cup. Strain into a jug and add the maple syrup. Blend a little of the liquid with the arrowroot, then return the mixture to the jug; mix well. Return to the pan and cook, stirring, until thick and clear. Cool.

COOK'S TIP

The cooking time will vary, depending upon the type and ripeness of the pears. They should be ripe, but firm; soft pears will not keep their shape.

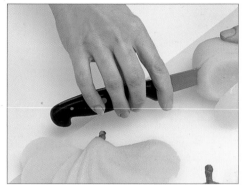

5 Slice each pear about three-quarters of the way through, leaving the slices attached at the stem end. Fan each pear out on a serving plate.

6 Stir 30ml/2 tbsp of the cooled syrup into the yogurt and spoon it around the pears. Drizzle with the remaining syrup and serve immediately.

NUTRITIONAL NOTES

Per portion:

Energy	136Kcals/573kJ
Fat, total	1.4g
Saturated fat	0.79g
Cholesterol	1.8mg
Fibre	3.3g

Blushing Pears

Pears poached in rosé wine and sweet spices absorb all the subtle flavours and turn a soft pink colour.

INGREDIENTS

Serves 6

6 firm eating pears

300ml/½ pint/1¼ cups rosé wine

150ml/¼ pint/⅔ cup cranberry juice
  or clear apple juice

strip of thinly pared orange rind

4 whole cloves

1 cinnamon stick

1 bay leaf

75ml/5tbsp caster sugar

small bay leaves, to decorate

2 Pour the wine and cranberry or apple juice into a large heavy-based saucepan. Add the orange rind, cloves, cinnamon stick, bay leaf and sugar.

4 Using a slotted spoon, gently lift the pears out of the syrup and transfer to a serving dish.

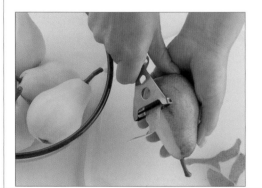

1 Thinly peel the pears with a sharp knife or vegetable peeler, leaving the stalks attached.

3 Heat gently, stirring all the time until the sugar has dissolved. Add the pears and stand them upright in the pan. Pour in enough cold water to barely cover them. Cover and cook very gently for 20–30 minutes, or until just tender, turning and basting occasionally to ensure even cooking.

5 Bring the syrup to the boil and boil rapidly for 10–15 minutes, or until it has reduced by half.

6 Strain the syrup and pour over the pears. Serve hot, decorated with bay leaves.

NUTRITIONAL NOTES
Per portion:

Energy	148Kcals/620kJ
Fat, total	0.16g
Saturated fat	0g
Cholesterol	0mg
Fibre	1.9g

COOK'S TIP

Check the pears by piercing with a skewer or sharp knife towards the end of the poaching time and carefully lift out any that have cooked more quickly than others.

Char-grilled Apples on Cinnamon Toasts

This yummy treat makes a fabulous finale to a summer barbecue, but it can also be cooked under the grill.

Serves 4

4 sweet dessert apples

juice of ½ lemon

4 individual muffins

15ml/1 tbsp low-fat spread, melted

30ml/2 tbsp golden caster sugar

5ml/1 tsp ground cinnamon

low-fat Greek yogurt, to serve (optional)

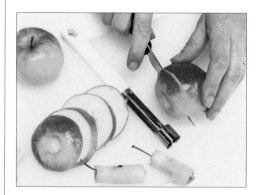

1 Core the apples and cut them horizontally in three or four thick slices. Sprinkle with lemon juice.

VARIATION

Other fruit in season could be used for this recipe. Try pears, peaches or pineapple for variety. Nutmeg or mixed spice could also replace the cinnamon.

NUTRITIONAL NOTES
Per portion:

Energy	241Kcals/1016kJ
Fat, total	4.9g
Saturated fat	1.63g
Cholesterol	0.2mg
Fibre	3.0g

2 Cut the muffins into thick slices. Brush sparingly with melted low-fat spread on both sides.

3 Mix together the sugar and ground cinnamon. Preheat the grill if not using the barbecue.

4 Place the apple and muffin slices on the hot barbecue or under the grill and cook them for 3–4 minutes, turning once, until they are beginning to turn golden brown.

5 Sprinkle half the cinnamon sugar over the apple slices and toasts and cook for 1 minute more, until they are a rich golden brown.

6 To serve, arrange the apple slices over the toasts and sprinkle them with the remaining cinnamon sugar. Serve hot, with low-fat Greek yogurt, if you like.

COOK'S TIP

To keep the quantity of fat within acceptable levels, make this simple, scrumptious dessert with muffins, but for a rare splurge, use brioche or a similar sweet bread.

Banana, Maple and Lime Pancakes

Pancakes are a treat any day of the week, and they can be made in advance and stored in the freezer for convenience.

INGREDIENTS

Serves 4

115g/4oz/1 cup plain flour

1 egg white

250ml/8fl oz/1 cup skimmed milk

60ml/4 tbsp cold water

spray oil, for frying

shreds of lime rind, to decorate

For the filling

4 bananas, sliced

45ml/3 tbsp maple syrup or golden syrup

30ml/2 tbsp fresh lime juice

1 Make the pancake batter by beating together the flour, egg white, milk and water in a bowl until smooth and bubbly. Cover and chill until needed.

2 Apply a light coat of spray oil to a non-stick frying pan. Heat the pan, then pour a little batter, swirling it around the pan to coat evenly.

3 Cook the pancake until golden, then toss and cook the other side. Slide on to a plate, cover with foil and keep hot while cooking all the pancakes.

4 Make the filling. Mix the bananas, syrup and lime juice in a pan and simmer gently for 1 minute. Spoon into the pancakes and fold into quarters. Decorate with lime rind.

NUTRITIONAL NOTES

Per portion:

Energy	282Kcals/1185kJ
Fat, total	2.79g
Saturated fat	0.47g
Cholesterol	1.25mg
Fibre	2.12g

COOK'S TIP

Pancakes freeze well. To store for later use, interleave them with non-stick baking paper, wrap and freeze for up to 3 months.

Chinese Chestnut Pancakes

Thin Chinese pancakes, spread with chestnut purée and fried in a little oil, make a deliciously different dessert.

INGREDIENTS

Serves 4

90g/3oz canned sweetened chestnut purée
15ml/1 tbsp vegetable oil, for frying
caster sugar, to serve

For the pancakes
150g/5oz/1¼ cups plain flour, plus extra
    for dusting
about 105ml/7 tbsp boiling water
2.5ml/½ tsp vegetable oil

1 Make the pancakes. Sift the flour and then pour in the boiling water, stirring as you pour. Mix in the oil and knead the mixture into a dough. Cover with a damp towel and leave to stand for 30 minutes.

2 Knead the dough until smooth, then roll it out into a long "sausage", cut into eight pieces and roll each into a ball. Flatten each piece, then roll it to a 15cm/6in pancake.

NUTRITIONAL NOTES

Per portion:

Energy	192Kcals/809kJ
Fat, total	3.8g
Saturated fat	0.47g
Cholesterol	0mg
Fibre	1.8g

3 Heat an ungreased frying pan until hot, then reduce the heat to low and place the pancakes, one at a time, in the pan. Turn them when small brown spots appear on the underside. Keep under a damp cloth until all are cooked.

4 Spread about 15ml/1 tbsp of the chestnut purée over each pancake, then roll it up.

5 Heat the oil in a non-stick wok or frying pan. Add the rolls in batches and fry them briefly until golden brown, turning once.

6 Cut each pancake roll into three or four pieces and sprinkle with caster sugar. Serve immediately.

Tropical Fruit Pancakes

Fresh fruit, coated with a citrus and honey sauce, makes the perfect pancake filling for this light and tasty dessert.

INGREDIENTS

Serves 4

115g/4oz/1 cup self-raising flour

pinch of grated nutmeg

15ml/1 tbsp caster sugar

1 egg

300ml/^{1}/2 pint/1^1/4 cups skimmed milk

15ml/1 tbsp melted low-fat spread

15ml/1 tbsp fine desiccated coconut (optional)

light sunflower spray oil for frying

icing sugar, for dusting

low-fat Greek yogurt, to serve (optional)

For the filling

225g/8oz ripe, firm mango

2 bananas

2 kiwi fruit

1 large orange

15ml/1 tbsp lemon juice

30ml/2 tbsp unsweetened orange juice

15ml/1 tbsp clear honey

1 Sift the flour, nutmeg and caster sugar into a large bowl. In a separate bowl, beat the egg lightly, then beat in most of the milk. Add to the flour mixture and beat to make a thick, smooth batter. Add the remaining milk, melted spread and coconut, if using, and continue beating until the batter is smooth and of a fairly thin, dropping consistency.

2 Spray a large non-stick frying pan with a very thin coating of oil. Heat, then pour in a little batter to cover the base. Fry until golden brown, then toss or turn with a spatula.

3 Repeat Step 2 with the remaining mixture to make about eight pancakes. Dice the mango, chop the bananas and slice the kiwi fruit. Peel the orange and cut into segments.

4 Place the fruit in a bowl. Mix the lemon and orange juices and honey, then pour over the fruit.

5 Spoon a little fruit down the centre of a pancake and fold over each side. Repeat with the remaining pancakes. Dust with icing sugar and serve solo or with low-fat Greek yogurt.

NUTRITIONAL NOTES
Per portion:

Energy	303Kcals/1280kJ
Fat, total	4.7g
Saturated fat	0.98g
Cholesterol	49.9mg
Fibre	4.2g

Blueberry Pancakes

*These fairly thick American-style
pancakes became popular as a breakfast
option, but are equally good as a dessert.*

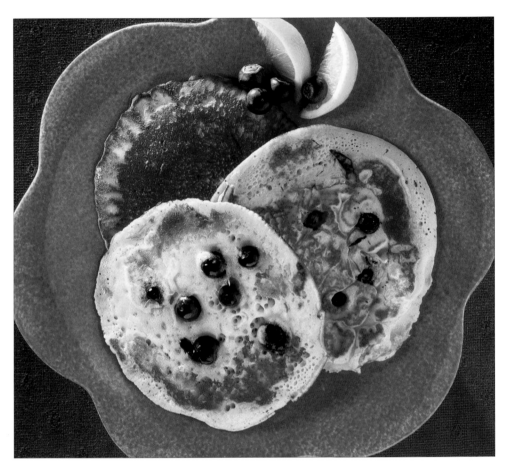

3 Heat a few drops of oil in a
pancake pan or heavy-based frying
pan until just hazy. Pour on about
30ml/2 tbsp of the batter and swirl it
around until it makes a neat pancake.

4 Cook for 2–3 minutes. When
almost set on top, sprinkle over
15–30ml/1–2 tbsp of the blueberries.
As soon as the base is loose and golden
brown, turn the pancake over.

5 Cook on the second side for only
about 1 minute, until golden and
crisp. Slide the pancake on to a plate
and keep warm while you make
17 more pancakes in the same way.
Serve drizzled with maple syrup, if you
like, and offer lemon wedges for
squeezing, if using.

INGREDIENTS

Serves 6

115g/4oz/1 cup self-raising flour

pinch of salt

40g/1¹/2 oz/3 tbsp caster sugar

2 eggs

120ml/4fl oz/¹/2 cup skimmed milk

15ml/1 tbsp vegetable oil

115g/4oz fresh or frozen blueberries

maple syrup and miniature lemon wedges, to
serve (optional)

1 Sift the flour and salt into a bowl.
Add the sugar. In a separate bowl,
beat the eggs thoroughly. Make a well
in the flour and stir in the eggs.

2 Gradually blend in a little of the
milk to make a smooth batter.
Whisk in the rest of the milk for
1–2 minutes. Rest for 20–30 minutes.

COOK'S TIP

Instead of blueberries you could use
fresh or thawed and drained frozen
blackberries or raspberries.

NUTRITIONAL NOTES
Per portion:

Energy	146Kcals/618kJ
Fat, total	3.9g
Saturated fat	0.76g
Cholesterol	64.6mg
Fibre	0.9g

Apple and Blackcurrant Pancakes

These pancakes are made with a whole-wheat batter and are filled with a delicious fruit mixture.

Serves 4

115g/4oz/1 cup wholemeal flour

300ml/¹/2 pint/1¹/4 cups skimmed milk

1 egg, beaten

15ml/1 tbsp sunflower oil

spray oil, for greasing

half-fat crème fraîche, to serve (optional)

toasted nuts or sesame seeds,
    for sprinkling (optional)

For the filling

450g/1lb Bramley or other cooking apples

225g/8oz/2 cups blackcurrants

30–45ml/2–3 tbsp water

30ml/2 tbsp demerara sugar

3 Quarter, peel and core the apples. Slice them into a pan and add the blackcurrants and water. Cook over a gentle heat for 10–15 minutes until the fruit is soft. Stir in enough demerara sugar to sweeten.

4 Apply a light, even coat of spray oil to a pancake pan. Heat the pan, pour in about 30ml/2 tbsp batter, swirl it around and cook for about 1 minute. Flip the pancake over with a palette knife and cook the other side. Keep the pancake hot while cooking the remaining pancakes (unless cooking to order).

5 Fill the pancakes with the apple and blackcurrant mixture and fold or roll them up. Serve with a dollop of crème fraîche, if using, and sprinkle with nuts or sesame seeds, if you like.

1 Make the pancake batter. Place the flour in a mixing bowl and make a well in the centre.

2 Add a little of the milk with the egg and the oil. Whisk the flour into the liquid, then gradually whisk in the rest of the milk, keeping the batter smooth. Cover the batter and put it in the fridge while you prepare the filling.

NUTRITIONAL NOTES	
Per portion:	
Energy	120Kcals/505kJ
Fat, total	3g
Saturated fat	0.5g
Cholesterol	25mg
Fibre	0g

Cherry Pancakes

These pancakes are virtually fat-free, and lower in calories and higher in fibre than traditional ones.

INGREDIENTS

Serves 4

50g/2oz/¹/2 cup plain flour

50g/2oz/¹/2 cup wholemeal flour

pinch of salt

1 egg white

150ml/¹/4 pint/²/3 cup skimmed milk

150ml/¹/4 pint/²/3 cup water

spray oil for frying

For the filling

425g/15oz can black cherries in syrup

7.5ml/1¹/2 tsp arrowroot

2 Apply a light coat of spray oil to a non-stick frying pan. Heat the pan, then pour a little batter, swirling the pan to cover the base evenly.

3 Cook until the pancake is set and golden, then turn to cook the other side. Slide on to kitchen paper and cook the remaining 8 pancakes.

4 Drain the cherries, reserving the syrup. Mix about 30ml/2 tbsp of the syrup with the arrowroot in a saucepan. Stir in the rest of the syrup. Heat gently, stirring, until the mixture boils, thickens and clears. Add the cherries and stir until heated. Spoon the cherries into the pancakes and fold them in quarters. Serve at once.

1 Sift the flours and salt into a bowl, adding any bran left in the sieve to the bowl at the end. Make a well in the centre of the flour and add the egg white, then the milk and water. Beat with a wooden spoon, gradually incorporating the surrounding flour mixture, then whisk the batter hard until it is smooth and bubbly.

NUTRITIONAL NOTES

Per portion:

Energy	190Kcals/800kJ
Fat, total	1.7g
Saturated fat	0.23g
Cholesterol	0.8mg
Fibre	2.2g

Summer Berry Crêpes

The delicate flavour of these fluffy crêpes contrasts beautifully with tangy summer berry fruits.

INGREDIENTS

Serves 4

115g/4oz/1 cup self-raising flour

1 large egg

300ml/¹/2 pint/1¹/4 cups skimmed milk

a few drops of pure vanilla essence

spray oil, for greasing

icing sugar, for dusting

For the fruit

15ml/1 tbsp low-fat spread

50g/2oz/¹/4 cup caster sugar

juice of 2 oranges

thinly pared rind of ¹/2 orange

350g/12oz/3 cups mixed summer berries, such as sliced strawberries, yellow raspberries, blueberries and redcurrants

45ml/3 tbsp Grand Marnier or other orange-flavoured liqueur

2 Apply a light, even coat of spray oil to an 18cm/7in non-stick frying pan. Whisk the batter, then pour a little of it into the hot pan, swirling to cover the base evenly. Cook until the mixture comes away from the sides and the crêpe is golden underneath.

3 Flip the crêpe over with a large palette knife and cook the other side briefly until golden. Slide the crêpe on to a heatproof plate. Make seven more crêpes in the same way. Cover the crêpes with foil or another plate and keep them hot in a warm oven.

1 Preheat the oven to 150ºC/300ºF/ Gas 2. To make the crêpes, sift the flour into a large bowl and make a well in the centre. Break in the egg and gradually whisk in the milk to make a smooth batter. Stir in the vanilla essence. Set the batter aside in a cool place for up to half an hour.

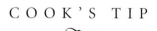

COOK'S TIP

For safety, when igniting a mixture for flambéing, use a long taper or long wooden match and stand back.

4 Melt the spread in a heavy-based frying pan, stir in the sugar and cook gently. Add the orange juice and rind and cook until syrupy. Then add the fruits and warm through (reserve some for decoration), add the liqueur and set it alight. Shake the pan until the flame dies down.

5 Fold the pancakes into quarters and arrange two on each plate. Spoon over the fruit mixture and dust with icing sugar. Serve the remaining fruit separately.

NUTRITIONAL NOTES
Per portion:

Energy	285Kcals/1203kJ
Fat, total	5g
Saturated fat	1.06g
Cholesterol	59.5mg
Fibre	3.5g

Blueberry and Orange Crêpe Baskets

Impress your guests with these fruit-filled crêpes. When blueberries are out of season, try raspberries.

INGREDIENTS

Serves 6

150g/5oz/1¼ cups plain flour

pinch of salt

2 egg whites

200ml/7fl oz/scant 1 cup skimmed milk

150ml/¼ pint/⅔ cup orange juice

spray oil, for greasing

For the filling

4 medium-size oranges

225g/8oz/2 cups blueberries

NUTRITIONAL NOTES

Per portion:

Energy	165Kcals/697kJ
Fat, total	1.4g
Saturated fat	0.16g
Cholesterol	0.7mg
Fibre	3.2g

1 Preheat the oven to 200ºC/400ºF/ Gas 6. Sift the flour and salt into a bowl. Make a well in the centre and add the egg whites, milk and orange juice. Beat the liquid, gradually incorporating the surrounding flour mixture, then whisk the batter until it is smooth and bubbly.

2 Apply a light, even coat of spray oil to a heavy or non-stick pancake pan and heat it. Pour in just enough batter to cover the base of the pan, swirling it to cover the pan evenly.

3 Cook until the pancake has set and is golden underneath and then turn it to cook on the other side. Slide the pancake on to a sheet of kitchen paper. Cook the remaining batter, to make six pancakes.

4 Invert six small ovenproof bowls or moulds on a baking sheet and drape a pancake over each. Bake them in the oven for about 10 minutes, until they are crisp and set into shape. Carefully lift the "baskets" off the moulds and set aside.

5 Pare a thin piece of orange rind from one orange and cut it in fine strips. Blanch the strips in boiling water for 30 seconds, rinse them in cold water and drain well. Cut all the peel and white pith from the oranges.

6 Cut the oranges into segments, working over a bowl to catch the juice. Add the segments and juice to the blueberries in a pan and warm through gently. Spoon the fruit into the baskets and scatter the shreds of rind over the top.

COOK'S TIP

Don't fill the pancake baskets until you are ready to serve them, because they will absorb the fruit juice and begin to soften.

Ginger and Honey Syrup

Particularly good for winter puddings, this virtually fat-free sauce can be served hot or cold with fruit salad.

Serves 4

1 lemon

4 green cardamom pods

1 cinnamon stick

150ml/¼ pint/⅔ cup clear honey

3 pieces stem ginger, plus
   30ml/2 tbsp syrup from the jar

60ml/4 tbsp water

3 Place the lemon rind, cardamoms, cinnamon stick, honey, ginger syrup and water lower in a saucepan Boil then simmer for 2 minutes.

4 Chop the ginger and stir it into the sauce with the lemon juice. Pour over a winter fruit salad or try it with a baked fruit compote. Chill to serve.

1 Thinly pare two strips of rind from the lemon with a potato peeler.

2 Lightly crush the cardamom pods with the back of a heavy-bladed knife. Cut the lemon in half. Reserve half for another recipe and squeeze the juice from the remaining half. Set the juice aside.

NUTRITIONAL NOTES
Per portion:

Energy	145Kcals/611kJ
Fat, total	0.1g
Saturated fat	0g
Cholesterol	0mg
Fibre	0g

Lemon and Lime Sauce

This tangy sauce goes well with pancakes or fruit tarts, or as an accompaniment to an orange or mandarin cheesecake.

INGREDIENTS

Serves 4

1 lemon

2 limes

50g/2oz/1/4 cup caster sugar

25ml/1 1/2 tbsp arrowroot

300ml/1/2 pint/1 1/4 cups water

freshly made pancakes, to serve

fresh lemon balm or mint leaves, to decorate

NUTRITIONAL NOTES

Per portion:

Energy	75Kcals/317kJ
Fat, total	0.1g
Saturated fat	0g
Cholesterol	0mg
Fibre	0g

1 Using a citrus zester, pare the rinds thinly from the lemon and limes. Squeeze the juice from the fruit.

VARIATION

This sauce can also be made with orange and lemon rind if you prefer.

2 Place all the rind in a pan, cover with water and bring to the boil. Drain through a sieve and set it aside.

3 Mix a little sugar and the arrowroot with enough water to give a smooth paste. Add to the remaining water, heat, and stir until the sauce boils and thickens.

4 Stir in the remaining sugar, the citrus juice and the reserved rind. Serve hot with freshly made pancakes. Decorate with lemon balm or mint.

Cold Low-fat Puddings & Desserts

✦✦✦

Rich Blackcurrant Coulis

There can be few more impressive desserts than this – port wine jelly with swirled cream hearts.

INGREDIENTS

Serves 8

6 sheets of leaf gelatine
475ml/16fl oz/2 cups water
225g/8oz/2 cups blackcurrants
225g/8oz/1 cup caster sugar
150ml/¼ pint/²/₃ cup ruby port
30ml/2 tbsp crème de cassis
120ml/4fl oz/½ cup single cream, to decorate

1 In a small bowl, soak the gelatine in 75ml/5 tbsp of the water until soft. Place the blackcurrants, sugar and 300ml/½ pint/1¼ cups of the remaining water in a large saucepan. Bring to the boil, lower the heat and simmer for 20 minutes.

2 Strain through a sieve and reserve the cooking liquid in a large jug. Put the blackcurrants in a bowl and pour over 60ml/4 tbsp of the reserved cooking liquid.

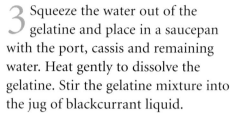

3 Squeeze the water out of the gelatine and place in a saucepan with the port, cassis and remaining water. Heat gently to dissolve the gelatine. Stir the gelatine mixture into the jug of blackcurrant liquid.

4 Run 6–8 jelly moulds under cold water, drain and place in a roasting tin. Fill with the port mixture. Chill for at least 6 hours until set. Tip the bowl of blackcurrants into a food processor, purée until smooth, then pass through a fine sieve.

5 Run a fine knife around each jelly. Dip each mould in hot water for 5–10 seconds, then turn the jelly out on to your hand. Place on a plate and spoon the coulis around the jelly.

6 To decorate, drop a little cream at intervals on to the coulis. Draw a cocktail stick through the cream dots, dragging each into a heart shape.

NUTRITIONAL NOTES
Per portion:

Energy	276Kcals/1163kJ
Fat, total	3.8g
Saturated fat	2.4g
Cholesterol	11mg
Fibre	2.7g

Raspberry Muesli Layer

As well as being a delicious, low-fat dessert, this muesli can be served for a quick, healthy breakfast.

Serves 4

225g/8oz/2 cups fresh or frozen and
   thawed raspberries
250ml/8fl oz/1 cup low-fat natural yogurt
75g/3oz/1/2 cup Swiss-style muesli

3 Sprinkle a layer of Swiss-style muesli over the yogurt.

4 Continue the layers until all the ingredients have been used. Top each dessert with a whole raspberry.

1 Reserve four raspberries to decorate, then spoon a few raspberries into four stemmed glasses or glass dishes.

2 Top the raspberries in each glass with a spoonful of yogurt.

NUTRITIONAL NOTES

Per portion:

Energy	114Kcals/481kJ
Fat, total	1.7g
Saturated fat	0.48g
Cholesterol	2.3mg
Fibre	2.6g

Strawberries in Spiced Grape Jelly

The spicy cinnamon combines with the sun-ripened strawberries to make a dessert for a summer dinner party.

Serves 4

475ml/16fl oz/2 cups red grape juice

1 cinnamon stick

1 small orange

15ml/1 tbsp powdered gelatine

225g/8oz/2 cups strawberries, chopped, plus
    extra to decorate

1 Pour the grape juice into a pan and add the cinnamon stick. Thinly pare the rind from the orange. Add most of it to the pan but shred some pieces and set them aside for the decoration. Place the pan over a very low heat for 10 minutes, then remove the flavourings from the grape juice.

2 Squeeze the juice from the orange into a bowl and sprinkle over the powdered gelatine. When the mixture is spongy, stir into the grape juice until it has completely dissolved. Allow the jelly to cool in the bowl until just beginning to set.

3 Stir in the strawberries and quickly tip into a 1 litre/1¾ pint/4 cup mould or serving dish. Chill until set.

4 Dip the mould quickly into hot water and invert on to a serving plate. Decorate with strawberries and shreds of orange rind.

NUTRITIONAL NOTES
Per portion:

Energy	85Kcals/355kJ
Fat, total	0.2g
Saturated fat	0g
Cholesterol	0mg
Fibre	1.04g

Chilled Oranges in Syrup

*This popular classic is light and
refreshing. A perfect dish to serve after
a heavy main course.*

2 Cut the peel into strips and boil in
fresh water several times to remove
the bitterness. Drain on kitchen paper.

3 Place the water, sugar and lemon
juice in a pan. Bring to the boil,
add the pared rind and simmer until
the syrup thickens. Add the orange-
flower or rose-water, stir and then cool.

INGREDIENTS

Serves 4

4 oranges

600ml/1 pint/2^1/$_2$ cups water

350g/12oz/1^1/$_2$ cups granulated sugar

30ml/2 tbsp lemon juice

30ml/2 tbsp orange-flower water or
rose-water

40g/1^1/$_2$ oz/^{1}/$_3$ cup unsalted pistachio nuts,
shelled and chopped

1 Peel the oranges with a potato
peeler, avoiding the pith.

NUTRITIONAL NOTES

Per portion:

Energy	467Kcals/1980kJ
Fat, total	4.9g
Saturated fat	0.59g
Cholesterol	0mg
Fibre	3.1g

COOK'S TIP

Almonds could be substituted for the
pistachio nuts, if you like, but don't
be tempted to increase the quantity
or you'll raise the level of fat.

4 Remove any pith and slice the
oranges. Arrange in a serving dish,
pour over the syrup and chill for
1–2 hours. Serve with pistachio nuts.

Grapes in Grape-yogurt Jelly

This light, refreshing combination makes a great special-occasion dessert, but takes very little time to make.

Serves 4

200g/7oz/1¾ cups white seedless grapes

450ml/¾ pint/scant 2 cups unsweetened white grape juice

15ml/1 tbsp powdered gelatine

120ml/4fl oz/½ cup low-fat natural yogurt

1 Set aside four tiny bunches of grapes for decoration. Pull the rest off their stalks and cut them in half.

2 Divide the grapes among four stemmed glasses and tilt the glasses on one side, propping them firmly in a bowl of ice.

3 Heat the grape juice in a pan until almost boiling. Remove it from the heat and sprinkle the gelatine over the surface, stirring until it dissolves.

4 Pour half the grape juice over the grapes and leave to set.

5 Cool the remaining grape juice until on the verge of setting, then stir in the low-fat natural yogurt.

6 Stand the set glasses upright and pour in the yogurt mixture. Chill to set, then decorate the rim of each glass with grapes, and serve.

NUTRITIONAL NOTES
Per portion:

Energy	113Kcals/480kJ
Fat, total	0.4g
Saturated fat	0.16g
Cholesterol	1.3mg
Fibre	0g

COOK'S TIP

For an easier version, stand the glasses upright rather than at an angle – then they can be put in the fridge to set rather than packed with ice in a container.

Fresh Citrus Jelly

Fresh fruit jellies really are worth the effort – they're packed with fresh flavour, natural colour and vitamins.

1 With a sharp knife, cut all the peel and white pith from one orange and carefully remove the segments. Arrange in the base of a 900ml/ 1½ pint/3¾ cup mould or dish. Chill.

2 Remove some shreds of citrus rind with a zester and reserve them for decoration. Grate the remaining rind from the lemon and lime and one orange. Place all the grated rind in a pan, with the water and sugar.

3 Heat gently, without boiling, until the sugar has dissolved. Take off the heat. Squeeze the juice from all the rest of the fruit and stir into the pan.

4 Strain the hot liquid into a measuring jug to remove the rind. You should have about 600ml/1 pint/ 2½ cups of liquid; if necessary, make up the amount with hot water. Sprinkle the gelatine over the liquid and stir until it has dissolved.

5 Pour a little of the jelly over the orange segments and chill until set. Leave the remaining jelly at room temperature to cool, but not set.

6 Pour the remaining cooled jelly into the dish and chill until set. To serve, turn out the jelly and decorate it with the reserved citrus rind shreds and extra slices of citrus fruit.

COOK'S TIP

To speed up the setting of the fruit segments in jelly, stand the dish in a bowl of ice. Or, if you're short of time, simply stir the segments into the liquid jelly, pour into a serving dish and set it all together.

NUTRITIONAL NOTES

Per portion:

Energy	137Kcals/580kJ
Fat, total	0.2g
Saturated fat	0g
Cholesterol	0mg
Fibre	2.1g

Orange-blossom Jelly

The natural fruit flavour of fresh orange juice in this smooth jelly has a wonderful cleansing quality.

INGREDIENTS

Serves 4

65g/2¹/2 oz/¹/3 cup caster sugar

150ml/¹/4 pint/²/3 cup water

25g/1oz powdered gelatine

600ml/1 pint/2¹/2 cups fresh orange juice

30ml/2 tbsp orange-flower water

NUTRITIONAL NOTES

Per portion:

Energy	135Kcals/573kJ
Fat, total	0g
Saturated fat	0g
Cholesterol	0mg
Fibre	0.2g

1 Place the caster sugar and water in a small saucepan and heat gently to dissolve the sugar. Pour into a heatproof bowl and leave to cool.

2 Sprinkle the gelatine over the surface of the syrup. Leave to stand until it has absorbed all the liquid.

3 Gently melt the gelatine over a saucepan of simmering water until it becomes clear and transparent. Leave to cool. When the gelatine is cold, mix it with the orange juice and orange-flower water.

4 Wet a jelly mould and pour in the jelly. Chill in the fridge for at least 2 hours, or until set. Turn out to serve.

Ground Rice Pudding

This delicious and light ground rice pudding, flavoured with almonds, is the perfect end to a spicy meal.

INGREDIENTS

Serves 4-6

50g/2oz/^{1}/2 cup coarsely ground rice

25g/1oz/2 tbsp ground almonds

4 green cardamom pods, crushed

900ml/1^1/2 pints/3^3/4 cups
    semi-skimmed milk

75g/3oz/6 tbsp caster sugar

15ml/1 tbsp rose water

1 tbsp crushed pistachio nuts and silver leaf
    (optional) to decorate

1 Place the ground rice and almonds in a saucepan with the green cardamoms. Add 600ml/1 pint/ 2^1/2 cups milk and bring to the boil over a medium heat, stirring occasionally.

3 Stir in the sugar and rose water and continue to cook for a further 2 minutes. Serve garnished with pistachio nuts and silver leaf, if wished.

2 Add the remaining milk and cook over a medium heat for about ten minutes or until the rice mixture thickens to the consistency of a creamy chicken soup.

NUTRITIONAL NOTES
Per portion:

Energy	201Kcals/844kJ
Fat, total	8.78g
Saturated fat	2.57g
Cholesterol	14.70mg
Fibre	0g

Clementine Jelly

This jelly has a clear fruity taste and can be made extra special by adding a little white rum or Cointreau.

INGREDIENTS

Serves 4

12 clementines

clear unsweetened white grape juice
   (see method for amount)

15ml/1 tbsp powdered gelatine

30ml/2 tbsp caster sugar

60ml/4 tbsp half-fat crème fraîche,
   for topping

VARIATION

Use ruby grapefruit instead of clementines, if you prefer. Squeeze the juice from half and segment the rest.

1 Squeeze the juice from eight of the clementines and pour it into a jug. Make up to 600ml/1 pint/2½ cups with the grape juice, then strain the juice mixture through a fine sieve.

2 Pour half the juice mixture into a pan. Sprinkle the gelatine on top, leave for 5 minutes, then heat gently until the gelatine has dissolved. Stir in the sugar and remaining juice; set aside.

3 Pare the rind very thinly from the remaining fruit and set it aside. Using a sharp knife, cut between the membrane and fruit to separate the citrus segments. Discard the membrane and pith.

4 Place half the segments in four dessert glasses and cover with some of the liquid fruit jelly. Place in the fridge to set.

5 Arrange the remaining segments on top. Pour over the remaining jelly and chill until set. Cut the clementine rind into shreds. Serve the jellies topped with a spoonful of crème fraîche scattered with clementine shreds.

NUTRITIONAL NOTES
Per portion:

Energy	142Kcals/600kJ
Fat, total	2.5g
Saturated fat	1.4g
Cholesterol	15.8mg
Fibre	1.5g

Mexican Lemony Rice Pudding

Rice pudding is popular the world over in many different guises. This Mexican version is light and attractive.

INGREDIENTS

Serves 4

75g/3oz/¹/₂ cup raisins

90g/3¹/₂ oz/¹/₂ cup short-grain (pudding) rice

2.5cm/1in strip of pared lime or lemon rind

250ml/8fl oz/1 cup water

475ml/16fl oz/2 cups skimmed milk

225g/8oz/1 cup granulated sugar

1.5ml/¹/₄ tsp salt

2.5cm/1in cinnamon stick

1 egg yolk, well beaten

15ml/1 tbsp low-fat spread

10ml/2 tsp toasted flaked almonds to decorate

orange segments to serve

3 Discard the cinnamon stick. Drain the raisins well. Add the raisins, egg yolk and low-fat spread, stirring constantly until the spread has been absorbed, the raisins evenly distributed and the pudding is rich and creamy.

4 Cook the pudding for a few minutes longer. Tip the rice into a serving dish and allow to cool. Decorate with the toasted flaked almonds and add a few orange segments to each serving.

NUTRITIONAL NOTES

Per portion:

Energy	450Kcals/1903kJ
Fat, total	4.9g
Saturated fat	0.88g
Cholesterol	53mg
Fibre	1.4g

1 Put the raisins into a small bowl. Cover with warm water and set aside to soak. Put the rice into a saucepan together with the pared lime or lemon rind and water. Bring slowly to the boil, then lower the heat. Cover the pan and simmer gently for about 20 minutes or until all the water has been absorbed.

2 Remove the rind from the rice and discard it. Add the milk, sugar, salt and cinnamon stick. Cook, stirring, over a very low heat until the milk has been absorbed. Do not cover the pan.

Fragrant Rice with Dates

Moroccan rice puddings are sprinkled with either nuts and honey or wrapped in pastry. This is a low-fat version.

INGREDIENTS

Serves 4

75g/3oz/¹/2 cup short-grain (pudding) rice

about 900ml/1¹/2 pints/3³/4 cups
   skimmed milk

30ml/2 tbsp ground rice

50g/2oz/¹/4 cup caster sugar

15g/¹/2 oz/2 tbsp ground almonds

5ml/1 tsp vanilla essence

2.5ml/¹/2 tsp almond essence

a little orange-flower water (optional)

30ml/2 tbsp chopped dates

30ml/2 tbsp unsalted, pistachio nuts, finely chopped

NUTRITIONAL NOTES
Per portion:

Energy	270Kcals/1135kJ
Fat, total	4.8g
Saturated fat	0.55g
Cholesterol	4.5mg
Fibre	0.4g

1 Place the rice in a saucepan with 750ml/1¹/4 pints/3 cups of the milk and gradually heat until simmering. Cook, uncovered, over a very low heat for 30–40 minutes, until the rice is completely tender, stirring frequently.

2 Blend the ground rice with the remaining milk and add to the pan, stirring. Slowly bring back to the boil and cook for 1 minute.

3 Stir in the sugar, ground almonds, vanilla and almond essences and orange-flower water, if using. Cook until the pudding is thick and creamy.

4 Pour into serving bowls and sprinkle with the chopped dates and pistachiosto decorate. Allow to cool before serving.

Rice Pudding with Mixed Berry Sauce

*A compote of red berries contrasts
beautifully with creamy rice pudding for
a richly flavoured cool dessert.*

INGREDIENTS

Serves 6

low-fat spread, for greasing

400g/14oz/2 cups short-grain
(pudding) rice

325ml/11fl oz/scant 1¹/2 cups
skimmed milk

pinch salt

115g/4oz/²/3 cup soft light brown sugar

5ml/1 tsp pure vanilla essence

2 eggs, beaten

grated rind of 1 lemon

5ml/1 tsp lemon juice

30ml/2 tbsp low-fat spread

strawberry leaves, to decorate

For the sauce

225g/8oz/2 cups strawberries, hulled
and quartered

225g/8oz/2 cups raspberries

115g/4oz/¹/2 cup granulated sugar

grated rind of 1 lemon

1 Preheat the oven to 160ºC/325ºF/
Gas 3. Grease a deep 2 litre/
3¹/2 pint/8 cup baking dish. Add the
rice to boiling water and boil for
5 minutes. Drain. Transfer the rice to
the prepared baking dish.

2 Combine the milk, salt, brown
sugar, vanilla, eggs, lemon rind
and juice. Pour over the rice and stir.

3 Dot the surface of the rice mixture
with the spread. Bake for 50 minutes
until the rice is cooked and creamy.

4 Meanwhile, mix the berries and
sugar in a saucepan. Stir over low
heat until the sugar has dissolved and
the fruit is becoming pulpy.

5 Transfer to a bowl and stir in the
lemon rind. Cool, then chill the
sauce until required.

6 Remove the rice pudding from the
oven. Leave to cool. Serve with the
berry sauce. Decorate with fresh
strawberry leaves.

NUTRITIONAL NOTES
Per portion:

Energy	474Kcals/1991kJ
Fat, total	4.9g
Saturated fat	0.95g
Cholesterol	65.5mg
Fibre	1.4g

Fresh Fruit with Caramel Rice

*This creamy rice pudding with a crisp
caramel crust sounds wickedly
indulgent, but is relatively low in fat.*

INGREDIENTS

Serves 4

50g/2oz/generous $^1/4$ cup short-grain
 (pudding) rice

low-fat spread, for greasing

75ml/5 tbsp demerara sugar

pinch of salt

400g/14oz can light evaporated milk made up
 to 600ml/1 pint/2$^1/2$ cups with water

2 crisp eating apples

1 small fresh pineapple

10ml/2 tsp lemon juice

1 Preheat the oven to 150ºC/300ºF/
Gas 2. Wash the rice under cold
water. Drain well and put into a lightly
greased soufflé dish.

2 Add 30ml/2 tbsp of the sugar to
the dish, with the salt. Pour on the
diluted evaporated milk and stir
gently. Bake for 2 hours, then leave to
cool for 30 minutes.

3 Meanwhile, peel, core and cut the
apples and pineapple into thin
slices, then cut the pineapple into
chunks. Toss the fruit in lemon juice,
coating thoroughly, and set aside.

4 Preheat the grill and sprinkle the
remaining sugar over the rice. Grill
for 5 minutes to caramelize the sugar.
Leave to stand for 5 minutes to harden
the caramel. Serve with the fresh fruit.

NUTRITIONAL NOTES
Per portion:

Energy	309Kcals/1293kJ
Fat, total	4.6g
Saturated fat	2.51g
Cholesterol	34mg
Fibre	2.8g

Rice Fruit Sundae

Cook a rice pudding on top of the stove instead of in the oven for a light creamy texture. Serve cold, topped with fruits.

INGREDIENTS

Serves 4

50g/2oz/^{1}/$_3$ cup short-grain
    (pudding) rice
600ml/1 pint/2^1/$_2$ cups skimmed milk
5ml/1 tsp pure vanilla essence
2.5ml/^{1}/$_2$ tsp ground cinnamon
25g/1oz/2 tbsp granulated sugar
200g/7oz/1^3/$_4$ cups strawberries, raspberries
    or blueberries, to serve

1 Put the rice, milk, vanilla essence, cinnamon and sugar into a medium-sized saucepan. Bring to the boil, stirring constantly, and then turn down the heat so that the mixture barely simmers.

2 Cook the rice for 30–40 minutes, stirring occasionally, until the grains are soft. Tip into a bowl and allow the rice to cool, stirring occasionally. Chill the rice in the fridge.

NUTRITIONAL NOTES
Per portion:

Energy	169Kcals/711kJ
Fat, total	3.3g
Saturated fat	0.1g
Cholesterol	3mg
Fibre	0.9g

3 Just before serving, stir the rice and spoon into four sundae dishes. Top with the prepared fruit.

VARIATION

Instead of simple pudding rice try using a Thai fragrant or jasmine rice for a delicious natural flavour. For a firmer texture, an Italian arborio rice makes a good pudding too. You could also use other toppings, such as toasted, chopped hazelnuts or toasted coconut flakes. Another fruit combination could be mango, pineapple and banana for a fresh tropical taste.

Summer Pudding

Summer pudding is an annual treat, and need not be high in fat if you avoid serving it with lashings of cream.

INGREDIENTS

Serves 6

1 loaf of white crusty bread,
   1–2 days old, sliced

675g/1½ lb/6 cups fresh redcurrants

75g/3oz/6 tbsp granulated sugar

60ml/4 tbsp water

450g/1lb/4 cups mixed berries, plus extra
   to decorate

sprig of mint, to decorate

juice of ½ lemon

NUTRITIONAL NOTES
Per portion:

Energy	272Kcals/1152kJ
Fat, total	1.6g
Saturated fat	0g
Cholesterol	0mg
Fibre	7.6g

1 Trim the crusts from the bread slices and cut a round to fit in the bottom of a 1.5 litre/2½ pint/6 cup pudding basin. Line the basin with bread slices, overlapping them slightly. Reserve enough to cover the top of the basin. Mix the redcurrants with 50g/2oz/¼ cup of the sugar and the water in a saucepan. Heat gently, lightly crushing the berries. When the sugar has dissolved, remove from the heat.

2 Tip the redcurrant mixture into a food processor and process until smooth. Press through a fine sieve set over a bowl. Discard the pressed fruit pulp left in the strainer.

3 Put the mixed berries in a bowl with the remaining sugar and the lemon juice. Stir well.

4 One at a time, remove the cut bread pieces from the basin and dip them in the redcurrant purée. Replace to line the basin evenly.

5 Spoon the berries into the lined basin, pressing them down evenly. Top with the reserved cut bread slices, which have been dipped in the redcurrant purée.

6 Cover the basin with clear film. Set a small plate, just big enough to fit inside the rim of the basin, on top of the pudding. Weigh it down with cans of food. Chill in the fridge for 8–24 hours.

7 To turn out, remove the weights, plate and clear film. Run a knife between the basin and the pudding to loosen it. Invert on to a serving plate. Decorate with a sprig of mint and a few berries. Serve in wedges.

Autumn Pudding

Here is an autumn version of the traditional summer pudding, served with apples, plums and blackberries.

INGREDIENTS

Serves 6

450g/1lb eating apples
450g/1lb plums, halved and stoned
225g/8oz/2 cups blackberries
60ml/4 tbsp apple juice
sugar or honey, to sweeten (optional)
8 slices of wholemeal bread, crusts removed
mint sprig and blackberry, to decorate
half-fat crème fraîche, to serve (optional)

1 Quarter the apples, remove the cores and peel, and slice them into a saucepan. Add the plums, blackberries and apple juice. Cover and cook gently for 10–15 minutes until tender. Sweeten, if necessary, with a little sugar or honey.

2 Line the bottom and sides of a 1.2 litre/2 pint/5 cup pudding basin with slices of bread, cut to fit. Press together tightly.

3 Spoon the fruit into the basin with enough juice to moisten.

4 Set aside any remaining juice. Cover the fruit completely with bread. Fit a plate on the top, resting just below the rim and stand the basin in a larger bowl to catch any juice. Weight the plate and chill overnight.

5 Turn the pudding out on a plate and pour the reserved juice over any areas that have not absorbed the juice. Decorate with the mint sprig and blackberry. Serve with crème fraîche, if you like.

NUTRITIONAL NOTES
Per portion:

Energy	141Kcals/595kJ
Fat, total	1.1g
Saturated fat	0.17g
Cholesterol	0mg
Fibre	5.4g

Two-tone Yogurt Ring with Tropical Fruit

A light and colourful dessert with a truly tropical flavour, combining mango, kiwi fruit and physalis together.

INGREDIENTS

Serves 6

175ml/6fl oz/³/4 cup tropical fruit juice

15ml/1 tbsp powdered gelatine

3 egg whites

150ml/¹/4 pint/²/3 cup low-fat
   natural yogurt

finely grated rind of 1 lime

For the filling

1 mango

2 kiwi fruit

10–12 physalis (Cape gooseberries),
   plus extra to decorate

juice of 1 lime

NUTRITIONAL NOTES
Per portion:

Energy	87Kcals/364kJ
Fat, total	0.5g
Saturated fat	0.13g
Cholesterol	1mg
Fibre	2.3g

1 Pour the tropical fruit juice into a small pan and sprinkle the powdered gelatine over the surface. Heat gently until the gelatine has completely dissolved.

2 Whisk the egg whites in a grease-free bowl until they hold peaks. Continue whisking hard, gradually adding the yogurt and lime rind.

3 Continue whisking hard and pour in the hot gelatine mixture in a steady stream, until evenly mixed.

4 Quickly pour the mixture into a 1.5 litre/2½ pint/6¼ cup ring mould. Chill the mould in the fridge until set. The mixture will separate into two layers.

5 Halve, stone, peel and dice the mango. Peel and slice the kiwi fruit. Remove the husks from the physalis (Cape gooseberries) and cut them in half. Toss all the fruits in a bowl and stir in the lime juice.

6 Run a knife around the edge of the ring to loosen the mixture. Dip the tin quickly into hot water, then turn it out on to a serving plate. Spoon all the prepared fruit into the centre of the ring, decorate with the reserved physalis and serve immediately.

VARIATION

Any mixture of fruit works in this recipe, depending on the season. Try using apple juice in the ring mixture and fill it with luscious, red summer fruits.

Fruited Rice Ring

This looks beautiful turned out of a ring mould, but you can stir the fruit into the rice and serve in individual dishes.

2 Meanwhile, mix the dried fruit salad and orange juice in a pan and bring to the boil. Cover, then simmer very gently for about 1 hour, until tender and no free liquid remains.

3 Remove the cinnamon stick from the rice and stir in the sugar and orange rind, mixing thoroughly.

4 Tip the fruit into the base of a lightly oiled 1.5 litre/2½ pint/ 6¼ cup ring mould. Spoon the rice over, smoothing down firmly. Chill.

5 Run a knife around the edge of the mould and turn out the rice carefully on to a serving plate.

INGREDIENTS

Serves 4

65g/2½ oz/5 tbsp short-grain (pudding) rice

900ml/1½ pints/3¾ cups semi-skimmed milk

1 cinnamon stick

175g/6oz/1½ cups dried fruit salad

350ml/12fl oz/1½ cups orange juice

45ml/3 tbsp caster sugar

finely grated rind of 1 small orange

low-fat oil, for greasing

1 Mix the rice, milk and cinnamon stick in a large pan and bring to the boil. Lower the heat, cover and simmer, stirring occasionally, for about 1½ hours, until no free liquid remains.

NUTRITIONAL NOTES
Per portion:

Energy	343Kcals/1440kJ
Fat, total	4.4g
Saturated fat	2.26g
Cholesterol	15.75mg
Fibre	1.07g

Dried Fruit Fool

This light, fluffy dessert can be made with a single dried fruit – try dried peaches, prunes, apples or apricots.

INGREDIENTS

Serves 4

300g/11oz/1¼ cups ready-to-eat
   dried fruit such as apricots, peaches, prunes
   or apples
300ml/½ pint/1¼ cups fresh orange juice
250ml/8fl oz/1 cup low-fat fromage frais
2 egg whites
fresh mint sprigs, to decorate

NUTRITIONAL NOTES
Per portion:

Energy	180Kcals/757kJ
Fat, total	0.63g
Saturated fat	0.06g
Cholesterol	0.5mg
Fibre	4.8g

3 Whisk the egg whites in a grease-free bowl until stiff enough to hold soft peaks, then slowly fold into the fruit mixture until it is all combined.

4 Spoon into four stemmed glasses or one large serving dish. Chill for at least 1 hour. Decorate with the mint sprigs just before serving.

COOK'S TIP
To make a speedier fool leave out the egg whites and simply swirl together the fruit mixture and fromage frais.

1 Put the dried fruit in a saucepan, add the orange juice and heat gently until boiling. Lower the heat, cover and simmer gently for 3 minutes.

2 Cool slightly. Tip into a food processor or blender and process until smooth. Stir in the fromage frais.

Passion Fruit and Apple Foam

Passion fruit have an exotic flavour that lifts this simple apple dessert. You could use two finely chopped kiwi fruit instead.

INGREDIENTS

Serves 4

450g/1lb cooking apples

90ml/6 tbsp unsweetened apple juice

3 passion fruit

3 egg whites

1 red-skinned eating apple, to decorate

5ml/1 tsp lemon juice

1 Peel, core and roughly chop the cooking apples. Put them in a pan with the apple juice.

2 Bring the liquid to the boil, then lower the heat and cover the pan. Cook gently, stirring occasionally, until the apple is very tender.

3 Remove from the heat and beat the apple mixture with a wooden spoon until it forms a fairly smooth purée (or purée the apple in a food processor if you prefer).

4 Cut the passion fruit in half and scoop out the flesh. Stir into the apple purée to mix thoroughly.

5 Place the egg whites in a grease-free bowl and whisk until they form soft peaks. Fold them into the apple mixture. Spoon the apple foam into four serving dishes. Leave to cool.

6 Thinly slice the red-skinned apple and brush the slices with lemon juice to prevent them from browning. Arrange the slices on top of the apple foam and serve cold.

COOK'S TIP
~
It is important to use a good cooking apple, such as a Bramley, for this recipe, because the fluffy texture of a cooking apple breaks down easily to a purée. You can use dessert apples, but will probably have to purée them in a food processor.

NUTRITIONAL NOTES
Per portion:

Energy	80Kcals/338kJ
Fat, total	0.2g
Saturated fat	0g
Cholesterol	0mg
Fibre	2.9g

Raspberry and Mint Bavarois

A sophisticated dessert that can be made a day in advance to impress guests at a special dinner party.

INGREDIENTS

Serves 6

450g/1lb/4 cups fresh or
    thawed frozen raspberries
30ml/2 tbsp icing sugar
30ml/2 tbsp lemon juice
15ml/1 tbsp finely chopped fresh mint
30ml/2 tbsp powdered gelatine
75ml/5 tbsp boiling water
300ml/¹⁄2 pint/1¹⁄4 cups low-fat custard
250ml/8fl oz/1 cup low-fat Greek yogurt
fresh mint sprigs, to decorate

2 Press the purée through a sieve to remove the raspberry seeds. Pour into a measuring jug and stir in the mint.

5 Mix the custard and low-fat Greek yogurt in a bowl and stir in the remaining fruit purée. Dissolve the rest of the gelatine in the remaining boiling water and stir it in quickly.

1 Reserve a few raspberries for decoration. Place the remaining raspberries in a food processor. Add the icing sugar and lemon juice and process to a smooth purée.

3 Sprinkle 5ml/1 tsp of the gelatine over 30ml/2 tbsp of the boiling water, stirring until it has dissolved. Stir into 150ml/¹⁄4 pint/²⁄3 cup of fruit purée.

6 Pour the raspberry custard into the mould and chill it until it has set completely. To serve, dip the mould quickly into a bowl of hot water and then turn it out on a serving plate. Decorate with the reserved raspberries and the mint sprigs.

4 Pour this jelly into a 1 litre/1³⁄4 pint/4 cup mould, and chill in the fridge until just setting. Tip the tin to swirl the setting jelly around the sides, and chill until set completely.

NUTRITIONAL NOTES

Per portion:

Energy	131Kcals/554kJ
Fat, total	2.4g
Saturated fat	1.36g
Cholesterol	4.1mg
Fibre	1.9g

COOK'S TIP

You can make this dessert using frozen raspberries, which have a good colour and flavour. Allow them to thaw at room temperature, and use any juice in the jelly.

Raspberry and Cranberry Jelly

Serves 6–8

142g/4¾oz packet raspberry jelly

150ml/¼ pint/⅔ cup boiling water

250ml/8fl oz/1 cup raspberry and
   cranberry juice

115g/4oz/1 cup fresh strawberries

115g/4oz/⅔ cup raspberries (fresh or frozen)

1 large red-skinned apple, cored and chopped

NUTRITIONAL NOTES
Per portion:

Energy	276Kcals/1163kJ
Fat, total	3.8g
Saturated fat	2.4g
Cholesterol	11mg
Fibre	2.7g

1 Break up the jelly into a heatproof measuring jug and pour over the boiling water. Stir until completely dissolved. Pour in the raspberry and cranberry juice and leave until the jelly is beginning to set.

2 Halve or quarter the strawberries, depending on their size. If using frozen raspberries, leave them in the freezer until you put the jelly to set. Prepare the apple at the last moment.

3 Have ready a pretty 1.2 litre/ 2 pint/5 cup mould, rinsed out with cold water. When the jelly is beginning to thicken, stir in the fruits. (With frozen raspberries it will set almost immediately, so you have to work quickly.) Spoon into the mould and chill until set.

4 Turn out the jelly on to a serving plate and serve with custard, fromage frais or frozen yogurt ice.

Blackberry and Apple Romanoff

Serves 6–8

350g/12oz (3–4) sharp eating apples, peeled,
   cored and chopped

45ml/3 tbsp caster sugar

250ml/8fl oz/1 cup half-fat double cream

5ml/1 tsp grated lemon rind

90ml/6 tbsp Greek-style yogurt

50g/2oz (4–6) crisp meringues,
   roughly crumbled

225g/8oz/2 cups blackberries (fresh or frozen)

whipped reduced-fat cream, a few blackberries
   and mint leaves, to decorate

1 Line a 1–1.2 litre/1¾–2 pint/ 4–5 cup freezerproof pudding basin with clear film. Toss the apples into a pan with 30ml/2 tbsp sugar and cook for 2–3 minutes, or until softening. Mash with a fork and leave to cool.

2 Whip the cream and fold in the lemon rind, yogurt, the remaining sugar, the apples and meringues.

3 Gently stir in the blackberries, then tip the mixture into the lined freezerproof pudding basin and freeze for 1–3 hours.

4 Turn out on to a plate and remove the clear film. Decorate with whirls of cream, blackberries and mint.

NUTRITIONAL NOTES
Per portion:

Energy	148Kcals/621kJ
Fat, total	7.0g
Saturated fat	4.3g
Cholesterol	17mg
Fibre	1.7g

Clementines in Cinnamon Caramel

The combination of sweet, yet sharp clementines and caramel sauce with a hint of spice is divine.

INGREDIENTS

Serves 4

8–12 clementines, about 450–500g/
   1–1¹/₄ lb

225g/8oz/1 cup granulated sugar

300ml/¹/₂ pint/1¹/₄ cups warm water

2 cinnamon sticks

30ml/2 tbsp orange-flavoured liqueur

25g/1oz/¹/₄ cup shelled, unsalted
   pistachio nuts

1 Using a vegetable peeler pare the rind from two clementines and cut it into fine strips. Set aside.

2 Peel the clementines, removing all the pith but keeping each fruit intact. Put the fruits in a heatproof serving bowl.

3 Gently heat the sugar in a pan until it dissolves and turns a rich golden brown. Immediately turn off the heat.

4 Protecting your hand with a dish towel, carefully pour in the warm water (the mixture will bubble and splutter). Bring slowly to the boil, stirring, until the caramel has completely dissolved.

5 Add the shredded peel and cinnamon sticks, then simmer for 5 minutes. Stir in the orange liqueur.

6 Cool the syrup for 10 minutes, then pour it over the clementines. Cover the bowl, cool, then chill for several hours or overnight.

7 Blanch the unsalted pistachio nuts in boiling water. Drain, cool and remove outer skins. Decorate the clementines by scattering the nuts over the top. Serve at once.

NUTRITIONAL NOTES

Per portion:

Energy	328Kcals/1392kJ
Fat, total	3.5g
Saturated fat	0.42g
Cholesterol	0mg
Fibre	1.4g

Yogurt with Apricots and Pistachios

Drain yogurt overnight to make it thick and more luscious. Add honeyed apricots and nuts for an exotic yet simple dessert.

INGREDIENTS

Serves 4

250ml/8fl oz/1 cup low-fat Greek yogurt
250ml/8fl oz/1 cup low-fat natural yogurt
175g/6oz/³⁄4 cup ready-to-eat dried apricots, snipped
15ml/1 tbsp clear honey
10ml/2 tsp roughly chopped unsalted pistachio nuts, plus extra for sprinkling
ground cinnamon, for sprinkling

1 Mix the yogurts and place in a sieve over a bowl. Drain overnight in the fridge.

2 Discard the yogurt whey. In a saucepan cover the apricots with water, simmer to soften. Drain, cool, then tip into a bowl and add the honey.

3 Add the yogurt to the apricot mixture, then add the nuts. Spoon into sundae dishes, sprinkle over a little cinnamon and nuts and chill.

NUTRITIONAL NOTES

Per portion:

Energy	164Kcals/689kJ
Fat, total	4.5g
Saturated fat	2g
Cholesterol	5.5mg
Fibre	2.8g

Raspberries and Fruit Purée

Three fruit purées, swirled together, make a kaleidoscopic garnish for a nest of raspberries.

INGREDIENTS

Serves 4–6·

200g/7oz/1 cup raspberries

120ml/4fl oz/¹/2 cup red wine

icing sugar, for dusting

For the decoration

1 large mango, peeled and chopped

400g/14oz kiwi fruit, peeled and chopped

200g/7oz/1 cup raspberries

icing sugar, to taste

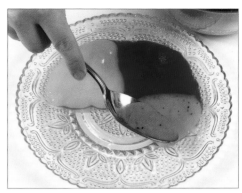

1 Place the raspberries in a bowl with the red wine and allow to macerate for about 2 hours.

2 Purée separately in a food processor, the mango, kiwi fruit, and the remaining raspberries, adding water if necessary. Press each purée through a sieve into a bowl. Sweeten the purées with sifted icing sugar.

3 Spoon each purée on to a serving plate, separating the kiwi and mango with the raspberry purée as if creating a four-wedged pie. Gently tap the plate on the work surface to settle the purées against each other.

4 Using a skewer, draw a spiral outwards from the centre of the plate to the rim. Drain the macerated raspberries, dust them heavily with icing sugar and pile them in the centre of the purées.

NUTRITIONAL NOTES

Per portion:

Energy	154Kcals/648kJ
Fat, total	0.9g
Saturated fat	0g
Cholesterol	0mg
Fibre	6.7g

Caramel with Fresh Fruit

A creamy caramel dessert is a wonderful way to end a meal. It is light and delicious, and this recipe is very simple.

INGREDIENTS

Serves 6
Caramel
25g/1oz/2 tbsp sugar
30ml/2 tbsp water

Custard
6 medium eggs
4 drops vanilla essence
90g/3½oz/½ cup caster sugar
750ml/1¼ pints/3 cups semi-skimmed milk
fresh fruit for serving

1 To make the caramel, place the sugar and water in a heatproof dish and place in a microwave. Cook for 4 minutes on high or until the sugar has caramelized. Alternatively, melt in a pan until pale gold in colour. Pour on to a 1.2 litre/2 pint/5 cup soufflé dish. Leave to cool.

2 Preheat the oven to 180°C/350°F/ Gas 4. To make the custard, break the eggs into a medium mixing bowl and whisk until frothy.

3 Stir in the vanilla essence and gradually add the sugar, then the milk, whisking continuously.

4 Pour the custard over the top of the caramel.

5 Cook in the preheated oven for 35–40 minutes. Remove from the oven and leave to cool.

6 Loosen the custard from the side of the dish with a knife. Place a serving dish on top of the soufflé dish and invert, giving a gentle shake.

7 Arrange any fruit of your choice around the caramel and serve.

NUTRITIONAL NOTES
Per portion:

Energy	229Kcals/964kJ
Fat, total	7.40g
Saturated fat	2.77g
Cholesterol	201.25mg
Fibre	0g

Crimson Pears

Poached pears in red wine are among the simplest of sweet treats, but look really spectacular.

Serves 4

1 bottle of red wine

175g/6oz/³/4 cup granulated sugar

45ml/3 tbsp clear honey

juice of 1/2 lemon

1 cinnamon stick

1 vanilla pod, split lengthways

5cm/2in piece of pared orange rind

1 whole clove

1 black peppercorn

4 firm, ripe pears

low-fat Greek yogurt, to serve (optional)

mint leaves, to decorate

1 In a large saucepan combine the wine, sugar, honey, lemon juice, cinnamon, vanilla pod, orange rind, clove and peppercorn. Heat gently, stirring, until the sugar dissolves.

2 Meanwhile, peel the pears, leaving the cores and stems intact. Slice a small piece off the base of each pear so it will stand upright.

3 Gently place the pears in the wine mixture. Simmer uncovered for 20–35 minutes, until the pears are evenly cooked and just tender.

4 With a slotted spoon, gently transfer the pears to a bowl. Continue to boil the poaching liquid until reduced by about half. Tip into a jug and leave to cool.

5 Strain the cooled liquid over the pears. Chill for at least 3 hours.

6 Place the pears in serving dishes, spoon over the liquid and decorate with a mint leaf. Serve solo or with low-fat Greek yogurt.

NUTRITIONAL NOTES

Per portion:

Energy	398Kcals/1681kJ
Fat, total	0.2g
Saturated fat	0g
Cholesterol	0mg
Fibre	3.3g

Apple Foam with Blackberries

This lovely light dish is perfect if you fancy a dessert, but don't want anything too rich or too filling.

INGREDIENTS

Serves 4

225g/8oz/2 cups blackberries

150ml/¼ pint/⅔ cup unsweetened apple juice

5ml/1 tsp powdered gelatine

15ml/1 tbsp clear honey

2 egg whites

1 Place the blackberries in a pan with 60ml/4 tbsp of the apple juice and heat gently until the fruit is soft. Remove from the heat, cool, then chill.

2 Sprinkle the gelatine over the remaining apple juice in a small pan and stir over low heat until dissolved. Stir in the honey.

3 Whisk the egg whites until they hold stiff peaks. Continue whisking hard and pour in the hot gelatine mixture gradually, until well mixed.

4 Quickly spoon the foam into rough mounds on individual plates. Chill. Serve with the blackberries and juice spooned around.

NUTRITIONAL NOTES
Per portion:

Energy	49Kcals/206kJ
Fat, total	0.2g
Saturated fat	0g
Cholesterol	0mg
Fibre	1.7g

Sensational Strawberries

Strawberries release their finest flavour when moistened with a sauce of raspberries and passion fruit.

Serves 4

350g/12oz/2 cups raspberries, fresh or frozen
45ml/3 tbsp caster sugar
1 passion fruit
675g/1½ lb/6 cups small strawberries
dessert biscuits, to serve (optional)

1 Mix the raspberries and sugar in a saucepan and heat gently until the raspberries release their juices. Simmer for 5 minutes. Leave to cool.

2 Cut the passion fruit in half and scoop out the seeds and juice into a small bowl.

3 Tip the raspberry mixture into a food processor, add the passion fruit and blend to a smooth purée.

4 Press the purée through a fine nylon sieve placed over a bowl, to remove the seeds.

5 Fold the strawberries into the sauce, then spoon into four stemmed glasses. Serve with the dessert biscuits, if you like, but these will increase the total fat content of the dessert.

NUTRITIONAL NOTES
Per portion:

Energy	115Kcals/484kJ
Fat, total	0.5g
Saturated fat	0g
Cholesterol	0mg
Fibre	4.2g

Crunchy Fruit Layer

This simple, almost instant, dessert contrasts smooth and crunchy textures. Other fruits can equally well be used.

INGREDIENTS

Serves 2

1 peach or nectarine

115g/4oz/1 cup muesli

150g/5oz/2/3 cup low-fat plain yogurt

15ml/1 tbsp jam

15ml/1 tbsp fruit juice

1 Remove the stone from the peach or nectarine and cut the fruit into bite-size pieces with a sharp knife.

2 Divide the fruit evenly between two tall glasses, reserving a few pieces for decoration.

3 Sprinkle the muesli over the fruit in an even layer, then top with the low-fat yogurt.

4 Stir the jam and the fruit juice together in a cup, then drizzle the mixture over the yogurt. Decorate with the reserved peach or nectarine pieces and serve immediately.

NUTRITIONAL NOTES

Per portion:

Energy	227Kcals/950kJ
Fat, total	2.7g
Saturated fat	0.98g
Cholesterol	3.0mg
Fibre	3.6g

Soft Fruit Pavlova

There is rather a lot of sugar in meringue, but for special occasions this is the queen of desserts.

INGREDIENTS

Serves 4

4 egg whites

pinch salt

175g/6oz/³/4 cup caster sugar

30ml/2 tbsp redcurrant jelly

15ml/1 tbsp rose water

300ml/¹/2 pint/1¹/4 cups low-fat
   Greek yogurt

450g/1lb/4 cups mixed soft fruits, such as
   blackberries, blueberries, redcurrants, raspberries or loganberries

10ml/2 tsp sifted icing sugar

1 Preheat the oven to 140ºC/275ºF/ Gas 1. Oil a baking sheet. Whisk the egg whites with a pinch of salt in a spotlessly clean bowl, until they are white and stiff. Slowly add the caster sugar and keep whisking until the mixture forms stiff, glossy peaks.

NUTRITIONAL NOTES

Per portion:

Energy	302Kcals/1280kJ
Fat, total	3.9g
Saturated fat	2.37g
Cholesterol	5.3mg
Fibre	3.1g

2 Spoon the meringue into a 25cm/10in round on the baking sheet, making a slight indentation in the centre to give it a swirled rim. Bake for 1–1¹/2 hours until the meringue is firm. Keep checking as the meringue can easily overcook and brown. Transfer the meringue to a serving plate.

3 Melt the redcurrant jelly in a small heatproof bowl resting over hot water. Cool slightly, then spread the jelly in the centre of the meringue. Gently mix the rose water with the low-fat Greek yogurt and spoon into the centre of the meringue. Pile the fruits on top and dust with icing sugar.

Figs with Ricotta Cream

Fresh, ripe figs are full of natural sweetness. This simple recipe makes the most of their beautiful, intense flavour.

Serves 4

4 ripe, fresh figs

115g/4oz/$\frac{1}{2}$ cup ricotta cheese

45ml/3 tbsp half-fat crème fraîche

15ml/1 tbsp clear honey

2.5ml/$\frac{1}{2}$ tsp pure vanilla essence

freshly grated nutmeg, to decorate

COOK'S TIP

The honey can be omitted and replaced with a little artificial sweetener.

1 Using a small sharp knife, trim the stalks from the figs. Make four cuts through each fig from the stalk-end, cutting them almost through but being careful to leave them joined at the base.

2 Place the figs on serving plates and open them out.

3 In a bowl, mix together the ricotta cheese, crème fraîche, honey and vanilla essence.

4 Spoon a little ricotta cream mixture on to each plate and sprinkle with grated nutmeg to serve.

NUTRITIONAL NOTES	
Per portion:	
Energy	97Kcals/405kJ
Fat, total	5.0g
Saturated fat	3.04g
Cholesterol	26.2mg
Fibre	0.8g

Low-fat Pastries, Cakes & Pies

⋅◆⋅

Spiced Mango Filo Fingers

Mangoes have a wonderful texture and look great simply sliced and fanned out next to these crunchy filo fingers.

INGREDIENTS

Serves 8

4 mangoes

6 filo pastry sheets

90g/3½oz/7 tbsp butter, melted

45g/3 tbsp soft light brown sugar

20ml/4 tsp ground cinnamon

icing sugar, for dusting

1 Preheat the oven to 200°C/400°F/ Gas 6. Set the most perfect mango aside for the decoration. Peel the remaining mangoes and slice the flesh. Cut the flesh across into 3mm/⅛in thick slices.

2 Keeping the rest of the filo covered with a damp cloth, lay one sheet on a baking sheet and brush with melted butter. Mix the brown sugar and cinnamon and sprinkle one-fifth of the mixture over the filo. Lay a sheet of filo on top and repeat for the other 5 sheets, ending with a filo sheet.

NUTRITIONAL NOTES

Per portion:

Energy	207Kcals/861kJ
Fat, total	5.0g
Saturated fat	2.75g
Cholesterol	11.5mg
Fibre	3.6g

3 Brush the top filo sheet with butter, trim off the excess pastry and lay the sliced mango in neat rows across the layered filo, to cover it completely. Brush with reserved butter and bake for 30 minutes. Allow to cool on the baking tray, then cut into fingers.

4 Slice the flesh from either side of the stone of the reserved mango. Cut each piece in half lengthways. Make four long cuts, almost to the end, in each quarter. Dust with icing sugar. Put on a plate and carefully fan out the slices. Serve with the mango fingers.

Filo Rhubarb Chiffon Pie

Filo pastry is low in fat and is easy to bake. Keep a pack in the freezer, ready to make impressive puddings like this one.

INGREDIENTS

Serves 3

500g/1¼ lb pink rhubarb

5ml/1 tsp mixed spice

finely grated rind and juice of 1 orange

15ml/1 tbsp granulated sugar

15ml/1 tbsp low-fat spread

3 sheets filo pastry, thawed if frozen

VARIATION

Other fruit such as apples, pears, peaches, cherries or gooseberries can be used in this pie – try it with whatever is in season.

1 Preheat the oven to 200°C/400°F/ Gas 6. Trim the leaves and ends from the rhubarb sticks and chop them in 2.5cm/1in pieces. Place them in a medium-sized mixing bowl.

2 Add the mixed spice, orange rind and juice and sugar; toss well to coat evenly. Tip the rhubarb into a 1 litre/1¾ pint/4 cup pie dish.

3 Melt the spread and brush over the filo sheets. Crumple the filo loosely and arrange over the filling.

4 Place the dish on a baking sheet and bake the pie for 20 minutes, until golden brown. Reduce the heat to 180°C/350°F/Gas 4 and bake for 10–15 minutes more until the rhubarb is tender. Serve warm.

NUTRITIONAL NOTES

Per portion:

Energy	118Kcals/494kJ
Fat, total	3g
Saturated fat	0.65g
Cholesterol	0.3mg
Fibre	2.4g

Apricot and Pear Filo Roulade

This is a very quick way of making a strudel – normally, very time consuming to do – it tastes delicious all the same!

INGREDIENTS

Serves 6

115g/4oz/1/2 cup ready-to-eat dried apricots, chopped

30ml/2 tbsp apricot conserve

5ml/1 tsp lemon juice

50g/2oz/1/3 cup soft light brown sugar

2 pears, peeled, cored and chopped

30ml/2 tbsp flaked almonds

30ml/2 tbsp low-fat spread, melted

8 sheets filo pastry, thawed if frozen

5ml/1 tsp icing sugar, for dusting

1 Put the apricots, apricot conserve, lemon juice, brown sugar and pears into a pan and heat for 5–7 minutes.

2 Remove from the heat and cool. Mix in the flaked almonds. Preheat the oven to 200ºC/400ºF/Gas 6. Melt the low-fat spread completely.

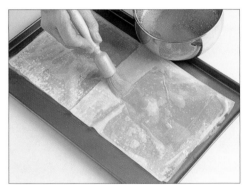

3 Lightly grease a baking sheet. Layer the pastry on the baking sheet, brushing each layer with the melted low-fat spread.

4 Spoon the filling down the filo, keeping it to one side of the centre and within 2.5cm/1in of each end. Lift the other side of the pastry up by sliding a palette knife underneath.

5 Fold this pastry over the filling, tucking the edge under. Seal the ends neatly and brush all over with spread again. Bake for 15–20 minutes, until golden. Dust with icing sugar and serve hot, cut into diamonds.

NUTRITIONAL NOTES
Per portion:

Energy	190Kcals/794kJ
Fat, total	4.1g
Saturated fat	0.54g
Cholesterol	0.1mg
Fibre	2.6g

Apricot Parcels

These filo parcels are a good way to use up mincemeat and marzipan that have been in your cupboard since Christmas!

NUTRITIONAL NOTES

Per portion:

Energy	234Kcals/982kJ
Fat, total	4.4g
Saturated fat	1.1g
Cholesterol	3.7mg
Fibre	1.5g

2 Place an apricot half, hollow up, in the centre of each pastry star. Mix together the mincemeat, crushed ratafias and marzipan and spoon a little of the mixture into the hollow in each apricot.

3 Top with another apricot half, then bring the corners of each pastry together and squeeze to make a gathered purse.

4 Place the purses on a baking sheet and brush each with a little melted spread. Bake for 15–20 minutes or until the pastry is golden and crisp. Lightly dust with icing sugar to serve.

INGREDIENTS

Serves 8

350g/12oz filo pastry, thawed if frozen

30ml/2 tbsp low-fat spread, melted

8 apricots, halved and stoned

60ml/4 tbsp luxury mincemeat

12 ratafias, crushed

30ml/2 tbsp grated marzipan

icing sugar, for dusting

1 Preheat the oven to 200°C/400°F/ Gas 6. Cut the filo into thirty-two 18cm/7in squares. Brush 4 of the squares with melted spread and stack them, giving each layer a quarter turn forming a star shape. Repeat to make 8.

COOK'S TIP

If you have run out of mincemeat, use mixed vine fruits instead.

Filo Fruit Scrunchies

Quick and easy to make, these pastries are ideal to serve at tea-time. Eat them warm or they will lose their crispness.

INGREDIENTS

Serves 6

5 apricots or plums

4 sheets filo pastry, thawed if frozen

20ml/4 tsp low-fat spread, melted

50g/2oz/^{1}/$_3$ cup demerara sugar

30ml/2 tbsp flaked almonds

icing sugar, for dusting

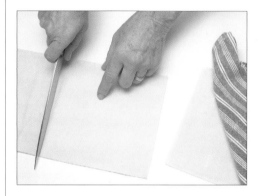

1 Preheat the oven to 190ºC/375ºF/ Gas 5. Halve the apricots or plums, remove the stones and slice the fruit. Cut the filo pastry into twelve 18cm/7in squares. Pile the squares on top of each other and cover with a damp cloth to prevent them drying out.

4 Place the scrunchies on a baking sheet. Bake for 8–10 minutes until golden brown, then loosen the scrunchies from the baking sheet with a palette knife and transfer to a wire rack. Dust with icing sugar and serve at once.

2 Remove one square of filo and brush it with melted spread. Lay a second filo square on top, then, using your fingers, mould into folds. Quickly make five more scrunchies in the same way so that the pastry does not dry out.

3 Arrange a few slices of fruit in the folds of each scrunchie, then sprinkle generously with the demerara sugar and flaked almonds.

NUTRITIONAL NOTES
Per portion:

Energy	132Kcals/555kJ
Fat, total	4.19g
Saturated fat	0.63g
Cholesterol	0mg
Fibre	0.67g

Plum Filo Pockets

Cheese-filled plums, baked in filo pastry, provide a wonderful mix of sweet and savoury tastes for the palate.

INGREDIENTS

Serves 4

115g/4oz/1/2 cup low-fat soft cheese

15ml/1 tbsp light muscovado sugar

2.5ml/1/2 tsp ground cloves

8 large, firm plums, halved and stoned

8 sheets filo pastry, thawed if frozen

sunflower oil, for brushing

icing sugar, for dusting

1 Preheat the oven to 220ºC/425ºF/ Gas 7. Mix together the low-fat soft cheese, muscovado sugar and ground cloves to make a firm paste.

2 Sandwich the plum halves together with a spoonful of the cheese mixture. Stack the filo pastry sheets and cut into 16 pieces, each 23cm/9in square. Brush each piece with oil and place them diagonally over each other.

3 Place a plum on each filo pastry square, lift up the sides and pinch the corners together. Place on a baking sheet. Bake for 15–18 minutes, until golden, then dust with icing sugar.

NUTRITIONAL NOTES
Per portion:

Energy	188Kcals/790kJ
Fat, total	1.87g
Saturated fat	0.27g
Cholesterol	0.29mg
Fibre	2.55g

Tropical Fruit Filo Clusters

These fruity filo clusters are ideal for a family treat or a dinner party dessert. They are delicious either hot or cold.

INGREDIENTS

Serves 8

1 banana, sliced

1 small mango, peeled, stoned and diced

lemon juice, for sprinkling

1 small cooking apple, coarsely grated

6 fresh or dried dates, stoned and chopped

50g/2oz/1/3 cup ready-to-eat dried pineapple, chopped

50g/2oz/1/3 cup sultanas

50g/2oz/1/3 cup soft light brown sugar

5ml/1 tsp ground mixed spice

8 sheets filo pastry, thawed if frozen

30ml/2 tbsp sunflower oil

icing sugar, for dusting

NUTRITIONAL NOTES

Per portion:

Energy	197Kcals/833kJ
Fat, total	3.58g
Saturated fat	0.44g
Cholesterol	0mg
Fibre	2.31g

1 Preheat the oven to 200ºC/400ºF/ Gas 6. Line a baking sheet with non-stick baking paper. In a medium-sized mixing bowl, toss the banana slices and diced mango in lemon juice to prevent discoloration.

2 Add the apple, dates, pineapple, sultanas, sugar and spice to the bowl and mix well.

3 To make each fruit cluster, cut each sheet of filo pastry in half crossways to make two squares or rectangles (16 pieces in total). Lightly brush two pieces of pastry with oil and place one on top of the other at a 45º angle to form a star shape.

COOK'S TIP

To prevent filo pastry drying out and crumbling, cover with a damp cloth before brushing with the oil.

4 Spoon some fruit filling into the centre, gather the pastry up over the filling and secure with string. Place the cluster on the prepared baking sheet and lightly brush all over with oil.

5 Repeat with the remaining pastry squares and filling to make a total of 8 fruit clusters. Bake for 25–30 minutes, until golden brown and crisp.

6 Carefully snip and remove the string from each cluster and serve hot or cold, dusted with icing sugar.

Redcurrant Filo Baskets

Filo pastry is low in fat and needs only a fine brushing of oil before use; a light oil such as sunflower is the best choice.

INGREDIENTS

Serves 6

3 sheets filo pastry, thawed if frozen
15ml/1 tbsp sunflower oil
175g/6oz/1½ cups redcurrants
250ml/8fl oz/1 cup low-fat Greek yogurt
5ml/1 tsp icing sugar

1 Preheat the oven to 200ºC/400ºF/ Gas 6. Cut the sheets of filo pastry into eighteen 10cm/4in squares.

2 Brush each filo square very thinly with oil, then arrange three squares in each of six small patty tins, placing each one at a different angle so that they form star-shaped baskets. Bake for 6–8 minutes, until crisp and golden. Lift the baskets out carefully and leave them to cool on a wire rack.

3 Set aside a few sprigs of redcurrants on their stems for decoration and string the rest. Stir the redcurrants into the low-fat Greek yogurt.

4 Spoon the yogurt into the filo baskets. Decorate with the reserved sprigs of redcurrants and sprinkle them with the icing sugar to serve.

NUTRITIONAL NOTES
Per portion:

Energy	80Kcals/335kJ
Fat, total	3.8g
Saturated fat	1.35g
Cholesterol	2.3mg
Fibre	1g

Filo Fruit Baskets

Crisp filo teamed with fruit in a straw-berry yogurt cream makes a fine finish for a summer meal.

INGREDIENTS

Serves 6

4 large or 8 small sheets of filo pastry, thawed
    if frozen
25g/1oz/5 tsp low-fat spread, melted
250ml/8fl oz/1 cup low-fat Greek yogurt
60ml/4 tbsp whole-fruit strawberry jam
15ml/1 tbsp Curaçao or other
    orange liqueur
115g/4oz/1 cup seedless red grapes, halved
115g/4oz/1 cup seedless green grapes, halved
175g/6oz/1 cup fresh pineapple cubes
225g/8oz/2 cups raspberries
30ml/2 tbsp icing sugar
6 small sprigs of fresh mint, for decorating

1 Preheat the oven to 180ºC/350ºF/ Gas 4. Grease 6 cups of a bun tin.

2 Stack the filo sheets and cut into twenty-four 12cm/4½ in squares.

NUTRITIONAL NOTES

Per portion:

Energy	207Kcals/867kJ
Fat, total	4.6g
Saturated fat	1.84g
Cholesterol	3.2mg
Fibre	1.4g

3 Lay 4 squares of pastry in each of the 6 bun tins, rotating to make star-shapes. Press the filo firmly down.

4 Brush the pastry baskets lightly with melted low-fat spread. Bake for 5–7 minutes, until the pastry is crisp and golden. Cool on a wire rack.

5 In a bowl, mix the yogurt with the strawberry jam and liqueur.

6 Just before serving, spoon a little of the cream mixture into each pastry basket. Top with the fresh fruit. Sprinkle with icing sugar and decorate each basket with a small sprig of mint.

Filo-topped Apple Pie

With its scrunchy filo topping and only a small amount of low-fat spread, this makes a really light and healthy dessert.

Serves 6

900g/2lb Bramley or other cooking apples

75g/3oz/6 tbsp caster sugar

grated rind of 1 lemon

15ml/1 tbsp lemon juice

75g/3oz/¹/2 cup sultanas

2.5ml/¹/2 tsp ground cinnamon

4 large sheets filo pastry, thawed if frozen

30ml/2 tbsp low-fat spread, melted

icing sugar, for dusting

1 Peel, core and dice the apples. Place them in a saucepan with the caster sugar and lemon rind. Drizzle the lemon juice over. Bring to the boil, stir well, then cook for 5 minutes or until the apples soften.

2 Stir in the sultanas and cinnamon. Spoon the mixture into a 1.2 litre/ 2 pint/5 cup pie dish and level the top. Leave to cool.

NUTRITIONAL NOTES
Per portion:

Energy	199Kcals/837kJ
Fat, total	2.5g
Saturated fat	0.56g
Cholesterol	0.3mg
Fibre	1.9g

3 Preheat the oven to 180ºC/350ºF/ Gas 4. Place a pie funnel in the centre of the fruit. Brush each sheet of filo with melted spread. Scrunch up loosely and place on the fruit to cover.

4 Bake for 20–30 minutes until the filo is golden. Dust the pie with icing sugar before serving.

VARIATION

To make filo crackers, cut the greased filo into 20cm/8in wide strips. Spoon a little of the filling along one end of each strip, leaving the sides clear. Roll up and twist the ends to make a cracker. Brush with more melted low-fat spread, bake for 20 minutes.

Pineapple and Strawberry Meringue

This is a gooey meringue that doesn't usually hold a perfect shape, but it has a wonderful marshmallow texture.

INGREDIENTS

Serves 6

5 egg whites, at room temperature
pinch of salt
5ml/1 tsp cornflour
15ml/1 tbsp distilled malt vinegar
few drops of vanilla essence
275g/10oz/1¼ cups caster sugar
250ml/8fl oz/1 cup low-fat Greek yogurt
175g/6oz fresh pineapple, cut into chunks
175g/6oz/1⅓ cups fresh strawberries, halved
strawberry leaves, to decorate (optional)

1 Preheat the oven to 160ºC/325ºF/ Gas 3. Line a baking sheet with non-stick baking paper.

2 Whisk the egg whites in a large grease-free bowl until they hold stiff peaks. Add the salt, cornflour, vinegar and vanilla essence; whisk again until stiff.

NUTRITIONAL NOTES

Per portion:

Energy	247Kcals/1050kJ
Fat, total	2.2g
Saturated fat	1.31g
Cholesterol	2.9mg
Fibre	0.7g

3 Gently whisk in half the sugar, then carefully fold in the rest. Spoon the meringue on to the baking sheet and swirl into a 20cm/8in round with the back of a large spoon.

4 Bake for 20 minutes, then reduce the temperature to 150ºC/300ºF/ Gas 2 and bake for 40 minutes more.

5 While still warm, transfer the meringue to a serving plate, then leave to cool. To serve, top with Greek yogurt, pineapple chunks and halved strawberries. Decorate with strawberry leaves, if you have them.

COOK'S TIP

You can also cook this in a deep, 20cm/8in loose-bottomed cake tin that is greased and lined.

Nectarine and Hazelnut Meringues

Sweet nectarines and yogurt paired with crisp hazelnut meringues make a really superb sweet.

Serves 5

3 egg whites

175g/6oz/³/4 cup caster sugar

50g/2oz/¹/2 cup chopped hazelnuts, toasted

300ml/¹/2 pint/1¹/4 cups low-fat
   Greek yogurt

15ml/1 tbsp sweet dessert wine

2 nectarines, stoned and sliced

fresh mint sprigs, to decorate

VARIATIONS

Use apricots instead of nectarines if you prefer, or you could try this with a raspberry topping.

1 Preheat the oven to 140ºC/275ºF/ Gas 1. Line two large baking sheets with non-stick baking paper. Whisk the egg whites in a grease-free bowl until they form stiff peaks. Gradually whisk in the caster sugar a spoonful at a time until the mixture forms a stiff, glossy meringue.

2 Fold in two thirds of the hazelnuts, then spoon five large ovals on to each baking sheet. Scatter the remaining hazelnuts over five of the meringue ovals. Flatten the remaining five ovals.

3 Bake the meringues for 1–1¼ hours until dry, carefully lift them off the baking paper and cool completely.

4 Mix the Greek yogurt lightly with the dessert wine. Spoon some of this mixture on to each of the plain meringues. Arrange a few nectarine slices on each. Put each meringue on a dessert plate with a hazelnut-topped meringue. Decorate each portion with mint sprigs and serve the meringues immediately.

NUTRITIONAL NOTES
Per portion:

Energy	293Kcals/1236kJ
Fat, total	4.9g
Saturated fat	2.34g
Cholesterol	4.2mg
Fibre	1.4g

Blackberry Brown Sugar Meringue

A brown sugar meringue looks very effective, especially when contrasted with a dark topping.

Serves 6

175g/6oz/1 cup soft light brown sugar

3 egg whites

5ml/1 tsp distilled malt vinegar

2.5ml/¹/2 tsp vanilla essence

For the topping

30ml/2 tbsp crème de cassis

350g/12oz/3 cups blackberries

15ml/1 tbsp icing sugar, sifted

300ml/¹/2 pint/1¹/4 cups low-fat
   Greek yogurt

small blackberry leaves, to decorate (optional)

1 Preheat the oven to 160ºC/325ºF/ Gas 3. Draw a 20cm/8in circle on a sheet of non-stick baking paper, turn over and place on a baking sheet.

2 Spread out the brown sugar on a second baking sheet and dry in the oven for 8–10 minutes. Sieve to remove lumps.

3 Whisk the egg whites in a clean grease-free bowl until stiff. Add half the dried brown sugar, 15ml/ 1 tbsp at a time, whisking well after each addition. Add the vinegar and vanilla essence, then fold in the remaining sugar.

4 Spoon the meringue on to the circle, leaving a central hollow. Bake for 45 minutes, turn off the oven but leave the meringue in the oven with the door slightly open, until cold.

5 In a bowl, sprinkle crème de cassis over the blackberries. Leave to macerate for 30 minutes.

6 When the meringue is cold, peel off the baking paper, carefully, and transfer the meringue to a serving plate. Stir the icing sugar into the low-fat Greek yogurt and spoon into the centre.

7 Top with the blackberries and decorate with small blackberry leaves, if you like. Serve at once.

NUTRITIONAL NOTES

Per portion:

Energy	199Kcals/833kJ
Fat, total	2.6g
Saturated fat	1.58g
Cholesterol	3.5mg
Fibre	1.8g

Floating Islands in Hot Plum Sauce

*The plum sauce for this pudding can be
made in advance, and reheated just
before you cook the meringues.*

Serves 4

450g/1lb red plums

300ml/1/2 pint/1 1/4 cups unsweetened
   apple juice

2 egg whites

30ml/2 tbsp concentrated apple juice

freshly grated nutmeg

3 Meanwhile, place the egg whites in
a grease-free bowl and whisk them
until they hold soft peaks.

5 Using a tablespoon, scoop the
meringue mixture into the gently
simmering plum sauce. You may need
to cook the "islands" in two batches.

1 Halve the plums and discard the
stones. Place them in a wide pan
with the unsweetened apple juice.

4 Gradually whisk in the
concentrated apple juice, whisking
continuously until the meringue holds
fairly firm peaks.

6 Cover and allow to simmer gently
for 2–3 minutes, until the
meringues are just set. Serve straight
away, sprinkled with a little freshly
grated nutmeg.

2 Bring to the boil, lower the heat,
cover and simmer gently for 15–20
minutes or until the plums are tender.

COOK'S TIP

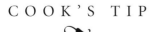

Concentrated apple juice is a useful
sweetener, or use a little honey.

NUTRITIONAL NOTES

Per portion:

Energy	77Kcals/324kJ
Fat, total	0.3g
Saturated fat	0g
Cholesterol	0mg
Fibre	1.7g

VARIATION

Add an extra dimension to this dessert
by using a fruit liqueur such as
Calvados, apricot brandy or Grand
Marnier instead of the concentrated
apple juice.

Raspberry Vacherin

Meringue rounds filled with orange-flavoured fromage frais and raspberries make a perfect dinner-party dessert.

INGREDIENTS

Serves 6

3 egg whites

175g/6oz/³/4 cup caster sugar

5ml/1 tsp chopped almonds

icing sugar, for dusting

raspberry leaves, to decorate (optional)

For the filling

175g/6oz/³/4 cup low-fat soft cheese

15ml/1 tbsp clear honey

15ml/1 tbsp Cointreau or other orange-flavoured liqueur

120ml/4fl oz/¹/2 cup low-fat fromage frais

225g/8oz/2 cups raspberries

2 Whisk the egg whites in a grease-free bowl until very stiff, then gradually whisk in the caster sugar to make a stiff meringue mixture.

3 Spoon the mixture on to the circles on the prepared baking sheets, spreading the meringue evenly to the edges. Sprinkle one meringue round with the chopped almonds.

5 To make the filling, cream the soft cheese with the honey and liqueur in a bowl. Fold in the fromage frais and raspberries, reserving three of the best for decoration.

1 Preheat the oven to 140°C/275°F/Gas 1. Draw a 20cm/8in circle on each of two pieces of non-stick baking paper. Turn the paper over so the marking is on the underside and use it to line two heavy baking sheets.

NUTRITIONAL NOTES
Per portion:

Energy	248Kcals/1041kJ
Fat, total	2.22g
Saturated fat	0.82g
Cholesterol	4mg
Fibre	1.06g

4 Bake for 1¹/2–2 hours, then lift the meringues off the baking sheets, peel away the paper and cool on a wire rack.

6 Place the plain meringue round on a board, carefully spread with the filling and top with the nut-covered round. Dust with icing sugar, transfer to a serving plate and decorate with the reserved raspberries, and a sprig of raspberry leaves, if you like.

COOK'S TIP
~

When making the meringue, whisk the egg whites until they are so stiff that you can turn the bowl upside-down without them falling out.

Baked Blackberry Cheesecake

This light, low-fat cheesecake is best made with wild blackberries, but cultivated ones will do.

INGREDIENTS

Serves 5

low-fat spread, for greasing

175g/6oz/³/4 cup low-fat cottage cheese

150ml/¹/4 pint/²/3 cup low-fat
    natural yogurt

15ml/1 tbsp wholemeal flour

25g/1oz/2 tbsp golden caster sugar

1 egg

1 egg white

finely grated rind and juice of ¹/2 lemon

200g/7oz/1³/4 cups fresh or thawed
    frozen blackberries

2 Place the cottage cheese in a food processor and process until smooth. Alternatively, rub it through a sieve, to obtain a smooth mixture.

5 Run a knife around the edge of the cheesecake, and then turn it out. Remove the lining paper, and place the cheesecake on a warm serving plate.

1 Preheat the oven to 180ºC/350ºF/ Gas 4. Lightly grease and base-line an 18cm/7in sandwich cake tin.

3 Stir in the yogurt, flour, sugar, egg and egg white. Add the lemon rind, juice and blackberries, reserving a few for decoration.

6 Decorate the cheesecake with the reserved blackberries, and serve it while still warm.

COOK'S TIP

If fresh blackberries are not in season, you can use canned blackberries. Choose those canned in natural juice and drain the fruit well before adding it to the cheesecake mixture.

4 Tip the mixture into the prepared tin and bake it for 30–35 minutes, or until it is just set. Turn off the oven and leave for a further 30 minutes.

NUTRITIONAL NOTES

Per portion:

Energy	95Kcals/402kJ
Fat, total	1.9g
Saturated fat	0.77g
Cholesterol	41.5mg
Fibre	1.4g

Tofu Berry Cheesecake

Strictly speaking, this isn't a cheesecake at all, as it is based on tofu – but who would guess?

INGREDIENTS

Serves 6

For the base

30ml/2 tbsp low-fat spread

30ml/2 tbsp unsweetened apple juice

115g/4oz/2^1/2 cups bran flakes or other high-fibre cereal

For the filling

275g/10oz/1^1/2 cups silken tofu

250ml/8fl oz/1 cup low-fat natural yogurt

60ml/4 tbsp apple juice

15ml/1 tbsp powdered gelatine

For the topping

175g/6oz/1^1/2 cups mixed summer soft fruit, such as strawberries, raspberries, redcurrants and blackberries

30ml/2 tbsp redcurrant jelly

30ml/2 tbsp hot water

1 For the base, place the low-fat spread and apple juice in a pan and heat them gently until the spread has melted. Crush the cereal and stir it into the pan, mixing well. Tip into a 23cm/9in round flan tin and press down firmly. Leave to set.

2 Make the filling. Place the tofu and yogurt in a food processor and process until smooth. Pour the apple juice into a cup and sprinkle the gelatine on top. Leave until spongy, then place over hot water until melted. Stir quickly into the tofu mixture.

3 Spread the tofu mixture over the chilled base. Chill until set. Remove the flan tin, place the "cheesecake" on a serving plate. Arrange the fruits on top.

4 Melt the redcurrant jelly with the hot water. Let it cool, then spoon over the fruit to serve.

NUTRITIONAL NOTES
Per portion:

Energy	163Kcals/688kJ
Fat, total	4.4g
Saturated fat	0.93g
Cholesterol	1.6mg
Fibre	3.2g

Angel Cake

Serve this light-as-air cake with low-fat fromage frais – it makes a perfect dessert or tea-time treat.

3 Gently fold in the flour mixture with a large metal spoon. Spoon into an ungreased 25cm/10in angel cake tin, smooth the surface and bake for about 45–50 minutes, until the cake springs back when lightly pressed.

4 Sprinkle a sheet of greaseproof paper with caster sugar and set an egg cup in the centre. Invert the cake tin over the paper, balancing it on the egg cup. When cold, the cake will drop out of the tin. Transfer to a plate, dust with icing sugar, or decorate and serve.

INGREDIENTS

Serves 10

40g/1¹/2 oz/¹/3 cup cornflour

40g/1¹/2 oz/¹/3 cup plain flour

8 egg whites

225g/8oz/1 cup caster sugar, plus extra
    for sprinkling

5ml/1 tsp pure vanilla essence

icing sugar, for dusting

1 Preheat the oven to 180ºC/350ºF/ Gas 4. Sift both flours on to a sheet of greaseproof paper.

2 Whisk the egg whites in a large grease-free bowl until very stiff, then gradually add the sugar and vanilla essence, whisking until the mixture is thick and glossy.

NUTRITIONAL NOTES

Per portion:

Energy	139Kcals/582kJ
Fat, total	0.08g
Saturated fat	0.01g
Cholesterol	0mg
Fibre	0.13g

COOK'S TIP

Make a lemony icing by mixing 175g/6oz/1¹/2 cups icing sugar with 15–30ml/1–2 tbsp lemon juice. Drizzle over the cake and decorate with physalis.

Chocolate and Orange Angel Cake

This light-as-air sponge with its fluffy icing is virtually fat-free, yet it tastes heavenly and looks great too.

INGREDIENTS

Serves 10

25g/1oz/¼ cup plain flour

15g/½ oz/2 tbsp fat-reduced
   cocoa powder

30ml/2 tbsp cornflour

pinch of salt

5 egg whites

2.5ml/½ tsp cream of tartar

115g/4oz/½ cup caster sugar

pared rind of 1 orange, blanched,
   to decorate

For the icing

200g/7oz/scant 1 cup caster sugar

75ml/5 tbsp water

1 egg white

2 Add the caster sugar to the egg whites a spoonful at a time, whisking for a few minutes each time. Sift a third of the flour and cocoa mixture over the meringue and gently fold in with a palette knife. Repeat the procedure, sifting and folding in the flour and cocoa mixture twice more.

5 Whisk the egg white in a grease-free bowl until soft peaks occur. Add the syrup in a thin stream, whisking all the time. Continue to whisk until very thick and fluffy.

6 Spread the icing over the top and sides of the cooled cake. Sprinkle the orange rind over the top of the cake and serve.

1 Preheat the oven to 180°C/350°F/ Gas 4. Sift the flour, cocoa powder, cornflour and salt together three times. Beat the egg whites in a large grease-free bowl until foamy. Add the cream of tartar, then whisk to soft peaks.

3 Spoon the mixture into a non-stick 20cm/8in ring mould and level the top. Bake for 35 minutes or until springy when lightly pressed. Turn upside-down on a wire rack and leave to cool in the tin. Remove the tin.

4 Make the icing. Put the sugar in a pan with the water. Stir over a low heat until dissolved. Boil until the syrup reaches a temperature of 120°C/250°F on a sugar thermometer, or when a drop of the syrup makes a soft ball when dropped into a cup of cold water. Remove from the heat.

COOK'S TIP

Do not over-beat the egg whites. They should form soft peaks, to allow for expansion during cooking.

NUTRITIONAL NOTES
Per portion:

Energy	153Kcals/644kJ
Fat, total	0.27g
Saturated fat	0.13g
Cholesterol	0mg
Fibre	0.25g

Cinnamon Apple Gâteau

Make this lovely cinnamon-spiced cake for an autumn celebration when apples are at their best.

INGREDIENTS

Serves 8

3 eggs

115g/4oz/$^{1}/_{2}$ cup caster sugar

75g/3oz/$^{3}/_{4}$ cup plain flour

5ml/1 tsp ground cinnamon

For the filling and topping

4 large eating apples

60ml/4 tbsp clear honey

15ml/1 tbsp water

75g/3oz/$^{1}/_{2}$ cup sultanas

2.5ml/$^{1}/_{2}$ tsp ground cinnamon

350g/12oz/1$^{1}/_{2}$ cups low-fat soft cheese

60ml/4 tbsp low-fat fromage frais

10ml/2 tsp lemon juice

45ml/3 tbsp smooth apricot jam, warmed

fresh mint sprigs, to decorate

1 Preheat the oven to 190°C/375°F/ Gas 5. Grease and line a 23cm/9in sandwich cake tin. Place the eggs and caster sugar in a bowl and whisk until thick and mousse-like (when the whisk is lifted, a trail should remain on the surface of the mixture for at least 15 seconds).

2 Sift the flour and cinnamon over the egg mixture and carefully fold in. Pour into the prepared tin and bake for 25–30 minutes or until the cake springs back when lightly pressed. Slide a palette knife between the cake and the tin to loosen the edge, then turn the cake on to a wire rack to cool.

3 To make the filling, peel, core and slice three of the apples and put them in a saucepan. Add 30ml/2 tbsp of the honey and the water. Cover and cook over a gentle heat for about 10 minutes until the apples have softened. Add the sultanas and cinnamon, stir well, replace the lid and leave to cool.

4 Put the soft cheese in a bowl with the remaining honey, the fromage frais and half the lemon juice. Beat until the mixture is smooth.

5 Halve the cake horizontally, place the bottom half on a board and drizzle over any liquid from the apple mixture. Spread with two-thirds of the cheese mixture, then top with the apple filling. Fit the top of the cake in place.

6 Swirl the remaining cheese mixture over the top of the sponge. Core and slice the remaining apple, sprinkle with the remaining lemon juice and use to decorate the cake edge. Brush the apple with apricot jam and decorate with mint sprigs.

NUTRITIONAL NOTES

Per portion:

Energy	244Kcals/1023kJ
Fat, total	4.05g
Saturated fat	1.71g
Cholesterol	77.95mg
Fibre	1.5g

Peach Swiss Roll

A feather-light sponge with a filling of peach jam – delicious at tea time or as a dinner-party dessert.

INGREDIENTS

Serves 6–8

low-fat spread, for greasing

3 eggs

115g/4oz/^{1}/2 cup caster sugar

75g/3oz/^{3}/4 cup plain flour, sifted

15ml/1 tbsp boiling water

90ml/6 tbsp peach jam

icing sugar, for dusting (optional)

NUTRITIONAL NOTES
Per portion:

Energy	178Kcals/746kJ
Fat, total	2.45g
Saturated fat	0.67g
Cholesterol	82.5mg
Fibre	0.33g

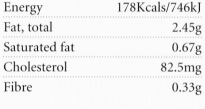

1 Preheat the oven to 200ºC/400ºF/ Gas 6. Grease a 30 × 20cm/12 × 8in Swiss roll tin and line with non-stick baking paper. Combine the eggs and sugar in a bowl. Whisk until thick and mousse-like (when the whisk is lifted, a trail should remain on the surface of the mixture for at least 15 seconds).

2 Carefully fold in the flour with a large metal spoon, then add the boiling water in the same way.

3 Spoon into the prepared tin, spread evenly to the edges and bake for about 10–12 minutes until the cake springs back when lightly pressed.

4 Spread a sheet of greaseproof paper on a flat surface, sprinkle it with caster sugar, then invert the cake on top. Peel off the lining paper.

5 Neatly trim the edges of the cake. Make a neat cut two-thirds of the way through the cake, about 1cm/^{1}/2in from the short edge nearest you.

6 Spread the cake with the peach jam and roll up quickly from the partially cut end. Hold in position for a minute, making sure the join is underneath. Cool on a wire rack. Decorate with glacé icing (see Cook's Tip) or simply dust with icing sugar before serving.

COOK'S TIP
~

Decorate the Swiss roll with glacé icing. Put 115g/4oz glacé icing in a piping bag fitted with a small writing nozzle and pipe lines over the top of the Swiss roll.

Apricot and Orange Roulade

This elegant dessert is very low in fat, so serving it with Greek yogurt or fromage frais would not be disastrous.

INGREDIENTS

Serves 6

low-fat spread, for greasing
4 egg whites
115g/4oz/¹/2 cup golden caster sugar
50g/2oz/¹/2 cup plain flour
finely grated rind of 1 small orange
45ml/3 tbsp orange juice

For the filling
115g/4oz/¹/2 cup ready-to-eat dried apricots, roughly chopped
150ml/¹/4 pint/²/3 cup orange juice

To decorate
10ml/2 tsp icing sugar, for sprinkling
shreds of pared orange rind, to decorate

1 Preheat the oven to 200ºC/400ºF/ Gas 6. Grease a 23 × 33cm/9 × 13in Swiss-roll tin and line it with non-stick baking paper. Grease the paper.

COOK'S TIP

Make and bake the sponge mixture a day in advance and keep it cool, rolled in the paper. Fill with the fruit purée 2–3 hours before serving. The sponge can also be stored frozen.

2 Place the egg whites in a large grease-free bowl and whisk them they hold soft peaks. Gradually add the sugar, whisking hard each time.

3 Fold in the flour, orange rind and juice. Spoon the mixture into the prepared tin and spread it evenly.

4 Bake for 15-18 minutes, or until the sponge is firm and pale gold in colour. Turn out on to non-stick baking paper, and roll it up loosely from one short side. Leave to cool.

5 Make the filling. Place the apricots in a pan, with the orange juice. Cover the pan and leave to simmer until most of the liqud has been absorbed. Purée the apricots in a food processor.

6 Unroll the roulade and spread with the apricot mixture. Roll up, arrange strips of paper diagonally across the roll, sprinkle lightly with lines of icing sugar, remove the paper and scatter with shreds of pared orange rind. Serve in slices.

NUTRITIONAL NOTES

Per portion:

Energy	154Kcals/652kJ
Fat, total	0.3g
Saturated fat	0.01g
Cholesterol	0mg
Fibre	1.5g

Lemon Chiffon Cake

Lemon mousse provides a tangy filling for this light lemon sponge, which is simple to prepare.

INGREDIENTS

Serves 8

low-fat spread, for greasing
2 eggs
75g/3oz/6 tbsp caster sugar
grated rind of 1 lemon
50g/2oz/1/2 cup plain flour, sifted
thinly pared lemon rind, cut in shreds

For the filling
2 eggs, separated
75g/3oz/6 tbsp caster sugar
grated rind and juice of 1 lemon
30ml/2 tbsp water
15ml/1 tbsp powdered gelatine
120ml/4fl oz/1/2 cup low-fat fromage frais

For the icing
115g/4oz/1 cup icing sugar, sifted
15ml/1 tbsp lemon juice

2 Bake for 20–25 minutes until the cake springs back when lightly pressed in the centre. Turn on to a wire rack to cool. Once cold, split the cake in half horizontally and return the lower half to the clean cake tin. Set aside.

3 Make the filling. Put the egg yolks, sugar, lemon rind and juice in a bowl. Beat with a hand-held electric whisk until thick, pale and creamy.

1 Preheat the oven to 180ºC/350ºF/ Gas 4. Grease and line a 20cm/8in loose-bottomed cake tin. Whisk the eggs, sugar and lemon rind until thick and mousse-like. Gently fold in the flour, then turn the mixture into the prepared tin.

4 Pour the water into a small heatproof bowl and sprinkle the gelatine on top. Leave until spongy, then place over simmering water and stir until dissolved. Cool slightly, then whisk into the yolk mixture. Fold in the fromage frais. When the mixture begins to set, quickly whisk the egg whites to soft peaks. Fold a spoonful into the mousse mixture to lighten it, then fold in the rest.

5 Pour the lemon mousse over the sponge in the cake tin, spreading it to the edges. Set the second layer of sponge on top and chill until set.

6 Slide a palette knife between the tin and the cake to loosen it, then transfer to a serving plate. Make the icing by adding enough lemon juice to the icing sugar to make a mixture thick enough to coat the back of a wooden spoon. Pour over the cake and decorate with the lemon rind.

NUTRITIONAL NOTES
Per portion:

Energy	202Kcals/849kJ
Fat, total	2.81g
Saturated fat	0.79g
Cholesterol	96.41mg
Fibre	0.2g

Tia Maria Gâteau

A feather-light coffee sponge with a creamy liqueur-flavoured filling and a hint of ginger.

INGREDIENTS

Serves 8

low-fat spread, for greasing
75g/3oz/³⁄4 cup plain flour
30ml/2 tbsp instant coffee powder
3 eggs
115g/4oz/¹⁄2 cup caster sugar
coffee beans, to decorate (optional)

For the filling
175g/6oz/³⁄4 cup low-fat soft cheese
15ml/1 tbsp clear honey
15ml/1 tbsp Tia Maria
50g/2oz/¹⁄4 cup stem ginger,
    roughly chopped

For the icing
225g/8oz/2 cups icing sugar, sifted
10ml/2 tsp coffee essence
15ml/1 tbsp water
5ml/1 tsp cocoa powder, preferably
    fat-reduced

2 Whisk the eggs and sugar in a bowl until thick (when the whisk is lifted, a trail should remain on the mixture's surface for 10–15 seconds).

3 Gently fold in the flour mixture with a metal spoon, being careful not to knock out any air. Turn the mixture into the prepared tin. Bake for 30–35 minutes or until it springs back when lightly pressed. Turn on to a wire rack and leave to cool completely.

5 Split the cake in half and sandwich them with the Tia Maria filling.

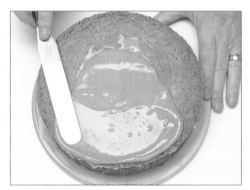

6 Make the icing. Mix the icing sugar and coffee essence with enough of the water to make an icing that will coat the back of a wooden spoon. Spread three-quarters of the icing over the cake. Stir the cocoa into the remaining icing until smooth. Spoon into a piping bag fitted with a writing nozzle and pipe the mocha icing over the coffee icing. Decorate with coffee beans, if you like.

1 Preheat the oven to 190ºC/375ºF/ Gas 5. Grease and line a 20cm/8in deep round cake tin. Sift the flour and coffee powder together on to a sheet of greaseproof paper.

4 Make the filling. Mix the soft cheese with the honey in a bowl. Beat until smooth, then stir in the Tia Maria and the chopped stem ginger.

NUTRITIONAL NOTES
Per portion:

Energy	226Kcals/951kJ
Fat, total	3.14g
Saturated fat	1.17g
Cholesterol	75.03mg
Fibre	0.64g

Low-fat Custards, Soufflés & Whips

• ◆ •

Bread and Sultana Custard

An old favourite gets the low-fat treatment and proves how successful this can be.

Serves 4

15ml/1 tbsp low-fat spread

3 thin slices of bread, crusts removed

475ml/16fl oz/2 cups skimmed milk

2.5ml/^{1}/$_2$ tsp mixed spice

45ml/3 tbsp demerara sugar

2 eggs, whisked

75g/3oz/^{1}/$_2$ cup sultanas

freshly grated nutmeg

a little icing sugar, for dusting

1 Preheat the oven to 180°C/350°F/
Gas 4. Lightly grease an ovenproof dish. Spread the bread with low-fat spread and cut into small pieces.

2 Place the bread in several layers in the prepared dish.

3 Whisk the skimmed milk, mixed spice, demerara sugar and eggs in a large mixing bowl. Pour the mixture over the bread, to cover. Sprinkle over the sultanas and stand for 30 minutes.

4 Grate a little nutmeg over the top and bake for 30–40 minutes until the custard is just set and golden. Serve sprinkled with icing sugar.

NUTRITIONAL NOTES

Per portion:

Energy	246Kcals/1037kJ
Fat, total	5g
Saturated fat	1.37g
Cholesterol	99.2mg
Fibre	0.7g

Poppyseed Custard with Red Fruit

Poppyseeds add a nutty flavour to this creamy custard without increasing the amount of fat too much.

INGREDIENTS

Serves 6

low-fat spread, for greasing

600ml/1 pint/2¹/₂ cups skimmed milk

2 eggs

15ml/1 tbsp caster sugar

15ml/1 tbsp poppyseeds

115g/4oz/1 cup each of strawberries, raspberries and blackberries

15ml/1 tbsp soft light brown sugar

60ml/4 tbsp red grape juice

1 Preheat the oven to 150°C/300°F/ Gas 2. Grease a soufflé dish very lightly with low-fat spread. Heat the milk until just below boiling point, but do not boil. Beat the eggs in a bowl with the caster sugar and poppyseeds until creamy.

2 Whisk the milk into the egg mixture until very well mixed. Stand the prepared soufflé dish in a shallow roasting tin, then pour in hot water from the kettle to come halfway up the sides of the dish.

VARIATION

If you don't like poppyseeds, sprinkle the surface of the custard with freshly grated nutmeg or ground cinnamon instead.

3 Pour the custard into the soufflé dish and bake in the preheated oven for 50–60 minutes, until the custard is just set and golden on top.

4 While the custard is baking, mix the fruit with the soft brown sugar and fruit juice. Chill until ready to serve with the warm baked custard.

NUTRITIONAL NOTES

Per portion:

Energy	109Kcals/460kJ
Fat, total	3.1g
Saturated fat	0.69g
Cholesterol	66.2mg
Fibre	1.3g

Orange Yogurt Brûlées

Luxurious treats, much lower in fat than classic brûlées, which are made with cream, eggs and lots of sugar.

INGREDIENTS

Serves 4

2 oranges

150ml/¼ pint/⅔ cup low-fat
   Greek yogurt

60ml/4 tbsp half-fat crème fraîche

45ml/3 tbsp golden caster sugar

30ml/2 tbsp light muscovado sugar

1 With a sharp knife, cut away all the peel and white pith from the oranges and segment the fruit, removing all the membrane.

2 Place the fruit in the bottom of four individual flameproof dishes. Mix together the yogurt and crème fraîche and spoon over the oranges.

3 Mix together the two sugars and sprinkle them evenly over the tops of the dishes.

4 Place the dishes under a preheated, very hot grill for 3–4 minutes or until the sugar melts and turns to a rich golden brown. Serve warm or cold.

NUTRITIONAL NOTES

Per portion:

Energy	154Kcals/648kJ
Fat, total	3.8g
Saturated fat	2.35g
Cholesterol	15.8mg
Fibre	1.4g

Tofu Berry Brûlée

Brûlée is usually out-of-bounds on a low-fat diet, but this version is perfectly acceptable as it uses tofu.

INGREDIENTS

Serves 4

300g/11oz packet silken tofu

45ml/3 tbsp icing sugar

225g/8oz/2 cups red berry fruits, such as raspberries, strawberries and redcurrants

about 75ml/5 tbsp demerara sugar

NUTRITIONAL NOTES

Per portion:

Energy	180Kcals/760kJ
Fat, total	3.01g
Saturated fat	0.41g
Cholesterol	0mg
Fibre	1.31g

1 Mix the tofu and icing sugar in a food processor or blender and process until smooth.

2 Stir in the fruits, then spoon into a 900ml/1½ pint/3¾ cup flameproof dish. Flatten the top.

3 Sprinkle the top with demerara sugar to cover evenly. Place under a very hot grill until the sugar melts and caramelizes. Chill before serving.

COOK'S TIP

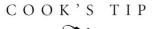

Choose silken tofu as it gives a smoother texture than firm tofu in this type of dish. Firm tofu is better for cooking in chunks.

Passion Fruit Brûlée

Fruit brûlées are usually made with double cream, but Greek yogurt works just as well.

INGREDIENTS

Serves 4

4 passion fruit

300ml/¹/2 pint/1¹/4 cups low-fat Greek yogurt

75g/3oz/¹/2 cup soft light brown sugar

15ml/1 tbsp water

COOK'S TIP

Watch the caramel closely. It is ready when it darkens to a rich golden brown. At this stage it will be very hot, so protect your hand and pour it with great care.

1 Cut the passion fruit in half, using a very sharp knife. Use a teaspoon to scoop out all the pulp and seeds and divide among four ovenproof ramekins.

2 Spoon equal amounts of the yogurt on the fruit and smooth the surface level. Chill for at least 2 hours.

3 Put the sugar in a small saucepan with the water and heat gently, stirring, until the sugar has melted and caramelized. Pour over the yogurt; the caramel will harden within 1 minute. Keep the brûlées in a cool place until ready to serve.

NUTRITIONAL NOTES

Per portion:

Energy	139Kcals/590kJ
Fat, total	3.8g
Saturated fat	2.37g
Cholesterol	5.3mg
Fibre	0.5g

Mango and Ginger Clouds

The sweet, perfumed flavour of ripe mango combines beautifully with ginger, and this dessert makes the most of them.

INGREDIENTS

Serves 6

3 ripe mangoes

3 pieces stem ginger, plus 45ml/3 tbsp syrup
   from the jar

75g/3oz/½ cup silken tofu

3 egg whites

6 unsalted pistachio nuts, chopped

1 Cut the mangoes' flesh off the stone, remove the peel and chop.

2 Put the mango flesh in a food processor and add the ginger, syrup and tofu. Process until smooth. Spoon into a bowl.

NOTE

Raw or lightly cooked egg whites should be avoided by young children and women during pregnancy.

3 Whisk the egg whites in a grease-free bowl to form soft peaks. Fold them lightly into the mango mixture.

4 Spoon the mixture into wide dishes or glasses and chill before serving, sprinkled with the pistachios.

NUTRITIONAL NOTES

Per portion:

Energy	141Kcals/592kJ
Fat, total	1.9g
Saturated fat	0.21g
Cholesterol	0mg
Fibre	3.9g

Raspberry Passion Fruit Swirls

If passion fruit is not available, this simple dessert can be made with raspberries alone.

2 Place alternate spoonfuls of the raspberry pulp and the fromage frais mixture into stemmed glasses or serving dishes.

3 Stir lightly to create a swirled effect. Decorate each dessert with a whole raspberry and a sprig of fresh mint. Serve chilled.

INGREDIENTS

Serves 4

300g/11oz/2¹/₂ cups raspberries

2 passion fruit

400ml/14fl oz/1²/₃ cups low-fat
   fromage frais

30ml/2 tbsp caster sugar

raspberries and fresh mint sprigs,
   to decorate

COOK'S TIP
~
Over-ripe, slightly soft fruit can be used in this recipe. Use frozen raspberries when fresh are not available, but thaw them first.

1 Using a fork, mash the raspberries in a small bowl until the juice runs. Place the fromage frais and sugar in a separate bowl. Halve the passion fruit and scoop out the seeds. Add to the fromage frais and mix well.

NUTRITIONAL NOTES
Per portion:

Energy	110Kcals/462kJ
Fat, total	0.47g
Saturated fat	0.13g
Cholesterol	1mg
Fibre	2.12g

Chocolate Vanilla Timbales

You really can allow yourself the occasional chocolate treat, especially if it's a dessert as light as this one.

INGREDIENTS

Serves 6

350ml/12fl oz/1¹/2 cups skimmed milk

30ml/2 tbsp cocoa powder, plus extra, for sprinkling

2 eggs, separated

5ml/1 tsp pure vanilla essence

45ml/3 tbsp caster sugar

15ml/1 tbsp powdered gelatine

45ml/3 tbsp hot water

For the sauce

120ml/4fl oz/¹/2 cup low-fat Greek yogurt

2.5ml/¹/2 tsp pure vanilla essence

1 Mix the milk and cocoa in a pan; stir over a moderate heat until the milk boils. Beat the egg yolks, vanilla and sugar in a bowl, until smooth. Pour in the chocolate milk, beating well.

2 Return the mixture to the pan and stir constantly over a gentle heat, without boiling, until it thickens slightly and is smooth. Dissolve the gelatine in the hot water and then quickly stir it into the milk mixture. Let it cool until on the point of setting.

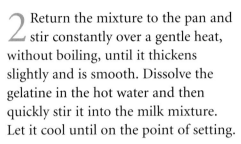

3 Whisk the egg whites in a grease-free bowl until they hold soft peaks. Fold them quickly into the chocolate milk mixture, then divide among six individual moulds. Chill until set.

4 To serve the timbales, run a knife around the edge of each mould, dip the moulds quickly into hot water and turn out on to serving plates. For the sauce, stir the yogurt and vanilla essence together, then spoon on to the plates. Sprinkle the sauce with cocoa powder just before serving.

NUTRITIONAL NOTES
Per portion:

Energy	118Kcals/497kJ
Fat, total	4.1g
Saturated fat	1.89g
Cholesterol	66.7mg
Fibre	0.7g

Peach and Ginger Paskha

This low-fat version of the Russian Easter favourite is made with peaches and stem ginger.

INGREDIENTS

Serves 4

350g/12oz/1¹/2 cups low-fat cottage cheese

2 ripe peaches or nectarines

90g/3¹/2oz/scant ¹/2 cup low-fat
    natural yogurt

2 pieces stem ginger in syrup, drained and
    chopped, plus 30ml/2 tbsp syrup
    from the jar

2.5ml/¹/2 tsp pure vanilla essence

To decorate

1 peach or nectarine, peeled and sliced

10ml/2 tsp slivered almonds, toasted

1 Drain the cottage cheese and rub it through a sieve into a bowl. Stone and roughly chop the fruit.

2 In a bowl, mix together the chopped peaches or nectarines, the low-fat cottage cheese, yogurt, stem ginger, syrup and vanilla essence.

3 Line a new, clean flower pot or a strainer with a piece of clean, fine cloth such as cheesecloth.

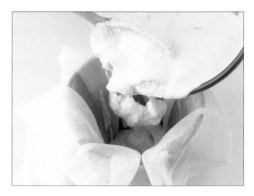

4 Tip in the cheese mixture, wrap over the cloth and weight down. Leave over a bowl in a cool place to drain overnight. Unwrap the cloth and invert the paskha on to a plate. Decorate with fruit slices and almonds.

NUTRITIONAL NOTES

Per portion:

Energy	147Kcals/621kJ
Fat, total	2.9g
Saturated fat	0.89g
Cholesterol	5.3mg
Fibre	1.1g

COOK'S TIP

For individual paskhas, line four to six ramekins with the clean cloth and divide the mixture among them.

Strawberry Rose-petal Paskha

This lighter version of a traditional Russian dessert is ideal for dinner parties – make it a day or two in advance.

INGREDIENTS

Serves 4

350g/12oz/1¹/2 cups low-fat cottage cheese
175ml/6fl oz/³/4 cup low-fat
   natural yogurt
30ml/2 tbsp clear honey
2.5ml/¹/2 tsp rose-water
275g/10oz/2¹/2 cups strawberries
handful of scented pink rose petals,
   to decorate

VARIATION

Use small porcelain heart-shaped moulds with draining holes for a pretty alternative.

1 Drain any liquid from the cottage cheese. Tip the cheese into a sieve. using a wooden spoon to rub it through the sieve into a bowl. Stir the yogurt, honey and rose-water into the cheese.

2 Roughly chop about half the strawberries and fold them into the cheese mixture.

3 Line a new, clean flowerpot or a sieve with fine muslin and tip the cheese mixture in. Drain over a bowl for several hours, or overnight.

4 Invert the flowerpot or sieve on to a serving plate, turn out the paskha and lift off the muslin. Cut the remaining strawberries in half and arrange them around the paskha. Scatter the rose petals over. Serve the paskha chilled.

NUTRITIONAL NOTES
Per portion:

Energy	133Kcals/561kJ
Fat, total	1.6g
Saturated fat	1g
Cholesterol	6.1mg
Fibre	0.8g

Lemon Hearts with Strawberry Sauce

These elegant little hearts are perfect for a romantic celebration, such as a Valentine's Day dinner.

INGREDIENTS

Serves 6

175g/6oz/3⁄4 cup low-fat cottage cheese

150ml/1⁄4 pint/2⁄3 cup half-fat crème fraîche

15ml/1 tbsp granulated sugar

finely grated rind of 1⁄2 lemon

30ml/2 tbsp lemon juice

10ml/2 tsp powdered gelatine

2 egg whites

low-fat spread, for greasing

For the sauce

225g/8oz/2 cups fresh or frozen and thawed strawberries, plus extra to decorate

15ml/1 tbsp lemon juice

1 Press the cottage cheese through a sieve into a bowl. Beat in the crème fraîche, sugar and lemon rind.

2 Pour the lemon juice into a small heatproof bowl and sprinkle the gelatine over the surface. When it has sponged, place the bowl over a pan of hot water and stir until dissolved.

3 Quickly stir the gelatine into the cheese mixture, mixing it in evenly.

4 Beat the egg whites in a grease-free bowl until they form soft peaks. Quickly fold them into the cheese mixture with metal spoon.

5 Spoon the mixture into six lightly greased, individual heart-shaped moulds, and chill the moulds until set.

6 Make the sauce. Mix the strawberries and lemon juice in a food processor or blender and process until smooth. Pour the sauce on to serving plates and invert the lemon hearts on top of the sauce. Decorate with slices of strawberry.

COOK'S TIP
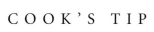

Don't worry if you haven't got heart-shaped (coeur à la crème) moulds. Simply use individual fluted moulds – or even ordinary teacups.

NUTRITIONAL NOTES

Per portion:

Energy	94Kcals/397kJ
Fat, total	4.2g
Saturated fat	2.60g
Cholesterol	27.7mg
Fibre	0.4g

Souffléed Rice Pudding

The fluffy egg whites in this rice pudding make the portions more substantial, without adding lots of extra fat.

INGREDIENTS

Serves 4

65g/2¹/2 oz/¹/3 cup short-grain (pudding) rice
45ml/3 tbsp clear honey
750ml/1¹/4 pints/3 cups semi-skimmed milk
1 vanilla pod or 2.5ml/¹/2 tsp vanilla essence
2 egg whites
5ml/1 tsp freshly grated nutmeg

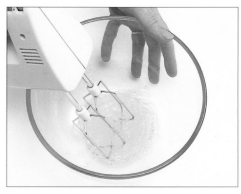

1 Place the rice, honey and milk in a heavy-based or non-stick pan and bring the milk to the boil. Add the vanilla pod, if using.

2 Lower the heat, cover and simmer over the lowest possible heat for approximately 1–1¹/4 hours, stirring occasionally to prevent sticking, until most of the liquid has been absorbed.

3 Remove the vanilla pod, or, if using vanilla essence, add this to the rice mixture now. Set the pan aside, so that the mixture cools slightly. Preheat the oven to 220ºC/425ºF/Gas 7.

4 Place the egg whites in a grease-free bowl and whisk until they hold soft peaks when the whisk is lifted.

5 Using a metal spoon or spatula, fold the egg whites evenly into the rice mixture, then tip it into a 1 litre/1³/4 pint/4 cup ovenproof dish.

6 Sprinkle with grated nutmeg and bake for 15–20 minutes, until the pudding has risen well and is golden brown. Serve hot.

NUTRITIONAL NOTES
Per portion:

Energy	186Kcals/782kJ
Fat, total	3.7g
Saturated fat	1.88g
Cholesterol	13.1mg
Fibre	0g

COOK'S TIP

If you like, use skimmed milk instead of semi-skimmed, but take care when it is simmering as, with so little fat, it tends to boil over very easily.

Cinnamon and Apricot Soufflés

Don't expect this to be difficult simply because it's a soufflé – it really couldn't be easier.

INGREDIENTS

Serves 4

low-fat spread, for greasing

plain flour, for dusting

3 eggs

115g/4oz/½ cup apricot fruit spread

finely grated rind of ½ lemon

5ml/1 tsp ground cinnamon, plus extra
  to decorate

NUTRITIONAL NOTES

Per portion:

Energy	134Kcals/560kJ
Fat, total	4.1g
Saturated fat	1.15g
Cholesterol	144.4mg
Fibre	0g

1 Preheat the oven to 190ºC/375ºF/ Gas 5. Lightly grease four individual soufflé dishes and dust them lightly with flour.

VARIATION

Other fruit spreads would be delicious in this soufflé. Try peach or blueberry for a change.

2 Separate the eggs and place the yolks in a bowl with the fruit spread, lemon rind and cinnamon.

3 Whisk hard until the mixture is thick and pale in colour.

4 Place the egg whites in a grease-free bowl and whisk them until they form soft peaks when the whisk is lifted from the bowl.

5 Using a metal spoon or spatula, gradually fold the egg whites evenly into the yolk mixture.

6 Divide the soufflé mixture among the prepared dishes and bake for 10–15 minutes, until well-risen and golden brown. Serve at once, dusted with a little extra ground cinnamon.

COOK'S TIP
∽

Puréed fresh or well-drained canned fruit can be used instead of the apricot spread, but make sure that the mixture is not too wet or the soufflés will not rise properly.

Fluffy Banana and Pineapple Soufflé

This light, low-fat mousse looks very impressive but is really very easy to make, especially with a food processor.

INGREDIENTS

Serves 6

2 ripe bananas

225g/8oz/1 cup low-fat cottage cheese

425g/15oz can pineapple chunks or pieces in juice

60ml/4 tbsp water

15ml/1 tbsp powdered gelatine

2 egg whites

1 Tie a double band of non-stick baking paper around a 600ml/ 1 pint/2½ cup soufflé dish, to come approximately 5cm/2in above the rim.

2 Peel and chop one banana and, with the cottage cheese, blend it in a food processor until smooth.

3 Drain the pineapple and reserve a few pieces for decoration. Add the remainder to the mixture and process until finely chopped.

4 Pour the water into a small heatproof bowl and sprinkle the gelatine on top. Leave until spongy, then place the bowl over hot water, stirring occasionally, until all the gelatine has dissolved.

5 Whisk the egg whites in a grease-free bowl until they hold soft peaks, then fold them lightly and evenly into the mixture. Tip the mixture into the prepared dish, smooth the surface and chill it in the fridge, until set.

6 When the soufflé has set, carefully remove the paper collar. Decorate the soufflé with the reserved slices of banana and chunks of pineapple.

NUTRITIONAL NOTES
Per portion:

Energy	106Kcals/452kJ
Fat, total	0.6g
Saturated fat	0.37g
Cholesterol	1.9mg
Fibre	0.7g

Hot Blackberry and Apple Soufflés

It's always worth freezing a bag of blackberries to have on hand for treats such as this delicious soufflé.

Serves 6

low-fat spread, for greasing

150g/5oz/²/3 cup caster sugar, plus extra
   for dusting

350g/12oz/3 cups blackberries

1 Bramley or other large cooking apple, peeled,
   cored and finely diced

grated rind and juice of 1 orange

3 egg whites

icing sugar, for dusting

COOK'S TIP

Running a table knife around the edge of the soufflés before baking helps them to rise evenly without any part sticking to the rim of the dishes.

3 Put a spoonful of the fruit purée into each prepared dish and smooth the surface. Set the dishes aside.

4 Whisk the egg whites in a large grease-free bowl until they form stiff peaks. Very gradually whisk in the remaining caster sugar to make a stiff, glossy meringue mixture.

5 Fold in the remaining fruit purée and spoon the flavoured meringue into the prepared dishes. Level the tops with a palette knife, and run a table knife around the edge of each dish.

6 Place the dishes on the hot baking sheet and bake for 10–15 minutes until the soufflés have risen well and are lightly browned. Dust the tops with icing sugar and serve at once.

1 Preheat the oven to 200ºC/400ºF/ Gas 6 and heat a baking sheet. Grease six 150ml/¼ pint/²/3 cup soufflé dishes and dust with caster sugar.

2 In a pan, cook the blackberries, diced apple, orange rind and juice for 10 minutes. Press through a sieve into a bowl. Stir in 50g/2oz/¼ cup of the caster sugar. Set aside to cool.

NUTRITIONAL NOTES
Per portion:

Energy	138Kcals/584kJ
Fat, total	0.3g
Saturated fat	0.5g
Cholesterol	0mg
Fibre	2.7g

Souffléed Orange Semolina

If your opinion of semolina is coloured by the memory of school puddings, treat yourself to a taste of this version.

INGREDIENTS

Serves 4

50g/2oz/¼ cup semolina

600ml/1 pint/2½ cups semi-skimmed milk

30ml/2 tbsp muscovado sugar

1 large orange

1 egg white

NUTRITIONAL NOTES

Per portion:

Energy	158Kcals/665kJ
Fat, total	2.67g
Saturated fat	1.54g
Cholesterol	10.5mg
Fibre	0.86g

1 Preheat the oven to 200°C/400°F/ Gas 6. Put the semolina in a non-stick pan and add the milk and sugar. Stir over a moderate heat until thickened and smooth. Remove from the heat.

COOK'S TIP

∾

When using the rind of citrus fruit, scrub the fruit thoroughly before use, or buy unwaxed fruit.

2 Scrub the orange rind and pare a few long shreds of rind, save for decoration. Finely grate the remaining rind. Cut all the peel and white pith from the orange and separate the flesh into equal segments. Stir the segments into the semolina, with the orange rind.

3 Whisk the egg white in a grease-free bowl until stiff, then fold lightly and evenly into the mixture. Spoon into a 1 litre/1¾ pint/4 cup ovenproof dish and bake for 15–20 minutes, until risen and golden brown. Scatter the orange shreds and serve.

Quick Apricot Blender Whip

One of the quickest desserts you could make – and also one of the prettiest with its delicate swirl of creamy apricot.

INGREDIENTS

Serves 4

400g/14oz can apricot halves in juice
15ml/1 tbsp Grand Marnier or brandy
175ml/6fl oz/³/4 cup low-fat Greek yogurt
15ml/1 tbsp flaked almonds

1 Drain the juice from the apricots and place the fruit and liqueur in a blender or food processor.

2 Process the apricots until the mixture is smooth.

3 Alternately spoon fruit purée and yogurt into four tall glasses or glass dishes, swirling them together slightly to give a marbled effect.

4 Lightly toast the almonds until they are golden. Let them cool slightly and then sprinkle them on top of each whip. Serve at once.

NUTRITIONAL NOTES
Per portion:

Energy	88Kcals/369kJ
Fat, total	4.4g
Saturated fat	1.38g
Cholesterol	3.1mg
Fibre	0.9g

Prune and Orange Pots

A simple, store-cupboard dessert, made in minutes. It can be served straight away, but it is best chilled before serving.

INGREDIENTS

Serves 4

225g/8oz/1¹/2 cups ready-to-eat
   dried prunes
150ml/¹/4 pint/²/3 cup orange juice
250ml/8fl oz/1 cup low-fat natural yogurt
shreds of thinly pared orange rind,
   to decorate

1 Remove the stones (if any), then roughly chop the prunes. Place them in a pan with the orange juice.

2 Bring the juice to the boil, stirring. Lower the heat, cover and simmer for 5 minutes, until the prunes are tender and the liquid is reduced by half.

3 Remove from the heat, allow to cool slightly, then beat well with a wooden spoon, until the fruit breaks down to a rough purée.

4 Transfer the mixture to a bowl. Stir in the yogurt, swirling the yogurt and fruit purée together lightly, to give an attractive marbled effect.

5 Spoon the mixture into stemmed glasses or individual serving dishes, smoothing the tops.

6 Top each pot with a few shreds of thinly pared orange rind, to decorate. Chill before serving.

COOK'S TIP

This dessert can also be made with other ready-to-eat dried fruit, such as apricots or peaches. If using dried apricots, try the unsulphured variety for a rich colour and flavour. For a special occasion, add a dash of brandy or Cointreau with the yogurt.

NUTRITIONAL NOTES

Per portion:

Energy	125Kcals/529kJ
Fat, total	0.7g
Saturated fat	0.28g
Cholesterol	2.3mg
Fibre	3.2g

Gooseberry Cheese Cooler

Gooseberries are one of the less common summer fruits, so they're well worth snapping up when you can get them.

INGREDIENTS

Serves 4

450g/1lb/4 cups fresh or frozen gooseberries

1 small orange

15ml/1 tbsp clear honey

250g/9oz/1 cup low-fat cottage cheese

NUTRITIONAL NOTES
Per portion:

Energy	93Kcals/392kJ
Fat, total	1.4g
Saturated fat	0.56g
Cholesterol	3.1mg
Fibre	3.4g

1 Top and tail the gooseberries and place them in a medium-sized saucepan. Finely grate the rind from the orange and squeeze out all of the juice; then add the orange rind and juice to the pan. Cover the pan and cook gently, stirring occasionally, until the fruit is completely tender.

2 Remove from the heat and stir in the honey. Purée the gooseberries with the cooking liquid in a food processor until almost smooth. Cool.

3 Press the cottage cheese through a sieve, or process it in a food processor, until smooth. Stir half the gooseberry purée into the cheese.

4 Spoon the cheese mixture into four serving dishes or glasses. Top each with a spoonful of the gooseberry purée. Serve chilled.

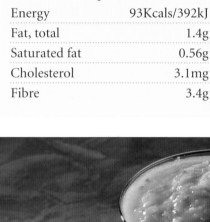

Grape Cheese Whips

A deliciously cool dessert of low-fat cheese and honey, topped with sugar-frosted grapes as decoration.

INGREDIENTS

Serves 4

150g/5oz/1¼ cups black or green seedless
  grapes, plus tiny bunches

2 egg whites

15ml/1 tbsp caster sugar

finely grated rind and juice of ½ lemon

225g/8oz/1 cup low-fat soft cheese

45ml/3 tbsp clear honey

30ml/2 tbsp brandy (optional)

1 Brush the tiny bunches of grapes lightly with egg white and sprinkle with sugar to coat. Leave to dry.

2 In a bowl, mix together the lemon rind and juice, cheese, honey and brandy if using. Chop the remaining grapes and stir them into the mixture.

3 Whisk the egg whites in a grease-free bowl until stiff enough to hold soft peaks. Fold the whites into the grape mixture, then spoon into four serving glasses.

4 Top with the sugar-frosted grapes and serve chilled.

NUTRITIONAL NOTES

Per portion:

Energy	135Kcals/563kJ
Fat, total	3g
Saturated fat	1.2g
Cholesterol	0.56mg
Fibre	0g

Apricot Delight

A fluffy mousse base with a layer of fruit jelly on top makes this dessert doubly delicious.

Serves 8

2 × 400g/14oz cans apricots in
    natural juice
60ml/4 tbsp fructose
15ml/1 tbsp lemon juice
25ml/1½ tbsp powdered gelatine
425g/15oz low fat ready-to-serve custard
150ml/¼ pint/⅔ cup low-fat natural yogurt,
    strained

To decorate
1 quantity yogurt piping cream
1 apricot, sliced
1 sprig of fresh apple mint

2 Drain the apricots, reserving the juice. Put the drained apricots in a food processor or blender. Add the fructose and 60ml/4 tbsp of the apricot juice. Blend to a smooth purée.

5 Sprinkle the remaining 15ml/ 1 tbsp gelatine over 60ml/4 tbsp of the apricot juice. Soak and dissolve as before. Mix the remaining purée with the custard, yogurt and gelatine. Pour on to the layer of set fruit purée and chill in the fridge for 3 hours.

1 Line the base of a 1.2 litre/2 pint/ 5 cup heart-shaped or round cake tin with non-stick baking paper.

3 Measure 30ml/2 tbsp of the apricot juice into a small bowl, add lemon juice, then sprinkle over 10ml/2 tsp of the gelatine. Leave for 5 minutes.

4 Stir the gelatine into half the apricot purée and pour into the tin. Chill in the fridge for 1½ hours.

6 Dip the cake tin into hot water for a few seconds and unmould the delice on to a serving plate. Decorate with yogurt piping cream, the sliced apricot and a sprig of fresh apple mint.

COOK'S TIP

Don't use a loose-bottomed cake tin for this recipe as the mixture may seep through before it sets.

NUTRITIONAL NOTES
Per portion:

Energy	155Kcals/649kJ
Fat, total	0.63g
Saturated fat	0.33g
Cholesterol	0mg
Fibre	0.9g

Low-fat Fruit Salads

⋄✦⋄

Strawberries with Cointreau

Strawberries at the height of their season are one of summer's greatest pleasures. Try this unusual way of serving them.

INGREDIENTS

Serves 4

1 unwaxed orange

40g/1¹/2 oz/3 tbsp granulated sugar

75ml/5 tbsp water

450g/1lb/3¹/2 cups strawberries, hulled

45ml/3 tbsp Cointreau or other orange-
　flavoured liqueur

250ml/8fl oz/1 cup low-fat Greek yogurt

1 With a vegetable peeler, remove wide strips of rind from the orange, taking care to avoid the pith. Stack two or three strips at a time and cut into very thin julienne strips.

2 Mix the sugar and water in a small saucepan. Heat gently, swirling the pan occasionally until the sugar has dissolved. Bring to the boil, add the julienne strips, then simmer for 10 minutes. Remove the pan from the heat and leave the syrup to cool.

3 Reserve four strawberries for decoration and cut the rest lengthways in halves or quarters. Put them in a bowl. Stir the Cointreau or chosen liqueur into the syrup and pour it over the fruit. Add the orange rind. Set aside for at least 30 minutes or for up to 2 hours.

NUTRITIONAL NOTES

Per portion:

Energy	155Kcals/653kJ
Fat, total	3.2g
Saturated fat	1.97g
Cholesterol	4.4mg
Fibre	1.2g

4 Whip the yogurt, then sweeten to taste with a little strawberry syrup.

5 Spoon the chopped strawberries into glass serving dishes and top with dollops of the sweetened Greek yogurt. Decorate with strawberries.

Fresh Figs with Honey and Wine

Fresh figs are naturally sweet, and taste wonderful in a honeyed wine syrup. Any variety can be used in this recipe.

Serves 6

450ml/³/4 pint/scant 2 cups dry white wine

75g/3oz/¹/3 cup clear honey

50g/2oz/¹/4 cup caster sugar

1 small orange

8 whole cloves

450g/1lb fresh figs

1 cinnamon stick

bay leaves, to decorate

For the sauce

300ml/¹/2 pint/1¹/4 cups low-fat
   Greek yogurt

5ml/1 tsp pure vanilla essence

5ml/1 tsp caster sugar

1 Put the wine, honey and sugar in a heavy-based saucepan and heat gently until the sugar dissolves.

2 Stud the orange with the cloves and add to the syrup with the figs and cinnamon. Cover and simmer until the figs are soft then leave to cool.

3 Flavour the low-fat Greek yogurt with the vanilla essence and sugar. Spoon it into a serving dish. Transfer the fruit to another serving dish. With a sharp knife cut one or two of the figs in half, if you like, to show off their pretty centres. Decorate with the bay leaves and serve with the yogurt.

NUTRITIONAL NOTES
Per portion:

Energy	201Kcals/845kJ
Fat, total	2.7g
Saturated fat	1.58g
Cholesterol	3.5mg
Fibre	1.5g

Persian Melon Cups

This typical Persian dessert uses delicious, sweet fresh fruits flavoured with rose-water and a hint of aromatic mint.

INGREDIENTS

Serves 4

2 small melons

225g/8oz/2 cups strawberries, sliced

3 peaches, peeled and cut into small cubes

1 bunch of seedless grapes, about 225g/8oz

30ml/2 tbsp caster sugar

15ml/1 tbsp rose-water

15ml/1 tbsp lemon juice

crushed ice

4 sprigs of mint, to decorate

COOK'S TIP
~
If you don't have a melon baller, scoop out the melon flesh using a large spoon and then cut into bite-size pieces.

1 Carefully cut the melons in half and remove the seeds. Scoop out the flesh with a melon baller, taking care not to damage the skin. Reserve the melon shells for later.

2 Reserve four strawberries and slice the rest. Place in a bowl with the melon balls, the peaches, grapes, sugar, rose-water and lemon juice.

3 Pile the fruit into the melon shells and chill in the fridge for 2 hours.

4 To serve, sprinkle with crushed ice and decorate each melon shell with a whole strawberry and a sprig of mint.

NUTRITIONAL NOTES
Per portion:

Energy	137Kcals/579kJ
Fat, total	0.4g
Saturated fat	0g
Cholesterol	0mg
Fibre	3.2g

Fragrant Mandarins with Pistachios

*Mandarins, tangerines, clementines,
mineolas: any of these lovely citrus fruits
could be used for this dessert.*

INGREDIENTS

INGREDIENTS

Serves 4

10 mandarins

15ml/1 tbsp icing sugar

10ml/2 tbsp orange-flower water

15ml/1 tbsp chopped pistachio nuts

1 Pare a little mandarin rind and cut into fine shreds. Squeeze the juice from two mandarins and set it aside.

2 Peel the remaining fruit, removing all the pith and place in a bowl.

3 Mix the reserved mandarin juice, icing sugar and orange-flower water and pour it over the fruit. Cover the dish and place in the fridge for at least an hour to chill.

4 Blanch the shreds of rind in boiling water for 30 seconds. Drain and cool on kitchen paper, then sprinkle them over the mandarins, with the pistachio nuts, to serve.

NUTRITIONAL NOTES
Per portion:

Energy	91Kcals/382kJ
Fat, total	2.2g
Saturated fat	0.25g
Cholesterol	0mg
Fibre	2g

Orange and Date Salad

This Moroccan dessert is simplicity itself, yet it is wonderfully fresh-tasting and light at the end of a rich meal.

INGREDIENTS

Serves 6

6 oranges

15–30ml/1–2 tbsp orange-flower water or rose-water (optional)

lemon juice (optional)

115g/4oz/²/3 cup stoned dates

40g/1¹/2 oz/scant ¹/2 cup pistachio nuts

15ml/1 tbsp icing sugar, plus extra for dusting

5ml/1 tsp toasted almonds

1 Peel the oranges with a sharp knife, removing all the pith. Cut into segments, catching the juice in a bowl. Place in a serving dish.

2 Stir in the juice from the bowl, with a little orange-flower or rose-water, if using, and sharpen with lemon juice, if liked.

3 Chop the dates and almonds and sprinkle over the salad with the icing sugar. Chill for 1 hour.

4 Just before serving, sprinkle the salad with the toasted almonds and a little extra icing sugar.

NUTRITIONAL NOTES
Per portion:

Energy	147Kcals/616kJ
Fat, total	4.3g
Saturated fat	0.45g
Cholesterol	0mg
Fibre	3.5g

COOK'S TIP

Use fresh dates, if you can, although if you can't get hold of them dried dates are delicious in this salad, too.

Fresh Fruit Salad and Almond Curd

This is a wonderfully light Chinese
dessert usually made from agar-agar or
isinglass, though gelatine can be used.

INGREDIENTS

Serves 6

10g/¹/4 oz agar-agar or isinglass
    or 25g/1oz gelatine
about 600ml/1 pint/2¹/2 cups water
50g/2oz/¹/4 cup caster sugar
300ml/¹/2 pint/1¹/4 cups semi-skimmed milk
5ml/1 tsp almond essence
fresh fruit salad

1 In a saucepan, dissolve the agar-
agar or isinglass in about half of the
water over a gentle heat. This will take
at least 10 minutes. If using gelatine,
follow the instructions on the sachet.

2 In a separate saucepan, dissolve the
sugar in the remaining water over
the heat. Add the milk and the almond
essence. Blend well, but do not boil.

3 Pour the agar-agar, isinglass or
gelatine mixture into a large
serving bowl. Add the flavoured milk
gradually, stirring all the time. When
cool, put in the fridge for 2–3 hours to
set. To serve, cut the curd into small
cubes and spoon into a serving dish or
into individual bowls. Spoon the fruit
salad over the curd and serve.

NUTRITIONAL NOTES
Per portion:

Energy	117Kcals/499kJ
Fat, total	1.2g
Saturated fat	0.75g
Cholesterol	5.3mg
Fibre	0g

Fresh Pineapple with Coconut

This refreshing dessert can also be made with vacuum-packed pineapple, and it is very simple to make and light to eat.

Serves 4

1 fresh pineapple, about
    675g/1¹/2 lb, peeled
few slivers of fresh coconut
300ml/¹/2 pint/1¹/4 cups unsweetened
    pineapple juice
60ml/4 tbsp coconut liqueur
2.5cm/1in piece stem ginger, plus 45ml/
    3 tbsp syrup from the jar

3 Thinly slice the stem ginger and add to the pan with the ginger syrup. Bring just to the boil, then simmer gently until the liquid is slightly reduced and the sauce is fairly thick.

4 Pour the sauce over the pineapple and coconut, leave to cool, then chill in the fridge before serving.

1 Peel and slice the pineapple, arrange in a serving dish and scatter the coconut slivers on top.

2 Place the pineapple juice and coconut liqueur in a saucepan and heat gently.

NUTRITIONAL NOTES
Per portion:

Energy	177Kcals/743kJ
Fat, total	2.2g
Saturated fat	1.55g
Cholesterol	0mg
Fibre	2.2g

Perfumed Pineapple Salad

Prepare this fruit salad ahead to give the fruit time to absorb the perfumed flavour of the orange-flower water.

INGREDIENTS

Serves 4

1 small ripe pineapple

15ml/1 tbsp icing sugar

15ml/1 tbsp orange-flower water, or
   more if liked

115g/4oz/²/3 cup fresh dates, stoned
   and quartered

225g/8oz/2 cups fresh strawberries, sliced

a few fresh mint sprigs, to serve

1 Cut the skin from the pineapple and, using the tip of a vegetable peeler, remove as many brown "eyes" as possible. Quarter the pineapple lengthways, remove the core from each wedge, then slice.

2 Lay the pineapple slices in a shallow glass serving bowl. Sprinkle with icing sugar and drizzle the orange-flower water over.

COOK'S TIP
~

Orange-flower water is available from Middle Eastern food stores or good delicatessens.

3 Add the dates and strawberries to the pineapple, cover and chill for at least 2 hours, stirring once or twice. Serve, decorated with a few mint sprigs.

NUTRITIONAL NOTES
Per portion:

Energy	127Kcals/534kJ
Fat, total	0.4g
Saturated fat	0g
Cholesterol	0mg
Fibre	2.9g

Iced Pineapple Crush

The sweet tropical flavours of pineapple and lychees combine well with richly scented strawberries.

INGREDIENTS

Serves 4

2 small pineapples

450g/1lb/4 cups strawberries

400g/14oz can lychees

45ml/3 tbsp kirsch or white rum

30ml/2 tbsp icing sugar

1 Remove the crown from both pineapples by twisting sharply. Reserve the leaves for decoration.

VARIATION

You could use other tropical fruit such as mango, papaya or guava as well as the pineapple.

2 Cut the fruit in half diagonally with a large serrated knife.

3 Cut around the flesh inside the skin with a small serrated knife, keeping the skin intact. Remove the core from the pineapple.

4 Chop the pineapple and combine with the strawberries and lychees, taking care not to damage the fruit.

5 Combine the kirsch or rum with the icing sugar, pour over the fruit and freeze for 45 minutes.

6 Turn the fruit out into the pineapple skins and decorate with the pineapple leaves. Serve chilled.

NUTRITIONAL NOTES
Per portion:

Energy	251Kcals/1058kJ
Fat, total	0.7g
Saturated fat	0g
Cholesterol	0mg
Fibre	5.2g

COOK'S TIP

A ripe pineapple will resist pressure when squeezed and will have a sweet, fragrant smell. In winter, freezing conditions can cause the flesh to blacken.

Pineapple Wedges with Allspice and Lime

Fresh pineapple is easy to prepare and always looks festive, so this dish is perfect for easy entertaining.

2 Loosen the flesh on each wedge by sliding a knife between the flesh and the skin. Cut the flesh into slices, leaving it on the skin.

3 Using a sharp-pointed or canelle knife, remove a few shreds of rind from the lime. Squeeze out the juice.

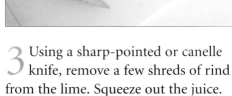

4 Sprinkle the pineapple with the lime juice and rind, sugar and allspice. Serve immediately, or chill for up to an hour.

INGREDIENTS

Serves 4

1 ripe pineapple, about 800g/1¾ lb

1 lime

15ml/1 tbsp dark muscovado sugar

5ml/1 tsp ground allspice

NUTRITIONAL NOTES

Per portion:

Energy	96Kcals/403kJ
Fat, total	0.5g
Saturated fat	0.03g
Cholesterol	0mg
Fibre	2.3g

1 Cut the pineapple lengthways into quarters and remove the hard core from each wedge.

Papaya and Mango Medley with Iced Yogurt

Tropical fruit with iced mango yogurt makes a wonderful dessert. Buy very ripe fruit for this dessert.

INGREDIENTS

Serves 4

2 large ripe mangoes, total weight about 675g/1¹/₂ lb

300ml/¹/₂ pint/1¹/₄ cups low-fat Greek yogurt

8 dried apricots, halved

150ml/¹/₄ pint/²/₃ cup unsweetened orange juice

1 ripe papaya, about 300g/11oz

1 Take one thick slice from one of the mangoes and, while still on the skin, slash the flesh with a sharp knife in a criss-cross pattern to make cubes.

3 Meanwhile, put the apricots and orange juice in a pan. Bring to boil, then simmer until the apricots are soft, adding a little water, if needed, so that the apricots remain moist. Remove from the heat and set aside to cool. Peel, stone and chop the mangoes.

4 Halve the papaya, remove seeds and peel. Dice the flesh and add to the mango. Pour the apricot sauce over.

5 Stir the mango yogurt a few times. Serve the fruit topped with the mango yogurt.

2 Turn the piece of mango inside-out and cut away the cubed flesh from the skin. Place in a bowl, mash to a pulp with a fork, then add the Greek yogurt and mix well. Spoon into a freezer tub and freeze for about 1–1¹/₂ hours until half frozen.

NUTRITIONAL NOTES

Per portion:

Energy	231Kcals/967kJ
Fat, total	4.3g
Saturated fat	2.44g
Cholesterol	5.3mg
Fibre	7.5g

Pineapple and Passion Fruit Salsa

Serve this fruity salsa solo or as a filling for halved baby cantaloupes. Either way, it is a cool and refreshing dessert.

INGREDIENTS

Serves 6

1 small fresh pineapple

2 passion fruit

150ml/¼ pint/⅔ cup low-fat
   Greek yogurt

30ml/2 tbsp light muscovado sugar

meringues, to serve (optional)

1 Cut off the top and bottom of the pineapple so that it will stand firmly on a chopping board. Using a large sharp knife, slice off the peel.

2 Use a small sharp knife to carefully cut out the eyes from around the pineapple.

VARIATION

Use low-fat fromage frais instead of the yogurt, if you like.

3 Slice the pineapple and use a small pastry cutter to stamp out the tough core. Finely chop the flesh.

4 Cut the passion fruit in half, remove the seeds and scoop out the pulp into a bowl.

NUTRITIONAL NOTES

Per portion:

Energy	82Kcals/342kJ
Fat, total	1.5g
Saturated fat	0.79g
Cholesterol	1.8mg
Fibre	1.3g

5 Stir in the chopped pineapple and yogurt. Cover and chill.

6 Stir in the muscovado sugar just before serving the salsa. Serve with meringues, if you like.

Grapefruit Salad with Campari and Orange

The bittersweet flavour of Campari combines especially well with citrus fruit for this sophisticated dessert.

INGREDIENTS

Serves 4

150ml/¹/4 pint/²/3 cup water

45ml/3 tbsp caster sugar

60ml/4 tbsp Campari

30ml/2 tbsp lemon juice

4 grapefruit

5 oranges

4 sprigs fresh mint

COOK'S TIP
~

When buying citrus fruit, choose brightly coloured varieties that feel heavy for their size.

1 Bring the water to the boil in a small saucepan, add the sugar and simmer until dissolved. Cool in a metal tray, then add the Campari and lemon juice. Chill until ready to serve.

2 Peel the grapefruit and oranges. Working over a bowl, to catch the juice, cut the fruit into segments. Add them to the bowl, stir in the Campari syrup and chill again.

3 Spoon the salad into four dishes and finish with a sprig of fresh mint.

NUTRITIONAL NOTES
Per portion:

Energy	182Kcals/764kJ
Fat, total	0.4g
Saturated fat	0g
Cholesterol	0mg
Fibre	5.3g

Muscat Grape Frappé

The flavour and perfume of the Muscat grape is rarely more enticing than when captured in this icy-cool salad.

2 Remove the seeds from the grapes with a pair of tweezers. If you have time, peel the grapes.

3 Scrape the frozen wine with a tablespoon to make a fine ice. Combine the grapes with the ice and spoon into four shallow glasses.

INGREDIENTS

Serves 4

1/2 bottle Muscat wine, Beaumes de Venise, Frontignan or Rivesaltes

150ml/1/4 pint/2/3 cup water

450g/1lb/4 cups Muscat grapes

COOK'S TIP
To make this frappé alcohol-free, substitute 300ml/1/2 pint/1 1/4 cups apple or grape juice for the wine.

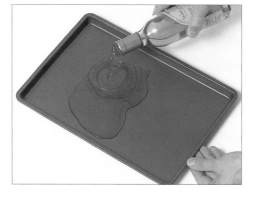

1 Pour the wine into a stainless-steel or non-stick tray, add the water and freeze for 3 hours or until solid.

NUTRITIONAL NOTES
Per portion:

Energy	155Kcals/651kJ
Fat, total	0g
Saturated fat	0g
Cholesterol	0mg
Fibre	1g

Cool Green Fruit Salad

A sophisticated, simple fruit salad, which would look wonderful served on a bed of crushed ice.

INGREDIENTS

Serves 6

3 Ogen or Galia melons

115g/4oz/1 cup green seedless grapes

2 kiwi fruit

1 star fruit, plus extra slices to garnish

1 green-skinned apple

1 lime

175ml/6fl oz/¾ cup unsweetened sparkling
   grape juice

3 Thinly pare the rind from the lime and cut it in fine strips. Blanch in boiling water for 30 seconds, and then drain them and rinse them in cold water. Squeeze the juice from the lime and pour it over the fruit. Toss lightly.

4 Spoon the prepared fruit into the reserved melon shells; then chill the shells until required. To serve, spoon the sparkling grape juice over the fruit and scatter with lime rind. Decorate with slices of star fruit.

1 Halve the melons and scoop out the seeds. Keeping the shells intact, scoop out the flesh and cut into bite-size cubes. Reserve the melon shells.

2 Cut any large grapes in half. Peel and chop the kiwi fruit. Slice the star fruit and set aside a few slices for decoration. Core and slice the apple and place in a bowl, with the melon, grapes and kiwi fruit.

NUTRITIONAL NOTES
Per portion:

Energy	91Kcals/382kJ
Fat, total	0.4g
Saturated fat	0.00g
Cholesterol	0.0mg
Fibre	1.6g

Blackberry Salad with Rose Granita

The blackberry is a member of the rose family and combines especially well with rose-water.

INGREDIENTS

Serves 4

600ml/1 pint/2¹/2 cups water

150g/5oz/²/3 cup caster sugar

petals from 1 fresh red rose, finely chopped

5ml/1 tsp rose-water

10ml/2 tsp lemon juice

450g/1lb/4 cups blackberries

icing sugar, for dusting

For the meringue

2 egg whites

115g/4oz/¹/2 cup caster sugar

2 Preheat the oven to 140°C/275°F/ Gas 1. Line a baking sheet with six layers of newspaper and cover with non-stick baking paper.

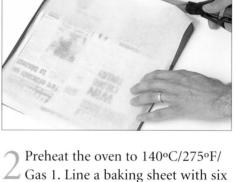

4 Spoon the meringue into a piping bag fitted with a 1cm/¹/2in plain nozzle. Pipe the meringue in lengths on the lined baking sheet. Dry in the bottom of the oven for 1¹/2–2 hours.

1 Bring 150ml/¹/4 pint/²/3 cup of the water to the boil in a stainless-steel or enamel saucepan. Add the sugar and chopped rose petals, then lower the heat and simmer for 5 minutes. Strain the syrup into a deep metal tray, add the remaining water, the rose-water and lemon juice; leave to cool. Freeze the mixture for approximately 3 hours or until solid.

3 Make the meringue. Whisk the egg whites in a grease-free bowl until they form soft peaks. Whisk in the caster sugar, a little at a time, then continue to whisk until the meringue forms stiff peaks when the whisk is lifted out of the bowl.

5 Break the meringue into 5cm/2in lengths and place three or four lengths on each of four large plates. Pile the blackberries next to the meringue. With a tablespoon, scrape the granita finely. Shape into ovals and place over the meringue. Dust with icing sugar and serve immediately.

COOK'S TIP
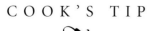
Serve the dessert as soon as possible after piling the granita on the meringue, or the meringue will soon go soggy.

NUTRITIONAL NOTES
Per portion:

Energy	310Kcals/1318kJ
Fat, total	0.2g
Saturated fat	0g
Cholesterol	0mg
Fibre	3.5g

VARIATION

Other soft fruits such as blueberries, raspberries or loganberries would work equally well with this dessert.

Blueberry and Orange Salad Meringues

What could be prettier than this simple salad of delicate blueberries, oranges and meringues flavoured with lavender?

Serves 4

6 oranges

350g/12oz/3 cups blueberries

8 sprigs fresh lavender

For the meringue

2 egg whites

115g/4oz/¹/₂ cup caster sugar

5ml/1 tsp fresh lavender flowers

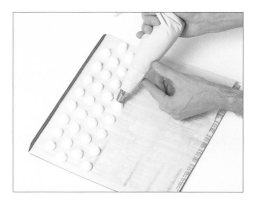

1 Preheat the oven to 140º/275ºF/ Gas 1. Line a baking sheet with six layers of newspaper and cover with non-stick baking paper. Whisk the egg whites in a large grease-free bowl until they hold soft peaks. Add the sugar a little at a time, whisking thoroughly after each addition. Fold in the lavender flowers.

2 Spoon the meringue into a piping bag fitted with a 5mm/¹/₄ in plain nozzle. Pipe small buttons of meringue on to the prepared baking sheet. Dry the meringue near the bottom of the oven for 1¹/₂–2 hours.

3 To segment the oranges, remove the peel from the top, bottom and sides with a serrated knife. Loosen the segments by cutting with a paring knife between the flesh and the membranes, holding the fruit over a bowl to catch the juice.

4 Arrange the segments on four plates, fanning them out.

5 Combine the blueberries with the lavender meringues and pile in the centre of each plate. Decorate with sprigs of lavender and serve immediately.

NUTRITIONAL NOTES
Per portion:

Energy	198Kcals/838kJ
Fat, total	0.3g
Saturated fat	0g
Cholesterol	0mg
Fibre	3.5g

COOK'S TIP

Lavender is used in both sweet and savoury dishes. Always use fresh or recently dried flowers, and avoid artificially scented bunches that are sold for dried flower displays.

VARIATION

You could use blackberries or firm raspberries with fresh rosemary leaves and flowers for this dessert. You would also make 7.5cm/3in circles of meringue instead of small buttons and layer the soft fruit in between circles of meringue.

Mixed Fruit Salad

A really good fruit salad is always refreshing, especially when it comes bathed in fresh orange and lemon juices.

Serves 4

juice of 3 large sweet oranges

juice of 1 lemon

1 banana

1–2 apples

1 ripe pear

2 peaches or nectarines

4–5 apricots or plums

115g/4oz/1 cup black or green grapes

115g/4oz/1 cup strawberries or raspberries

any other fruits in season

sugar, to taste (optional)

30–45ml/2–3 tbsp Kirsch, Maraschino or other liqueur (optional)

COOK'S TIP

For a herb infused flavour add chopped fresh herbs, try pineapple mint, lemon balm or borage flowers.

NUTRITIONAL NOTES

Per portion:

Energy	133Kcals/558kJ
Fat, total	0.4g
Saturated fat	0.03g
Cholesterol	0mg
Fibre	3.8g

---

1 Place the fresh orange and lemon juices in a large serving bowl.

2 Prepare all the fruits by washing or peeling them as necessary. Cut them into bite-size pieces. Halve the grapes and remove any seeds. Core and slice the apples. Stone and slice soft fruits and leave small berries whole. As soon as each fruit is prepared, add it to the juices in the bowl.

3 Taste the salad, adding sugar if needed. Liqueur can also be added, if you like. Cover the bowl and put it in the fridge for at least 2 hours. Mix well before serving.

Spiced Fruit Platter

The spicy sour flavour of chat masala
may seem a little strange at first, but this
Indian dessert can become addictive!

INGREDIENTS

Serves 6

1 pineapple

2 papayas

1 small melon

juice of 2 limes

2 pomegranates

chat masala, to taste

sprigs of fresh mint, to decorate

NUTRITIONAL NOTES

Per portion:

Energy	102Kcals/429kJ
Fat, total	0.5g
Saturated fat	0g
Cholesterol	0mg
Fibre	4.8g

1 Peel the pineapple. Remove the core and any remaining "eyes", then cut the flesh lengthways into thin wedges. Peel the papayas, cut them in half, and then into thin wedges. Halve the melon and remove the seeds from the middle. Cut it into thin wedges and remove the skin.

2 Arrange the fruit on six individual plates and sprinkle with the lime juice. Cut the pomegranates in half and scoop out the seeds, discarding any pith. Scatter the seeds over the fruit. Serve, sprinkled with a little chat masala to taste. Scatter over a few sprigs of mint, to decorate.

Ruby Fruit Salad

After a rich main course, this port-flavoured fruit salad is light and refreshing. Use any fruit available.

Serves 8

300ml/^{1}/$_2$ pint/1^1/$_4$ cups water

115g/4oz/^{1}/$_2$ cup caster sugar

1 cinnamon stick

4 cloves

pared rind of 1 orange

300ml/^{1}/$_2$ pint/1^1/$_4$ cups port

2 oranges

1 small ripe Ogen, Charentais or
   honeydew melon

4 small bananas

2 dessert apples

225g/8oz/2 cups seedless grapes

1 Put the water, sugar, spices and pared orange rind into a pan and stir over a gentle heat to dissolve the sugar. Then bring to the boil, lower the heat, cover and simmer for 10 minutes. Leave to cool, then add the port.

NUTRITIONAL NOTES
Per portion:

Energy	212Kcals/895kJ
Fat, total	0.2g
Saturated fat	0.04g
Cholesterol	0mg
Fibre	1.9g

2 Strain the liquid into a bowl. With a sharp knife, cut off all the skin and pith from the oranges. Then, holding each orange over the bowl to catch the juice, cut it into segments, and drop them into the syrup. Squeeze the remaining pulp to release any juice.

3 Cut the melon in half, remove the seeds and scoop out the flesh or cut it in small cubes. Add it to the syrup.

4 Peel the bananas and cut them diagonally in 1cm/^{1}/$_2$in slices. Quarter and core the apples and cut the wedges in small cubes. Leave the skin on, or peel them if it is tough. Halve the grapes if large or leave them whole. Stir all the fruit into the syrup, cover with clear film and chill for an hour before serving.

Winter Fruit Salad

A colourful, refreshing and nutritious fruit salad, this makes an excellent choice for a winter buffet.

INGREDIENTS

Serves 6

225g/8oz can pineapple cubes in fruit juice

200ml/7fl oz/scant 1 cup fresh orange juice

200ml/7fl oz/scant 1 cup unsweetened
   apple juice

30ml/2 tbsp orange- or
   apple-flavoured liqueur

30ml/2 tbsp clear honey (optional)

2 oranges, peeled

2 green-skinned eating apples

2 pears

4 plums, stoned and chopped

12 fresh dates, stoned and chopped

115g/4oz/1/2 cup ready-to-eat
   dried apricots

fresh mint sprigs, to decorate

2 Segment the oranges, catching any juice in the bowl, then add the orange segments and pineapple to the fruit juice mixture.

3 Core and chop the apples and pears and add them to the bowl.

4 Stir in the plums, dates and apricots. Cover and chill for several hours. Decorate with fresh mint sprigs to serve.

1 Drain the pineapple, reserving the juice in a large serving bowl. Add the orange juice, apple juice, liqueur and honey, if using, and stir.

NUTRITIONAL NOTES
Per portion:

Energy	227Kcals/967kJ
Fat, total	0.37g
Saturated fat	0g
Cholesterol	0mg
Fibre	5.34g

Mixed Melon Salad

Several melon varieties are combined with strongly flavoured wild or woodland strawberries for a delicious salad.

NUTRITIONAL NOTES
Per portion:

Energy	91Kcals/381kJ
Fat, total	0.7g
Saturated fat	0g
Cholesterol	0mg
Fibre	2.7g

1 Cut the cantaloupe or charentais melon, Galia melon and watermelon in half.

2 Using a spoon, scoop out the seeds from the cantaloupe or charentais, and the Galia.

3 With a melon scoop, take out as many balls as you can from all three melons. Mix them together in a large bowl, cover and put the bowl in the fridge. Chill for 2–3 hours.

4 Just before serving, add the wild strawberries and mix lightly. Spoon into four stemmed glass dishes.

5 Decorate with sprigs of mint and serve at once.

Fresh Fruit with Mango Sauce

This bright, flavourful sauce is easy to prepare and turns a simple fruit salad into something very special.

INGREDIENTS

Serves 6

1 large ripe mango, peeled, stoned and
    chopped
rind of 1 unwaxed orange
juice of 3 oranges
caster sugar to taste
2 peaches
2 nectarines
1 small mango, peeled
2 plums
1 pear or ¹/2 small melon
juice of 1 lemon
25–50g/1–2oz/2 heaped tbsp wild strawberries
    (optional)
25–50g/1–2oz/2 heaped tbsp raspberries
25–50g/1–2oz/2 heaped tbsp blueberries
small mint sprigs, to decorate

1 In a food processor fitted with a metal blade, process the large mango until smooth. Add the orange rind, juice and sugar to taste and process again until very smooth. Press through a sieve into a bowl and chill the sauce.

2 Peel the peaches if liked, then slice and stone the peaches, nectarines, small mango and plums. Quarter the pear and remove the core and seeds, or, if using, slice the melon thinly and remove the peel.

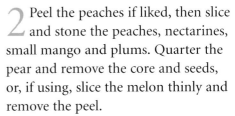

3 Place the sliced fruits on a large plate, sprinkle with lemon juice and chill, covered with clear film, for up to 3 hours before serving. (Some fruits may discolour if cut too far ahead of time.)

4 To serve, arrange the sliced fruits on individual serving plates, spoon the berries on top, drizzle with a little of the mango sauce and decorate with the mint sprigs. Serve the remaining sauce separately.

NUTRITIONAL NOTES

Per portion:

Energy	229Kcals/997kJ
Fat, total	0.6g
Saturated fat	0g
Cholesterol	0.0mg
Fibre	4.9g

Marzipan Figs with Dates

Sweet Mediterranean figs and dates combine well with crisp dessert apples. A hint of almond unites the flavours.

Serves 4

6 large apples

juice of $1/2$ lemon

150g/5oz/1 cup fresh dates

25g/1oz white marzipan

5ml/1 tsp orange-flower water

60ml/4 tbsp low-fat natural yogurt

4 green or purple figs

4 almonds, toasted

1 Core the apples. Slice thinly and cut into fine matchsticks. Moisten with lemon juice to prevent them browning.

2 Remove the stones from the dates and cut the flesh into fine strips, then mix with the apple matchsticks in a bowl.

3 Soften the marzipan with orange-flower water and combine with the low-fat yogurt. Mix well.

4 Pile the apples and dates in the centre of four plates. Remove the stem from each of the figs and cut the fruit into quarters without slicing the base. Squeeze the base with the thumb and forefinger to open the fruit.

5 Place a fig in the centre of the salad, spoon in the yogurt filling and decorate each portion with a toasted almond.

NUTRITIONAL NOTES

Per portion:

Energy	210Kcals/884kJ
Fat, total	3.1g
Saturated fat	0.15g
Cholesterol	0.6mg
Fibre	5.4g

Dried Fruit Salad with Summer Berries

This is a wonderful combination of fresh and dried fruit. In the winter you can use frozen raspberries or blackberries.

INGREDIENTS

Serves 4

115g/4oz/^{1}/2 cup dried apricots

115g/4oz/^{1}/2 cup dried peaches

1 fresh pear

1 fresh apple

1 fresh orange

115g/4oz/^{2}/3 cup mixed raspberries
   and blackberries

550ml/18fl oz/2^1/2 cups water

1 cinnamon stick

50g/2oz/^{1}/4 cup sugar

15ml/1 tbsp honey

1 Soak the apricots and peaches in water for 1–2 hours until plump, then drain and halve or quarter.

2 Peel and core the pear and apple and cut into cubes. Peel the orange with a sharp knife, removing all the pith, and cut into wedges. Place all the fruit in a large saucepan with the raspberries and blackberries.

NUTRITIONAL NOTES

Per portion:

Energy	190Kcals/811kJ
Fat, total	0.4g
Saturated fat	0g
Cholesterol	0.0mg
Fibre	5.1g

3 Add the water, the cinnamon, sugar and honey.

4 Bring to a boil, then cover the pan and simmer very gently for 10–12 minutes, until the fruit is just tender, stirring occasionally.

Tropical Fruit Salad

Like all nuts, coconut is a significant source of fat, so go easy on the strips used to decorate this delicious salad.

INGREDIENTS

Serves 4–6

1 medium pineapple, about 600g/1lb 5oz

400g/14oz can guava halves in syrup

2 medium bananas, sliced

1 large mango, peeled, stoned and diced

115g/4oz stem ginger, plus 30ml/2 tbsp of the syrup from the jar

60ml/4 tbsp thick coconut milk

10ml/2 tsp granulated sugar

2.5ml/1/2 tsp freshly grated nutmeg

2.5ml/1/2 tsp ground cinnamon

a few fine strips of coconut, to decorate

1 Peel, core and cube the pineapple, and place in a serving bowl. Drain the guavas, reserving the syrup, and chop. Add the guavas to the bowl with half the sliced banana and the mango.

2 Chop the stem ginger and add to the fruit mixture.

3 Pour 30ml/2 tbsp of the ginger syrup, and the reserved guava syrup, into a blender or food processor. Add the remaining banana slices with the coconut milk and the sugar. Blend to a smooth purée.

NUTRITIONAL NOTES

Per portion:

Energy	340Kcals/1434kJ
Fat, total	1.8g
Saturated fat	0.83g
Cholesterol	0mg
Fibre	8.1g

4 Pour the banana and coconut mixture over the tropical fruit. Add a little grated nutmeg and a sprinkling of cinnamon on the top. Serve chilled, decorated with fine strips of coconut.

Melon and Strawberry Salad

This colourful fruit salad can be served either as a dessert or as a refreshing appetizer before a meal.

INGREDIENTS

Serves 4

1 Galia melon

1 honeydew melon

1/2 watermelon

225g/8oz/2 cups fresh strawberries, halved if large

15ml/1 tbsp lemon juice

15ml/1 tbsp clear honey

15ml/1 tbsp water

15ml/1 tbsp chopped fresh mint

NUTRITIONAL NOTES

Per portion:

Energy	139Kcals/584kJ
Fat, total	0.84g
Saturated fat	0g
Cholesterol	0mg
Fibre	2g

2 Mix the lemon juice, honey and water in a jug and stir into the fruit.

3 Sprinkle the chopped mint over the fruit and serve.

1 Prepare the melons by cutting them in half and scraping out the seeds. Use a melon baller to scoop out the flesh into balls or a knife to cut it into cubes. Place these in a fruit bowl and add the fresh strawberries.

Papaya and Green Grapes with Mint Syrup

This wonderful combination of textures and flavours makes the perfect dessert to follow a spicy main course.

INGREDIENTS

Serves 4

2 large papayas

225g/8oz/2 cups seedless green grapes

juice of 3 limes

2.5cm/1in fresh root ginger, peeled and
 finely grated

15ml/1 tbsp clear honey

5 fresh mint leaves, cut into thin strips, plus
 extra whole leaves, to decorate

1 Peel the papaya and cut into small cubes, discarding the seeds. Cut the grapes in half.

2 In a bowl, mix together the lime juice, grated root ginger, clear honey and shredded mint leaves.

3 Add the papaya and grapes and toss well. Cover and leave in a cool place to marinate for 1 hour.

4 Serve in a large dish or individual stemmed glasses, garnished with the whole fresh mint leaves.

NUTRITIONAL NOTES
Per portion:

Energy	120Kcals/507kJ
Fat, total	0.2g
Saturated fat	0g
Cholesterol	0mg
Fibre	4.4g

Papaya Skewers with Passion Fruit Coulis

Tropical fruits make a simple, exotic dessert. The passion fruit flesh can be used without puréeing or sieving.

Serves 6

3 ripe papayas

10 passion fruit or kiwi fruit

30ml/2 tbsp fresh lime juice

30ml/2 tbsp icing sugar

30ml/2 tbsp white rum

lime slices, to garnish

NUTRITIONAL NOTES

Per portion:

Energy	94Kcals/399kJ
Fat, total	0.3g
Saturated fat	0g
Cholesterol	0mg
Fibre	4.1g

3 Press the fruit pulp through a sieve placed over a bowl; discard the seeds. Add the lime juice, icing sugar and rum, then stir the coulis well until the sugar has dissolved.

4 Spoon a little coulis onto plates and place the skewers on top. Scoop the flesh from the remaining passion or kiwi fruit and spoon over. Serve at once, garnished with lime slices.

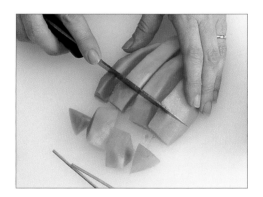

1 Cut the papayas in half and scoop out the seeds. Peel them and cut the flesh into even-size chunks. Thread the chunks on to six bamboo skewers.

2 Halve eight of the passion fruit or kiwi fruit and scoop out the flesh. Purée the flesh for a few seconds in a blender of food processor.

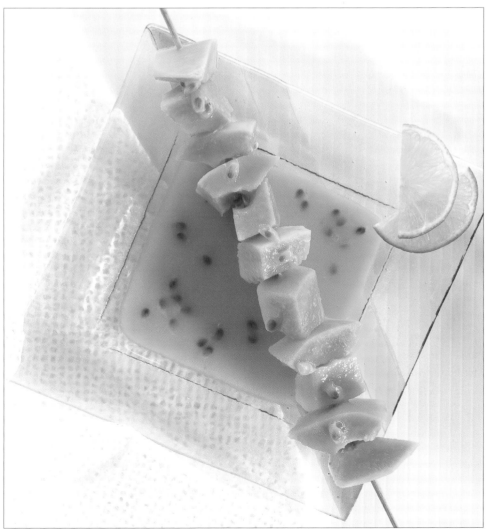

Three-fruit Compote

Mixing dried fruits with fresh ones makes a good combination, especially if flavoured with orange-flower water.

INGREDIENTS

Serves 6

175g/6oz/1 cup ready-to-eat dried apricots

300ml/½ pint/1¼ cups water

1 small ripe pineapple

1 small ripe melon, about 450g/1lb

15ml/1 tbsp orange-flower water

mint sprigs, to decorate

NUTRITIONAL NOTES
Per portion:

Energy	86Kcals/360kJ
Fat, total	0.4g
Saturated fat	0g
Cholesterol	0mg
Fibre	3.2g

2 Peel and quarter the pineapple, cut the core from each quarter and discard. Cut the flesh into chunks.

3 Cut the melon in half and out the seeds. Working over a bowl to catch the juices, scoop balls from the flesh. Tip the juices into the apricots.

4 Put the apricots, with the juices, into a bowl. Stir in the orange-flower water. Add the pineapple and melon and mix all the fruits gently.

5 Pour into a serving dish or individual dishes. Decorate with a mint sprig and chill before serving.

1 Put the apricots into a saucepan and pour in the water. Bring to the boil, then lower the heat and simmer for 5 minutes. Leave to cool.

VARIATION

A good fruit salad needn't consist of a mixture of fruits. For a delicious red fruit salad, try berry fruits with sliced plums, or for green fruits, try apple, kiwi fruit and green grapes.

Apricot and Banana Compote

This compote is delicious with low-fat custard or ice cream. Served for breakfast, it makes a tasty start to the day.

3 Spoon the fruit and juices into a large serving dish.

4 Serve immediately, or cover and chill for several hours first. Sprinkle with flaked almonds just before serving.

INGREDIENTS

Serves 4

225g/8oz/1 cup ready-to-eat dried apricots

300ml/^{1}/2 pint/1^1/4 cups unsweetened
  orange juice

150ml/^{1}/4 pint/^{2}/3 cup unsweetened
  apple juice

5ml/1 tsp ground ginger

3 medium bananas, sliced

25g/1oz/^{1}/4 cup toasted flaked almonds

1 Put the apricots in a saucepan with the fruit juices and ginger and stir. Cover, bring to the boil and then simmer gently for 10 minutes, stirring.

2 Set aside to cool, leaving the lid on. Once the compote is cool, stir in the sliced bananas.

COOK'S TIP

Use other combinations of dried and fresh fruit such as prunes or figs and apples or peaches.

NUTRITIONAL NOTES
Per portion:

Energy	241Kcals/1022kJ
Fat, total	4.18g
Saturated fat	0.37g
Cholesterol	0mg
Fibre	4.91g

Spiced Fruits Jubilee

Based on the classic Cherries Jubilee, this is a great way to use a glut of pitted fruit. The spiced syrup is a delicious bonus.

2 Add the fruit, cover the pan and simmer for 5 minutes. Drain the fruit and set it aside; return the syrup to the pan. Boil it, uncovered, for 2 minutes or until thick and syrupy.

3 Put the arrowroot in a small bowl and stir in 30ml/2 tbsp of the brandy. Stir the mixture into the syrup. Continue cooking and stirring, until the sauce thickens. Return the fruit to the pan.

4 If serving with ice cream, place a scoop in each serving bowl and spoon the hot fruit over the top. Warm the remaining brandy in a small pan, then set it alight. For maximum dramatic effect, ladle it over the fruit at the table.

INGREDIENTS

Serves 6

115g/4oz/^{1}/2 cup caster sugar

thinly pared rind of 1 lemon

4 whole cloves

1 cinnamon stick

300ml/^{1}/2 pint/1^1/4 cups water

225g/8oz tart red plums, stoned and sliced

225g/8oz nectarines, stoned and chopped

225g/8oz/2 cups cherries, stoned

5ml/1 tsp arrowroot

75ml/5 tbsp brandy

low-fat vanilla ice cream, to serve (optional)

1 Put the sugar, lemon rind, cloves, cinnamon stick and water in a pan. Bring to the boil, stirring, then simmer for 5 minutes. Lift out the spices with a slotted spoon and discard.

NUTRITIONAL NOTES	
Per portion:	
Energy	151Kcals/639kJ
Fat, total	0.1g
Saturated fat	0g
Cholesterol	0mg
Fibre	1g

Italian Fruit Salad and Ice Cream

Macerated soft fruits are delectable on their own, and also make a wonderful ice cream.

INGREDIENTS

Serves 6

900g/2lb/8 cups mixed soft fruits, such as
   strawberries, raspberries, loganberries, redcurrants, blueberries, peaches,
   apricots, plums and melons

juice of 6–8 oranges

juice of 1 lemon

15ml/1 tbsp liquid pear and apple concentrate

60ml/4 tbsp very low-fat fromage frais

30ml/2 tbsp orange-flavoured
   liqueur (optional)

fresh mint sprigs, to decorate

1 Prepare the fruit according to type. Cut it into reasonably small pieces, large enough to hold their shape.

2 Put the fruit pieces in a serving bowl and pour over enough orange juice to cover. Add the lemon juice, stir gently, cover and chill for 2 hours.

3 Set half the macerated fruit aside to serve as it is. Purée the remainder in a blender or food processor.

4 Gently warm the pear and apple concentrate and stir it into the fruit purée. Whip the fromage frais and fold it in, then add the liqueur, if using.

NUTRITIONAL NOTES	
Per portion:	
Energy	60Kcals/254kJ
Fat, total	0.2g
Saturated fat	0.01g
Cholesterol	0.1mg
Fibre	3.2g

5 Churn in an ice-cream maker. Alternatively, place in a container and freeze until ice crystals form around the edge, then beat until smooth. Repeat once or twice, then freeze until firm. Soften slightly before serving decorated with mint. Serve accompanied by the macerated fruit.

Low-fat Ices & Sorbets

◆ ✦ ◆

Redcurrant and Raspberry Coulis

A dessert sauce to serve with meringues and fruit sorbets. Make it pretty with a decoration of fresh flowers and leaves.

3 Blend the cornflour with the orange juice, then stir into the fruit purée. Transfer to a saucepan and bring to the boil, stirring continuously, and cook for 1–2 minutes until smooth and thick. Leave until cold.

4 Spoon the sauce over each plate. Drip the cream from a teaspoon to make small dots evenly around the edge. Draw a cocktail stick through the dots to form heart shapes. Scoop or spoon sorbet into the middle and decorate with flowers.

INGREDIENTS

Serves 6

225g/8oz/2 cups redcurrants

450g/1lb/4 cups raspberries

50g/2oz/1/2 cup icing sugar

15ml/1 tbsp cornflour

juice of 1 orange

30ml/2 tbsp low-fat cream

edible flowers, to decorate

1 Strip the redcurrants from their stalks. Place them in a blender with the sugar and raspberries, and blend to a purée.

2 Press the fruit mixture through a fine sieve into a bowl and discard the seeds and pulp.

NUTRITIONAL NOTES
Per portion:

Energy	81Kcals/340kJ
Fat, total	1.2g
Saturated fat	0.6g
Cholesterol	0mg
Fibre	3.2g

Christmas Cranberry Bombe

This alternative to Christmas pudding is light and low in fat, but still very festive and luxurious.

Serves 6

250ml/8fl oz/1 cup buttermilk

60ml/4 tbsp low-fat crème fraîche

1 vanilla pod

2 eggs

30ml/2 tbsp clear honey

30ml/2 tbsp chopped angelica

30ml/2 tbsp mixed peel

10ml/2 tsp flaked almonds, toasted

For the sorbet centre

175g/6oz/1¹/2 cups fresh or
   frozen cranberries

150ml/¹/4 pint/²/3 cup fresh orange juice

finely grated rind of ¹/2 orange

2.5ml/¹/2 tsp mixed spice

50g/2oz/¹/4 cup golden caster sugar

1 Heat the buttermilk, crème fraîche and vanilla pod until the mixture is almost boiling. Remove the vanilla pod.

NUTRITIONAL NOTES
Per portion:

Energy	153Kcals/644kJ
Fat, total	4.6g
Saturated fat	1.58g
Cholesterol	75.5mg
Fibre	1.5g

2 Place the eggs in a heatproof bowl over a pan of hot water and whisk until they are pale and thick. Pour in the heated buttermilk in a thin stream, whisking hard. Continue whisking over the hot water until the mixture thickens slightly.

3 Whisk in the honey and then cool. Spoon the mixture into a freezer container and freeze until slushy, tip into a bowl and stir in the chopped angelica, mixed peel and almonds.

4 Pack into a 1.2 litre/2 pint/5 cup pudding basin and hollow out the centre. Freeze until firm.

5 Meanwhile, make the sorbet centre. Put the cranberries, orange juice, rind and spice in a pan and cook gently until the cranberries are soft. Set some cranberries aside for decorating. Add the sugar to the rest, then purée in a food processor until almost smooth, but still with some texture. Leave to cool.

6 Fill the hollowed-out centre of the bombe with the cranberry mixture, smooth over and freeze until firm. To serve, allow to soften slightly at room temperature, then turn out and serve in medium-sized slices, decorated with the reserved cranberries.

Summer Fruit Salad Ice Cream

What could be more cooling on a hot summer day than fresh summer fruits, lightly frozen in this irresistible ice?

INGREDIENTS

Serves 6

900g/2lb/6 cups mixed soft summer fruit, such as raspberries, strawberries, blackcurrants or redcurrants

2 eggs

250ml/8fl oz/1 cup low-fat Greek yogurt

175ml/6fl oz/¾ cup red grape juice

15ml/1 tbsp powdered gelatine

1 Reserve half the fruit for the decoration; purée the rest in a food processor, then sieve it over a bowl to make a smooth purée.

VARIATION

You could use other combinations of summer fruit such as apricots, peaches and nectarines, with apple or orange juice for a more delicate ice cream.

2 Separate the eggs, whisk the yolks and the yogurt into the fruit purée.

3 Heat the grape juice until almost boiling, then remove it from the heat. Sprinkle the gelatine over the grape juice and stir to dissolve the gelatine completely.

4 Whisk the dissolved gelatine mixture into the fruit purée. Cool, then pour the mixture into a freezerproof container. Freeze until half-frozen and slushy in consistency.

5 Whisk the egg whites in a grease-free bowl until stiff. Quickly fold them into the half-frozen mixture.

6 Return the ice cream to the freezer and freeze until almost firm. Scoop into individual dishes and decorate with the reserved soft fruits.

NUTRITIONAL NOTES
Per portion:

Energy	116Kcals/489kJ
Fat, total	3.9g
Saturated fat	1.69g
Cholesterol	66.8mg
Fibre	3.6g

COOK'S TIP

Red grape juice has a good flavour and improves the colour of the ice, but if it is not available, use cranberry, apple or orange juice instead.

Frozen Apple and Blackberry Terrine

This pretty, three-layered terrine can be frozen, so you can enjoy it at any time of year.

INGREDIENTS

Serves 6

450g/1lb cooking or eating apples

300ml/½ pint/1¼ cups sweet cider

15ml/1 tbsp clear honey

5ml/1 tsp pure vanilla essence

200g/7oz/scant 2 cups fresh or frozen and
   thawed blackberries

15ml/1 tbsp powdered gelatine

2 egg whites

fresh apple slices and blackberries,
   to decorate

1 Peel, core and chop the apples and place them in a pan with half the cider. Bring the cider to the boil, then lower the heat, cover the pan and let the apples simmer gently until tender.

2 Tip the apples into a food processor and process to a smooth purée. Stir in the honey and vanilla essence. Add half the blackberries to half the apple purée, and process again until smooth. Sieve to remove the pips.

3 Heat the remaining cider until almost boiling, then sprinkle the gelatine over and stir until the gelatine has dissolved completely. Add half the gelatine mixture to the apple purée and half to the blackberry purée.

4 Leave both purées to cool until almost set. Whisk the egg whites until they are stiff. Quickly fold them into the apple purée. Remove half the purée to another bowl. Stir the remaining whole blackberries into half the apple purée, and then tip this into a 1.75 litre/3 pint/7½ cup loaf tin, packing it down firmly.

5 Top with the blackberry purée and spread it evenly. Finally, add a layer of the plain apple purée and smooth it evenly. If necessary, freeze each layer until firm before adding the next.

6 Freeze until firm. When ready to serve, remove from the freezer and allow to stand at room temperature for about 20 minutes to soften. Serve in slices, decorated with fresh apple slices and blackberries.

VARIATION

For a quicker version the mixture can be set without the layering. Purée the apples and blackberries together, stir the dissolved gelatine and whisked egg whites into the mixture, turn the whole thing into the tin and leave the mixture to set.

NUTRITIONAL NOTES
Per portion:

Energy	83Kcals/346kJ
Fat, total	0.2g
Saturated fat	0g
Cholesterol	0mg
Fibre	2.6g

Key Lime Sorbet

Cool and refreshing, this traditional American sorbet is ideal for serving after a curry or similar spicy dish.

INGREDIENTS

Serves 4

275g/10oz/1¼ cups granulated sugar

600ml/1 pint/2½ cups water

grated rind of 1 lime

175ml/6fl oz/¾ cup fresh lime juice

15ml/1 tbsp fresh lemon juice

30ml/2 tbsp icing sugar

lime shreds, to decorate

1 In a small heavy saucepan, dissolve the granulated sugar in the water, without stirring, over medium heat. When the sugar has dissolved, boil the syrup for 5–6 minutes. Remove from the heat and leave to cool.

2 Mix the cooled sugar syrup and lime rind and juice in a jug or bowl. Stir well. Sharpen the flavour by adding the lemon juice. Stir in the icing sugar.

3 Freeze the mixture in an ice-cream maker, following the instructions of the machine's manufacturer. Decorate with lime shreds.

NUTRITIONAL NOTES
Per portion:

Energy	300Kcals/1278kJ
Fat, total	0g
Saturated fat	0g
Cholesterol	0mg
Fibre	0g

COOK'S TIP

To make ice cream by hand, pour the mixture into a freezerproof container and freeze until softly set, about 3 hours. Spoon into a food processor and process until smooth. Return the mixture to the freezer container and freeze again until set. Repeat this process 2 or 3 times, until a smooth consistency is obtained.

Ruby Grapefruit Sorbet

On a hot day, nothing slips down more easily than a smooth sorbet. This one looks as good as it tastes.

INGREDIENTS

Serves 8

175g/6oz/³/4 cup granulated sugar

120ml/4fl oz/¹/2 cup water

1 litre/1³/4 pints/4 cups strained freshly squeezed ruby grapefruit juice

15ml/1 tbsp fresh lemon juice

15ml/1 tbsp icing sugar

mint leaves, to decorate

1 In a small heavy saucepan, dissolve the granulated sugar in the water over a medium heat, without stirring. When the sugar has dissolved, boil the syrup for 3–4 minutes. Remove from the heat and leave to cool.

2 Pour the cooled sugar syrup into the grapefruit juice. Stir well. Taste the mixture and adjust the flavour by adding the lemon juice or the icing sugar, if necessary, but do not make it over-sweet.

NUTRITIONAL NOTES
Per portion:

Energy	133Kcals/568kJ
Fat, total	0.1g
Saturated fat	0g
Cholesterol	0mg
Fibre	0g

3 Pour the mixture into a metal or plastic freezer container and freeze for about 3 hours, or until softly set.

4 Remove from the container and chop roughly into 7.5cm/3in pieces. Place in a food processor and process until smooth. Return the mixture to the freezer container and freeze again until set. Repeat this freezing and chopping process 2 or 3 times, until a smooth consistency is obtained.

5 Alternatively, freeze the sorbet in an ice-cream maker, following the manufacturer's instructions. Serve, decorated with mint leaves.

Mango Sorbet with Mango Sauce

After a heavy meal, this Indian speciality makes a refreshing dessert. Remove from the freezer 10 minutes before serving.

INGREDIENTS

Serves 4

900g/2lb/5 cups mango pulp

2.5ml/^{1}/2 tsp lemon juice

grated rind of 1 orange and 1 lemon

4 egg whites

50g/2oz/^{1}/4 cup caster sugar

120ml/4fl oz/^{1}/2 cup low-fat Greek yogurt

50g/2oz/^{1}/2 cup icing sugar

1 In a large, chilled bowl that can safely be used in the freezer, mix half of the mango pulp with the lemon juice and the grated citrus rind.

NUTRITIONAL NOTES
Per portion:

Energy	259Kcals/1090kJ
Fat, total	1.7g
Saturated fat	0.79g
Cholesterol	1.8mg
Fibre	5.9g

2 Whisk the egg whites in a grease-free bowl to soft peaks and fold into the mango mixture with the caster sugar. Cover, freeze for at least 1 hour.

3 Remove the sorbet from the freezer and beat again. Transfer to an ice-cream container, and freeze until solid.

4 Lightly whisk the yogurt with the icing sugar and the remaining pulp. Spoon into a bowl and chill for 24 hours. Scoop individual servings of sorbet and cover with mango sauce.

Lychee and Elderflower Sorbet

The flavour of elderflowers is famous for bringing out the essence of gooseberries, and it complements lychees wonderfully.

Serves 4

175g/6oz/3/4 cup caster sugar

400ml/14fl oz/1²/3 cups water

500g/1¹/4 lb fresh lychees, peeled
   and stoned

15ml/1 tbsp undiluted elderflower cordial

dessert biscuits, to serve (optional)

NUTRITIONAL NOTES

Per portion:

Energy	249Kcals/1058kJ
Fat, total	0.1g
Saturated fat	0g
Cholesterol	0mg
Fibre	0.9g

1 Heat the sugar and water until the sugar has dissolved. Then boil for 5 minutes and add the lychees. Lower the heat and simmer for 7 minutes. Remove from the heat and allow to cool.

2 Purée the fruit and syrup. Place a sieve over a bowl and press the purée through it with a spoon.

3 Stir the elderflower cordial into the strained purée, then pour the mixture into a freezerproof container. Freeze for approximately 2 hours, until ice crystals start to form around the edges.

4 Remove the sorbet from the freezer and process briefly in a food processor or blender to break up the crystals. Repeat this process twice more, then freeze until firm.

5 Transfer to the fridge for 10 minutes to soften slightly before serving in scoops. Crisp dessert biscuits can be served with the sorbet, but aren't really necessary. If you do serve them, remember that they will increase the fat content of the dessert.

Plum and Port Sorbet

Rather a grown-up sorbet, this one, but you could use still red grape juice instead of port if you prefer.

Serves 6

900g/2lb ripe red plums, halved
   and stoned
75g/3oz/6 tbsp caster sugar
45ml/3 tbsp water
45ml/3 tbsp ruby port or red wine
crisp, sweet biscuits, to serve (optional)

1 Put the plums in a pan with the sugar and water. Stir over a gentle heat until the sugar has melted, then cover and simmer gently for about 5 minutes, until the fruit is soft.

2 Tip into a food processor and purée until smooth, then stir in the port or wine. Cool completely, then tip into a container that can safely be used in the freezer and freeze until firm around the edges.

3 Spoon into the food processor and process until smooth. Return to the freezer and freeze until solid.

4 Soften slightly at room temperature then serve in scoops, with sweet biscuits if you like, but they will add fat content.

NUTRITIONAL NOTES
Per portion:

Energy	166Kcals/699kJ
Fat, total	0.25g
Saturated fat	0g
Cholesterol	0mg
Fibre	3.75g

Raspberry Sorbet with a Soft Fruit Garland

This stunning fresh fruit and herb garnish creates a bold border for the scoops of sorbet.

INGREDIENTS

Serves 8

175g/6oz/³/4 cup caster sugar

250ml/8fl oz/1 cup water

450g/1lb fresh or thawed
frozen raspberries

strained juice of 1 orange

For the decoration

1 bunch mint

selection of soft fruits, including strawberries,
raspberries, redcurrants
and blueberries

1 Heat the caster sugar with the water in a saucepan, until dissolved, stir occasionally. Bring to the boil, then set aside to cool. Purée the raspberries with the orange juice, then sieve, to remove any seeds.

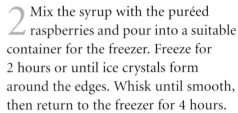

2 Mix the syrup with the puréed raspberries and pour into a suitable container for the freezer. Freeze for 2 hours or until ice crystals form around the edges. Whisk until smooth, then return to the freezer for 4 hours.

3 About 30 minutes before serving, transfer the sorbet to the fridge to soften slightly. Place a large sprig of mint on the rim of a serving plate, then build up a garland, using more mint sprigs.

4 Leaving on the leaves, cut the strawberries in half. Arrange on the mint with the other fruit. Place the fruits at different angles and link the leaves with strings of redcurrants. Place scoops of sorbet in the centre.

NUTRITIONAL NOTES

Per portion:

Energy	158Kcals/669kJ
Fat, total	0.4g
Saturated fat	0g
Cholesterol	0mg
Fibre	3.4g

Blackcurrant Sorbet

If not serving immediately, cover this blackcurrant sorbet tightly and freeze it again, for up to one week.

INGREDIENTS

Serves 4

100g/3¹/2 oz/scant ¹/2 cup caster sugar

120ml/4fl oz/¹/2 cup water

450g/1lb/4 cups blackcurrants

juice of ¹/2 lemon

15ml/1 tbsp egg white

1 Mix the sugar and water in a small saucepan. Heat gently, stirring until the sugar dissolves, then boil the syrup for 2 minutes. Remove the pan from the heat and set aside to cool.

2 Remove the blackcurrants from the stalks by pulling them through the tines of a fork. Wash thoroughly and drain.

3 Using a metal blade, process the blackcurrants and lemon juice until smooth. Or, chop the blackcurrants coarsely, then add the lemon juice. Stir in the sugar syrup.

4 Press the purée through a sieve to remove the seeds.

5 Pour the blackcurrant purée into a non-metallic dish that can safely be used in the freezer. Cover the dish with clear film or a lid and freeze until the sorbet is nearly firm, but still slushy.

6 Cut the sorbet into pieces and process in a food processor until smooth. With the machine running, add the egg white through the feeder tube and process until well mixed. Tip the sorbet back into the dish and freeze until almost firm. Chop the sorbet again and process until smooth. Serve immediately.

NUTRITIONAL NOTES

Per portion:

Energy	132Kcals/558kJ
Fat, total	0g
Saturated fat	0g
Cholesterol	0mg
Fibre	4.1g

Mango and Lime Sorbet in Lime Shells

This richly flavoured sorbet looks pretty served in the lime shells, but is also good served in traditional scoops.

Serves 4

4 large limes

1 ripe mango

7.5ml/1¹/2 tsp powdered gelatine

2 egg whites

15ml/1 tbsp caster sugar

strips of pared lime rind, to decorate

1 Slice the top and bottom off each lime. Squeeze the juice, keeping the shells intact, then scrape out the shell.

2 Halve, stone, peel and chop the mango. Purée in a food processor with 30ml/2 tbsp of the lime juice.

3 Sprinkle the gelatine over 45ml/ 3 tbsp of the lime juice in a small heatproof bowl. Set aside until spongy, then place over a pan of hot water and stir until the gelatine has dissolved. Stir it into the mango mixture.

4 Whisk the egg whites in a grease-free bowl until they hold soft peaks. Whisk in the sugar. Fold the egg white mixture quickly into the mango mixture. Spoon the sorbet into the lime shells. Any leftover sorbet can be frozen in small ramekins.

NUTRITIONAL NOTES
Per portion:

Energy	83Kcals/350kJ
Fat, total	0.4g
Saturated fat	0g
Cholesterol	0mg
Fibre	2.3g

5 Place the filled shells in the freezer until the sorbet is firm. Overwrap the shells in clear film. Before serving, allow the shells to stand at room temperature for about 10 minutes; decorate them with knotted strips of pared lime rind.

Watermelon Sorbet

A slice of this refreshing sorbet is the perfect way to cool down on a hot day. Ensure the watermelon is perfectly ripe.

INGREDIENTS

Serves 6

1/2 small watermelon, about 1kg/2 1/4 lb
75g/3oz/6 tbsp caster sugar
60ml/4 tbsp unsweetened cranberry
   juice or water
30ml/2 tbsp lemon juice
sprigs of fresh mint, to decorate

1 Cut the watermelon into six equal-size wedges. Scoop out the pink flesh, discarding the seeds but reserving the shell.

2 Select a bowl that is about the same size as the melon and which can safely be used in the freezer. Line it with clear film. Arrange the melon skins in the bowl to re-form the shell, fitting them together snugly so that there are no gaps. Put in the freezer.

3 Mix the sugar and cranberry juice or water in a saucepan and stir over a low heat until the sugar dissolves. Bring to the boil, then lower the heat and simmer for 5 minutes. Leave the sugar syrup to cool.

4 Put the melon flesh and lemon juice in a blender and process to a smooth purée. Stir in the sugar syrup and pour into a freezer-proof container. Freeze for 3–3 1/2 hours, or until slushy.

5 Tip the sorbet into a chilled bowl and whisk to break up the ice crystals. Return to the freezer for another 30 minutes, whisk again, then tip into the melon shell and freeze until solid.

6 Carefully remove the sorbet-filled melon shell from the freezer and turn it upside down. Use a sharp knife to separate the segments, then quickly place them on individual plates. Decorate with mint sprigs and serve.

NUTRITIONAL NOTES
Per portion:

Energy	125Kcals/525kJ
Fat, total	0.52g
Saturated fat	0g
Cholesterol	0mg
Fibre	0.26g

COOK'S TIP

Watermelon seeds make a delicious and nutritious snack if toasted in a moderate oven until brown and hulled to remove the outer shell.

Rhubarb and Orange Water-ice

Pink rhubarb, with sweet oranges and honey – the perfect summer ice. Add more honey or sugar if needed, to taste.

INGREDIENTS

Serves 4

350g/12oz pink rhubarb

1 orange

15ml/1 tbsp clear honey

5ml/1 tsp powdered gelatine

orange slices, to decorate

NUTRITIONAL NOTES
Per portion:

Energy	38Kcals/158kJ
Fat, total	0.1g
Saturated fat	0g
Cholesterol	0mg
Fibre	2g

3 Heat the remaining orange juice and stir in the gelatine to dissolve. Stir it into the rhubarb. Tip the whole mixture into a rigid container that can safely be used in the freezer; freeze for about 2 hours or until slushy.

4 Remove the mixture from the freezer, tip into a bowl and beat well to break up the ice crystals. Freeze until firm. Soften slightly at room temperature before serving in scoops, decorated with orange slices.

1 Trim the rhubarb and slice into 2.5cm/1in lengths. Place the rhubarb in a non-reactive pan.

2 Finely grate the rind from the orange and squeeze out the juice. Add about half the orange juice and the grated rind to the rhubarb in the pan and simmer until the rhubarb is just tender. Stir in the honey.

Orange Ice with Strawberries

Juicy oranges and really ripe strawberries make a flavoursome ice that does not need any additional sweetening.

Serves 4

6 large juicy oranges

350g/12oz/3 cups ripe strawberries

finely pared strips of orange rind,
   to decorate

NUTRITIONAL NOTES

Per portion:

Energy	124Kcals/518kJ
Fat, total	0.4g
Saturated fat	0g
Cholesterol	0mg
Fibre	5.6g

1 Squeeze the juice from the oranges and pour into a shallow freezer-proof bowl. Freeze until ice crystals form around the edge of the mixture, beat thoroughly and freeze again. Repeat this process at 30-minute intervals over a 4-hour period.

2 Halve the strawberries and arrange them on a serving plate. Scoop the ice into serving glasses, decorate with strips of orange rind and serve immediately with the strawberries.

COOK'S TIP

The ice will keep for up to 3 weeks in the freezer. Sweet ruby grapefruits or deep red blood oranges can be used for a different flavour and colour.

Iced Oranges

These little sorbets served in the fruit shell are easy to eat – just the thing for serving at a barbecue or patio picnic.

NUTRITIONAL NOTES
Per portion:

Energy	167Kcals/703kJ
Fat, total	0.3g
Saturated fat	0g
Cholesterol	0mg
Fibre	4.3g

3 Grate the rind of the six remaining oranges and add this to the syrup. Squeeze the juice from the oranges, and from the reserved flesh. There should be 750ml/1¼ pints/3 cups. Top up with water, if necessary.

4 Stir the orange juice into the syrup, with the remaining lemon juice and water. Pour the mixture into a shallow container that can safely be used in the freezer. Freeze for 3 hours.

5 Turn the mixture into a bowl, and whisk to break down the ice crystals. Return to the freezer container and freeze for 4 hours more, until firm, but not solid.

6 Pack the mixture into the orange shells, mounding it up, and set the "hats" on top. Freeze until ready to serve. Just before serving, make a hole in the top of each "hat", using a skewer, and push in a bay leaf as decoration.

INGREDIENTS

Serves 8

150g/5oz/⅔ cup granulated sugar
juice of 1 lemon
200ml/7fl oz/scant 1 cup water
14 oranges
8 fresh bay leaves, to decorate

1 Put the sugar in a heavy-based pan. Add half the lemon juice, then pour in 120ml/4fl oz/½ cup of the water. Heat gently, stirring occasionally, until the sugar has dissolved, then bring to the boil, and boil for 2–3 minutes, until the syrup is clear. Leave to cool.

2 Slice the tops off eight of the oranges, to make "hats". Scoop out the flesh from inside each, taking care not to damage the shell, and set it aside. Put the empty orange shells and the "hats" on a baking sheet and place in the freezer until needed.

COOK'S TIP
~

Use crumpled foil to keep the shells upright on the baking sheet.

Fresh Orange Granita

A granita is like a water ice, but coarser and quite grainy in texture. It makes a refreshing dessert after a rich meal.

INGREDIENTS

Serves 6

4 large oranges

1 large lemon

150g/5oz/²/3 cup granulated sugar

475ml/16fl oz/2 cups water

dessert biscuits, to serve (optional)

pared strips of orange and lemon rind,
   to decorate

1 Thinly pare the orange and lemon rind, avoiding the white pith, and set aside for the decoration. Cut the fruit in half and squeeze the juice into a jug. Set aside.

2 Heat the sugar and water in a heavy-based saucepan, stir until the sugar dissolves. Bring to the boil, and boil without stirring, until a syrup forms. Remove from the heat, add the orange and lemon rind and shake the pan. Cover and allow to cool.

3 Strain the sugar syrup into a shallow freezer container, add the fruit juice. Stir well then freeze, uncovered, for 4 hours until slushy.

COOK'S TIP
❧

Slice orange and lemon rind into thin strips. Blanch for 2 minutes, refresh in cold water and dry.

---

4 Remove the half-frozen mixture from the freezer and mix with a fork, return to the freezer and freeze again for 4 hours or until frozen hard.

5 To serve, turn into a bowl and leave to soften for about 10 minutes, break up again and pile into long-stemmed glasses. Decorate with the orange and lemon rind. Serve with dessert biscuits, if you like, but the fat content must be taken into account.

NUTRITIONAL NOTES
Per portion:

Energy	139Kcals/589kJ
Fat, total	0.2g
Saturated fat	0g
Cholesterol	0mg
Fibre	1.6g

Lemon Granita

Nothing is more refreshing for dessert on a hot summer's day than a fresh lemon granita.

INGREDIENTS

Serves 4

475ml/16fl oz/2 cups water

115g/4oz/½ cup granulated sugar

2 large lemons

NUTRITIONAL NOTES
Per portion:

Energy	114Kcals/488kJ
Fat, total	0g
Saturated fat	0g
Cholesterol	0mg
Fibre	0g

1 In a large saucepan, heat the water and sugar together over a low heat until the sugar dissolves. Bring to the boil, stirring occasionally. Remove from the heat and allow to cool.

2 Grate the rind from one lemon, then squeeze the juice from both. Stir the grated rind and juice into the sugar syrup. Place it in a shallow container or freezer tray, and freeze until solid.

3 Plunge the bottom of the frozen container or tray in very hot water for a few seconds. Turn the frozen mixture out, and chop it into large chunks.

4 Place the mixture in a food processor fitted with metal blades, and process until it forms small crystals. Spoon into serving glasses.

Coffee Granita

A granita is a cross between a frozen drink and a flavoured ice, and can be made at home with the help of a food processor. The consistency should be slushy, not solid.

INGREDIENTS

Serves 4

475ml/16fl oz/2 cups water

115g/4oz/½ cup granulated sugar

250ml/8fl oz/1 cup very strong espresso coffee, cooled

NUTRITIONAL NOTES
Per portion:

Energy	115Kcals/488kJ
Fat, total	0g
Saturated fat	0g
Cholesterol	0mg
Fibre	0g

1 Heat the water and sugar together gently until the sugar dissolves. Bring to the boil, stirring occasionally. Remove from the heat and allow to cool.

2 Stir the coffee and sugar syrup together. Place it in a container and freeze until solid. Plunge the bottom of the frozen container or tray in very hot water. Turn the mixture out, and chop into chunks.

3 Place the mixture in a food processor and process until it forms small crystals. Spoon into tall glasses and serve.

COOK'S TIP

To store a granita, pour the processed mixture back into a container, cover, and freeze again. Allow to thaw slightly before serving.

Index